I0129536

Children Everywhere

by
Florence Koenderink

Books by Florence Koenderink

Children Everywhere Book 1:
Essential Elements of Childcare in Institutions

Sick Children Everywhere Book 2:
Basic Medical Care for Children in Institutions

Volunteering with Children Everywhere Book 3:
Manual for Volunteers in Children's Homes

Children Everywhere

How to Provide Good Institutional Care

Book 1:
Essential Elements of Childcare in Institutions

Second Edition

by
Florence Koenderink

Orphanage Projects

First Edition published in 2013 by Orphanage Projects
Second Edition published in 2017

www.orphanageprojects.org
ISBN: 978-0-9935023-2-3

Copyright © Florence Koenderink 2013, 2017

Photos by Florence Koenderink
With the exception of photos on p23, 24 top, 38, 40, 68, 81, 119 bottom, 129,
208, 223, 343 Bert Koenderink; p60 Tom van der Meer; p69 Tijl Koenderink;
p119 top Yolanda Koenderink; p224 Marjolijn Koenderink; p263 bottom right Kausthubh;
p310 Miranda Hudson; p322 Vaijnath Lohar; p353 U&I

Lay-out, cover design and cover photo by Bert Koenderink

Icon design by Claartje van der Meer

Editing by Willow Editing

Contents

Acknowledgements

Accumulating the knowledge that eventually led to the writing of this manual has been a process of many years. And I have by no means finished learning and finding better ways. There are so many people that I am immensely grateful to for the ways in which they have helped me, supported me, taught me, and in some cases obstructed me, helping me grow in understanding and skill. It would take a separate book to name them all. Not doing so does nothing to diminish my gratitude to these people.

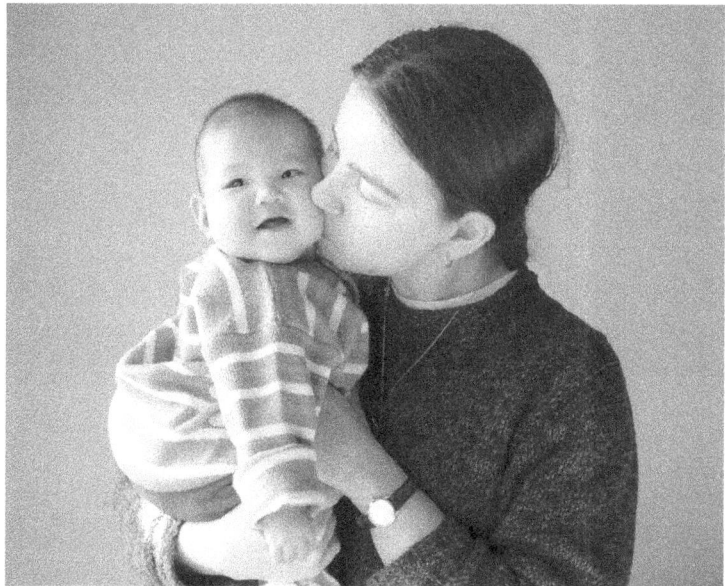

I want to thank my parents who have been amazingly supportive and have helped me infinitely by encouraging me to not worry about them worrying about me. Not many parents would show the confidence and calm that my parents did when I announced that I was going to China to volunteer for a year for the first time. Instead of going into a panic, they said: 'That sounds really interesting. Do you know what you will be doing there?' The rest of my family too have always been a beacon of support to me, even if it is not always easy for all of them to keep up with where I am at any given moment.

People who unlike any others have been an inspiration to work alongside, whose friendship I treasure and who taught me so incredibly much without it seeming like teaching, are Brent and Serena Johnson, Ajit Sivaram, Satish Manchikanti, Lily Lu and Sun Yu Lan.

The paediatricians, neurologists, GPs, nurses, physiotherapists, occupational therapists, speech therapists, and psychologists from various continents who have taken me by the hand, taught me how to deal with situations, let me work as their assistant or let me observe their work are literally too many to name. They have given me a tremendous gift, which I will always cherish and continue to build on.

For their advice and feedback on this book, I am indebted to Dr. Ronald S. Federici and David B. Werner. Their encouragement and suggestions for ways to tackle things have been invaluable. I want to thank Bert Koenderink for doing an amazing job on the cover design and lay-out, Claartje van der Meer for designing the icons, Isa McKechnie for editing, and Malika v.d. Kooij for making the illustrations, all of which was done voluntarily.

Every effort has been made to obtain permission for the use of all the materials. If by unintended oversight something has been used without your approval, please contact me to rectify this situation.

Finally my eternal gratitude goes out to the hundreds of children that I have worked with over the years. No one has taught and shown me more than they have. It will always continue to be a privilege to be awarded the trust and love of a child, especially in a difficult situation. I will continue to try to be worthy of the trust and to improve their world bit by bit.

Foreword to the Second Edition

As I wrote in the acknowledgements to the first edition of *Children Everywhere*, as I continue to do projects all over the world, I continue to learn and I discover more issues and solutions. This is the reason why only a few years after the bringing out the first edition, I have decided to write a second edition. New examples will be given, and more issues will be addressed. I have rearranged the order of certain chapters for a clearer overview. Certain parts have been removed: these are things that I thought to be of higher priority than they have since turned out to be. By removing them, including Part 3, Chapter 7, which was mostly a summary, I hope the focus on the most important subjects will be stronger. I have also further simplified the language throughout the manual, to make it even more accessible for people whose first language is not English.

One way in which this edition particularly distinguishes itself from the first one, is that while the first edition was very much focused on the needs of babies and toddlers, in this edition most subjects have been expanded to include more information relevant to older children. Over the years, since I first started writing the first edition, I have come across a number of issues involving older children that turned out to be a serious challenge in many places. Plus, I discovered that certain things, which I—perhaps naively—thought flowed naturally from the information given in *Children Everywhere*, did not go without saying at all. This second edition also contains a complete new chapter, Part 3, Chapter 2, about some of the ethical issues involved in starting and running a children's home. All of this in the hope of improving the lives of even more children.

Aside from the people already mentioned in the acknowledgements, I would like to thank Elzevera Koenderink for cleaning up the language in this second edition.

Introduction

✳ ————————— **Reasons for this book**
Institutional childcare encompasses more than you might think.
Orphanages come to mind first for many people, but really, standard
day care, boarding schools, and intensive care in a hospital fall under
the same category. Any situation where groups of children are cared
for by people not related to them who are paid to take care of them,
is institutional childcare. This means that even in rich countries
there is more institutional childcare than many people would like to
admit. The impact of the standard of care on the children is enormous in all these places. However, it is greatest in situations where
children have no contact at all with their parents or family. So that is
what I focus on.

I have visited many orphanages, children's homes, respite care
homes, medical children's homes and hospice care facilities in various parts of the world. Some of these institutions were very good,
some were extremely bad–to the point where you wonder how any
of the children survive. In some children's homes, practical needs
were looked after very well, while emotional needs were ignored
completely. However well-organised places were, there was room
for improvement everywhere.

To my great surprise I found
that there was no book with
overall guidelines for practical
care of children in institutional
situations. Apparently, no one
had yet decided to look at the
universal needs of children in
children's homes, to write down
some of these needs and to
make sure that the information
reached the people who could
apply it. For the benefit of all
those involved in institutional
childcare anywhere in the world,
and for the benefit of those in
their care.

This can probably partly be explained by the fact that most major
organisations, such as UNICEF and Save the Children, do not believe
in institutional childcare and refuse to get involved in it, or be vocal
about it. They concentrate their efforts on trying to put an end to institutional childcare, by providing families and communities with as
much help as possible to continue looking after children themselves,

and by stimulating local foster care and adoption in cases where there really is no possibility of the child being taken care of by family members. This is to be applauded. No matter how well-organised and lovingly given, institutional care is not good for children. The fewer children in children's homes, the better. However, I feel that we cannot close our eyes to the millions of children worldwide who are currently in children's homes. It is a fact that, unfortunately, institutional childcare is not redundant yet, however much we might want it to be so. There are still situations where institutional care is not desirable, but where it is the only alternative to the child dying by the side of the road. Until this has changed, I feel that we must do whatever we can to ensure the quality of care within existing institutions, and the quality of life of those who live there.

I do not believe putting in effort to improve care in children's home, for the time being, confirms their right to exist any more than giving money for treatment of measles and malaria is an indication that we do not want to get rid of these diseases. On the other hand, I do believe that the policy of large international organisations to ignore institutional childcare is at least in part to blame for the fact that the word 'care' hardly applies to what takes place in some children's homes–the number of which, when taken worldwide, is shocking.

Children waiting for caregivers.

I believe that we can work on putting an end to institutional childcare *alongside* working to improve the lives of children currently in children's homes. Writing a book like this, and going to visit children's homes where management is interested in improvement to help train people, will by no means be the end to the current situation. However, hopefully my endeavours will improve the quality of life and survival chances for some children, and for their caregivers.

To improve things in children's homes, usually all that is needed is awareness and knowledge of certain issues and a real interest in the well-being of the children on the part of the management and care-givers. Unfortunately, in some places, that interest is lacking. When there is no real interest in the well-being of the children, nothing any outsider can do will make any difference. However, for those who do have the interest of the children at heart, but lack aware-ness and knowledge on certain issues, this book may be of help. It may reach more people and will certainly travel faster than I personally can by visiting children's homes.

While children of all ages are being cared for in children's homes around the world, in this book I mainly concentrate on infant and toddler care. There are two reasons for this. One is that I have much more experi-ence with this age group than with older children. The other, more important reason is that this is an extremely vulnerable age group. While school-aged children without a doubt are in great need of receiving prop-er care and nutrition and having psychologi-cal needs met, and they will suffer if they lack these things, the youngest age group is much more sensitive to any of those lacks. Any degree of sub-standard infant or toddler care is very likely to lead to **morbidity** and even **mortality** quite fast.

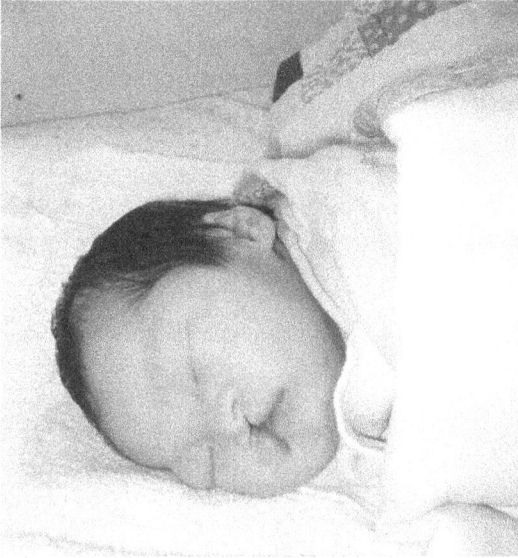

Here the baby is very well, a week later he had passed away due to dehydration.

The first part of this book focuses quite closely on the practical care of babies and toddler specifically, while the second part of the book looks at global and psychological development throughout child-hood. The third part of the book focuses on aspects of setting up and running a children's home; this is relevant to anyone involved in managing a children's home, and more examples will be given that specifically apply to homes for older children.

To many people, some of the issues I raise in this book will seem obvious, or even silly. Unfortunately, I have to assure the reader that these things were only included because I saw them go badly wrong somewhere, or because I was asked to explain them by people who quite sincerely did not know or understand them. So congratulate yourself on the knowledge you already possess when you come across something like that. Hopefully some of what you find among the rest will provide you with new information.

Cultural Differences

Childcare, like many aspects of life, is very different across cultures. One cannot objectively say that one way is better than another. I have no desire whatsoever to impose my cultural values—whatever they may be by now; I do not think they can be called strictly European anymore–on anyone. What I enjoy most in my work is an exchange of thoughts, ideas and handy tricks, by all involved.

Aside from the cultural aspects to childcare, there are universal needs that are overlooked in many places, also in rich countries. I have found that many issues such as lying to children, not allowing babies to play on their belly, and not brushing first teeth are universal and need to be addressed worldwide. On issues that can be seen as cultural, such as discipline and communication, I will make a case for the reasoning behind my approach and you can decide for yourself what you choose to do with it. I consider it a good sign that wherever I have been I have always been considered far too soft and sweet with children by a certain group of people, while being considered excessively strict by another group. To have accomplished that, I must be somewhere in the middle.

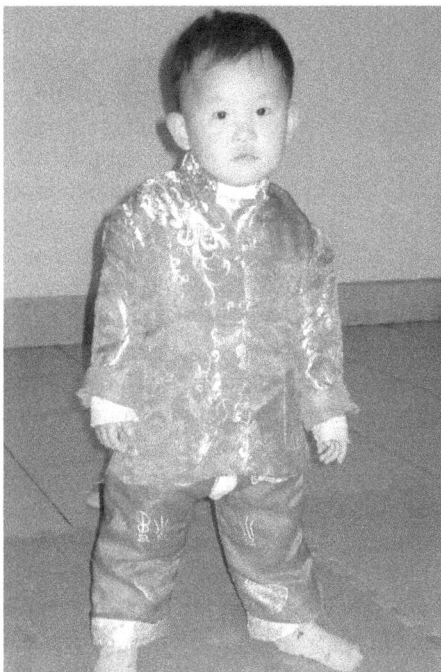

In the case of children's homes run by foreigners, ideally they should stick as closely to local values and social rules as possible in caring for the children. That way, the children do not receive conflicting messages or risk becoming unfamiliar with their own culture. Personally, I prefer it when children are not given Western names–for the 'convenience' of the foreigners–and are spoken to in their native language as well as being exposed to native music and storytelling. Because all these things are an **essential** part of their identity. This is particularly important for children who can be expected to live their lives in their own country, and every effort should be made to make sure this is the case for as many children as possible.

Purpose of the book

What I try to do in this book is to provide boundaries–concerning safety, health and a basic understanding of child development and psychology–within which to try things out. To give advice and suggestions about how you can go about finding the right course of action for a specific child. When it comes down to it, all that is really needed to provide good care is a bit of background knowledge and a lot of creativity, patience, an open mind, and a real interest in the children's well-being.

The needs of children individually should be considered.

Of course, life and care in a children's home limit the possibilities and the freedom to experiment in certain ways. It is important for health and safety that there are set rules about various aspects of care. Because of the number of children cared for at any given time, children will have to conform more to the group and the way things are done than they would in a family situation. Nevertheless, I think it is important that whenever possible, caregivers still try to observe the small, non-disruptive ways in which a child has slightly different needs from the rest and give in to them whenever possible. This can strengthen the child's self-esteem and feeling of well-being a lot.

This is not your standard reference book about childcare with lots of theoretical and scientific lectures. My aim is to make the solutions I offer as widely accessible as possible. I will give a lot of examples of why things do or do not work, to illustrate why I came to certain conclusions. Especially with the things that pose dangers and might be taken for granted by some, I use examples to illustrate why I focus on those things. Where necessary, I will give an explanation about the research that indicates the effects of certain methods of care.

Cases studies are divided into several categories that are indicated by the use of an icon. The icons and their meaning are:

A situation well handled   *A situation poorly handled*   *An example to give a more concrete idea of an abstract concept that was just introduced*

Something that is essential to keep in mind   *A quote*   *General information*

The books and the articles used to get this information are all listed in the reference section of this book. However, I have chosen not to complicate the text in the book with footnotes or other referencing tools to indicate what came from where, paragraph by paragraph.

There is also a word list at the back of the book, to explain the more complicated words used in the text. Words that appear in the word list will be bold the first time they appear in the text. If one of the Guidelines that the UN has dictated for care of children in children's homes, or in 'alternative care' as they call it, is relevant to a part of the book, these guidelines will be included at the end of the section or chapter, to allow you to access them without making a complicated search. You will find most of these guidelines in Part 3 of the book.

While this book is written for people who run a children's home to instruct them on the standard to aim for and the instructions to give to their caregiving staff, it may also be of use to other people in some way involved in institutional childcare—for example volunteering organisations. The advice given here is not aimed at creating a utopia for children. Doing nothing but following the guidelines of this book will not lead to the ideal children's home. It will just improve conditions in critical areas. While they might not always be easy to fulfil, the needs given here are basic needs that must be met for a child to have a reasonable quality of life. Any less will endanger life, health and wellbeing. Any child who is being cared for in a children's home for more

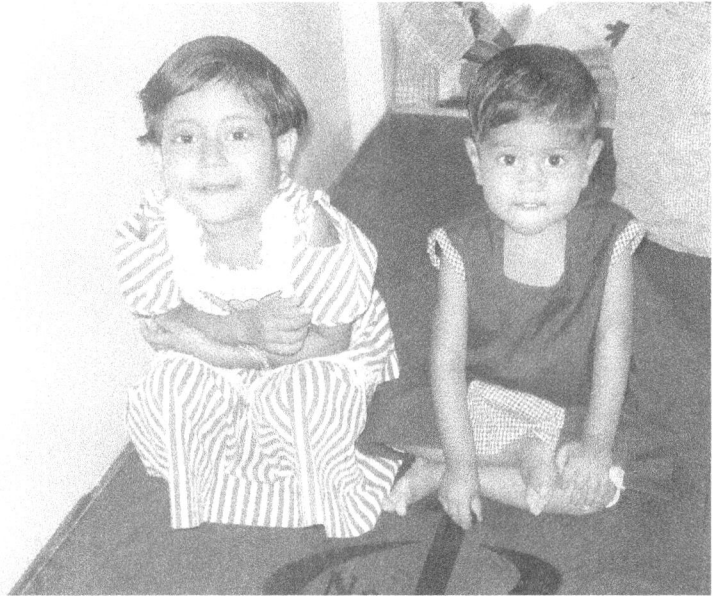

These girls can expect to live here untill they are adults.

than a few weeks will start to show 'damage' if those essential basic needs are not met. I am aware that money is usually very tight and that it is not easy to get everything done all the time, but what I describe here are standards that need to be met to get basic health and safety on the rails. Whenever I describe a situation and I say 'at least', I am talking about the absolute minimum requirement, even if resources are very scarce. If you are unable to meet those standards, maybe you should rethink the decision to run a children's home.

Throughout the book, I have chosen to address the reader directly, as if the reader is the person who will actually take care of the situation discussed. On the subject of personal pronouns, I have chosen to refer to all adults involved in the running of things and the caring for children in children's homes as 'she' and 'her', because in my experience the vast majority of people working at institutions is female. If any adults outside the children's home are referred to, I will designate them male, simply for clarity and distinction. I will alternately refer to the children as 'he' and 'she' in different parts, while sticking to one of the two throughout a section.

It is my hope that these books will help you improve the care in your children's home. My motto, and that of Orphanage Projects, is: I cannot change the world, but I can change the world for one child, and then another, and another…. And so can you!

Part 1:
Basic Childcare

Chapter 1:   Hygiene

Good **hygiene** is extremely important for children's health and their chances of survival. This is true in general for babies and **toddlers** because they are still building up their **immune system** and are more **vulnerable** to illnesses and **infection** than older children. However, it is especially true when children live in children's homes. Many people living close together in itself increases the chance of someone carrying a virus, bacteria or other infections, as well as increasing the chance of whatever one person has spreading to others through close contact. When you add to this that children living in a children's home almost always have a weaker immune system than children who live in families–because all their essential basic needs are not met–you will realise that doing your best to protect these children from infection through good hygiene is a top priority. Making changes to achieve a higher standard of hygiene will generally show a big **improvement** in the children's health within a few weeks' time.

It is useful to be aware of the things that undermine a child's immune system, so that you know what to avoid. The main factors for children in children's homes are:
- **Lack** of good hygiene
- Lack of enough food
- Lack of the right food
- Lack of enough sleep
- Lack of physical contact
- Lack of safe water
- Depression

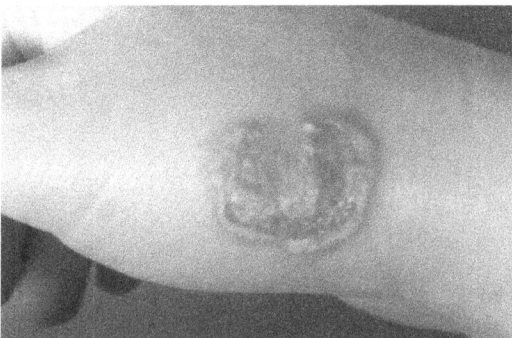

A tiny scratch that turned into a major infection, because of bad hygiene conditions. It needed antibiotics to resolve.

Through good hygiene, a lot of infections can be **prevented**, and when infection does take place, the effects can be minimised. While in conditions of poor hygiene, any disease is very likely to spread to all the children, and minor infections often become much more serious, sometimes even life-threatening. So, while it takes a bit more work–in other words, an investment of time and energy–to make sure good hygiene is maintained, you will benefit from it. Good hygiene practice saves you the considerable time and energy involved in having to care for sick children, as well as saving you a lot of money on medical bills. Finally, good hygiene can quite simply save lives, which I think we can all agree is the most valuable saving that can be made.

✳ ———————————— **General Hygiene**

✳ ———————————— *Washing Hands*

The simplest and at the same time most complicated way to keep up good hygiene is by thorough hand washing with soap. It is the simplest because everyone knows how to do it and it is a very cheap and effective way to prevent the spread of bacteria, viruses and fungi. It is complicated because it is very hard to make people understand how important it is and to make sure that they do it **consistently**.

Making sure that hands are washed consistently means that *any-one*–including management–setting foot in the children's home should go straight to the tap and soap, before they touch any of the children. Using soap to wash your hands is important, because just rinsing them with water will not get rid of all bacteria and dirt. While mixing liquid soap with water may save money, watered down soap will not clean your hands well enough to save the children's health.

Next comes a rule that is even harder to enforce: hands should be washed in between handling different children, especially if they are babies or sick children. When a caregiver is sitting in the middle of a group of children, playing, she does not need to wash her hands between one child and the other. It would be better if she did, but it is not practical. However, she should wash her hands before she moves to another group, or to a child from another group.

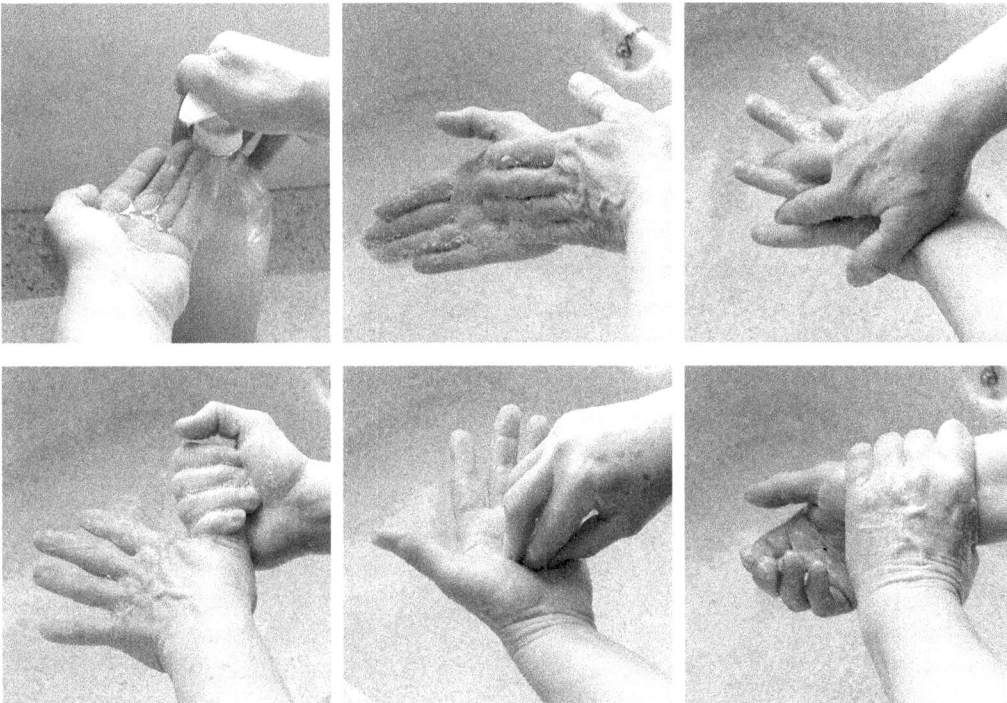

Washing Hands

To give a simple overview:

- *Before preparing meals or bottles, hands should be washed.*
- *Before preparing or handling medication, hands should be washed.*
- *Before handling sterilised bottles etc., hands should be washed.*
- *After EVERY **nappy** changed, hands should be washed.*
- *After helping a child on the toilet, hands should be washed.*
- *After every bath given, hands should be washed.*
- *After handling vomit, hands should be washed.*
- *After having been drooled on, hands should be washed.*
- *Before and after touching any wound, sore, **rash**, hands should be washed.*
- *Before and after touching a child with a fever or other signs of illness, hands should be washed.*
- *Before and after handling one of the youngest babies, hands should be washed.*
- *After visiting the toilet, hands should be washed.*
- *After eating, hands should be washed.*

It is time consuming, it is annoying, it is hard to get caregivers to **co-operate**, and it is hard on your hands. I know all these things, because I practice constant hand washing. The reason why I keep washing my hands so often despite the inconvenience–and in some cases despite the pain–is that I have seen the enormous difference hand washing makes in the children's health and the health of the caregivers. Providing people with hand lotion to use after they wash their hands can help against dry hands.

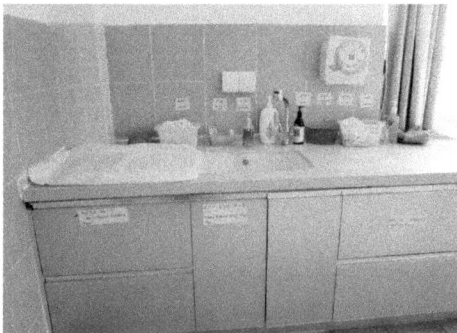

Area for handwashing, changing and bathing.

An eye infection broke out. There were two groups in this children's home: one baby group and one toddler group. At the start, one or two of the children in each group had the infection. In the toddler group, it soon spread a lot faster, and within three days, two or three of the caregiving staff also had the eye infection. This solved the riddle: in the baby group, hands were washed consistently and the infection was kept relatively limited. In the toddler group, hands were not washed as well as they should be, and the infection did not only reach more children, but also the caregivers who did not wash their hands.

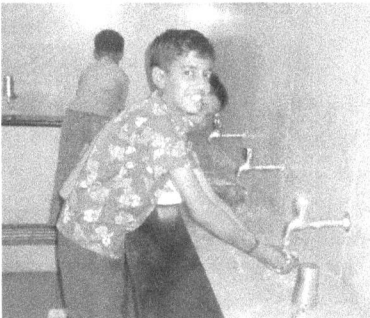

The children have been taught to wash their hands before they eat.

From about two years old onwards, children should be taught to wash their own hands every time before they eat—any food they put in their mouth, so snacks as well as meals—and after they have been to the toilet or on the **potty**.

If washing hands with water and soap is not possible because of shortage of (safe) water or a great inconvenience in reaching the place to wash your hands, hand sanitiser can be used instead. If washing hands is very inconvenient, or if water cuts are frequent, every room in the children's home should have a bottle of hand sanitiser, placed outside of the children's reach, but easily accessible to the staff.

Washing Clothes

Making sure that clothes, playing mats, sleeping mats and bed linen are washed regularly and thoroughly is an important part of maintaining good hygiene. The use of soap and hot water, if available, makes sure they are properly cleaned.

What is important and sometimes overlooked, is making sure that clothes are hung out to dry in a room other than the room where the children sleep or play. Hanging clothes outside is ideal, if weather conditions allow it. Having clothes hang out in the sun can kill a lot of bacteria and **mould** spores. However, wherever you choose to hang the clothing and bed linen to dry, under no circumstances should they be hung to dry over the sides of the children's beds. The constant

Drying clothes outside whenever and however possible.

nearness of damp clothes is a serious health risk for children because depending on the temperature and humidity (the amount of water in the air), the clothes may take a long time to dry indoors and are likely to form mould before they are completely dry.

It is important to make sure that clothes are completely dry before they are stored away in a closet. If a little dampness remains when clothes are locked away, there is a chance of mould forming in the material. The typical smell of cloth that has been wet for too long is an indication of the presence of mould. Bed linen needs to be completely dry before it is put on a bed, because otherwise the dampness may seep into the mat or mattress and cause mould to form there.

The rainy season had started, which meant that it was much harder to get clothes to dry. It also meant that the temperature had dropped and that the children were feeling cold more often. One morning, before breakfast, a ten-year-old girl came up to me to say good morning. She was shivering and complaining she was cold. When I gave her a hug, I noticed that the T-shirt she was wearing was still wet.

Clothes should be completely dry before they are put on a child, because the dampness will use the child's body heat to dry. This removal of body heat can put a child at risk for **hypothermia** (more information about hypothermia can be found in *Sick Children Everywhere*) and make him more vulnerable to the bacteria and viruses he is exposed to at any given moment. This is because his body will give priority to the energy needed to keep his body warm, instead of the energy needed to fight attacks on his health. This means he will get sick more easily.

The laundry room.

Cleaning Rooms

Children do not live in little bubbles. They live in the world. They live in the rooms you provide them with and between the things

Toddlers too may put whatever they find in their mouths.

you surround them with. While at times we would all like to say 'just sit on that chair and do not move for a few minutes', anyone who is involved with children knows that not only is this not a realistic request, it is not good for the child either. Children move around, and that means they will create a mess and they will be affected by dirt in their environment.

Children move around in whatever area they can move around in. Whether it is their cot, their bedroom, the playroom, or a whole house and garden, they will go exploring as far as they can. Exploring means looking at, feeling and holding, and often tasting too. It does not matter how many times you tell babies and toddlers not to put things in their mouths: they will still do it. Not because they are bad, but because for them tasting something and finding out how it feels in their mouth is an important way of discovering what something is. Up to two years of age, a child's brain finds it much easier to interpret information coming from the mouth than information coming from the eyes. So he uses his mouth to 'look' at things. This is called **oral** exploration. It is why you may see a baby lick the floor or even the carpet, to find out what exactly it is.

Bedbugs were a big problem in a particular children's home. The children were scratching the bites until they opened the skin and caused little wounds that became infected. Fumigators were brought in to spray poison to kill all the bedbugs. That night no one got bitten by bedbugs, but after a few days the problem started again.
The poison cannot kill the eggs that the bedbugs have laid. So the place needs to be sprayed again after four or five days to kill all the bedbugs that have come out of the eggs in the meantime. If this is not done, the problem will be as bad as it was before. And the money spent on the first round of fumigation will have been wasted.

People know that it is important to keep their houses and the surrounding grounds clean to prevent **infestations** of insects or rodents, and to make sure no one gets sick. This is equally true in a children's home. However, as mentioned at the start of this chapter, in a place where there are a lot of people and small children together, standards need to be higher to get the same result.

The rooms in which the children live and the objects with which they come into contact—which can be toys, but also furniture and so on—need to be kept especially clean. This is because the toys go from hand to hand and from mouth to mouth, and the children will lick their beds and the floor and the wall. Plus, having a large group of small children in a space will cause a lot more mess than in an average home: they spill, **throw up** and leak their various toilet wastes everywhere.

One of the babies has thrown up most of the milk he has just drunk; his caregiver takes him away to change his clothes, because everything is wet with thrown up milk. As soon as the caregiver has left the room, another baby, who so far seemed totally focused on the cups with which she was banging, puts down the cups and crawls over to where the puddle of thrown up milk is. She looks at it, then puts her hand into it to feel what it is and she moves her fingers around in the puddle. After a while, she starts splashing the milk around by beating her hand into the puddle. Her face, her clothes and a big area on the floor are now wet with the milk. The funny sound of splashing has caught the attention of the other children who are playing on the floor; they start to make their way over to join in the fun. Just as the caregiver walks back into the room with the boy who was sick earlier, all clean now, she sees the little girl put her hand—covered in thrown up milk mixed with dirt from the floor—in her mouth.

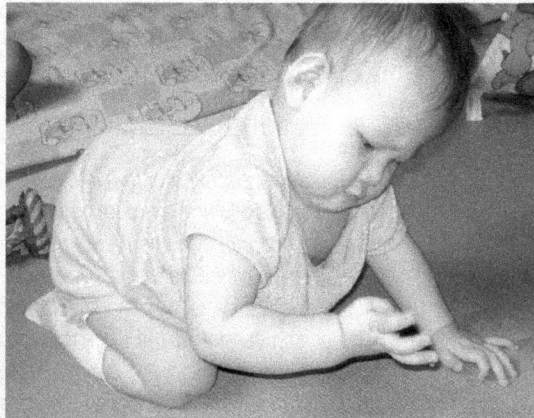

She has got something stuck to her hand, first she will take a look, and then a taste.

This means that sweeping once a day or once every other day, which is enough to keep everyone healthy in a normal household, is not enough in a children's home. It is essential that a mess is cleaned up thoroughly as soon as it is discovered, while placing the children out of reach. It means that floors need to be swept at least once or twice a day and the floors as well as the furniture need to be wiped with a wet cloth regularly too. If you do not do this, bacteria will multiply in these places and will spread very rapidly among all the children, causing illness and infection.

Whenever an infestation such as rodents, or bedbugs, fleas, or lice is discovered, action should be taken straight away to get rid of the problem. If you have experience with getting rid of a problem like this and your methods have been effective—that is to say the problem did not return for at least six to twelve months after you solved it—you can handle it yourself. If you are not entirely sure how to get rid of the infestation or if before your methods only helped for a short time, it is best to get in help from someone who has more knowledge and success in handling the problem. No time should be lost after discovering an infestation, because these kinds of problems usually get out of control quite quickly and they pose a serious risk to the children's health, as well as that of the caregiving staff.

A children's home had a rat problem, like most other places in the slum that surrounded it. At first, there were just a few rats, running over the wooden beams below the roof. However, foods like cornflour, rice and beans were stored in sacks rather than plastic or metal containers, making them easy to get for the rats. This meant that the rats were essentially being fed and very quickly, the rat population grew enormously. The management was warned

Especially when there are many, rats form a danger to the children.

to make sure the food was stored in containers the rats could not get into and to get someone to get rid of the rats, but they thought that just bringing in a cat would be enough. As the rat population grew from just a few to several dozens, the rats became bolder and more aggressive. At first, they started running over the children's legs while they were asleep. Eventually, they started biting children and chewing on their feet while they were in bed. What initially seemed like a minor problem had become a big danger.

While these boys have special needs, they also have regular needs, such as fresh air and daylight.

Having a door or window open whenever possible.

Having good ventilation and plenty of light is important for healthy living conditions. When Florence Nightingale first suggested the need for this in the nineteenth century, it was a revolutionary new concept in nursing to let light and air into a patient's room. However, it proved very effective and it is now common knowledge that light and air are important. But it does not apply only to hospital care. Light and fresh air are important in any living environment. When it comes to children's homes, this is often overlooked. Either because of the belief that small children need to be protected from the outside world or because people just do not think about it. After all, the caregivers and management go in and out of the house during the day. They may not even notice or realise that the children never get to be outside or to have fresh air, since the adults have a different experience.

It is true that babies should not lie in a stream of moving air and that it is important to keep them warm enough. However, they need fresh air and light to **thrive**. It is almost always possible to find a way to make sure that fresh air comes into the room without having babies lying in moving air or getting too cold. Make sure that there are windows in the rooms where the children spend most of their time, and do not cover those windows up. This makes life more pleasant and brighter not only for the children, but also for the caregivers.

Allowing children to be exposed to sunlight is also a way of making sure that they get enough Vitamin D, which prevents problems with the bones, such as rickets. And the great part is: it does not cost a thing.

✳ ──────────── **Nappy Hygiene**

It is very important that nappies or wet/**soiled** clothes are changed very regularly. Both **urine** and **poop** literally break down the skin, if the skin stays in contact with them for some time. How often nappies need to be changed depends on the type of nappy used.

✳ ──────────── *Kinds of Nappies*

These days, most **disposable** nappies make sure that the contact between skin and urine is minimal. So it is usually not a problem to wait up to four hours between changes when the nappy is only wet. A dirty nappy (one with poop in it) should always be changed as soon as possible, because poop acts more aggressively towards the skin than urine. If you use cloth nappies (they should preferably be made of absorbent cotton) or no nappies but only clothes around the child's bottom, there is no barrier between the urine and the skin, plus the nappy becomes saturated more quickly. So cloth nappies should be changed every 2 to 3 hours at least. And clothes should be changed whenever they are wet or soiled.

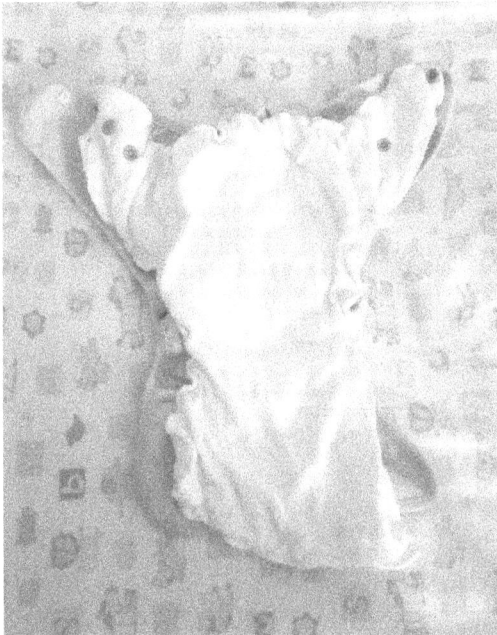

Preformed cloth nappy with snaps and cover.

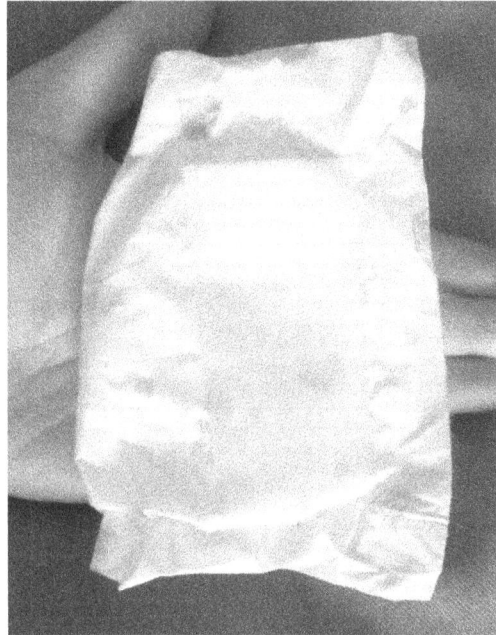

Disposable nappy for a premature baby.

In either case, unless the baby's bottom is already red or the skin in the nappy area is broken, you can usually leave changing nappies longer at night. How long mainly depends on how absorbent the nappy you use is.

What kind of nappies are used, will depend on the location, circumstances and what is affordable:

Disposable nappies	Advantage	Disadvantage
	Very easy to put on	Expensive
	Very absorbent	Can cause heat rash in the nappy area because of little ventilation
	No extra laundry	Cause a lot of waste, not always easy to throw away hygienically

Square Cloth nappies	Advantage	Disadvantage
	Only a periodic investment	Takes practice and time to fold and put on right
	Cheaper than disposable nappies	Needs to be changed more often than disposable nappies and is more likely to leak unless covered by a plastic layer
	Less waste than disposable nappies	Needs to be washed and dried very thoroughly to avoid infections
	Kinder to the skin in heat	Poses an infection risk during times of infectious diseases unless nappies are not exchanged between children, so everyone has their own pile, to be washed separately

Preformed Cloth nappies	Advantage	Disadvantage
	Only a periodic investment	Needs to be changed more often than disposable nappies and is more likely to leak unless covered by a plastic layer
	Cheaper than disposable nappies, more expensive than square cloth nappies	Needs to be washed and dried very thoroughly to avoid infection
	Less waste than disposable	Takes longer to dry than square cloth nappies
	Easy to put on	Poses an infection risk during times of infectious diseases unless nappies are not exchanged between children, so everyone has their own pile, to be washed separately

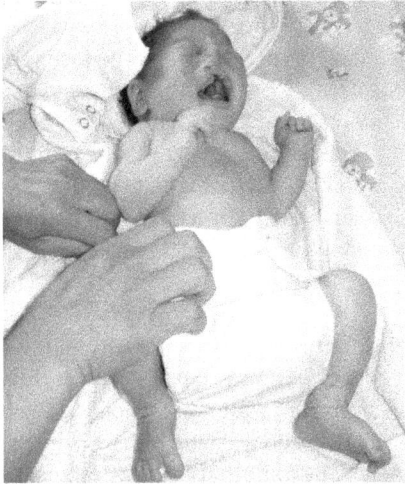

A pre-formed cloth nappy with a cover to prevent leakage.

Cloth nappies arranged by size.

Cloth nappies need to be washed after every use, which will require either a washing machine or hiring someone who washes and dries the nappies full-time in any place with many babies. It is very important that the nappies are washed very thoroughly and that any traces of urine and poop are removed to prevent the **development** of bacteria or the spread of infections. To make sure the nappies are really clean, they need to be washed with a detergent with germicidal (= kills bacteria) properties, or a sterilising agent needs to be added to the water (they can often be bought in tablet form). If these things are not available in your area or are unaffordable, the nappies will need to be boiled after every use.

In a particular adoption centre, the babies are given cloth nappies, but they are made of a single layer of very thin, smooth cotton. Since this material is unable to absorb more than a few drops of liquid, the urine runs out as if the cloth was not there, and because it is attached very loosely, most of the poop also tends to escape. This means that every time a baby relieves herself, all of her clothes and bedding get wet and need to be changed. While it will certainly do the babies no harm to use these nappies, for the caregivers it causes more work–the nappies need to be washed–without bringing any benefit, since the result is exactly the same as when the baby would not use any nappy. My advice would be either to stop using the useless nappies and save yourself at least the work of having to wash them, or start using nappies that absorb well enough to save you having to change–and wash–the babies' clothing and bedding every time.

Depending on the location and climate, you can also choose to let babies go without nappies. It saves the money on buying nappies and work on washing them. However, a very strict hygiene standard needs to be maintained in this case. Every time a baby pees or poops, it needs to be cleaned up immediately and the location needs to be wiped with disinfectant, to prevent the spreading of diseases. If the baby is not wearing something to absorb urine and poop, it is also very important to make sure you check the baby's bedding and change it every time it is soiled or wet. In cases of bad nappy rash, it is a good idea to leave the baby with a bare bottom for at least a few hours a day, to let the skin dry and heal.

Cleaning Bottoms

Whether you clean a baby's bottom with disposable baby wipes–preferably ones without any kind of perfume, because the perfume can lead to allergies–, a wash cloth with water, or by holding the baby's bottom under the tap and washing it there with your hands, it is extremely important that you wash the baby's bottom very thoroughly every time she has pooped. Just wiping the bottom with a dry cloth or toilet paper, or with the nappy you have just removed, is not enough. The material you use to clean the baby's bottom needs to be damp to effectively remove all remaining poop. Whenever the nappy area is very damp after removing a wet nappy, it should also be wiped clean.

Changing table: everything needed is within reach.

Not properly cleaning a baby's bottom can literally kill her. Remains of poop on the skin will eat away at it. This will cause slight redness at first, which will steadily get worse, in a process which progresses faster and faster if it is not stopped by proper care. The redness will get bright and become very painful. Then the skin will break and wounds with liquid coming out and blisters will appear. This will progress to open, bleeding wounds, which will get infected when the bacteria from the poop enter them, and this can–and probably will, if nothing is done–lead to septicaemia (a blood infection), which can lead to death if not treated promptly in hospital. This is why it is so extremely important to clean the baby properly after she pooped, every time, and to take action straight away if a nappy rash starts to develop.

Due to circumstances, a three-year-old boy with special needs, who was generally very healthy, had to be transferred back from a children's home where he was well cared for, to the orphanage that had originally accepted him when he was found abandoned. It was known that the care standard at the original orphanage was not very high, but it had been decided that this boy was robust enough to withstand the circumstances for what would only be a few months. Only nineteen days after arriving in the original orphanage, the boy passed away. Cause of death was septicaemia–a dangerous blood infection–caused by severe wounds and sores on his bottom.

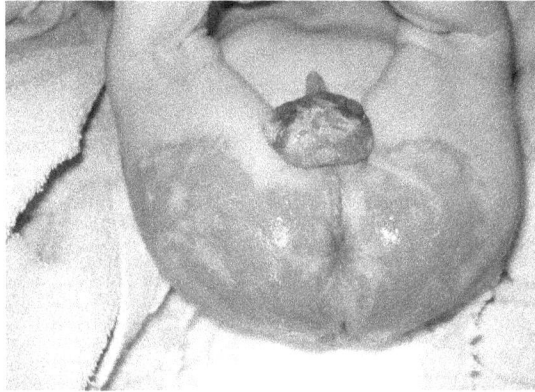

Result of not changing nappies often enough, after only a few days.

When cleaning a girl after a dirty nappy, make sure you wipe front to back, to prevent poop from reaching the vaginal and urinal openings and possibly causing infections there. Both with boys and girls, make sure you check all the hiding places. This is not sexual assault: it is proper hygiene. Little boys tend to hide some of the poop between their penis and their scrotum, so check there and clean it, but do not pull back the foreskin. Another hiding place is under the scrotum, so check and clean there. Girls sometimes manage to store poop in between their labia, so this also needs to be cleaned to prevent breaking skin.

When you use a bowl of water–make sure the water is safe to use, if there are a lot of parasites in the water in your area, strain the water through a clean cloth before you use it to wash children and their bottoms with–and a clean cloth to clean a bottom, avoid dipping the soiled cloth in the water again. Use a different cloth for the second wiping. Otherwise poop will get into the water and will be wiped onto bottoms, increasing the chance of spreading infection.

Always use a cotton swab to take cream from a jar or tube.

If you are applying any creams, especially when more than one child uses the contents of the tube or jar, apply the cream with a cotton swab, not with your finger, and use a new cotton swab every time you want to get more out of the tube or jar. This prevents bacteria getting into the cream and spreading onto the next child.

If the baby has a nappy rash, zinc oxide is the most effective barrier. Applying a generous layer of zinc oxide will prevent the skin from coming into contact with urine and poop; this allows the skin time to heal. If there is no zinc oxide or other barrier cream, very fine cornflour can also be used.

If the baby's rash is not a red area, but separate red dots, it is probably a fungal infection instead of a regular nappy rash–especially if the baby has thrush in her mouth too (this looks like white patches on the inside of her cheeks and on her tongue). In this case, a doctor should have a look at the rash, so that an **appropriate** anti-fungal cream can be prescribed to treat it.

Fungal infection, combined with too few nappy changes.

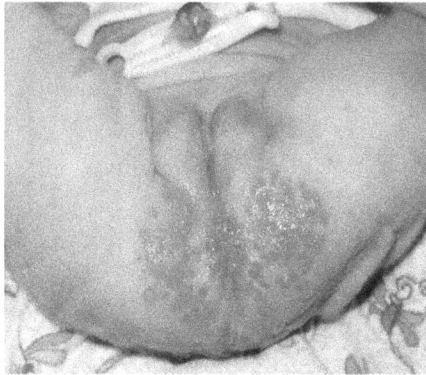

When you put the clothes back on the baby, check that they are still dry and that nothing has leaked out of the nappy onto them. If there is any wetness or staining, the clothes should be changed.

Finally, ALWAYS wash your hands after you finish changing a baby's nappy.

Older Children in Nappies

Sometimes, a physical handicap or severe **mental retardation** makes it impossible for a child to learn to control his bladder and **bowels**. In such a case, I would strongly recommend using some form of absorbent nappy, whether it is disposable or washable. With the larger bladder and bowels, the mess caused can be quite big if there is nothing in place to catch and absorb most of the waste.

If the child is able to move and understand well enough, he should gradually be taught to clean himself up after relieving himself, as much as possible. Not as a punishment for soiling himself, but to give him a sense of **independence** and dignity. Anything he cannot do for himself, he should receive help with without blaming him.

With older children who are still dependent on the use of nappies, it is just as important as with babies to clean thoroughly to prevent sores and infections in the nappy area. Once puberty starts, nappy hygiene is further complicated by the growth of hair, the excretion of 'new' bodily fluids and increased sweating. During each nappy change, thorough cleaning as well as very thorough drying is essential to prevent infection and sores.

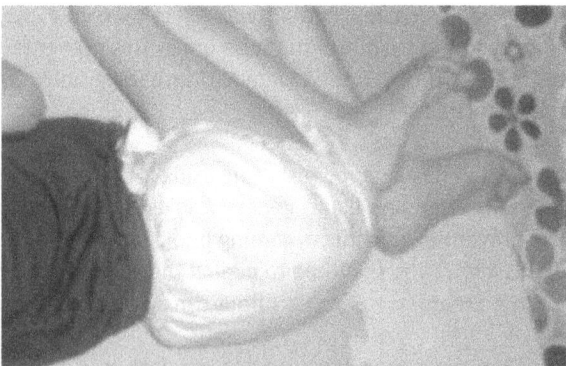

A young adult with cerebral palsy in cloth nappies.

Although these children continue to require nappy changes, this does not mean they should be treated like babies. When it comes to changing them, their dignity should be respected. They should not be undressed in front of other people, and no one should make humiliating remarks about their lack of bladder and bowel control. Nappy changing should be done by someone of the same sex as the child, if possible.

All human beings have the right to basic respect and dignity.

Potty training

Moving from using a nappy to wearing underwear and using a potty or a toilet is a big step. Not just for the people in charge of buying or washing the nappies, whose expenses and efforts decrease, but especially for the toddler. It is very important for his sense of growing independence, **self-esteem**, and the feeling that he is growing up and no longer a baby.

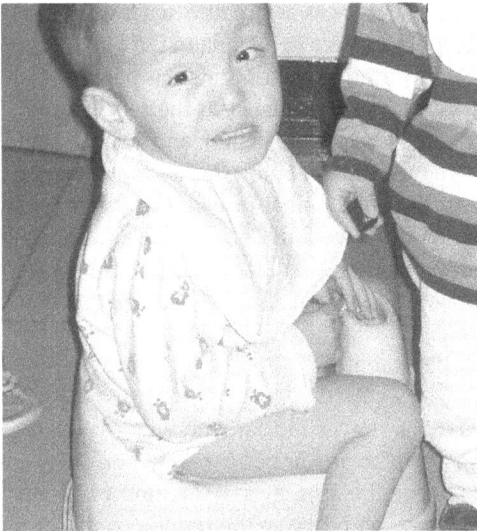

Sitting on the potty, waiting for something to happen.

Both in families and in children's homes, it is not uncommon for the caregivers to wait with starting potty training for quite some time, even if the toddler is well past the age where he can be expected to understand the concept, and sometimes despite a clearly indicated wish to stop using his nappy. This is very unfortunate. It is true that potty training is time-consuming, and that accidents will happen for some time, which may cause extra laundry. However, this step is essential for the toddler's development and self-esteem. Plus, if he is **discouraged** at a time when he shows an interest in using a potty or the toilet, it is entirely possible that when the 'more convenient' time has arrived in the eyes of the caregiver, the toddler is no longer willing to cooperate.

It is very hard to say what is the 'right' age to start potty training. This depends on a combination of the child and the circumstances. One indication that a child is ready to start learning to use a potty, is when you notice that he stops walking, or doing what he is doing right before he relieves himself. This indicates that he is aware that something is coming before it is happening. On the other hand, if you see a child continue to do what he was doing and only stop once he notices urine or poop running down his legs, that is a sign that he does not realise when something is on its way yet, and that he is not ready for potty training.

It being called potty training does not mean that a potty needs to be involved. Some children go straight to the toilet. Sometimes, the child needs to learn to go to a certain outdoor area to relieve himself. For the sake of ease, I will continue to speak of potty training and potties, but you know your own situation well enough to fill in the best approach.

In northern China, most babies go without nappies and wear split pants. From almost the very start of life, they are regularly held over a little bucket, while a 'ssshhh' sound is made. They learn to pee at these moments quite quickly, and while accidents certainly happen, they are not as common as you would think. Not long after the toddler starts walking, they are taught to go outside when they feel they need to pee, squatting out in the garden. Initially, this is anywhere outside the door, gradually the skill is perfected to where the child will go to a specific place and eventually to the outhouse. This is a labour-intensive process, but it shows that it is possible to have babies and toddlers go without nappies with fewer accidents than you might expect.

Allowing the child to go as soon as she indicates that she has to, is key to avoiding accidents.

If a toddler shows he is aware of when he is peeing, at whatever age, it is a good idea to put him on the potty whenever he indicates that he is peeing or is about to start. This way he learns the relation between the feeling and the action, and you can start asking him to warn you before he starts peeing. Do not become angry if he has not warned you in time, this will make him anxious and less likely to cooperate. Just remind him every time you put him on the potty, or when you change his wet nappy, that you would really like him to tell you when he thinks he needs to pee soon.

When he does start to indicate more or less reliably when he needs to pee or poop, put him on the potty whenever he asks, even if the timing is inconvenient. This is both to give the toddler confidence and to avoid accidents. Accidents caused by ignoring a request to go on the potty are not his fault, but may still make the toddler feel bad. If he sits on the potty and nothing comes, let him stay there a minute or two to see if something may come after all. If it does not, help him pull up his trousers again and send him off to play, reminding him to let you know when he thinks he does need to pee. Do not become irritated or angry with him; that is not likely to improve the situation. The stress of knowing he might be **reprimanded** or punished if he has an accident, makes it harder for him to **focus** on signals that he needs the potty, which in turn makes accidents more likely to happen.

If you notice that he is asking to go on the potty a lot without doing anything, this is most likely because he has found this is a way to get individual attention. In this case, make sure that going on the potty becomes rather a boring experience, by not giving attention while the child is on the potty. Becoming angry about it will not help, because becoming angry will still give him attention. Every time that he does do something on the potty, provide him with a couple of minutes of extra attention, while praising the fact that he has done something, and washing his hands and yours. This way, the situation should resolve itself quite quickly, as there is not much to be gained by asking to go when nothing comes and everything when something does come.

Once the toddler is mostly dry, having no more than one accident a day and not every day, stop using nappies and move on to underwear, as encouragement. It can be very discouraging for a toddler to be made to wear nappies when he does not really need them anymore. Moving on to underwear may just be the boost he needed to make sure the accidents become even rarer.

A two-and-a-half-year-old girl was put on the potty just once in a while, when I first arrived. Basically only when the caregiver remembered. Then the caregiver went away for her holidays and I took over care of the group of toddlers for two weeks. From the start, I encouraged the little girl to use the potty and to warn me when she needed to use it, and within two days she was in underwear during the day and after a week during the night as well. It happened to be the right time for her and she needed only a little encouragement to take charge of it by herself. When she wore underwear day and night you could see her beaming with pride at being such a big girl and accidents were extremely rare. A little boy of the same age, in the same group, showed interest and curiosity about the whole potty-business, so I allowed him to sit on a potty for two or three minutes a few times a day too. He did not have any awareness of his bodily functions yet, but he was enthusiastic about being on a potty. Even more so when after a few days he did something on the potty–by chance–and got praised for it. So, all in all, the potty training of these two went very well... until their caregiver returned.

She put the little girl back in nappies during the night, because she said she had no intention of dealing with any accidents (there had so far not been a single accident at night), which visibly deflated the little girl's joy, and indeed the nappies did not always stay dry anymore during the night. As for the little boy, just after having experienced what it was like to do something on the potty and being very enthusiastic about trying again, his chances were dashed when the caregiver put a stop to attempts to train him. She said this was because she had tried a few months before and it had not worked, so there was no point.

It is usual for children–and especially boys–to need more time to become dry at night than to stay dry during the day. For some children it is a question of a few weeks, but it is not uncommon for a child to

Playing with potties to get used to them.

wet the bed until he is five to seven years old. Particularly if the child is anxious about something, or if his essential basic needs are not met (more about this will be explained in Part 1, Chapter 5: 'Essential Psychological Needs'), the likelihood of having problems with bed-wetting goes up. Most children older than three or four years old are very ashamed about having accidents in the night. It is something that is completely out of their control: if they were able to do something about it, they would. Just like with the initial potty training, reprimanding and punishing children who wet their bed at night is more likely to make the problem worse than to make it better.

While the child is still unable to stay dry at night, you can use nappies during the night and underwear during the day. It often helps to wake up a child who is dry during the day somewhere between 10 p.m. and midnight to use the potty or the toilet, making the rest of the night shorter. When he usually stays dry six nights a week, it is a good idea to move on to underwear during the night. While it might be more convenient for the caregiver to use nappies during the night, for the child's confidence and pride it is very important that you show confidence in him and his **ability** to stay dry. After all, if you do not believe in him, why should he bother to make the effort? The nappy is there anyway.

Do not scold the child when accidents happen, and they will. Start by asking if he needs to do more, and put him on the potty–or in the case of an older child, send him to the toilet–to let him try and make sure. Then just change his clothes and move on, simply reminding him to let you know when he needs to do something again. **Praise** him whenever he stays dry–for example in the evening before going to bed, tell him how proud you are that he has stayed dry all day– and whenever he does something on the potty. Having his caregiver angry with him whenever he has an accident causes insecurity and stress. Insecurity and stress make accidents more likely to happen, so this is a vicious circle (a situation that continues getting worse), which becomes hard to escape.

If an older child is normally completely dry and suddenly starts having accidents, it is worth finding out whether there is a pattern to be discovered behind the accidents. It could be because of a **traumatic** experience, or fear of a particular person. Although it could also be something much simpler, such as a bladder infection; it is worth having this checked. It could also be something even more innocent.

ⓘ

A girl of about two and a half years old was completely dry, day and night. Except when she was dressed in clothes she did not like. In that case, she could be expected to be wet within the hour. As long as she was given some choice or say in what she was to wear, everything was fine. A small price to pay in exchange for not having to do a lot of extra laundry

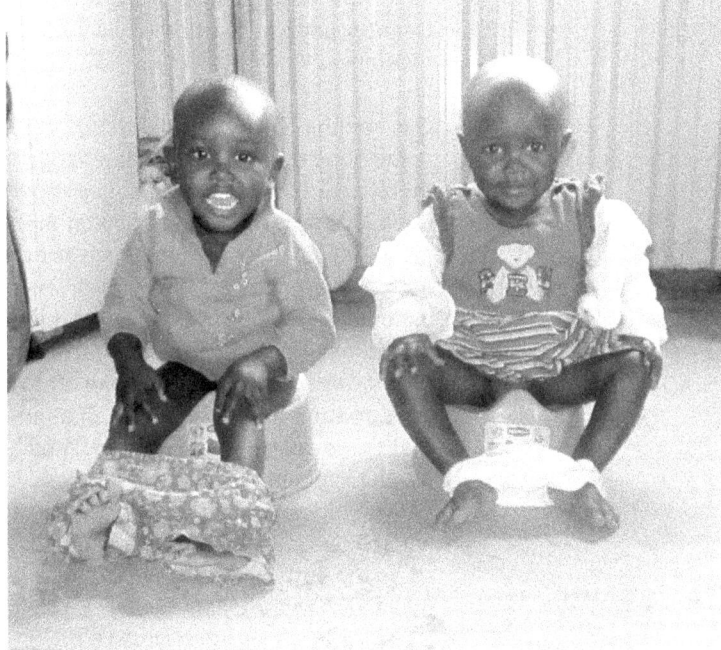

Practising together makes it more exciting and fun.

It is not uncommon for toddlers to take longer getting the hang of pooping on the potty than of peeing there. As long as they still use a nappy during the night, many children wait until then to poop, and some toddlers will even ask to have a nappy put on them so that they can poop. It is usually more effective to give in to their wish than to try to force them to do it on the potty. As he gets more familiar and comfortable with the potty, the toddler usually gradually loses the need for a nappy to poop.

It will be necessary for an adult to clean the toddler's bottom after having pooped for quite some time. If the child wishes to try to wipe his own bottom, let him try–from about three years onward, before that it is not likely to be more than messy– but most children will need to be wiped again by an adult after their own attempts until they are five or six years old.

If there is no indication that there is a **physiological** lack of control of the sphincters (the muscles that need to be controlled to stop urine and poop coming out) or a learning disability that makes an understanding of the process unlikely, and the toddler is still unaware of his bodily functions at about two and a half years old, it can help to put him on the potty regularly, to give him the experience. Allowing children to see one of their friends on the potty and see the praise and attention received when something is done, can be a great motivator to try it out for themselves. Only put a child on the potty if it can be done without a big battle, as a battle will likely create an **aversion** to potty training. If there appears to be a real aversion or fear of the potty, then allowing the child to play with a–thoroughly cleaned–potty or to sit on it fully clothed can help overcome this resistance.

Once on the potty, the child should be left there for a few minutes, in the hope that he will do something. He should not be abandoned there, or left to feel excluded. It is important that the potty-experience is a positive one. Put him on the potty at times when he is most likely to do something, such as right after waking up. If he does nothing during the set time–which should not be more than five minutes, especially if he has never done anything on a potty yet–help him put his nappy back on, arrange his clothes properly, both of you wash hands, and send him off to play without comment. If he does do something, give plenty of attention. Praise him and tell him that this is peeing (or doing a poo) and how wonderful and 'grown-up' this is of him, to create **awareness**. Once he starts to show signs of awareness, you can start encouraging him to warn you in advance when he needs the potty. If it is not possible to get the toddler to sit on the potty without a big struggle, leave it for another month or two and then try again.

After the potty routine has been finished, everything has been cleaned and clothes are back in their proper place, both child and caregiver will of course need to wash their hands, every time.

Bathing

It is very important for health and hygiene that children are kept clean. Mouths and hands should be wiped with a damp cloth regularly throughout the day. The whole face and nappy area should be given a wash at least once a day. If enough safe water is available, all children should be given a bath at least twice or three

The morning wash. Those who are able to, wash themselves.

times a week. If this is not an option, giving them a full-body wash with water that has been thoroughly boiled–and cooled–could be an alternative.

If there is plenty of water and time available, having a daily bath is good. However, more than once a day–as I have encountered–may be excessive. It is not a good idea to use soap more than once a day on the whole body because soap dries out the skin. Especially with babies, whose skin is even thinner, using soap very often causes skin problems.

Do not, under any circumstances, leave a child under four years old alone in the bath. Children up to eight or nine years old should be within hearing range of an adult when they are in the bath. A child needs only a couple of minutes and a couple of centimetres of water to drown. What many people do not realise is that there may not necessarily be a big splash or scream to warn you that something has gone wrong.

In a particular children's home, the little children were bathed in a small baby bath that was put on a slightly unstable stool, to bring it to a height that was easier on the caregiver's back. The caregiver had the habit of putting a baby who was able to sit up by herself in the bath and then go to one of the bedrooms to get clean clothes for the baby to sleep in, while the baby was allowed to play in the water. One evening, I was giving this baby a bath in the same construction. At one point, the baby decided to try if she could stand up. Pulling herself up changed the balance of the bath and caused it to shift, which in turn caused one of the legs to break off the old stool on which the bath was placed. I was just in time to catch her. If no one had been standing beside her, she would have crashed to the floor, together with the bath and the remains of the stool, and she might have gotten hurt very badly.

A few things become clear in this example. One is that even if a situation has not caused any problems for a long time, it does not mean that something will not suddenly happen. Especially when it involves a baby who may decide to try out something new at any moment. Secondly, while it is a good idea to try to find a way to spare your back while caring for a baby, only do so if it can be done in a very secure way, not on an unstable stool.

If you realise that you have left the baby's towel in the other room and there is no one you can call to get it for you, it is better to take the baby out of the bath and bring her with you dripping wet–if she is very small, hold her against you for warmth, even if this means you get wet–than to leave her in the tub by herself while you go get the towel.

*In a home for mentally challenged boys, bathing occurred very rarely when I first arrived. Boys were told to wash, but not much attention was paid to whether it actually happened. Some of the boys were not able, or had not learned, to control where and when they relieved themselves, and many of them would just sit in their own urine or poop. Skin infections and infected wounds were everywhere, as well as problems like **scabies**. So, one of the first things I did when I got to work there was to introduce daily supervised washing, assisted if necessary. The staff at the home grumbled that there was no need for this excessive cleanliness; they thought that giving the children a bath every day was too much of a good thing and a waste of time. However, after two or three weeks of daily washing, some of the staff came up to me and pointed out that the skin infections were starting to disappear and that small cuts and other wounds were not getting infected anymore. I explained that that is the difference made by regular washing.*

As they get older, children should be encouraged to gradually do more and more of their self-care. For bathing, this means initially showing her how to dress and undress, how to soap herself properly, how to rinse the soap off again, how to dry off, and helping her when needed. As she gets better at it, allow her to do more of it herself. In time, she will only need supervision to make sure it is done properly and eventually she will only need to have an occasional check afterwards to see if anything was missed. It is tempting to just do it all yourself, because for the first few years that is much quicker than letting the child do it. However, in the end it will save you a lot of time. While it is only possible to wash one child at a time, you can easily supervise several children. And once the child is able to wash herself properly, you will not need to spend any time on her during bathing.

Placing the baby's bath on the floor is most secure.

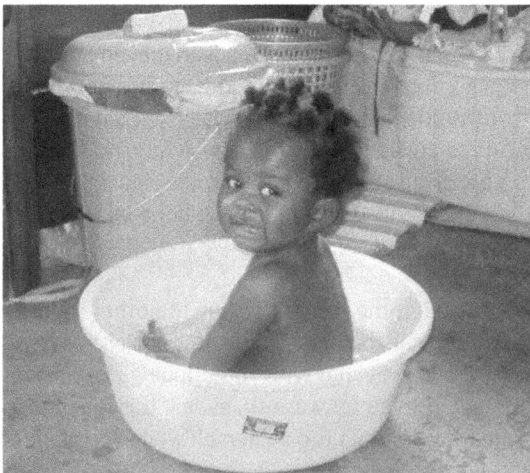

Up to the age of about nine or ten years old, it is not **inappropriate** for boys and girls to bathe or wash in the same place together. After that their bodies start to grow and develop and it is more appropriate for boys and girls not to see each other naked anymore. From that age, if possible, bathing should be overseen by someone of the same sex. Also, while there is no problem with small children bathing in relatively public areas, once children start to develop into men and women, they should be given the same opportunities for washing in private that adults have.

In many places, washing takes place outside. And if the temperature is high enough, there is nothing against this. For babies not to cool down too much, the outside temperature should be at least around 30°C. A baby being wet at lower temperatures outside, where there is usually a breeze, is likely to lead to hypothermia. For older children, washing outside is fine above temperatures of about 20°C. If it is colder than that, or if there is a strong cool wind, even older children can get hypothermia when they are wet, and they may be more likely to get ill. So, if it is colder than 20°C, it is a good idea to see if it is possible to wash indoors. Or, if there is no possibility for washing indoors, to at least see if you can build a simple structure that keeps out the wind while washing.

✳ ——————————— **Grooming**

Making sure that nails are kept short is an important part of children's hygiene. Dirt and germs gather underneath fingernails—and they are very hard to get out from under those tiny nails—and get transferred onto food and into the mouth. Babies and children with long nails are also more likely to scratch themselves or others, either by accident or on purpose, and break the skin, which in turn leads to a greater chance of infections.

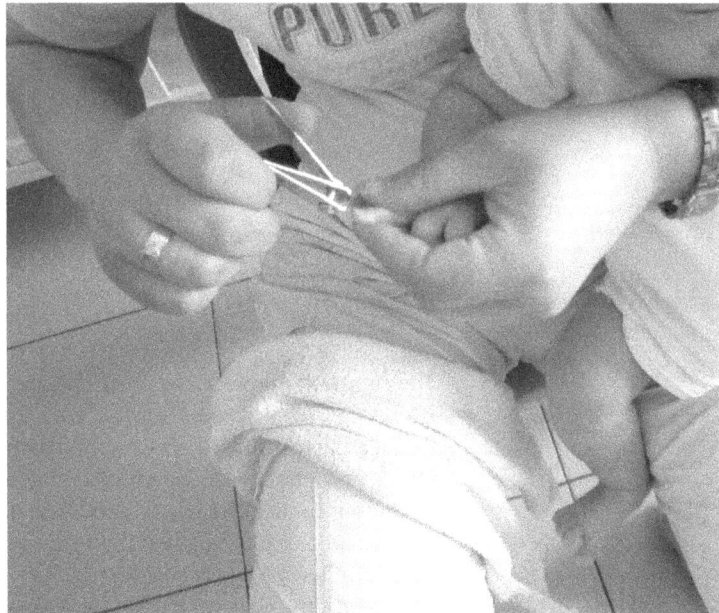

Cut nails regularly.

Children should also be checked for lice very regularly, and treated for it if lice are found. There is no shame in having lice. In fact, in any place where a lot of people live close together, it is extremely hard to avoid. Having lice is not a sign of being dirty: lice are just as happy to live in clean hair as they are to live in dirty hair.

In a children's home, nothing much was done about grooming. From time to time the children would get coconut oil rubbed into their hair, to prevent lice. But this is only effective if it is done every day, so all the children did have lice. They were always scratching their heads. Because nothing at all was being done about the lice, it got worse and worse, until eventually the children even had lice in their eyelashes and their eyelashes were caked with lice eggs.

However, steps should be taken to eliminate this problem as much as possible. Aside from the annoying itch, which can make children quite difficult to deal with, there is a risk of infection if scratching reaches the point of breaking the skin. Also, do not think that it will be possible to make sure that the lice will not pass from the children to the staff. If the children have lice, the staff will get them too, and the other way around.

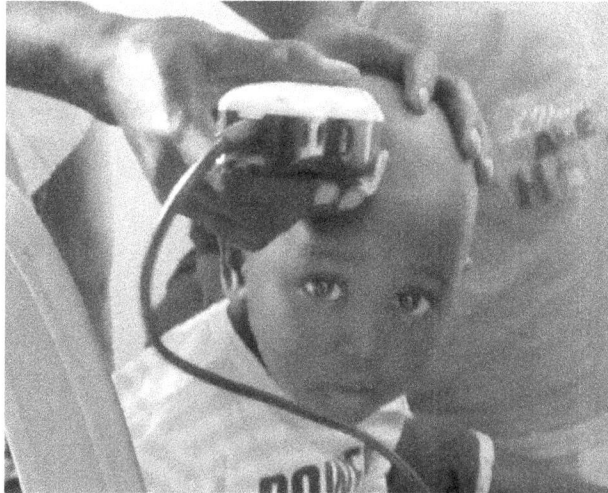

Lice have no interest in a shaven head.

The simplest, quickest and most effective way to get rid of lice and to keep them away, is to take off a child's hair. This means to cut/shave the head leaving only a couple of millimetres of hair, at the most. This is only effective if everyone's hair is shaved at the same time, because if some children still have hair, lice can live there and spread back to other children when their hair grows back. However, in many parts of the world it is considered to be unacceptable, humiliating, or bad luck to shave off hair. In this case, you will have to look for special shampoos to get rid of lice and make sure you follow the whole course of the treatment for all the children, as well as washing all clothes and bed linen in very hot water, at the same time. Otherwise louse (one louse, two lice) eggs will be left behind and the whole thing will start again. Also make sure that the treatment you were given in the shop is safe to use for children of the age you are dealing with and that there are no warnings against using it for children who are using any of the medications your children use, or have any of the medical conditions your children have.

Dental Hygiene

Brushing teeth is also part of hygiene for children. Although at first teeth are very few and really tiny, they do, right from the start, come into contact with foods and liquids that can damage them. So, is it very important to start brushing the baby's teeth right from the moment the first one appears.

You can use a small toothbrush, but even a piece of gauze wrapped around your finger will do. In some countries, special toothpaste is available for children under six years old who swallow everything they get in their mouths instead of spitting out the toothpaste. If this is available where you are, you can use a tiny amount of it—about the size of the baby's pinky nail. If it is not available, just brushing with a toothbrush or gauze with water also works well. Babies and toddlers should not use adult toothpaste. The amount of fluoride in it is not safe for them to swallow.

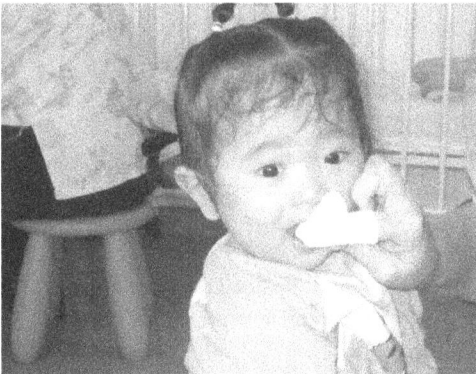

Brushing teeth can also be done with a wet piece of gauze around your finger

Small toothbrushes and special toothpaste.

From about two years old, children should brush their teeth twice a day. Ideally after breakfast and before bed. Just like with bathing, it is helpful to gradually allow children to brush their own teeth. Until they are six years old, you will need to brush their teeth yourself, after they have finished brushing, to make sure that it was done properly.

Food Hygiene

In any kind of institutional situation, it is very important to have very high standards of food hygiene. Not only for the preparation of food, but also with regard to the bottles, bowls and plates, utensils and eating surfaces. Having a lot of children close together will always make the spreading of any disease or infection easy, but no method of spreading these is quite as effective as through what the children put in their mouths.

'But she only has eight teeth!' I am often told in disbelief when I recommend the brushing of baby teeth. Well, that means that she has eight teeth which need cleaning, because all eight teeth may get cavities (holes) in them, which can lead to serious infection, which can spread to other parts of the body.

It is important to:

- *Always wash your hands before preparing a bottle or any food.*
- *Thoroughly wash your hands after having handled raw meat, fish or eggs.*
- *Make sure that work surfaces, cutting boards, bowls, pans and anything else that comes into contact with the food is clean before you use them.*
- *Make sure that all the food you make is cooked through and through.*
- *Regularly clean the fridge, containers and any places where food is kept.*
- *Store food that spoils fast in the fridge or freezer and throw it away if it has been left outside the fridge or freezer for too long–or if a power cut has let things in the fridge or freezer warm up or thaw.*
- *Throw away food if insects, larvae, eggs or mould are found in the dry-stored goods; in some cases, mould may be safe to eat for adults, but children could get very ill from eating the same thing.*

All these measures are there to prevent food poisoning and para-sites, which especially in the case of babies and toddlers can lead to dangerous medical problems quite fast. In *Sick Children Everywhere*, Part 1, Chapter 2: 'Problems of Digestion', information is given about the dangers of diarrhoea and vomiting, and about how to deal with those things when they happen.

Plates and bowls drying after being thoroughly washed.

Where babies are bottle-fed, all bottles, nipples and caps should be thoroughly washed with soap and a brush after every feed. If bottles are shared by all children, they need to be sterilised after every use. Even in situations where all babies have their own bottle and nipple, which are both clearly marked with their name to avoid any mistakes, bottles for babies under five months old should be sterilised after every use. At times when the temperature is high–26°C and over–bottles, nipples and caps should be sterilised after every time they have contained milk, for all children, even if they do not share bottles. For babies over five months, when it is not hot, bottles, nipples and caps should be sterilised at least twice a week.

Bottles etc. in a UV light sterilizer.

When the child starts eating **solids** bowls, cups and spoons should be thoroughly washed with soap after every use. Every child should use a separate bowl and a separate spoon.

A caregiver would feed three or four children from the same bowl, using only one spoon. When she was offered one spoon for each child, she said she would not use the other spoons, because it would save on the dishes having to be washed. Unfortunately, one of the four children had a throat infection, and this was known. When the other children also got the throat infection, much more time was needed to take them to the doctor and to care for them than it takes to wash a few more bowls and spoons. And the cost was also considerably higher.

Very, very few children eat without making a mess. If spilled food is left where it falls, it can start to rot or a mould will form, and then a child may pick it up, eat it and get ill. So, it is important to thoroughly clean the area where the children eat. That includes the floor, the wall, the chairs and table—and the little ridges where food gets trapped—and possibly toys or other things that a child may have grabbed while her hands were still covered in food. A quick wipe is usually not enough to get it all clean. Check that everything has really come off.

Chapter 2: Food

Most of the time caregivers in children's homes are very busy, and their aim is to do things as quickly and efficiently as possible. There is nothing wrong with this, as long as they remember that there are some things that cannot be rushed without endangering the health

Waiting impatiently for food.

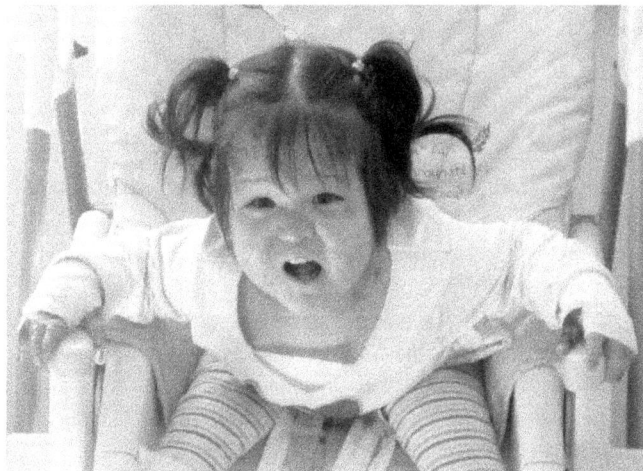

and well-being of the children. Feeding is one of these things. The feeding of babies and young children is time-consuming and can be messy. However, it needs to be done properly. If you cannot find a way to make sure there is time and attention for each individual child's feeding, you should ask yourself if it is a good idea to keep the children's home going. Because excellent care in other areas will be a waste of time and **resources** if feeding is not done properly.

UN GUIDELINES:

83. Carers should ensure that children receive adequate amounts of wholesome and nutritious food in accordance with local dietary habits and relevant dietary standards, as well as with the children's religious beliefs. Appropriate nutritional supplementation should also be provided when necessary.

✳ ———————— **Bottle Feeding**

✳ ———————— *How to Feed*

Time needs to be made to feed a baby. Often, making time to feed a baby in a calm way saves you time. A baby needs to be held while she drinks and should never be allowed to drink while lying down flat. Being fed while lying flat can cause very serious infections and choking. Feeding flat can lead to pneumonia and ear infection because the milk may flow from the throat up into the ear canals, instead of down into the stomach. Or, it might flow in the right direction, but go into the lungs instead of into the stomach. When the milk reaches the nice, warm, wet surroundings of the ear canal or the lungs, the bacteria in the milk feel right at home and start growing very fast, causing infection. **Preventing** middle ear infection and **pneumonia** saves time and expenses–and in some cases lives.

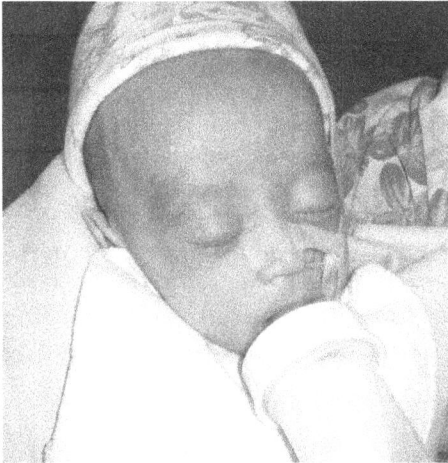

Taking time to feed saves time and lives.

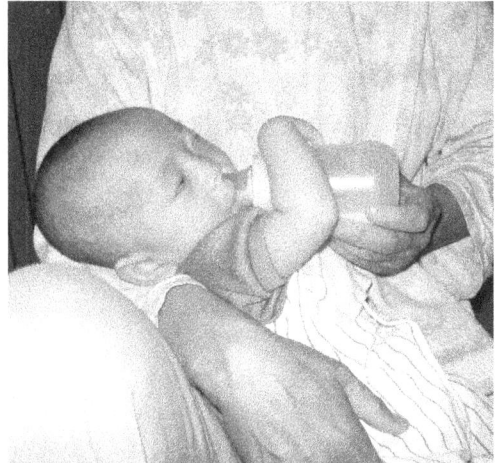

Tired but not allowing the bottle to go.

Between twenty and thirty babies are cared for by one caregiver, who is also expected to hand-wash the babies' clothes as part of her duties. There is quite simply no time for holding babies, or even for feeding them. So, the babies are left lying in their cots and with a variety of small cushions and cloths the bottles are propped up in the corner of the cot and after a while the bottles are all taken away again. If a baby drank from the bottle in the meantime, excellent! If a baby was unable to find the nipple, was too weak to drink more than a few sips, or was simply asleep, well, that is too bad. Maybe she will drink better next time. The effects of feeding like this are clearly visible by just glancing around the room: dehydration, ear infection, pneumonia and severe malnutrition are seen in several of the babies. How many of them have choked while being fed like this is hard to say.

The **dehydration** mentioned in the example with the propped-up bottles is not caused by the bottles themselves, but by there being no one there to check if the baby is drinking. Some babies need someone to remind them that they should drink, others cannot find the nipple and some of them are just too weak to make any effort to keep the nipple in their mouth and keep sucking. This means that the baby does not get enough milk and gets malnourished and dehydrated.

Giving a baby the time to burp halfway through the feed and at the end may prevent her throwing up large amounts of milk, which means she can go three or four hours between feeds, instead of needing more after only two hours. Preventing throwing up also helps prevent infection. When the milk goes up from the stomach, much of it comes out of the mouth while throwing up, but some of it will slide down again, and it might slide down the airway into the lungs instead of down the oesophagus to the stomach, leading to the same situation as lying flat: choking and pneumonia.

Taking the bottle away immediately at the first cough, to allow the baby time to catch her breath again before continuing instead of pushing on until the cough turns into a choking episode, saves time. Because a choking episode takes a long time to resolve itself—plus, this too can lead to **aspiration** and pneumonia. If the baby really starts choking you need to hold her face down and slap her back hard-with a hollow hand-until she stops coughing. If milk has reached the lungs (=aspiration), there is nothing you can do. It will not come out, and it will cause bronchitis or pneumonia This is why you need to do what you can to prevent this from happening. After coughing, it a good idea to allow the baby to take at least two calm breaths before continuing, otherwise she is likely to start coughing again. So, invest time to save time.

Time was taken to feed the seven-month-old baby. Her caregiver would get the buggy, strap the baby into it and then sit down on the bench opposite the buggy and hold the bottle. When the baby would start coughing or choking, it was difficult to get her out quickly to pat her back because of all the straps. Still, her caregiver insisted that it was better this way. The caregiver felt that the baby probably would not be comfortable being held, because it was so hot and sweaty. The caregiver said this was a difficult baby: she cried a lot throughout the day 'for no reason at all'.

If you sit down with a baby in a relaxed way and let her have as much time as she needs to take her bottle—while helping her, making sure she does not get distracted or drinks less than she is able to—the

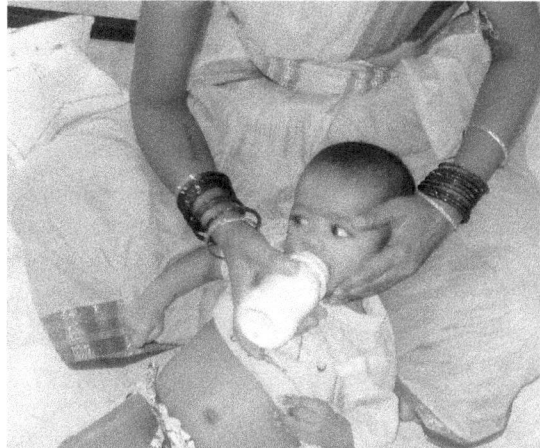

Sitting down to feed a baby.

baby will drink better and more. But not only that. In the course of a long, busy day with many things to do, getting to sit down with a baby, to feed her, taking the weight off your feet, can be a very good way to get a little rest while still doing an essential part of your job. In Part 1, Chapter 5: 'Essential Psychological Needs' I will explain some of the other reasons, aside from not letting babies lie flat, why it is important to hold babies when you feed them.

Despite the heat, the caregiver would sit down and hold the five-month-old baby on her arm to feed him his bottle. She put a cotton cloth between her arm and his body, so that neither of them would get too sweaty. The baby would smile at her when she gave him his bottle and drank well. If he started coughing, she would sit him up straighter immediately and pat his back, and he would soon stop again. The caregiver said that he was a very good baby; he seemed happy almost all the time and only cried when something was really the matter.

What to Give

During the first five to six months of life, babies should not receive any food other than milk. Their digestive system is not yet ready to process other things. Giving babies regular food too young can lead to kidney and liver failure. Even water–always boiled and then cooled down, if given–should be given as little as possible. If the climate is very hot and the baby is at risk of dehydration if he does not get extra liquids, water can be given. However, in a more temperate or cold climate, it is not a good idea to give water during the first four months of life. Drinking water (or rice water) will make a small baby feel full and he will drink less milk. If he drinks less milk, he does not receive all the calories he needs to grow, because water does not contain any calories.

Ideally, babies should be given breast milk, as this is made especially for human babies and provides antibodies to help build up the baby's immune system. However, in children's homes, this is almost never an option. When there is no breast milk, regular cow's milk is not an acceptable alternative for children under one year old. For babies younger than six months old, giving regular cow's milk is dangerous and for children between six months and one year old it does not give the nutrition they need. Regular cow's milk is too rich in **protein,** saturated fat and sodium for human babies, and lacks other important components. It does have high concentrations of essential minerals like iron, but because of the make-up of cow's milk, it is very difficult for a baby to absorb enough of any of them, which leads to a lack of these essential minerals. If they are given regular cow's milk, most babies, especially those under six months old, will develop severe diarrhoea, which can quickly lead to dehydration, which can be fatal in a very short time span. In *Sick Children Everywhere* Part 1, Chapter 2: 'Problems of Digestion' more information is given about dehydration and diarrhoea. Babies who do survive drinking cow's milk are more likely to develop an allergy to either the lactose or the protein in it.

This is why it is so important to use **infant formula**, which is especially made to meet the needs and abilities of a human baby's digestive system. Although it is more expensive than regular cow's milk, infant formula is essential to keep babies healthy, and using it saves lives.

A three-month-old girl was HIV-positive, dehydrated and malnourished. When I asked what she was given to eat I was told formula, which I was very glad to hear. However, later I found out that they fed the girl porridge (made with fortified flour, water and sugar, no milk) first and then she was offered milk. This was much cheaper, because after eating the porridge, the girl felt quite full and could not drink very much expensive milk, made from baby formula. However, the porridge did not have much in it that the baby's body was able to use for growing and gaining weight. So, doing this was causing the girl to become malnourished and dehydrated. She needed more milk!

If there is absolutely no way to get infant formula for the babies, cow's milk should be diluted: add 50ml of clean boiled water to every 100ml of cow's milk then add 10gr of sugar to it.

Giving goat's milk is not a safe alternative, it needs complicated adaptation and should not be given undiluted.

To prepare infant formula, the instructions on the tin or box should always be followed. It is important to use the exact number of level scoops—using the scoop provided with the formula—in combination with the stated amount of water. Because if you use less milk powder with an equal amount of water, the baby may feel satisfied and full, but he will not receive the calories he needs and become thin and malnourished. If you use more milk powder with an equal amount of water, the baby's kidneys will need to work much harder than normal, which can damage them and cause dangerous conditions.

Bottles prepared long in advance and not kept cool are a danger.

Left over milk stored in fridge, with name labels.

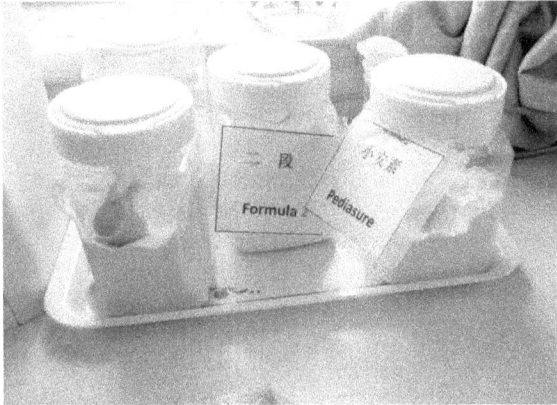

Formula in sealed containers with labels to show what is inside.

Infant formula should always be pre-pared with safe drinking water. If there is a lot of diarrhoea or there are a lot of parasites where you live, the water commonly used as drinking water in your area is probably unsafe. In this case, the water should be filtered and boiled for at least 30 minutes before it is used to make infant formula, or used for any food or drink. If using bottled water is an option, it is preferable in such a situation. However, with bottled drink-ing water it is important to use a brand with as few minerals as possible in it, to avoid putting the baby's kidneys under too much pressure.

If the drinking water in your area *is* safe to drink, it should still be boiled and left to cool down for a while before using it to make a bottle of milk for a baby. However safe your drink-ing water may be, under no circumstances should bottles be made from warm tap water, anywhere in the world. Pipelines for hot tap water are a breeding ground for bacteria. This water is fine for bathing and wash-ing, but should never be used for drinking.

An option if tap water is not safe to drink.

The exact temperature at which you make a bottle can vary. Babies also vary in their preferences for the temperature of their bottle, anywhere from having it as hot as is still safe to drink to barely luke-warm. Just make sure that the temperature is in fact safe to drink. If a drop of milk stings when it touches the back of your hand or the inside of your wrist, it is still too hot. If it does not, it is safe. When the water is still boiling or when it is too cold, the milk powder does not dissolve very well. So it is easier to make a bottle when the wa-ter temperature is somewhere between 85°C and 20°C.

Formula bottles should not be made a long time in advance and left to stand until the time comes for the baby to drink it. Leaving for-mula bottles at room temperature makes it likely that bacteria start to multiply in the milk and the baby could get very sick from drinking this milk. The bottle should be cooled down quickly to the right drinking temperature, for example by holding it under cold water and then giving it to the baby as soon as the temperature is right. Or it should be placed in a refrigerator and left there until it is time for the baby to drink. The milk can then be heated up quickly by placing the bottle in a bowl with hot water. If you use a microwave to heat up bottles, the bottle needs to be shaken thoroughly after it comes out of the microwave and the temperature must be tested. A microwave can cause pockets of extremely high temperatures, while other parts of the milk are still quite cool. If you do not shake and test the bottle, and give it to the baby straight from the microwave, the milk can cause very serious burns.

Any formula milk that has been outside the refrigerator for an hour or more should be thrown away. The same goes for any milk left over from a feed. If milk like this is reheated and used again, or given to a baby again without reheating, there is a great risk of the baby becoming seriously ill.

Examples of formulas used in case of lactose intolerance.

If a baby has diarrhoea a lot despite being exclusively fed with infant formula for his age, correctly prepared with safe drinking water, the cause of this could be lactose intolerance. In this case, switching to lactose-free infant formula usually puts an end to the diarrhoea within a few days. If it is hard to get lactose-free formula, or if the expense of this is hard to bear, once the baby has been free from diarrhoea for two weeks, you can try to reintroduce regular infant formula again. If the diarrhoea does not return, you can continue feeding him with regular infant formula. If the diarrhoea does return, the baby's health and possibly his life will depend on being fed with a lactose-free formula.

How Much to Give

Unlike parents who have known their baby from the very start and have watched his intake of milk naturally increase over time, when the baby first arrives, a children's home has no information about how much a baby normally drinks, how often and for how long. So, how do you determine how much he should be given?
To start with, you can go with 150ml per kilo of bodyweight, per day (ml/kg/day), and divide this amount over the number of feeds. The number of feeds will be eight—one every three hours—for babies up to two to three months and for older babies who are very weak or sick. For older, healthy babies, five to six feeds a day is often enough—one every four hours—and if the baby sleeps through the night, once he weighs more than 5kg he does not need to be woken up anymore.

A baby who arrives and appears to be about two weeks old is weighed. His weight is 3.5kg, so you calculate that he should be given 3.5x150ml=525ml per day. At his age, he will need to drink every 3 hours, which is 8 feeds a day. 525ml divided over eight feeds is 65ml per feed. With most formulas, that is what you get when you use 60ml of water and 2 scoops of powder for each feed.

After calculating this initial amount, you need to watch the baby and see if it is the right amount. All babies are different, after all. If the baby is very weak and unable to drink 50ml in one go, you can try to give him 30ml every two hours, if that is more manageable for him. Also, if the baby throws up a lot after every feed, it is better to give less milk each time and feed more often, to try to reduce the amount that comes back up. The overall daily amount can also be reduced a little bit, if necessary, but not below 100ml/kg/day, because less would cause dehydration. An average of about 120ml/kg/day is needed to avoid **malnutrition** and lack of growth over time.

If a baby always finishes all the milk in the bottle and shows signs of needing more–such as finishing the bottle very quickly and trying to continue sucking on an empty bottle, or becoming restless and fussy quickly after a feed–and he does not throw up, you can increase the amount of milk given per feed. Usually, the best way is to increase by one scoop of milk powder, plus the appropriate amount of water–which generally means about 30ml–at a time. If the baby starts throwing up regularly after the increase, it is a sign he is getting too much and does not know when he has reached his limit, so he needs you to set the limit for him. When you offer a baby 30ml more because you think he was not getting enough, it does not mean you need to force the entire 30ml into him from now on. You are just offering the opportunity to drink more if the baby wants to. If he only drinks as much as he used to before you offered more, or only a little bit more than that, that is all right too.

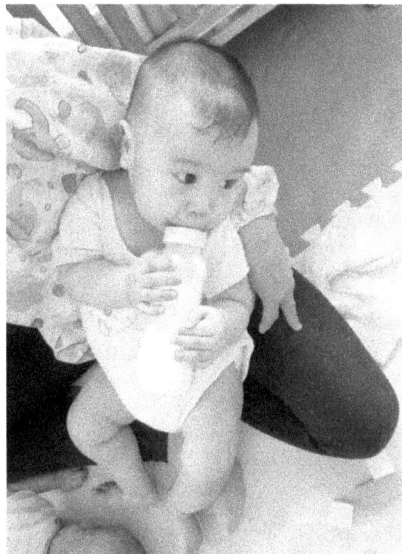

Until a baby weighs about 5kg he will need regular feeding throughout the day and night. Once he reaches 5kg, if he does not have any

An example of follow-up formula.

health problems that require him to be fed around the clock, it is all right to allow the baby to sleep at night and only feed him if he wakes up hungry. As he gets older and bigger, the baby will sleep longer stretches during the night, until he stops waking up altogether until morning.

It is extremely important that small babies, and particularly premature babies and those weighing less than 3kg, are woken up for all their feeds, day or night, and that they are fed no less than once every three hours. In babies this small, there is a danger of the sugar level in their blood getting very low, very quickly, which will make the baby very sleepy and uninterested in eating, maybe even too weak to suck. If you put the baby back to bed because you think he is just very tired and wants to sleep some more instead of trying very, very hard to get him to drink something, a life-threatening situation could develop surprisingly quickly.

Monitor the amount the baby drinks very closely, especially if she uses something other than a bottle with a nipple to drink from. If the baby does not take in the minimum required amount of milk, she should be taken to a doctor, because she will probably need to have a feeding tube placed to make sure that she receives enough liquids and calories and does not become dehydrated or malnourished.

After six months, there is a different kind of infant formula, usually called 'follow-up' or '**stage** 2' milk. This formula has been made to suit the needs of older babies, who need a different make-up of calories, vitamins and minerals. It is recommended to change babies of six months old to follow-up formula, except for babies who are premature. In their case, a doctor should be consulted to see when is the right time to change to the next kind of formula. Babies under six months should NOT be given this formula, because it does not have all the nutrients they need in the right amounts for their age.

In a children's home with a care unit for premature babies, they ask nursing mothers they know—only those whom they know to be healthy and not on medication—to donate some breast milk for the premature babies. This way, they are able to give premature babies some natural milk, with antibodies, from time to time. When breast milk is available, it is kept frozen and is only defrosted as needed. The babies receive alternating bottles of breast milk and premature formula whenever possible.

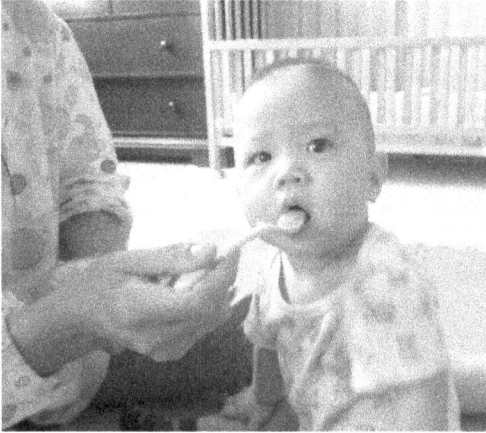

Starting solids.

Premature babies often need more frequent, smaller feeds in the first few months, because they cannot process the milk if it comes in large amounts. There is a special formula for premature babies, which contains more calories, while not being too hard on the kidneys and liver. If you are caring for premature babies and you have a way of getting this special formula, it is highly recommended that you use it.

Preemie formula, if available, can also be very helpful in helping very thin or malnourished young babies gain weight. Another option to help these babies is to give them slightly more concentrated formula, but this should only be done at a doctor's advice, with specific instructions as to how much water and formula to use for that baby, to avoid damaging his kidneys. To illustrate how easy it is to get this wrong: in my experience doctors usually prescribe using 27.5ml or 28ml of water for one scoop instead of 30ml, to provide more calories. When such a tiny amount can make such a big difference, the smallest mistake can also have serious **consequences**, so do not do this without a doctor's advice.

Weaning

When to Start

From six months onwards, just drinking milk is no longer enough for a baby to stay healthy. For example, the iron reserves that the baby received in the mother's womb are running out by six months, and there is not enough iron in milk to make up for that. This is one of the reasons why **weaning**–the transition from drinking

Trying out apple sauce.

only milk to starting to eat solid foods–needs to be started by six months of age. It should not start too early, however. Some children indicate a need or desire for eating things other than milk earlier than others. Generally speaking, weaning can be started between about four and a half and six months.

While it is important not to start babies on any other food than infant formula until close to six months of age, it is just as important not to wait too long after the six-month mark to start introducing other sources of food. If you wait until after seven or eight months, you are likely to encounter a very uncooperative baby, and the baby will start to suffer from lack of iron in her **diet**.

After six months, the baby becomes more aware of things. This is explained more in Part 2: 'Basic Child Psychology and Child Development'. As far as food is concerned, babies at this age start to get suspicious of the unknown, and unwilling to try things they are not familiar with. Plus, they become better at resisting you.

In other words, by the time the baby reaches this stage, if she is already familiar with a range of tastes and **textures**, she is more likely to accept a greater variety of foods. And she may be more inclined to try out new things, because she has already learned that there are many things that taste good. If she does not have any experience with eating solids yet, she is likely to be very resistant to giving it a try.

At first, the baby will not consider being fed with a spoon to be really eating. For her, eating is drinking a bottle, which fills you up nice and quickly. When she just starts taking solids, it takes too much effort and goes too slowly for her to feel satisfied by it. This means that if you try to feed her solids at a time when she is hungry, she is likely to get impatient and uncooperative. With time this will change, and eventually the solid feed will become a meal in itself, and will replace a bottle feed. However, to begin with, it is usually best to offer solid food at a time in-between two bottle feeds, when she is not hungry and is not tired or sleepy either. Choosing a time like this to introduce new foods will make the experience more pleasant and more likely to be successful.

If at the age of six to seven months you are unable to get anything into her that does not come out again right away, initially you should take a few weeks to allow the child to gradually get used to the new experience of having solids, to see if the situation im-

Eating is a messy business at first.

proves. Even if a lot of the food seems to come out, do not conclude that this means the baby cannot eat. As long as the baby does not get upset with eating, having the chance to practise every day makes it more likely that the eating will improve. If this is not the case, or a baby is physically unable to eat solids, then just continuing with 'follow up' or 'stage 2' milk formula will not be enough to give the baby all she needs. You will need to look for a specialised formula that provides everything a baby of the age you are dealing with needs, in the form of milk with additives, such as for example PediaSure®. You can ask advice from a doctor about what the best option is for your baby.

How to Feed

When a baby first starts eating solids, it will be messy. She will work quite a large amount of the food out of her mouth with her tongue. This is normal. It does not mean that she is unable to eat, nor does it mean that she does not like the food. To indicate that she does not like something a baby is more likely to turn her head away when you try to give her more, or to keep her mouth closed. The reason why the baby often moves more food to the front of her mouth and out than to the back of the mouth to be swallowed, is that she has a different swallowing technique than adults and older children do. A baby's swallowing technique, which involves moving the tongue forward over the palate, is the most effective way to get milk from a breast or bottle and swallow it in an on-going, rhythmic movement. It is very efficient for milk, but not very effective when you use it on food. Over time, most babies will automatically learn to use a different swallowing technique that uses the tongue to move food to the back of the mouth, and less of the food will be actively pushed out of the mouth.

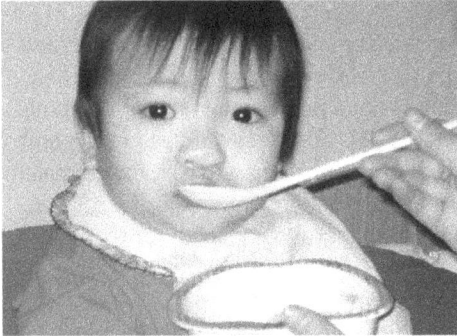

A boy with a cleft lip and palate–lip repaired already–eating his fruit.

A two-year-old boy who had Down's Syndrome was only given milk. When asked why, the caregivers explained that he was not able to eat at all. When I tried–with yoghurt and mashed fruit–I found that he opened his mouth very well for the spoon. Quite a lot came out of his mouth again, but that seemed more than it was, because it was mixed up with saliva. He did swallow some of it and when you scraped what flowed out of his mouth up with a spoon and put it back into his mouth, he would take that just fine too. It was messy, but he was eating. What was more, he enjoyed eating. He would cry when he had finished his food, wanting more.

I encouraged the caregivers to try feeding him at least twice a day. Whenever they did, I heard them complaining constantly about the boy not being able to eat. And they would spend a lot of time wiping his face with a cloth, which he did not like and made him cry. Whenever I fed him, he enjoyed it and he gradually improved. After a while, the first two or three bites would be swallowed without anything running out of his mouth, showing that he could do that. And as long as I did not wipe his face until the end of the feed, he kept on trying.

Until that time, you will simply have to put up with a bit of a mess. If you want, you can protect the baby's clothes—and your own—by covering them with a bib or some other cloth. Just be very aware of the fact that reprimanding the child for being a messy eater is not going to change the way she swallows and eats. In the first few months of eating solids the baby is simply physically unable to do it any other way. The only thing you may accomplish by constantly reprimanding a baby while she is learning to eat, is to make her feel bad about the whole eating experience and less willing to cooperate.

Babies with a cleft palate have an opening between the mouth and nose. This means that when you feed her solids, some of it is likely to come out of her nose. This is not a problem and it is not painful, only messy. It is better to start solids at the regular age of six months and have some of it come out of her nose than to wait for her palate to be repaired, as this will leave her dependent on milk for far too long. Plus, it is very hard for her to learn to eat solids for the first time at a much later age.

Be patient and encouraging when you first start feeding a baby solids. If the baby cries a lot the first time you try to feed her solids, wait a day or two and try again. Never force-feed a baby. Holding the baby's mouth open to force food into it and holding it closed and pinching her nose to force her to swallow will make her feel very afraid and is likely to create an aversion to eating. This can make it almost impossible to get the child to eat again for a long, long time.

It can sometimes be helpful to make a baby open her mouth through distracting her or playing a game and putting some food in her mouth when she forgets to protest, if this does not lead to her panicking. However, it is not a good idea to put food into her mouth when she opens it for crying or yawning. In these cases, she probably hardly notices you putting the food into her mouth. So instead of swallowing, she is likely to take a breath and inhale the food. This usually leads to choking and possibly aspiration.

Unable to sit up, still able to eat.

When a baby or child—with or without feeding problems—does not swallow, there is no point in loading more food into her mouth, even if she opens her mouth to allow you to do so. This will increase the amount of the food in her mouth, often to a point where the food becomes too big and dry to be able to chew and swallow anymore. So this only increases the chance of everything being spat out again. It can also cause gagging and even vomiting. Instead of continuing to add food to what is already there, give the child positive encouragement to swallow. Threats are usually not effective and may make the situation worse.

If verbal encouragement alone is not enough to get the child to start swallowing, you can gently touch her cheek, chin and/or lips to trigger the sucking and swallowing reflexes that may still be present. Touching the lips or tongue with an empty spoon, as if you are placing more food in the mouth, can remind the child that she was eating and is supposed to continue. If this happens regularly towards the end of the meal, and touching her lips or cheeks does not help any more, it is likely that she has had enough and has lost interest in eating.

A young woman in her early twenties had the abilities of a toddler. She needed to be spoon-fed very soft food. Sometimes, she would be in a playful or in a difficult mood and would refuse to open her mouth to allow her caregiver to put the spoon into it. At these times her caregiver often got impatient and would force the spoon past the young woman's lips. Since it was not possible to force the spoon past her teeth, the caregiver put the food between the woman's lips and teeth. This almost never led to the food being eaten; usually the food would come running out together with saliva or it would be spat out. On other days, when the caregiver was in a more patient mood and talked to the young woman, persuading her to open her mouth and accept the food, almost everything would be swallowed.

In a later section of this chapter, I will give some more detailed information about feeding children who are difficult to feed.

A baby is usually not trying to **manipulate** you when she refuses to open her mouth. It simply means that either she has not yet swallowed what she had in her mouth, that she is not hungry (anymore), or that she truly does not like what you give her. Especially at the start, the enjoyment of eating is much more important than how much the child eats. Making eating a positive experience from the start saves a lot of time in battles and fussy eating later on.

While feeding a baby solids, she should not be lying down. Just like with bottle feeding, the danger of choking and aspiration is great when a baby eats lying down. If she is able to sit up well, without falling to the side, the baby can be put on the floor opposite you or in a (high) chair. If she is not able to sit up well enough yet, the easiest thing to do is usually to take the baby on one of your legs, hold her against your body with one of her arms stuck between your body and the arm that is supporting her back, and her other hand held in your hand, while feeding her with your other hand. Use a small spoon for feeding, not a big one. A spoon that can easily fit in the child's mouth works best. Go slowly, watch for the child's signals that she is ready for more. Touch her bottom lip with the spoon. If the mouth does not open, the child is not ready to take the next bite. Wait a little while and touch the lip again. There is no need to urge the child to open her mouth. While you wait, you can comment on how well the child is eating and how tasty the food is.

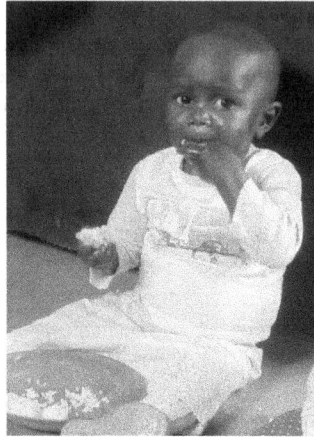

Putting food in his mouth with his left hand.

When you first start feeding a baby solids, everything should be mashed until it is almost liquid, so that the step from drinking milk to eating other things is as small as possible. While this is the right way to start, it is important to remember that over the course of the next four to six months, the texture of the food should gradually become less like a liquid and contain more small bits. Eventually, the child will eat food that is just cut up in small pieces. Most children are able to eat regular food, as long as it is cut up small, by twelve to eighteen months of age. Allowing them to gradually eat more chunky food is not only important for the development of their ability to eat and chew, it is also important for their speech development.

A group of twelve children aged six months to five years was cared for by four caregivers. Although five of the children were over two years old and able to eat regular food and to feed themselves, they did not get that opportunity. All food was put in a blender and mashed so fine that the six-month-old could eat it, and then all the children were fed a bowl of this liquid food by their caregiver.

When there are children of varying ages including both babies and older children, it can be tempting to just make food into a soft thin mash for everyone and feed it like that, to save time. However, this is not going to help the child's development. Also, it may lead to a five-year-old child who is not willing to chew anything.

Self-Feeding

When babies first start eating solids, they do not have the motor **skills** to feed themselves. The only ability they have when it comes to eating is to open their mouth when the spoon approaches and to close it around the spoon to take the food from it. Their **motor development** progresses very rapidly, however. From about eight to nine months, they are able to bring food to their mouth with their fingers, to enjoy sucking on rice cakes and rusks and to bring small bits of soft fruits to their mouth. As they get teeth, they become able to chew things and bite things off.

While it will take quite some time before toddlers are able to eat with chopsticks, with a fork or with their right hand only, most of them have no problem eating with their fingers, and from about one year onward with a spoon. Although it is very messy and time-consuming to have toddlers eat by themselves and it may not be possible all the time, it is important that at least some of the time they are allowed to feed themselves. At least at one meal a day. Or, when they only just start to learn, maybe let them have a snack by themselves, once they are able to get most of the food to their mouth. This is important for the development of their motor skills, their self-esteem, their self-confidence and their growing sense of independence.

A group of two-year-olds–some of them closer to three–were always spoon-fed by their caregiver. Although she got annoyed with the children's impatience at having to wait their turn and at having to wait for them to finish chewing something before she could put the next spoonful in their mouth, she felt this was by far the easiest method. During her time off, I gave each of the toddlers a bib, a plate and a spoon at mealtime and let them try by themselves. They did quite well, sometimes asking for help getting food on to the spoon. And surprisingly, they ate more than usual, because they enjoyed the act of eating, even if the food was not nicer than before. Now four toddlers were able to eat at the same time, without having to wait, supervised by just one adult.

Toddlers happy to be allowed to try to eat by themselves for the first time.

Even if at times it seems like there is food everywhere except in the toddler's mouth and you feel close to despair, try to make an effort to give **compliments** for good behaviour–for instance whenever food does happen to reach the mouth–and as much as possible overlook or ignore the less desirable behaviour. A lot of the spilling and smearing is due to lack of motor control rather than bad behaviour. However, if the toddler finds out that she can gain a lot more (negative) attention by throwing food across the room or spitting it out, she is likely to start doing that more and more. At times, you will have to correct bad behaviour, but try to make sure that the toddler knows that good behaviour will get her more and better attention than bad behaviour. This issue will be dealt with in more detail in Part 2, Chapter 6: 'Discipline'. Other, psychological issues to do with mealtimes are addressed in Part 2, Chapter 3: 'How Children Think'.

> The caregiver from the previous example came back from her days off and was happy to see the children eat well by themselves. However, she did not find it easy to sit through a meal just watching the children eat. So, to occupy herself, she started to comment on everything the children were doing wrong while they ate. This took some of the joy of eating by themselves away for all the children, and one of the toddlers was particularly sensitive to these kinds of comments. He started to do worse and worse when it came to eating by himself. Whenever the caregiver was not looking at him, he would eat very well, with very little mess. The moment she looked at him, he would start to eat more slowly, make a big mess, or just refuse to put his spoon to his mouth. To him this was like a hidden treasure full of attention.

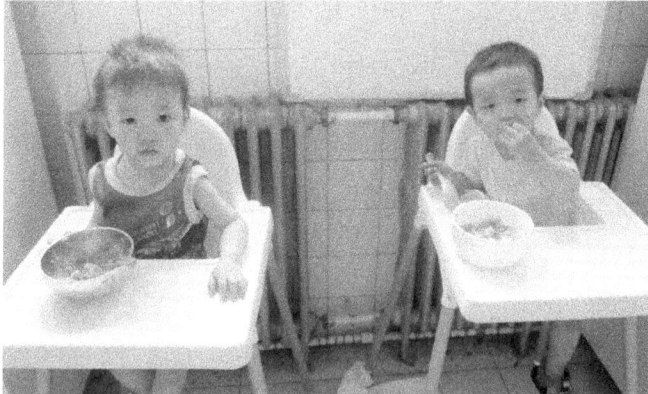

He knows how to use the spoon, but still prefers his hand.

Around the same time that a baby starts to become able to feed herself, she should start drinking liquids from a sipping cup, instead of from a bottle. This helps the development of the motor skills of her mouth, which helps her speech development. Plus, it is less damaging for her teeth to drink from a cup than from a bottle.

Weaning Foods
The ideal food to start with when introducing solids is rice flakes. These are made of pure rice, with nothing added to them. Rice flakes are added to the formula that the baby is familiar with, to

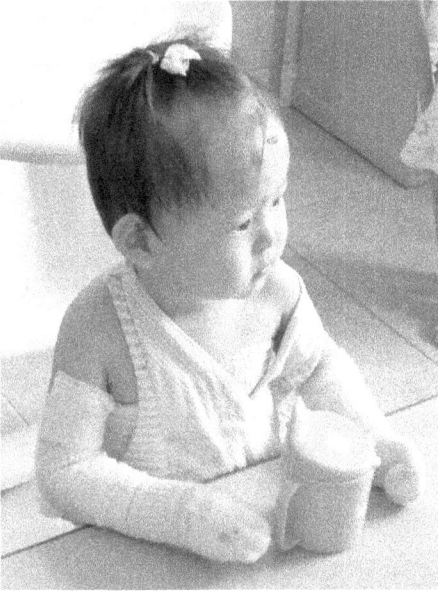

Drinking from a cup.

become a kind of porridge which you can make as thick or runny as you want—to start with, not so runny that it is hard to give with a spoon, but not so thick that the baby needs to make a big effort to swallow it. This hardly changes the familiar flavour of milk, while it does change the consistency, providing the first experience of eating solids. Another reason that rice flakes are a good choice as a first solid food is that it is the most hypoallergenic option available, so even for allergic children, this is a relatively safe start.

It is important that once the baby has accepted the concept of eating from a spoon, you introduce new flavours regularly. However, this does not mean that she needs to get something different at every meal or every day. Repetition is very reassuring to babies. While adults will quickly become bored with eating the same thing day in day out, for babies it provides a sense of comfort. So, a balance must be found between these two sides.

If the baby does not accept a certain food the first day she gets it, this does not necessarily mean that she does not like it. It could simply be that she finds it strange. Often, if you give the same thing again the day after and the day after that, she can get used to it and end up eating it happily. If the baby clearly outright refuses to eat a certain food, even after repetition, or becomes very upset when you offer a certain food, but not with all food, leave that food for a while and try to introduce it again after about a month or so, to see if you get a different response.

From rice flakes you can move on to fruits and vegetables. To start with, all fruits and vegetables should be boiled (or steamed), cut up, and **liquidised** to make them easier to swallow and digest. Good foods to start with are carrots, apples, pears, butternut squash, sweet potato (although this one not for babies

Food mash made in large amounts is easier.

with diarrhoea as it works as a mild laxative-something that makes you poo softer and thinner, in high doses it can cause diarrhoea), peach, and cauliflower. Shortly after, introduce beans, peas, broccoli, potatoes, and rice. Combinations of different flavours can also be made, once a new flavour has been accepted. Because babies need a lot of calories to provide them with the energy they need, a little butter or oil should be added to the vegetable mixtures. Citrus fruit and onions should be avoided at the start, as they are more likely to cause bellyaches than other fruits and vegetables.

Once the baby enjoys eating more than a few bites, you can start increasing the amount to a small bowl. This can then be increased to two meals of solids a day—for instance once fruit and once vegetables—and later on once the child is comfortable eating two meals a day, you can increase to three. Usually, this all develops over the course of only a few weeks. Once a baby eats two to three meals a day of solid food, one of the milk bottles is dropped. Especially if the baby gets porridge made from milk, for instance for breakfast. Up to about eight months of age, milk should be the main source of nutrition. After that, the balance starts to shift to solid food being the main source and milk becoming a drink.

Up to seven to eight months, the baby should not eat meat, as it is hard to digest. After this time, meat can be added in very small amounts, without spices and preferably boiled, the first few months always liquidised, because the baby is not able to chew meat yet. If meat is not part of the local diet, make sure that enough other protein and iron sources are included in the diet. Up to eight to nine months of age, food with gluten should be avoided if possible, to prevent the possible development of a lifelong gluten allergy. Gluten is found in grains such as wheat, barley, and rye, from which for instance bread, chapatti, pasta, and noodles are made.

At no point during the first year of a baby's life is it necessary to add salt or sugar to ANYTHING at all—the only exception is on doctor's prescription, for example in case of dehydration, or when you have to dilute cow's milk because there is no formula available. While adults consider the baby's diet quite bland, this is only in compari-

Eating finger food: a piece of bread.

son to what we are used to. Babies do not have the experience of tasting seasoned, spicy, salty or sugary foods, so they do not miss those tastes. Giving sugar to a baby this early in life increases the risk of obesity, caries, and diabetes later in life. Adding salt to a baby's food, even in what we consider to be small amounts, can cause kidney damage and even kidney failure, which can lead to death. Baby kidneys are the size of large pebbles, so even a little bit of salt is a lot to deal with for them. Also, before their first birthday, babies should not be given honey, as this can cause a type of botulism in babies, a disease which is rare, but almost always fatal if they get it.

Baby stomachs are very small, and babies need a lot of energy. Ideally, once a baby gets most of her energy from solid food, she should be getting five 'meals' a day. That means three main meals: breakfast, lunch and dinner, plus two–healthy–snack moments in-between. As a snack she could, for instance, be given some fruit or yoghurt or something made of nuts or a cracker–with crackers, read the label to make sure they do not contain salt or sugar.

Once they reach one year of age, toddlers are allowed to drink regular cow's milk. But only if it has been pasteurised or sterilised (boiled) and can be stored in a reliable refrigerator.

Feeding Difficulties

Colicky Babies

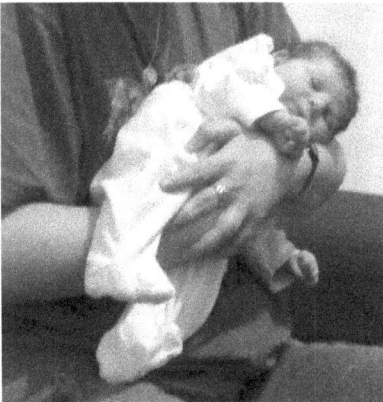

Some babies, especially in the first three months of life, suffer a lot from colic–painful cramping of the bowels–because their bowels have not fully developed yet and have trouble getting used to having to digest things. These babies may spend several hours a day screaming in pain. Carrying them around while providing some pressure and warmth on their belly can provide some relief, but is often hard to do in a children's home because it is very time-consuming.

In some cases, changing the formula–to another brand or to a lactose-free variety–can be a solution. It is worth trying out.

Giving relief to a colicky baby.

Four babies aged between two and three months:
The first baby always drinks her bottle very calmly, and when she is done, her caregiver holds her upright for a few minutes and pats her back, but she almost never burps. After two or three minutes, she is put down either on a mat to look around for a while if she is wide awake, or else in bed. In either case, she will lie there quietly and be quite content.

The second baby usually drinks his bottle as if he has never been fed before. Even though he had a bottle just three hours ago, he gulps his milk down, taking in a lot of air with it. His caregiver holds him upright against her shoulder for a few minutes after he has finished his bottle and pats his back. He almost always lets out one or two really big burps and sometimes a little bit of milk. After he has done his burps, he is very content when he is put down to sleep or to play

The third baby also usually gulps her bottle down as quickly as she can. After she has finished the bottle, her caregiver holds her upright for two or three minutes and gently pats her back, but usually no burps come out. When this baby has been put down in bed or on the mat, she starts out quite content, but after a few minutes she will start to cry and scream and violently kick her legs. She can easily go on for an hour or longer. Sometimes when you pick her up after a while, she will suddenly let out a burp, or occasionally she will vomit when you pick her up. Once she has done that, she calms down.

The fourth baby drinks his bottle calmly, but noisily. Every time he sucks and swallows there is a sound. His caregiver also started by just holding him upright for a few minutes and then putting him down again regardless of whether he did a burp or not. But he would almost always get very, very upset and she had heard somewhere that sometimes babies need more help or more time to get their burp out. So now, the caregiver keeps sitting with him upright, rubbing and patting his back with some force until she has heard at least three burps. This sometimes takes more than ten minutes, but she feels it is worth it, because once the baby gets his burps out, he is quiet and content and he sleeps much better.

One other thing that can be done and that almost always provides some relief, is burping. A lot of people seem to be under the impression that a baby will let the air she takes in while drinking back out by herself, or that when no burp is produced after patting her back for a minute, there is no air to get out. This is not always true. Certainly, there are babies who appear to need little or no burping. They are quite comfortable, eat well and sleep well without anyone taking the time to hold them upright and pat them. There are also babies who only need to be held upright for a moment or two, or need to be patted lightly on their back for a moment, to let the air they have collected in their stomach out. However, there is also a group of babies who seem to get their air 'trapped' inside their body and have great difficulty getting rid of it. They need help to get rid of this air, and if they do not get help, they will spend a lot of time crying in pain, feeling bloated and getting bowel cramps. These babies are also at risk of not getting enough to eat, because with all

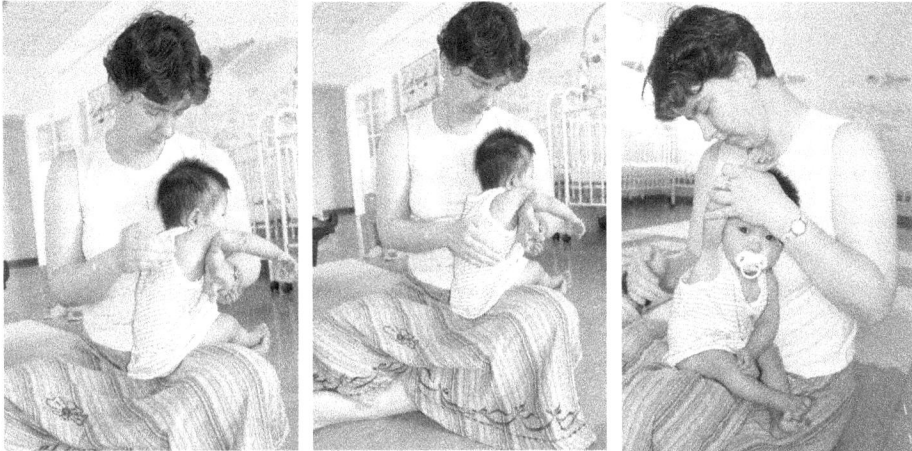

the air they have collected in their stomach, they feel quite full and do not want to eat anymore. However, since what is filling them up is air and not food, they will become very hungry again, very soon. It is important to help these babies get rid of their air, both for their well-being and for your own. I am sure you will agree that your job becomes a lot easier when you do not have one or more babies screaming loudly for hours.

To help a baby get rid of air trapped in his stomach, you need to hold him upright with his spine as straight as possible. Especially in the first two to three months of life, it is very effective to hold the baby over your shoulder, with his arms hanging over your shoulder. Or you can hold the baby in a sitting position on your leg, using one hand to support his chest, with your thumb and forefinger holding up his head, and holding him as straight as possible, while using the other hand to rub or pat his back.

With a baby who takes in quite a lot of air while he drinks and who has trouble getting rid of it without help, it helps to give a bottle in stages. Have the baby drink for a few minutes and then stop and help to get a burp up. Then continue giving the bottle and if the baby becomes restless or drinks less well after another few minutes, take another break to get some air out. This will allow him to drink more than he would if you would just continue without letting him burp. Usually it takes less time to get burps out after a shorter time drinking than when trying to get all of the air out at the end of the feed.

After the bottle is finished, time should be taken to get as many burps out as possible. After a while you will know how many burps you can expect before the baby will stay quiet and settle down. It can sometimes take as long as 10 to 20 minutes to get all the burps up. Still, it is worth the time and energy, because proper burping leads to better eating and better sleeping.

✳ ———————————

Difficulties with Bottles

Some babies have great difficulty drinking from a bottle. This could be because they have become too weak to suck because of an illness, such as pneumonia or dehydration. They may have been born too weak to suck, something you see in premature babies. Or they may have a medical condition that causes a lack of control of the mouth and throat muscles, a lack of reflexes for sucking and swallowing or shortness of breath, which can make it hard, and in some cases entirely impossible, for them to drink from a bottle or to take anything in through their mouth.

The issues and solutions described in this section come mostly from extensive experience with children with **cerebral palsy**. (In *Sick Children Everywhere*, Part 2, Chapter 9: 'Cerebral Palsy' more information is given about the care for these children). However, the methods can also be used in other cases. So, even if the child with feeding difficulties that you are dealing with does not have cerebral palsy, it is worth having a look to see if the advice may be of use to you.

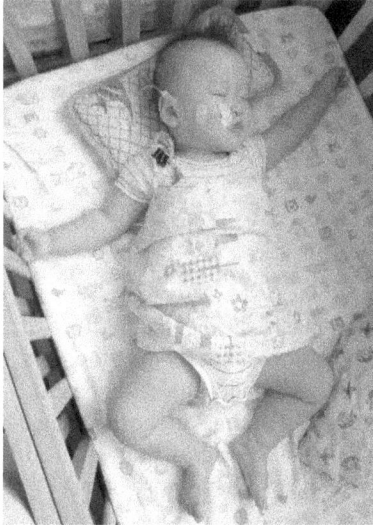

One year old and dependent on a feeding tube for food.

In most cases, babies with cerebral palsy or other special needs are able to bottle-feed normally like other babies. However, depending on the location of the damage in the brain, there can be some problems.

These problems can include:

- Muscle weakness, leading to a lack of power to suck milk from the bottle
- A tongue thrust that is so strong that it is (almost) impossible to place a nipple in the baby's mouth or that causes almost all of the milk to be pushed out of the mouth
- Other problems with the muscles of the mouth and throat that cause movement that go against what is needed to swallow or do not regulate swallowing and breathing in a way to prevent aspiration

In rare cases a complete absence of a sucking and/or swallowing reflex

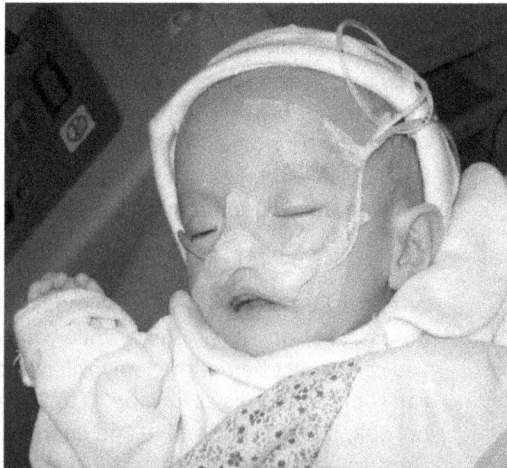

A baby needing a feeding tube (and oxygen) due to weakness from pneumonia.

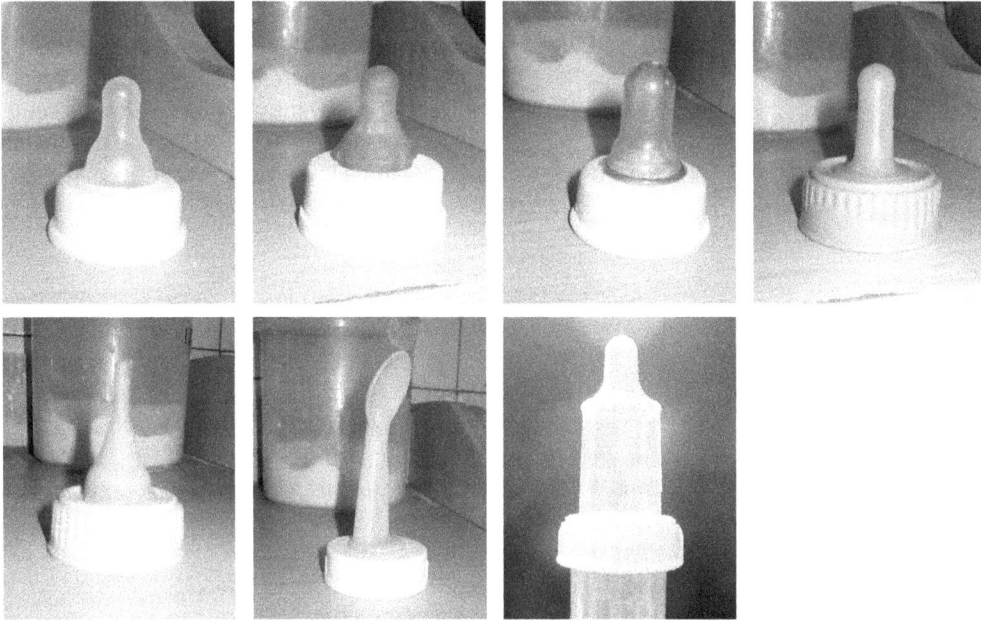

When there are problems with feeding, one of the first things you can try is to use different kinds of nipples. The size, shape and texture of a nipple can make a big difference for some children. Nipples designed for use by babies with a cleft palate have a much slower flow and require less force to get a milk flow going. They also allow milk to emerge without sucking, using a chewing movement instead. There are also spoons that can be attached to bottles, where the milk flows from the bottle onto the spoon which can then be poured into the baby's mouth. Haberman feeders allow you to regulate the speed of the flow of milk, and help you get milk from the nipple into the mouth by squeezing. There are also nipples that end in a narrow tube, from which milk slowly pours into the mouth. Sometimes a nipple that has become soft with use works better than a new, rigid, one. You can try using a sipping cup if no nipple works. You can also try to drip milk into the baby's mouth with a spoon or a syringe. However, you have to be careful that the flow is not too fast, because that can cause choking and aspiration.

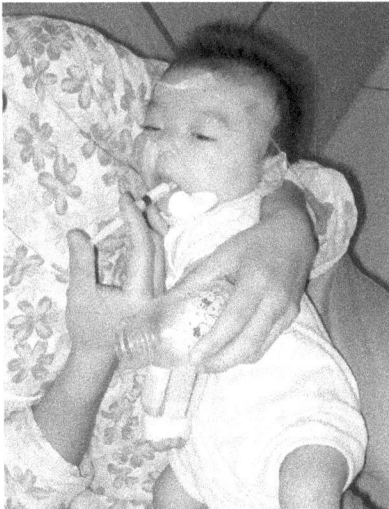

If no nipple works, you can try putting milk in the baby's mouth with a syringe

If none of these strategies work, or with children who clearly have no swallowing reflex, it will be necessary to feed the baby through a feeding tube. This is a tube that enters through a nostril and passes through the oesophagus directly into the stomach. This tube will in most cases need to be placed by a doctor or health worker, who can then teach you how to feed the baby with this method. Without this, a baby who does not drink will die of dehydration and malnutrition.

However, it is important not to give up on feeding by mouth too soon, even if it looks quite hopeless at the start. By trying different possibilities from time to time, there is a chance that you will succeed in getting the child to eat by mouth again. If you succeed in getting as much as 5ml into the child, you know that he has the ability to eat and swallow, and with a lot of work and effort that can be stretched to whole meals.

> A baby boy had been accepted in the children's home with signs of a very difficult birth. It soon became clear that he had cerebral palsy and that he did not have a swallowing reflex, which meant that he was unable to eat by himself. A feeding tube was placed and for several months all his milk was put through that. When he was five and a half months old, it started becoming very difficult to feed through the feeding tube, because he put up a big fight every time. He was also starting to move his mouth more, and seemed to be making sucking movements. Until five to six months of age sucking and swallowing depend mostly on reflexes; after that, eating starts to become driven by voluntary action. So, it was decided to see if there might be any hope of this boy taking milk by mouth. First a few drops were put on his lips while he received the rest of the milk through the feeding tube. He sucked these drops into his mouth and swallowed them. So at least it was clear that he was able to swallow now. The next stage was giving him milk from a syringe (without a needle), so he would have to swallow, but did not need to suck. Then he was given milk from a bottle with a nipple for cleft lip and palate; he drank a little from that and then the rest from a syringe. After two to three weeks, the little boy was drinking all his milk from a bottle, and the feeding tube could be removed.

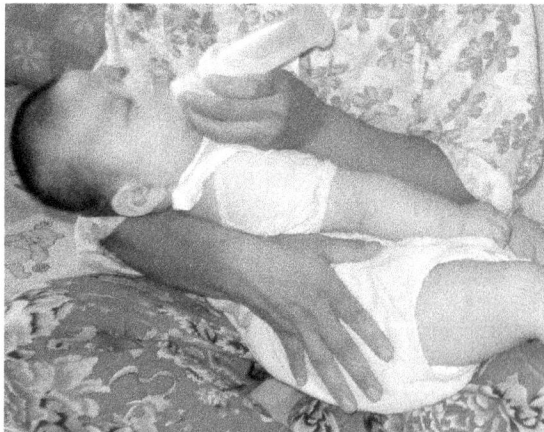

Feeding a girl who until recently depended on a feeding tube.

Getting a baby to eat by mouth if she has been fed through a feeding tube for quite some time is very hard work and requires tremendous patience and stamina. It is essential to be creative in thinking of ways to offer milk and to always be encouraging towards the baby.

That not everyone is suited to feeding babies with feeding difficulties became very clear when a little girl of one year old, who had been dependent on a feeding tube for most of her life, was finally able to take milk through her mouth from a bottle. Once I had gotten her to the point where her milk intake was enough and it looked reasonably certain that she would continue to allow people to feed her by mouth, she was put back in the care of her regular caregivers. One of these caregivers was particularly good with the little girl; she would take time, encourage her and keep her entertained through the feeds–which took up to 45 minutes each at this point. Quite soon the little girl drank more per feed for this caregiver than she did for me. However, in this location caregivers worked in shifts, so the 'ideal caregiver' was only available seven hours a day, six days a week. Another caregiver was also given a chance to try. She spent most of the feeding time reprimanding the little girl for drinking badly, drinking too slowly and dribbling too much. The little girl became more and more upset and less and less willing to drink. We tried to explain to this caregiver the importance of patience and encouragement, but she really did not understand what she was doing wrong. So in the end, someone else was chosen to feed the little girl during her shifts.

Oral Aversion

Oral aversion means that a child will not let anything go near, let alone into, her mouth. She may not even allow people to touch her face at all, without going into a complete panic. This situation can develop if the child has been force-fed.

Similarly, in cases where feeding has been associated with pain for a long time,

Encouraging putting her hand in her mouth to overcome her oral aversion.

either because of a physical condition or a post-surgery situation, the child's fear may grow into oral aversion. In a case like this, for some time at least, it might be necessary to feed through a feeding tube, because continuing the fight is likely to only make things

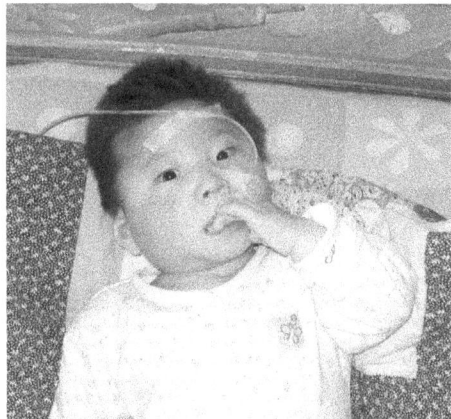

worse, and the amount of food that goes into the child is almost certainly not enough to keep her healthy.

> *A six-month-old girl with cerebral palsy had difficulties eating, partly because of her spasticity. Her caregivers were very anxious that she should start solids and they felt that she needed to eat something to stay healthy. So, once or twice a day, two of the caregivers would come together to get her to eat. Whenever the little girl showed no interest, one would force her mouth open, the other would put a spoonful of fruit into her mouth and then they would hold her mouth closed and would try to force her to swallow. After a few days, the little girl was in a complete panic from the moment someone would sit down with her, especially when she saw a spoon. It even got to the stage that she would start crying and get very spastic whenever anyone touched her face. Trying to feed her was abandoned by the caregivers and seen as impossible.*

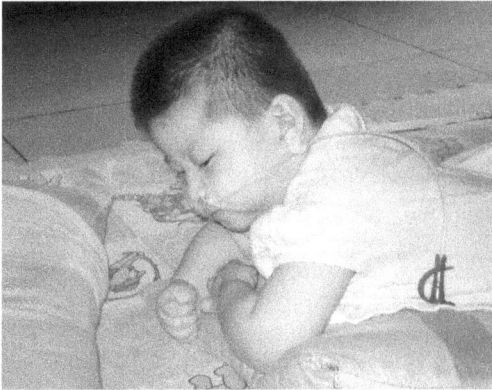

It took almost 6 months to get her off the feeding tube...

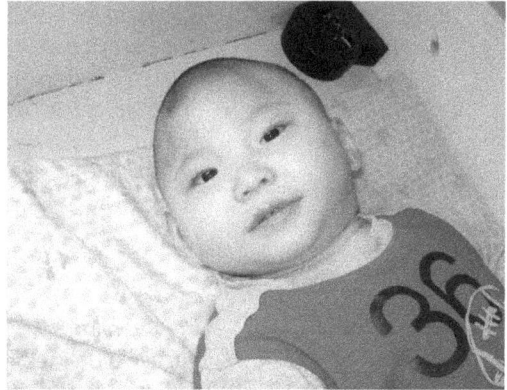

...partly because of setbacks caused by impatience.

In a case of oral aversion, if at all possible, the first step is to let the child 'rest' for a few days. During this time, no attempts should be made at all to feed orally, or to touch her mouth. This can only be done if the child has a feeding tube through which food can be given in the meantime. If at all possible, even keep washing of the face and wiping away of dribble to a minimum.

The next step is to provide oral stimulation in a non-threatening way not related to food. It is very important to let the child set the limits and not to cross them. When the child starts to try to get away or even cry, stop and wait for another time when she is happy again. Ideally, this stimulation should take place twice or three times a day. It can start by simply lightly and briefly touching the face. Start away from the mouth, for instance on the forehead, and move towards the mouth if the sensation is tolerated. Later, if the child allows, stroke her lips with your finger and make a game of it. It can be helpful to put her hand on your mouth to let her explore, to make it an exchange situation.

If the child is in any way inclined to put her hands or other objects in her mouth, this should be encouraged, not discouraged. Oral exploration is a very important step in getting her to accept oral feeding. Playing with nipples, either pacifiers or the nipples from the bottles, is another step. Allow her to explore them with her hands, mouth, or whatever she wants. And for instance, see if she will allow you to make a 'hopping' trail with the nipple over her arm, over her face and eventually over her lips, *without* attempting to put the nipple in her mouth.

If she tolerates you touching her lips quite well you can start **experimenting** with wetting her lips with either water or milk. Again, do not try to push your finger into her mouth unless she invites you to do so. If she grabs your finger and wants to put it into her mouth, let her do that and encourage it. But do not attempt to force your finger in. You do not put anything at all into her mouth, until she herself opens her mouth to accept it. And then you only do it tentatively, ready to withdraw the moment she starts to feel unhappy about it.

If she accepts your finger, you can try if she will accept a nipple or a spoon by gently tapping on her lip with it and seeing if she opens her mouth–this is after she is already completely used to and comfortable with the feel of the nipple or the spoon. If she opens her mouth, do not push the nipple or the spoon in all the way, only a little, gently, up to about a centimetre, and see how she reacts. If she tolerates it and seems relaxed, you can go slightly further.

If she completely accepts the nipple in her mouth, the next time you can try to have the nipple attached to a bottle with a little milk in it, to see if she will accept it. But again, be very tentative and withdraw at the very first sign of discomfort or distress. When there is milk in the bottle, you also need to make sure that she is sitting upright enough to prevent coughing and choking, which could make the experience traumatic again.

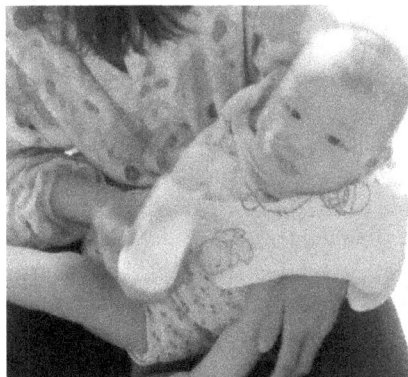

Her chin is not cleaned until after she is done, or she will not drink anymore.

Once she is comfortable drinking from a bottle again, slowly increase the amount she drinks at any given feed and reduce the amount given through the feeding tube. When she is able to feed on her own entirely, the feeding tube can be removed.

Similarly, with an older child, once the spoon is accepted, you can try carefully having something on the spoon to taste and so gradually working towards actually taking bites without panicking.

A fourteen-month-old girl had been dependent on her feeding tube for a very long time, and her oral aversion was quite severe. Now she started to accept milk from a bottle, and during the daytime she was drinking increasingly well. Night-times were very challenging, however, because during the long months in which she was fed through the tube that led to her stomach, she had not needed to wake up to get food. In her mind, there was no relation between being awake and being fed. During the night, it was extremely difficult to wake her up and get her to drink, but if she did not drink at all during the night, she would also drink less in the morning. It was as if she forgot how to drink if there was too much time between two feeds.

For some time, I would get up at night to make sure the girl would take at least a little bit of milk. One evening I was assured by the night supervisor that she could handle it and that I should get some sleep. I agreed, but at midnight I went to check to see how things were going anyway, for my own peace of mind. I found the night supervisor with the little girl half-awake on her lap, calling out the girl's name. I asked what she was doing and was told that the little girl was very sleepy and she was trying to get her to wake up more. I explained that this was really the best you could hope for at night and that she should start to try to get milk into the girl before she went back into a deep sleep. The supervisor nodded and continued trying to wake the girl. In the end, I took the girl and fed her, and got up for the next feed, until the day the other night supervisor came on shift and did well.

With difficult feeders, it is best to be open to working with what you get to make sure the child eats something at least. If you wait for the perfect situation to occur, the child may not eat at all.

It is very tempting to go through the different steps as quickly as possible or to try to skip a step or two. However, in many cases, moving forward too fast will risk losing the progress you made and having to start all over again. The most important thing you have is the child's trust, which you will have to win at the start. If you lose that trust by going too far, you will have to start all over again. In some cases, if you are unable to re-establish the bond of trust, you may even be forced to hand over the attempt to someone else. To maintain the trust, try to distance yourself from inevitable, potentially traumatic procedures so that the child does not associate you with the cleaning of eyes, the placing of feeding tubes or medical procedures that must take place.

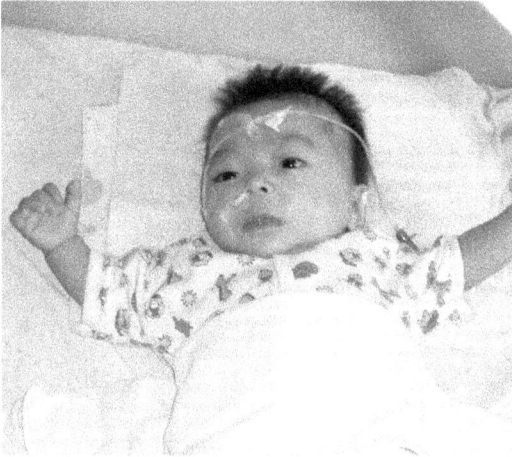

No swallowing reflex and yet...

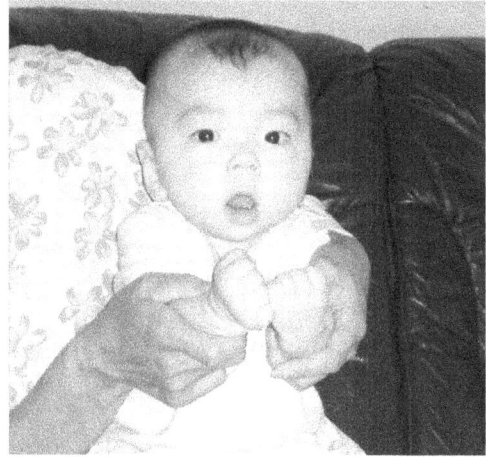

...it took less than a month to lose the feeding tube.

I regularly place feeding tubes, clean noses and perform other interventions on children if necessary. However, when I am in the early stages of helping a child overcoming oral aversion, I ask other people to do these things for me, whenever possible. I even try to stay out of the room, or if I need to supervise what is being done, I at least stay out of the child's line of sight. This helps me strengthen the trust the child puts in me, until we reach the point where that trust is so great that it will even last through my doing something that is unpleasant for a moment.

There is no set timeline for how long these steps will take. You need creativity in trying different things and close observation as to what works, what is accepted by the child, and what is not. Both the time needed and the way by which you will get to the end goal have to be determined by the child. To be on the safe side, it is always much better to go too slow than to risk everything by going too fast.

When a child has overcome her oral aversion, it is important to remember that eating will probably always remain a sensitive area for her. Any negative experiences with, for example, being force-fed medication, or a forceful transition to solids can cause a big step back and may even lead to an absolute refusal to accept anything by mouth again.

One more issue which needs to be considered, closely related to oral aversion, is motivation. Some children quite simply lack the motivation to eat. Not everyone gets the same stimulation and satisfaction from the experience of eating and tasting. If this is the case, you will need to think of ways to encourage the child to eat.

A little boy started out making excellent progress when he started learning to drink from a bottle instead of being fed through a feeding tube. It was clear that he had no difficulty sucking or swallowing anymore, nor did he show any signs of weakness or tiredness. Still, after the good start, it seemed impossible to get him to drink enough to be able to stop using his feeding tube. He would refuse to go on drinking after the first half of the bottle was gone. Until one day, more or less in desperation, his caregiver started to walk around the room with him while feeding. While he was looking around to see all the different things present in the room and visible through the window, he continued sucking and finished his bottle. He simply thought drinking from a bottle was too boring to bother with after the worst of the hunger was gone. When you would walk around with him, or have another person dangle a toy in front of his face, he would drink just fine.

A girl with some physical problems that had caused feeding difficulties as well as oral aversion was finally starting to accept milk from a bottle. However, it was not easy to get her to keep drinking. If you just sat with her and put the bottle in her mouth, she would suck once or twice and then just lie there with her mouth around the nipple, looking around. Over time it was discovered that to keep her drinking meant to keep her entertained by singing almost non-stop to encourage her, and to remind her now and again that she was meant to be drinking by squirting some milk into her mouth by squeezing the nipple. If you did that, she drank very well.

Held with his knees over a leg and his bottom hanging down to break spasticity.

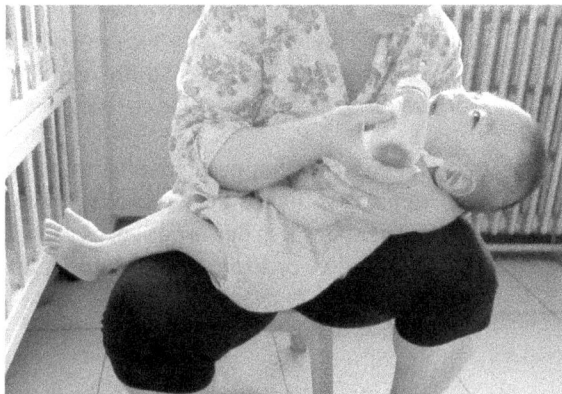

Overcoming Problems with Eating Solids
Positioning is very important. Hold the child upright, as close to a sitting position as is possible. If the child is spastic, take some time

before you start feeding him to help him relax. Also, if he stretches out rigidly during feeding, pause for a moment to help the child relax and come back to a sitting position. If the child has a problem with being held, it is all right to have him sit by himself. Just make sure he is not lying down flat. His head needs to be elevated and preferably his upper body too.

Allowing the child to try for herself may motivate her, even if it is messy.

With older children, if the child absolutely refuses to be fed but is willing and able to eat if he can feed himself, allow him to do so. Even if he eats with both his hands rather than with a spoon or just his right hand and makes a big mess. Do wash his hands before eating.

If the child starts crying, stop feeding and play with him until he is happy again. Then try again. If the child still cries, stop altogether until the next feeding time. Making meals a positive experience is much more important than finishing what is in the bowl. Do not try to push past the child's limits. Even if there are only two more spoonfuls left, do not try to make him finish them. A small thing like this can undo a lot of good work. When you have found a type of food that is accepted by the child, still try to introduce new flavours and textures from time to time—at least once a week at the start—to increase the number of different foods given. If there is a clear dislike for a certain food, do not give this food again for at least a month.

If the child is very sensitive to having his face touched—resisting, crying, going into spasm—do not clean the face at all until the meal is finished completely, no matter how dirty it gets.

It might help to change the consistency of the food. Thicker textures are often easier to deal with than watery ones, but some children prefer the other way around. So you could, for instance, add rice flakes to mashed fruit. This might make a big difference. Or, in the opposite case, you can add some more cooking juices to the mixture to make it wetter and thinner. If this goes well, you can start trying mashed vegetables, and eggs. If that goes well, keep experimenting with different foods. Do not use too much salt, and no salt at all if the child is less than one year old!

More than once I have been called to look at a child 'who would not eat' to see if something could be done, only to be told that all the child will eat are biscuits. If a child is able to eat biscuits, that is, bite off a piece and chew it, not inhale the crumbs and swallow it, there is clearly very little wrong with his ability to eat. This is almost always a case of a picky eater, not of feeding difficulties. In most cases, attempts to make him eat something else have been half-hearted. If he can keep from being hungry by eating his favourite food, why try anything less appealing?

Important points in helping a child eat are:

- *Do not force the child's mouth open or hold her head so she cannot move.*
- *Even if the child spits out food, DO NOT cover her mouth with your hand to prevent her from spitting. This can make her **choke** and can traumatise her.*
- *Do not criticise the child when something does not go right; praise her when something does go right.*
- *Do not rush the child.*
- *Do not keep adding food if the child does not swallow. This will only increase the chance of choking and gagging. It can even lead to vomiting. Eventually the lump of food will become so big and dry in her mouth that it is impossible to swallow. Instead, encourage the child verbally to swallow, and if this does not work, gently touch her lips or tongue with the empty spoon, to remind her that she was eating.*

Take time to feed the child. The most important thing is for meals to be fun for the child.

Mealtimes
Babies do not have set mealtimes yet. They need to be given bottles regularly, at intervals that can range between every two hours to every four hours, depending on the size and the age of the baby and on any medical conditions she might have. When the baby first starts eating solids, this is still mostly placed within the—possibly varying—schedule of her bottle feeds. Once a child becomes

mostly dependent on regular food, in most children's homes the day becomes more structured, with mealtimes set at more or less the same time every day.

Lining up for ART after prayer; they cannot eat for at least half an hour after they take their medication.

Although most children's homes have more or less set routines with everyone getting up at a certain time, having breakfast at a certain time, and so on, there is often still some variation in mealtimes. For example, if there is an important visitor–such as a government official or a big donor–a meal may be pushed back a bit, to suit the convenience of the guest. Or if there is an unexpected delay in getting the firewood or the ingredients needed to make the meal, this can cause the time of the meal to change. In most cases this is not a very big problem. Children may be hungry for a little while longer, but healthy children are able to deal with this.

However, there are cases where set mealtimes, without *any* variation, are extremely important. This is especially the case if you care for children with medical conditions that require medication to be taken at set times, with food or on an empty stomach, or for children who have an unstable blood sugar level. So, in the case of children with diabetes and children who are HIV-positive and are taking **ART** treatment, for example, it is essential that there is no change in mealtimes, for any reason. Also, if you have malnourished children in your care, they should never have to go longer between meals than usual, because they do not have the reserves in their body to help them cope with this situation like healthy, well-fed children do.

In a children's home where a lot of children are HIV-positive, dinnertime is officially at 7:30 p.m. Children receive their ART medication at 6:30 p.m., so that they will have an empty stomach for at least an hour after taking the medication. They finish their dinner no later than 8:00 p.m., which allows the children who need to take another kind of medication at 10:00 p.m. to not eat for at least two hours before taking that medication, as instructed by the doctor. It is important to make sure these instructions are followed, because if they are not, the medication is not effective. Taking the medication the wrong way has a similar effect to not taking it at all and when you skip doses of ART medication, a resistance to the medication can build up very quickly and it will no longer be useful.

While the official routine looks perfect, in practice it is not uncommon for something to happen–a function or a visit from important people–that leads to dinner being pushed back. This causes a big problem, because ART medication has to be taken at the same time every day, in the correct way, to be effective. When dinner is later than usual either the 10:00 p.m. medication has to be given at a later time, to make sure of at least two hours without food beforehand–but that means it is not given at the right time. Or it is given at the regular time, but that means it will not be given on a completely empty stomach.

I explained to the manager of a children's home for HIV-positive children that it was extremely important not to move mealtimes around for children on ART, because to do so is literally to play with these children's lives. I was told that he understood this, but that sometimes the situation was quite simply out of his control. If some important person came and demanded to be received at a certain time, there was nothing he could do. I suggested to at least make sure that all the children who needed to receive the 10:00 p.m. medication–only a small group–could be fed separately at the right time, to make sure that they did not get into trouble. The manager still kept saying that this was very complicated and that he just could not help it. Then I asked him a different question: 'How often has it happened that the children did not go to school on time because there was a function or a VIP guest?' The answer was 'never'. So, I told him, it is possible to make these things happen. It is not really about whether it is hard or complicated. What it is about is whether you find it important enough to make sure it happens. So now you have to decide whether keeping these children alive is as important as giving them an education.

Giving Medication

Getting children to take medication is not always easy. This not only goes for children with feeding difficulties, but for many children. Sometimes small children will like the extremely sweet taste of an antibiotic or other medication. But often they do not like the taste at all, and they will fight to avoid having to take it. Still, I would advise anyone to start out trying if the child will take the medicine without any extra measures. I have regularly seen caregivers presume that a child would be uncooperative, and by trying to avoid problems they actually caused them.

While the baby initially was quite curious to taste what he was given, he soon became unhappy and started to struggle. Not because he had decided that he did not want the medicine, but because someone was squeezing his cheeks to force his mouth open. That made him decide that this must be a bad thing, not the taste of the medicine. The next time he saw someone coming with the medicine, he started crying and resisting before anyone had even touched him.

If you have a baby who has decided that he will not take any more medicine from a spoon or syringe, one option is a special pacifier in which you can put medicine and when the baby sucks on it, he sucks the medicine up automatically. Though if the medicine tastes very bad, that is likely to only work once or twice. Then the baby probably will not accept any pacifiers anymore.

If the doctor allows you to give the medicine with food, if the child has started eating solids, you can try to mix it with some mashed fruit or something else to hide the taste. Again, how effective this is likely to be will depend on how strong the taste of the medicine is. With older children, you can try to bribe the child. You bargain with him that if he takes the medicine, he can eat something that he likes to take away the taste, or he can do an activity that he likes a lot. This can be very effective, but it only has a chance of success if you keep your promise to the child every single time.

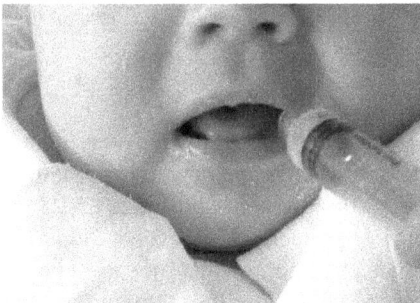

In the end, if there is really no other way to get the child to take the medication, the only way is to force him. You do this by forcing his mouth open—by squeezing the cheeks between the jaws—and putting the medicine to the side of the back of the mouth (in the cheek, towards the back) with a syringe (without needle). Then close his mouth and hold it closed and if the child does not swallow, close off the nostrils by pinching for an older child and by putting your finger up against them for a baby. This will force him to swallow, because

Squirting the medicine into the back of the cheek.

otherwise he cannot breathe. Be careful not to do this too long; if he still does not swallow, he needs to be allowed to breathe again within a minute. This should *only* be done if there is absolutely no other way, because if you do it this way, he will fight even harder the next time you arrive with the medicine. And if this is a baby who has feeding difficulties or problems with oral aversion, giving medicine like this will be a great setback in getting him to cooperate with oral feeding.

With children who have medical conditions that require medication every day for months, years or even their entire life—as opposed to children who only need to take a few days of antibiotics—it is even more important to try, at all costs, to make sure giving the medication does not turn into a struggle or a traumatic event. Because the struggle will continue and get fiercer every time. Eventually, as the child grows bigger and stronger, it will become almost impossible to force him anymore. In other words, you really need his voluntary cooperation.

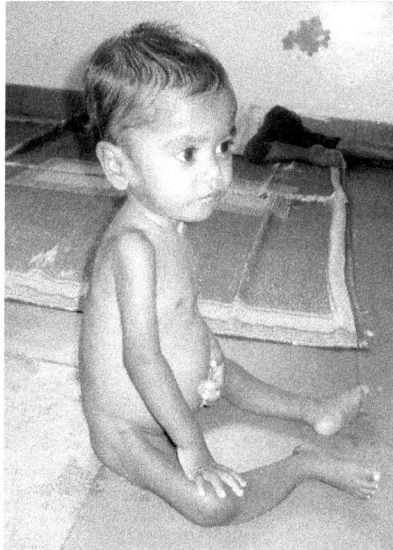

18 months old, the size of a three-month-old, the weight of a newborn.

Preventing Malnutrition

While this book does not deal with medical issues, I think it is important to touch lightly on what malnutrition is and how to prevent it. More complete information about this can be found in *Sick Children Everywhere* Part 1, Chapter 2: 'Problems of Digestion'. When thinking about malnourishment in children, the first thought people usually have is of children who are starving because there is not enough food for them. It is certainly true that these children are also malnourished, and that a situation like this might arise in a children's home when there is an extreme drought or failure of crops in the area. However, it is not the only way for children to get malnourished, and it is essential to be aware of that.

16 children aged between one and six years old are cared for by one caregiver. The vegetarian diet given to the children is not well-balanced, so all of the children show various degrees of malnutrition. One child is much worse off than the others. She is eighteen months old, weighs 4.5kg and is 63cm tall. Her arms, legs and buttocks have lost all muscles and her belly is very bloated. She sits quietly on the floor, not really moving. Occasionally, she makes a hand gesture to indicate that she wants to eat or drink, but usually no one notices and if they don't, she gives up immediately. She has fallen into a vicious cycle. The caregiver is extremely busy trying to take the best care possible of all 16 children and has her hands full. The little girl got weakened by a diet that is not quite balanced–but also not terrible. Getting weaker, she needed more care, but was too weak to demand it and the caregiver is only able to go from one demand to the next. This caused the little girl to weaken further, making it even less likely that she would find the energy to fight for her needs, and so it continued until the present stage was reached: severe malnutrition, serious dehydration and bronchitis, all on top of being HIV-positive.

Malnutrition means a diet that is wrong in some way. This can both mean too much or not enough. In this book, the word malnutrition is only used to indicate that a person does not get enough food. This can be not enough food over-all, or not enough of a certain kind of food, which means that the body lacks some-thing–a building block–that it needs to stay healthy. While it is possible for malnutrition to be caused by a simple inability to get enough food to give to the children–because of local shortages or because of lack of funds at the children's home–, in children's homes around the world, malnutrition is more often caused by incomplete knowledge of what children need in their diet to stay healthy and strong. Beliefs, tradition, religion, local cook-

A seven-month-old girl weighing 2.5kg.

ing practices and local childrearing practices can also lead to a poor diet, while the right foods are available locally.

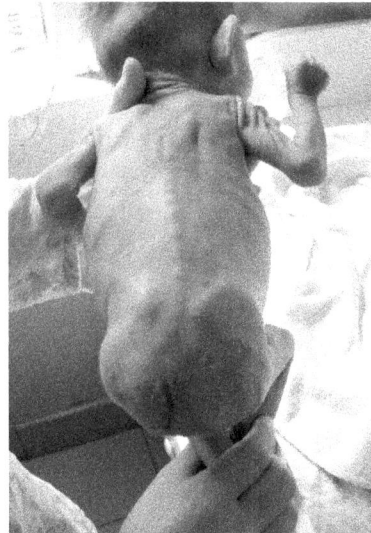

Even though the children in a children's home often get more or less the same kinds of things to eat as the children in families who live in the same area, the 'more or less' can make a bigger difference than you might think. While children in a family often receive the best or most nutritious parts of the food available and extra bits from their mother's plate and a little extra treat from someone in their extended family from time to time, this does not happen with children in a children's home. This small difference between just being given what everyone else gets and getting a few little extras from time to time can make the difference between being healthy and being malnourished.

The foods children need to stay healthy, and how much they need per day for each age:

Food Group	1-3yrs	4-6yrs	7-9yrs	10-12yrs		13-18yrs	
				Girls	Boys	Girls	Boys
Cereal & Millets	120gr	210gr	270gr	270gr	330gr	300gr	420gr
Chicken, Meat, Eggs or Pulses	30gr	45gr	60gr	60gr	60gr	60gr	60gr
Milk	500ml	500ml	500ml	500ml	500ml	500ml	500ml
Roots & Tubers	50gr	50gr	100gr	100gr	100gr	100gr	100gr
Green Leafy Vegetables	50gr	50gr	100gr	100gr	100gr	100gr	100gr
Other Vegetables	50gr	50gr	100gr	100gr	100gr	100gr	100gr
Fruits	100gr	100gr	100gr	100gr	100gr	100gr	100gr
Sugars	25gr	30gr	30gr	30gr	35gr	30gr	35gr
Fat/Oils (visible)	20gr	25gr	25gr	25gr	25gr	25gr	25gr

Children who are malnourished will get sick much more easily than children who get all the food they need. If a well-nourished and a malnourished child get the same illness, the malnourished child is almost certain to get much sicker from it, because her body does not have the strength and resources to fight the illness. Sometimes she even lacks the energy to cause a fever, which is needed to activate more white blood cells to help fight the disease. It is possible that while the well-nourished child only gets a little bit ill, the malnourished child dies of the same illness. Malnutrition is recognised as the most common cause of immuno**deficiency** (a weakened immune system) worldwide. If the malnutrition was severe and lasted for a long time, it can **permanent**ly slow down brain development.

A seven-month-old girl arrived at a children's home from another orphanage. The orphanage she came from said that she was basically all normal, except for a mild heart condition. She only weighed 2.5kg and had clearly been deprived of food for many months. She was fed high-energy formula and quite soon she started to drink well and gain weight. However, as soon as she started to become more active, it became apparent that she was not just a little delayed developmentally: she had cerebral palsy with severe mental retardation, spasticity and epilepsy. If these symptoms were not present on the initial examination when she was admitted to the orphanage where she spent at least six months and became malnourished, it seems likely that her deprivation caused damage to her brain.

Once a baby gets to the point where her diet depends more on solid food than on milk, it becomes especially important that she receives a well-balanced diet to continue to grow well and stay healthy. A well-balanced diet means that aside from the cheaper energy foods such as rice, maize, cassava, and millet, children need a variety of other foods to get everything they need. Protein is very important to help them build their muscles and strength, and particularly if their diet is vegetarian, it is easy to accidentally give them too little protein and iron, which leads to malnutrition.

I mentioned to the management of a children's home that although they provided their children with enough food, the diet was not well-balanced and it lacked in certain things, particularly protein and iron. Their defence was that it is almost impossible to force the children to eat everything they are given. They will eat their favourite food and leave or trade what they do not like. This is certainly true. However, one thing is certain: regardless of likes and dislikes, a child will never be able to eat something that he is not given. Not giving food because you expect–some of–the children not to eat it, is not going to make any of the children healthier.

Children under five years old, and in some cases older than that, cannot be made responsible for what they eat. They need to receive a plate with good, varied food and they need to be supervised while eating it. They need to be encouraged–but not forced–to eat, or to least try, everything on their plate. This is because young children have no idea of what a balanced diet is and why it is important to have one. Plus, a lot of rejection of food comes simply from not trusting the unfamiliar. Once the child has tasted something a few times, she may come to like it.

In a children's home, I had my meals together with the children and ate exactly what they ate. It became apparent quite quickly that some elements of a balanced diet were missing. When I reported this to the management, they were greatly surprised. They showed me the meal plan for the month, which the kitchen supervisor had submitted for approval. I had to admit that it looked very good. However, I knew that some of the items mentioned on the meal plan had never made it onto the plates of the children. When the kitchen supervisor was confronted, he said that sometimes when he went to the market to get the food, certain things would not be available or they would be very expensive, so he would make a change. There is nothing wrong with that, as long as you get another protein source when your protein source is not available and different dark leafy vegetables when the ones you were planning to get are too expensive. Otherwise, quite serious lacks can appear in the diet.

INDICATIONS OF MALNUTRITION:

Mid-arm circumference of children aged one to five years old:
> 13.5cm   normal
12.5cm-13.5cm   moderate malnutrition
< 12.5cm   severe malnutrition

If a child's weight is less than 70% of what would be expected for his age, this is considered an indication of high risk of morbidity and mortality

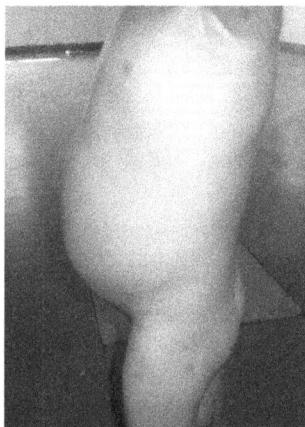

The amount of food is enough, but not all the child needs is in it, causing the bloated belly and lack of buttocks.

To make sure that you will find out early if there is any problem with malnutrition, it is important to regularly weigh the children and keep records of their weight. How to keep these records will be discussed in more detail in Part 3, Chapter 6: 'Day-to-Day Issues'. To sum up the most important thing: healthy growing children do not lose weight, they gain weight steadily. So, if your regular weighing shows that one of the children is losing weight, it is important to have this child looked at by a doctor to try to figure out what causes the weight loss. If you find that several of the children in your care are losing weight, you need to start looking at the children's diet and if you are unable to improve it by yourself, you should find help to make sure that you provide the children with a diet that provides everything they need.

In a children's home, the children in one of the dorms were weighed once a week and their weights were all written down in a growth overview. Generally, most of the children gained weight well, but at certain times suddenly most of the children would lose weight. After some time, it was discovered that these periods of weight loss were always at times when one of the supervisors was not present to make sure that the people who cooked for this dorm were providing the quality of food needed. Having discovered this, it was possible to organise a replacement for the supervisor, whenever he could not be there, to avoid this situation in the future.

Children who are HIV-positive or who suffer from other serious infections require more calories and more protein in their diet than healthy children to keep up or get back their health. In *Sick Children Everywhere* Part 1, Chapter 2: 'Problems of Digestion' you can find a lot of information on how to recognise malnutrition, how to prevent it and how to deal with it when you have a malnourished child in your care.

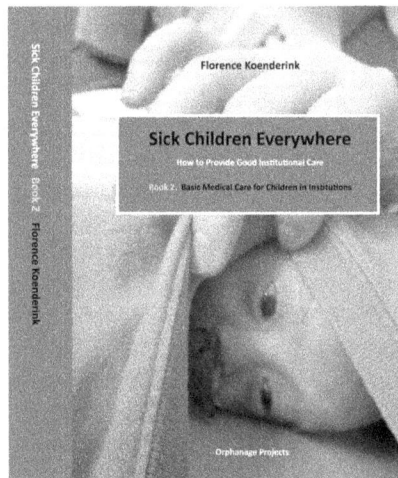

Chapter 3: Sleeping

It is essential for children's health and development that they get enough sleep. Plus, children are easier to deal with when they are well rested. In the first months of their lives, babies sleep most of the day and night. They wake up to eat and play for a little while, and then they are ready for more sleep. As he gets older, the child will start to spend more and more time awake, using his awake-time to learn how to use his body.

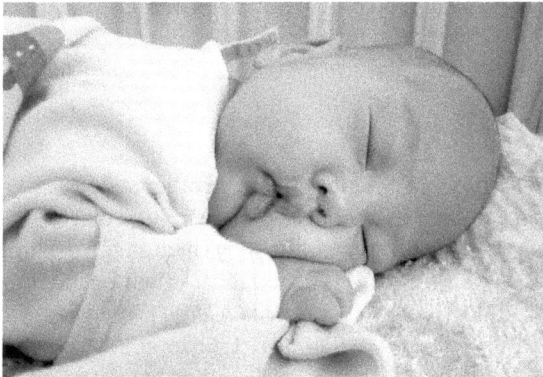

Allowed to sleep on his belly because there is always someone in the room.

It is important to let the child have as much sleep as he needs, because children do their growing while they sleep, not while they are awake. So, if a child is not allowed to sleep as much as he needs–usually because he is made to be awake when other, possibly older, children are also awake–he is unable to grow as much as he should. Not sleeping enough is also likely to make a baby so tired that he does not to eat well, because he is too sleepy. This can lead to a vicious cycle of the baby getting weaker and weaker, and his health getting worse.

However, when they are well, it is also important to allow babies to spend awake-time actively. For good development, they need to have the opportunity to spend time outside of their cots. If they get no stimulation or attention, some babies will just go back to sleep, to shut out the world. This does not help their development. In Part 1, Chapter 5: 'Psychological Essentials', the importance of stimulation and the effects of getting no stimulation will be discussed in more detail.

When a child arrives at the children's home, especially if he is over six months old, he is likely to have a hard time sleeping well, at first. He is in an unfamiliar place, and it is likely he is not used to sharing a room with several

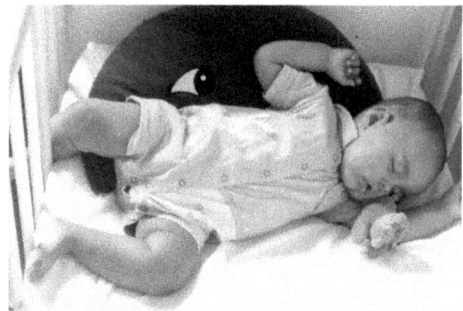

Sleep is essential for growth and health.

other children who all wake and sleep in their own time. When he is 'abandoned' in his bed, in the first weeks, he may feel a strong sense of loss for the people who used to take care of him before he arrived here. It is not reasonable to presume that he is a difficult child or that he is intentionally disruptive if he has trouble sleeping during the first month or two. He simply needs some time to adjust to his new situation and to grieve for the loss of what used to be his world and his life, even if he might not have conscious knowledge of it.

Sleeping Arrangements

When it comes to sleeping arrangements, there are several things that need to be considered to keep babies and toddlers safe. To make sure that they sleep peacefully and as undisturbed as possible, it is helpful if the sleeping area is separated from the living/playing area. This way, whenever some of the children are sleeping while others are awake, sleep will not be disturbed. The sleeping area should always be within hearing range of an adult so that crying, but also other suspicious sounds like 'thumps', are heard straight away. If it is not possible to hear the bedroom from the living room, a baby monitor of some sort should be used, or an adult should be posted within hearing range of the bedroom.

Safe cots adjustable in height and the sides can be put down.

A cot which is sturdy and constructed to avoid accidents.

If the babies sleep in cots, these must be constructed safely. The cot has to be sturdy enough to withstand the force of a baby or toddler pulling himself up by the bars and rocking back and forth holding on to those bars, sometimes quite violently. The bars must be close enough together that no baby can stick their head through them–if the head fits through, the baby will be able to come out all the way– yet you must also make sure that arms or legs cannot get trapped between them.

The higher the bottom of the cot is secured, the easier it is on the back of the caregiver who puts the child down. However, it is essential to make sure that the child cannot fall out. A baby's head is very heavy compared to the rest of his body, so if a baby is able to bend over the top, at about armpit level or lower, he is likely to fall out of the cot. Since reaching the next developmental **milestone** usually happens suddenly, it is important to make sure that you are always one step ahead by installing the mattress low enough to make sure the baby is safe.

From the very start, a cot should have sides high enough to not allow the baby to fall out if he rolls over. Once he can more or less sit–but not yet get into a sitting position by himself–the sides should be so high that they reach just over his head when he is sitting up in bed. From about seven to nine months, the mattress should be at the lowest setting, to prepare for the day when the baby will pull himself up to standing by the bars. While rocking cots can be very helpful for calming babies down and helping them go to sleep when they are quite small, with these kinds of beds it is even more important to make absolutely sure that the baby cannot fall out. The sides need to be high enough to guarantee that even if he decides to roll over, the baby will not fall out while the cot is swinging.

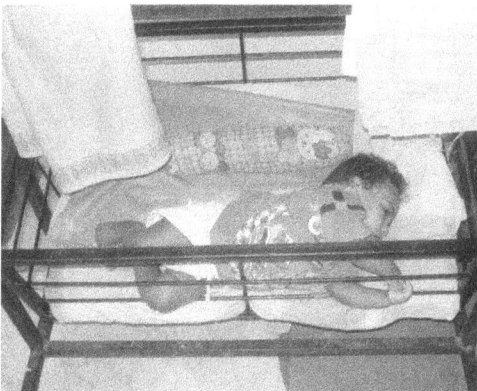

A rocking cot with low sides, suitable for newborns, but not for older children.

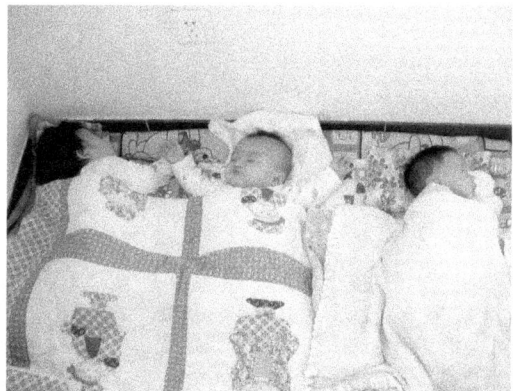

Babies sleeping on a mat on the floor.

If the babies and toddlers sleep on the floor on mats, or in hammocks, they should never be left alone in the room. A caregiver always needs to be present because if one of the babies wakes up and starts moving around, he can easily hurt himself or another child. In a children's home for babies with serious medical conditions or illnesses, it is always a good idea to have a caregiver present, or at least very regularly make a round through the area where the babies sleep. This is because very small and/or weak children do not always cry out when they get into trouble or when they get sick.

When a baby is put to bed, all bibs, pacifier-chains and other string-like things should be taken off him. Because when he starts moving or turning in his sleep, there is a risk of these things wrapping around his neck and strangling him. There is nothing wrong with a pacifier being used to soothe the baby to sleep. However, a bottle of milk or juice in bed is not a good idea. This is very bad for the baby's teeth and could cause choking.

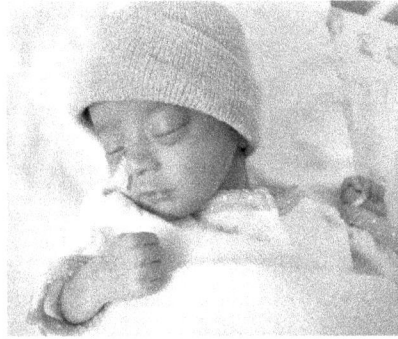

The temperature is 30°C, still she needs the hat and blanket.

Making sure that babies are dressed appropriately for the climate is always important, but especially so when it comes to sleeping time. For the first few weeks, newborn babies may have difficulty regulating their body temperature. So, it is important to make sure that they are dressed and covered neither too warmly nor too coldly. This is because both overheating and cooling down too much can cause dangerous and even life-threatening situations for small babies.

The temperature both outside and inside is 33°C, yet the little baby boy of about one week old who just arrived in the children's home has a temperature of 32.7°C: hypothermia to a dangerous degree. He needs to be warmed up quickly and for several days he needs to wear warm clothes and a hat, and have a warm water bottle in his cot to make sure he does not get too cold again, despite the warm weather.

To sleep well, a child should neither be too hot nor too cold. If the temperature is very high, dress the child in only one very thin layer of clothing or even nothing but a nappy. If it is cold, the child should be dressed for it, with a hat if necessary, and tucked in under blankets. Very young babies may need a hot water bottle to keep them warm in bed when it is cold. If a child is sweating a lot, he is dressed too warmly.

It was the cold season and in this country this meant temperatures around 18°C outside. Afraid that the ten-month-old baby would get cold in the night, her caregiver dressed her in thick, warm clothes, a woollen jumper and a snowsuit that had been donated over that. The girl was put in bed and covered with a thick duvet. I found her dressed and covered like this in the morning. The little girl was hot and covered in sweat. When I said that she was dressed rather warmly and that she was sweating, I was told that the girl was just like that, she was always sweaty. I explained that the way she was dressed and covered she was able to safely be outside at temperature of -15°C, and I explained the dangers of overheating a baby.

Older babies and children are more likely to let you know if they are too warm or too cold when you put them to bed–they will be restless and have trouble getting to sleep. When you notice this happening, check the room temperature and the way the children are dressed and covered, and adjust the way they are dressed and covered to make them more comfortable. This will mean more sleep for the children, and more peace and quiet for the caregivers.

Mosquito-tents for babies.

If a baby has a wet or dirty nappy or if he is hungry or thirsty, he is not likely to fall asleep quickly or sleep well either, because he is uncomfortable. So, before putting a baby to bed it is a good idea to check if he needs a nappy change and if he is due a bottle. If he takes longer to fall asleep than usual it is also worth checking if one of these things need to be taken care of. If you leave a baby lying in discomfort and he does not sleep well because of it, you are likely to have to deal with a very grumpy, demanding baby for the rest of the day.

Whether the children sleep on mats, in hammocks or in cots, if there is dengue fever, malaria or even just a lot of mosquitoes in any season, they should be protected by mosquito nets. This is to prevent serious illnesses, and in the case of regular mosquitoes, restlessness due to itching and in some cases allergic reactions.

When one of the children has a serious infectious illness–for example pneumonia, tuberculosis, measles, or diphtheria–he should sleep separated from other children. If at all possible, he should be put to sleep in a different room, but in any case he cannot share a bed or mat with healthy children. If he does, the children surrounding him will almost certainly get the same illness.

Sleeping Positions

Babies should not be placed on their stomach to sleep, because this increases the risk of cot death. The reason for this is that babies sleep very deeply when they are on their bellies and so are less likely to wake up if something happens while they are asleep. Also, they may accidentally turn their head entirely facedown and not move it to the side again in time to allow for breathing. Generally speaking, it is advised to place babies on their backs for sleeping. There are a few issues with this, however.

The reason why sleeping on their backs is preferred for babies, is that they sleep much lighter in this position, which means that if something happens, they are likely to wake up and cry out. However, quite a lot of babies sleep so lightly when put on their backs, that they do not get proper sleep, because everything and anything wakes them up. Also, if a baby spends a lot of time lying on his back

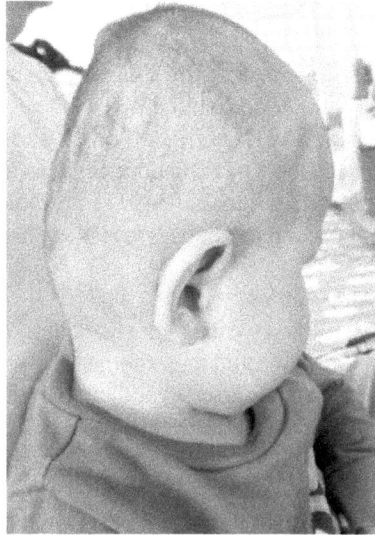

A head flattened by sleeping on it in the same position for a long time.

and his head is not positioned alternatingly facing left and facing right, his head is likely to develop a favourite position, which in time leads to his head flattening at the point where it rests on the mattress. This can make it harder to get the baby to turn his head to the other side at all, after some time. So, if a baby does sleep on his back, it is important to place his face towards his left shoulder for one nap and towards his right on for the next one, and so on.

A third option, and a good compromise for a baby who will not sleep on his back, is to place the baby on his side. This allows for a sleep that is deeper than when the baby is on his back, but not as deep as when he is lying on his belly. It is important, however, to place the baby securely, with a small rolled-up cloth behind his back and one in front of his belly, to prevent him from rolling over to either side–rolling onto his back would wake him up, rolling onto his belly would put him at risk of cot death. When the baby sleeps on his side, like when he sleeps on his back, it is important to change sides every time the baby is put down in his bed, to prevent deformation of the head. Choosing the position in which a baby sleeps is only relevant until he is able to roll over by himself. From then on, there is little

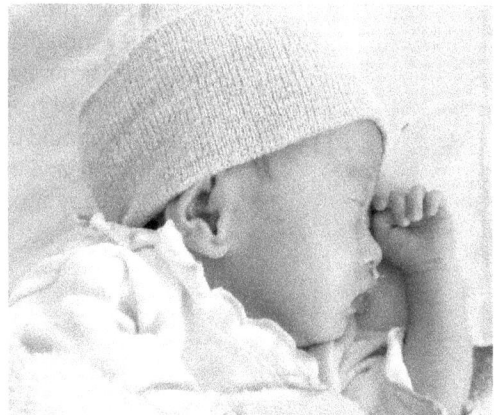

A premature baby sleeping on her side.

you can do, even if he chooses to sleep on his belly, except for keeping an eye on him, because whatever way you place him, he will roll over to his preferred position.

For a baby who throws up often, it safer to sleep on his side than to sleep on his back: lying on his back, he may choke on the vomit, while lying on his side, the vomit can flow away from his mouth and nose.

Unless they have breathing difficulties or severe reflux, babies should lie flat while sleeping. They do not need a pillow—they could suffocate (die because they are unable to breathe for a long time, usually because something closes off their nose and mouth or because an airway is obstructed on it)—and they should not be left to sleep in car seats or baby bouncers, because this puts a lot of strain on their backs, which can lead to problems later in life. This is true especially when the baby is less than five months old.

Swaddling Babies

There is nothing wrong with swaddling babies. In some cases, it can calm them down and help them sleep better because they feel more secure. When it is cold, swaddling is helpful in keeping them warm. There are a few things to take note of, however, to make sure that the swaddled baby is safe and comfortable:

- The baby should be able to stretch and kick her legs within the swaddling. If not, spending a lot of time swaddled can lead to weakening and even deformation of the legs.
- The swaddling should not force the baby's legs to remain stretched, nor should it be knotted tightly around the knees—which can cause the legs to scissor—to prevent deformation of the legs.
- The cloth should be wrapped in such a way that there is no risk of part of it covering the baby's face. Nor should there be a risk of the baby's head slowly moving down into the cloth-bundle.
- Babies should never be left on their bellies unsupervised, but they should most definitely never be put on their bellies with their arms swaddled to their bodies, as this gives them no chance of helping themselves if they get into difficulties.
- Care should be taken that the baby is not wrapped up too warmly and in danger of overheating.
- The baby should be allowed some time without being swaddled every day, to give him the chance to move his arms and legs freely and to learn new skills.

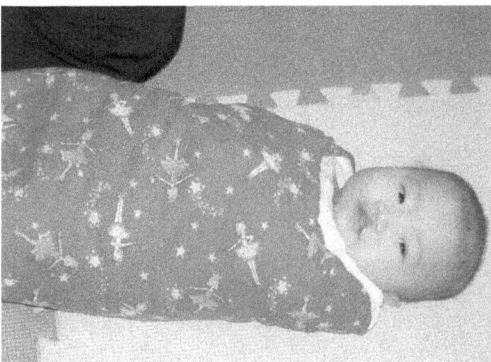

A swaddled baby.

Toddlers choose their own sleeping position.

The oldest two fell asleep before dinner after a busy day.

✱ ————————— **Routine**

In any situation where a lot of children are cared for together, the stricter the routine, the easier things are for the caregivers. For toddlers, a set routine is as useful as it is for the caregivers. It helps them know what to expect and to feel safe and secure within the familiar pattern—once they have become used to doing things a certain way.

With babies, things are different. For most babies, you can settle on an individual routine once you get to know them a little and find out their needs. However, it is almost impossible to force a group of babies into a set routine. At least, if you have any thought for the well-being of the babies. Even if you do not consider that some newborn babies sleep 20 hours out of 24 and others only 14, and that at six months, one baby still sleeps close to 18 hours, while another barely needs 12 hours, babies' needs also change as they grow older. That change comes surprisingly quickly, so their routine needs to evolve.

So, if you have a group of babies to care for, you need to allow for some flexibility. You can steer the individual babies towards what is seen as a good routine in your home, but you will have to make allowances for individual differences, at least up to about six months of age. After that it becomes a little bit easier, because from there on, some babies will start to become able to play in their beds if they are put down at nap time but do not need as much sleep as their companions.

After all the toddlers had been put to bed for the night in the bedrooms, the caregiver would tidy up the living/playing area of the home. During the process of tidying she would find several things that belonged in a toy box or in one of the wardrobes in the bedrooms. Every time she found such a thing, she went into the bedroom–where the toddlers were just starting to fall asleep–, turned on the light and placed the toy or the shoes, or whatever she found, where it belonged. Each time, the children in the room would be wide awake again and often they would start to play or call out to her, or sometimes cry because they were so tired. The caregiver was annoyed by this and did not understand why the children would not just go to sleep.

Like with any aspect of childcare, common sense is an important ingredient when it comes to dealing with babies and their sleeping.

A seven-month-old girl was cared for in a group home among toddlers. She would wake up a little before 6 a.m. and be left in her bed until near 7:30 a.m. when all the children were getting up. By 9 a.m. she would already be very tired and she would be put to bed close to 9:30. Generally she slept until 11:30, got up just in time to have lunch together with the other children, and at 12:00 it was nap time for everyone. The baby was put to bed as well. She would spend most of 'nap time', which lasted until 2 p.m., screaming, because she was wide wake, well-rested and upset at being left alone in her bed. When everyone was up again, they would get a snack and go outside to play around the house, and after a couple of hours of playing, the baby would become very tired again. By about 5 p.m. she was back in bed again, and usually she woke up at about 6 p.m.

However, the caregiver was determined that the baby should not be taken out of bed straight away, because she needed to learn that she was not the boss. After about 15 minutes of crying, the baby would be asleep again and sleep until 7 p.m.: dinnertime. After dinner, everyone was changed into their pyjamas and 8 p.m. was bedtime for everyone. The baby would spend some considerable time crying again before going to sleep. The caregiver did not understand why the baby would not just sleep when she was told to.

It really is too much to expect from a baby that she spends all of the 'official awake time' (the time your schedule says she can play) *and* the naptime assigned by your routine asleep. If you insist on certain nap times and bedtimes to be followed, you need to plan the rest of the day around them.

EXAMPLE

> *I solved the situation from the previous box within one day. I let the baby sleep in the morning from 9 a.m., but no more than 1 hour. Then she went down with the others for nap time and slept on average just over an hour, and after 2 p.m. she was not allowed another nap. So, in the evening she would be very tired, would usually get her dinner just before the others and go to bed somewhere between 7 p.m. and 7:30 and fall asleep immediately, until 6:30-7:00 a.m. in the morning.*

Playing in the shade because of the heat.

Once a baby is about four to five months old, there is nothing wrong with letting a baby cry for a while before going to sleep. Some babies need it to calm down and get ready for sleep. However, letting a baby scream hysterically serves no purpose at all. She will only get herself more and more upset, make the other babies restless, and she will be likely to start associating 'going to bed' with stress and anxiety. So, it is preferable to help her calm down and then let her try again. Or at least to look in on her every ten minutes or so, so that she realises she is not all alone and forgotten.

Exactly what the routine of a baby or child looks like will depend a lot on her age and the situation in the home in which she is cared for. Generally speaking, a daily routine should contain time for feeding, sleeping, changing nappies or using the potty or toilet, washing, playing outside her bed, receiving attention and physical contact, and going outside.

Spending time outside, getting direct daylight, fresh air and in the case of children who are mobile, exercise, is very important. Sometimes weather conditions do not allow it, during the rainy season or in extremes of cold or heat. However, it is usually possible to find a moment in the day when the children can spend some time outside if they are dressed properly. Especially in places where mostly babies are cared for, this is something that is often forgotten. However, whatever their age, unless children are quite ill or extremely weak, they benefit from spending some time outside, even if it is only to lie on a blanket or mat, taking in a different environment, fresh air and daylight. Make sure that when they go outside, they are appropriately dressed and shielded from the wind and direct sun.

Sleep for Older Children

Once a child reaches the age of about three years old, she usually needs less sleep. However, sleep continues to be extremely important for the child's well-being. Just like with babies and small children, older children will not grow and develop well and will be less healthy if they do not get the sleep they need.

The amount of sleep that an individual child needs varies. Some children need more sleep than others. However, here is an indication of how much sleep children of different ages need to stay healthy and develop normally:

- 0-3 months old: 14-18 hours per day
- 4-12 months old: 12-15 hours per day
- 1-2 years old: 11-14 hours per day
- 3-5 years old: 10-13 hours per day
- 6-13 years old: 9-11 hours per day
- 14-18 years old: 8-10 hours per day

Something that is important to be aware of, is that for older children, one of the effects of not getting enough sleep is that they do less well in school. When you are not properly rested, it becomes much harder to concentrate in class and to absorb the knowledge given by teachers and read in books. This is particularly unfortunate, because in many places it is the determination to make sure that children do well in school that causes the lack of sleep.

Older children also need sleep to grow and stay healthy.

The sixteen-year-old children in the children's home, who are in their exam year, are constantly reminded that this is a very important year and that they need to study hard to get good grades on their exams. Tuition and study groups are organised to help them do well. So, for the entire school year their routine is as follows: They are woken up at 5:00 a.m. to start studying, until breakfast. After breakfast, they leave for school. They arrive back at the home late afternoon and are allowed to have one hour of free time before prayer assembly and dinner. After dinner, they have tuition and study groups until midnight, when they are allowed to go to bed. For an entire year, these children are only allowed five hours of sleep per day. If they spent a few extra hours sleeping, they would get much better results from the remaining hours of study.

So, both to save yourself money on doctor's bills for sleep **deprived** children who are getting ill all the time, and to help them do well in school, please make sure that all the children in your care are getting the sleep they need to be properly rested and to stay healthy.

Chapter 4:   Safety

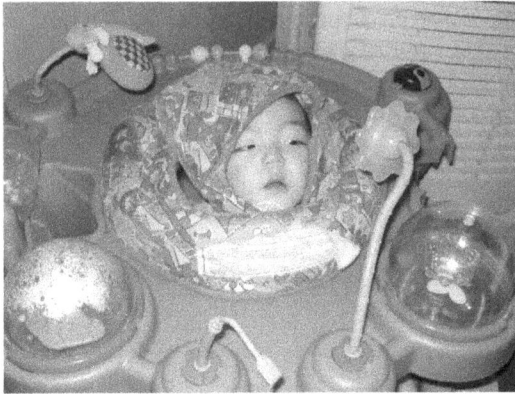

Exploring: easier to get into than to get out of again.

Especially once they start moving around, children have an almost endless ability to get into trouble. This is not out of badness or stupidity, but out of curiosity, a sense of adventure, and a lack of understanding of danger. If you explain to them why something is not allowed whenever you tell them they cannot do something, their ability to predict what is dangerous or unacceptable will–very slowly–grow over time. If you do not give them an explanation, or simply say 'because I am telling you!', it will take them a lot longer to find out what is dangerous and what is not, through trial and error. Unfortunately, error can have very serious, dangerous consequences.

Safe Surroundings

Children's curiosity about their surroundings and their amazing ability to get in, onto, under, around, and behind things make it very important to create a safe environment where they can explore without being in constant danger. In some children's homes, as well as in some families, the choice is made that the children need to learn to stay safe and out of trouble in circumstances that have not been changed to make them safer.

> *A lady led a group home for children up to six years old. The children who were put in her care were taken away from their families by Social Services because they had been neglected or abused. The law in the country in question states that children cannot be in institutional care for more than two years. So, the caregiver saw the children like guests who came and went, while to her where she lived and cared for them, was her home. She felt that to feel at home, she needed to surround herself with her own things and decorations. The children were under no circumstances allowed to touch any of the delicate figurines that were placed around the living area. Nor were they allowed to touch–let alone sit on–the two sofas that were there, because they would only get them dirty. The caregiver felt she had a right to a certain kind of life and the children were allowed to be present, but they should not interfere too much.*

This is certainly a possibility. However, it is good to keep in mind that this creates a situation in which both the children and your **possessions** are at risk unless they are watched all the time. The children

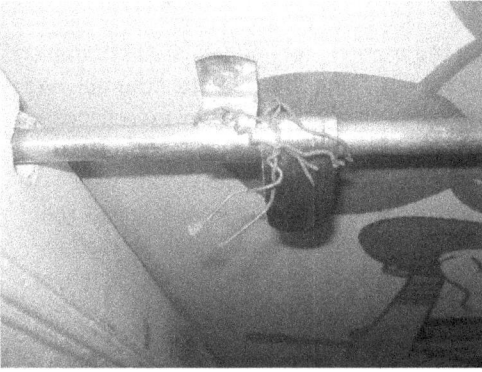

Door secured with sharp metal wire at children's eye level.

Making a situation safe does not always require a complicated, expensive solution.

Medication kept on a desk where children can easily reach them.

may learn, in time, not to touch certain things, but this will not come naturally to them, and they will not learn it from being told just once. That means that this situation is also a lot more stressful for the caregivers, who have to constantly watch and reprimand the children, never having a moment of peace. Plus, in a learning process like this, a child can get hurt and precious items can be irreparably broken. Young children are not aware that the colourful 'toy' on the dresser is an expensive, fragile object. They just want to play with it and hear what kind of sound it makes when it is banged on the floor repeatedly. Not to hurt you or to break something you value, but to discover how the world, and everything in it, works. If all expensive, fragile and dangerous items are kept out of children's reach—which is often as simple as putting them on higher shelves—everyone can be more relaxed, and loss and injury are prevented.

Providing basic safety requires:
- Removing any objects that are small enough to be put entirely in a child's mouth and can be choked on.
- Removing objects with sharp edges or spikes, or objects that come apart in small or sharp pieces.
- Removing dangerous tools from where children can reach them.
- Removing anything that might be toxic or unhygienic from children's reach.
- Closing electrical sockets with a special safety device or by taping it closed whenever there is no plug in it.
- Moving electrical wiring out of sight and out of reach.
- Blocking unaccompanied access to stairs, kitchen and other rooms where a lot of dangerous things can be found.
- Securing cupboards, wardrobes and toy shelves so they will not fall over if a child attempts to climb them.
- Keeping medication and medical equipment outside of children's reach at all times, preferably locked away.

Fire and Other Disasters

Naturally, when choosing the property for your children's home, or when having it built, you need to think about safety. Attention needs to be paid to construction: is it solid enough to prevent collapsing walls–potentially on top of children? Is there a danger of the roof leaking, or dampness in the house? Are there dangerous steps? Is it possible to close all exits to prevent children from leaving a room on their own, or from getting into the kitchen? Things like wiring and plumbing also need to be checked for risks of short circuits or flooding.

However many precautions you take to prevent fires and flooding or other natural disasters, they may still happen. No one has any power over them. Because there is always a possibility of something major going wrong, it is a good idea to put some thought into what should be done in case a natural disaster happens.

> A major earthquake thankfully did not cause anything to collapse in the orphanage and there was time to bring all 18 babies safely outside. However, the building had become very weak, so the babies could not go back inside. For a few weeks, the caregivers took care of the babies in tents outside the orphanage building. Then the babies were all brought to a children's home of the same organisation, in a different location, before the weather started to turn colder.

How complicated a scenario like that is, depends on your situation. A lot of the time the children's home is built on the ground floor with several exits. If you have enough staff to look after the children, this means that everyone should be able to get out all right and carry the smallest babies out with them. However, sometimes the situation is more complicated.

> Say your children's home has 34 babies aged from newborn to two years old, with only one of the children able to walk by himself, and is located on the third floor with a big, indoor staircase on one end of the hallway and a narrow fire escape outside on the other side of the hallway. How are you going to get all the babies down quickly and safely when there is a fire on the indoor staircase?

This is going to take some planning, and staff will need to be instructed what to do to be able to get most of the children out alive in case of a fire or something similar. It also makes sense to take some time to think about the following, for example: if your building has several floors, is it sensible to put the offices on the ground floor and the smallest babies on the top floor? Of course it is convenient for visitors if they do not have to climb stairs to visit the offices. But from a safety point of view, bringing the babies down and placing the offices upstairs might be better.

A new building was being planned for the adoption centre. The plans had the offices on the ground floor and the babies on the second floor. Questions were asked about the safety of this arrangement in the case of a fire. However, these were countered by concerns for the safety of the children if people could reach the babies too easily and take one of them away. Because of this last concern, management thought it would be safer if visitors who came to see the babies had to pass through the office space first so they could not reach the babies unseen. For fire safety, they considered specially designed aprons, which are also used in children's hospitals. These have four very large pockets sewn onto them, allowing each adult to carry down four or five babies.

In the case of older children, it is important to inform them of the plans you have for safely getting out of the building in case of a fire, and of what to do in case of an earthquake. It is also useful to practise with the children what they should do in such an event. Knowing what to do can help keep the panic to a minimum if something happens, and it may save lives.

Supervision

Even when a place has been made safe for children, small children should never be left entirely alone. A child under three years old should have someone come to see what she is doing every five minutes or so while she is awake, at the very least. And no child under five years old, awake or asleep, should ever be out of hearing range of at least one adult. As children grow older and learn to obey the rules of what they are and are not allowed to do, you can gradually allow them to have more freedom of movement and more time without constant close supervision. However, it should be judged per child whether she can be trusted not to do something dangerous if she is left on her own or with only other children.

That all children are healthy when you leave them behind, does not guarantee that they will not get ill or hurt themselves while you are away, even in a relatively safe environment. Trying to climb out of bed may go wrong, even if it has gone right many times. A child can choke on something. In all of these cases, if help is immediate, the situation may not become too serious. But if the problem is not discovered until an hour or more afterwards, the consequences can be very serious.

I was able to catch one of these children just in time to stop him falling head-first into the hole with the spikes when a ball rolled into the hole and he wanted to reach down to try to grab it.

I provided a training for the caregivers of a very large children's home, which had various dorm buildings spread out over a big compound. During the training I asked the caregivers if they had children of their own, and many of them did. Then I asked individual caregivers whether they would allow their six-year-old or their ten-year-old to walk freely wherever they wanted on the compound, on their own. The answer was a shocked 'No! That would not be safe, they would make their child stay where they could see of hear them.' So my next question was: 'Then why are children in your care, some of whom are as young as three years old, allowed to wander wherever they please, without any supervision? What is the difference?'

At lunchtime, the toddlers were all put to bed, their bedroom door was locked and the door to the building they were in was locked too. Then their caregiver would go to have her lunch in one of the other buildings on the compound, about a five-minute walk from where the toddlers were left alone. Sometimes the caregiver would also take the car after lunch to run some errands in the nearby town, leaving the children locked in on their own.

Children who are too young—or too handicapped mentally and/or physically to save themselves or take action to get help—should never be left alone without an adult close by. And no one—adult or child—should ever be locked in a space without someone right outside the door to let them out in case of an emergency.

While it seems self-evident, it still needs to be mentioned: never leave a baby or a toddler on their own on a high surface—such as the changing table, a table top, a bed without high sides, a garden wall, or a stepladder. While most people are aware of the risk, it is hard to realise exactly how little time children need

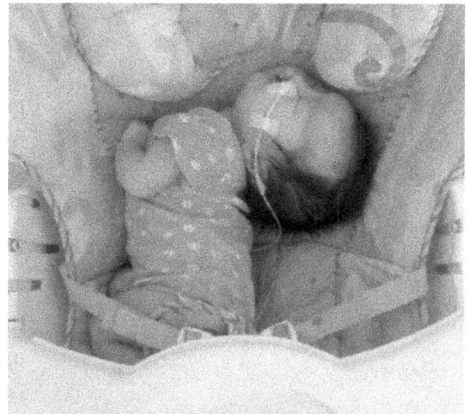

Safety is also about not putting a newborn in an upright seat, where she will end up like this.

to come crashing down from something, even when they are only a few months old. Accidents usually happen when a caregiver has been closely watching the child the whole time, but then has to step away for just a very short moment. Even if you do not stop paying attention, you may be surprised.

> *I was changing a baby on the changing table. He was about four months old and had just started rolling over, but only over his left side, which on that changing table would have brought him over towards the wall. I took one step back, to open one of the drawers below the changing mat and grab a clean pair of pants for him. The next moment, I held him in my hands. He had rolled over and fallen so quickly, that I did not realise what had happened until after I had caught him.*

So, whenever a baby or toddler is on an elevated surface, an adult should be not just nearby, but close enough to catch her if she decides to do something dangerous. The reason why very small children do things like these is a combination of a lack of understanding of the danger, and an infinite trust that the caregiver will catch her and make things right, no matter what.

> *An eighteen-month-old girl, who was never any trouble, walked over to see what the caregiver was doing. While she was watching the caregiver take care of something, the little girl held on to the door on the side of the hinges. The caregiver had not noticed the girl there and when she had finished what she needed to do, she closed the door and the little girl's fingers were caught between the door and the doorpost on the other side. She only very narrowly escaped broken bones, and still needed a trip to the hospital to have her hand treated.*

In situations where small babies and young children who are able to crawl and walk are together in one room, safety issues occur. Children under four years old who are able to move around, often have an interest in, or even a fascination with, small babies, but they do not know how vulnerable the babies are. Even though the older child only wants to play, pulling the arm of a small baby, hitting the baby on the head or stumbling and falling onto the baby by accident can all have very

A one-year-old, just able to walk, left by himself up there.

serious results. Constant supervision is needed in these situations. Toddlers should *never* be left alone in a room with small babies.

In most cases where small babies and toddlers are in the same room, the caregivers are mostly focused on protecting the babies from the older children and taking care of their needs. This leads to the older children being seen as a **nuisance**. Either they constantly get shouted at and punished for hurting the babies, or they are kept in their bed all day or prevented from moving around in some other way. This is not a great way to deal with this situation. After all, the toddlers are being punished for acting the way they always do, just in a situation that does not allow that behaviour. The toddlers were not the ones who chose that situation. By not allowing them to move around and play, their opportunity to develop properly and to build up self-confidence is taken away.

> In a particular adoption centre, they usually care for babies aged newborn to about six months old. Most of the children are adopted before they become much older than that. However, at a certain time, by coincidence, they were asked to take in three children of around one year old, one shortly after the other. Now they suddenly had three toddlers walking around in between the babies' beds and crawling over the babies playing on the floor. Because the toddlers were seen as not needing as much intensive care as the babies, no caregiver was specifically assigned to them, but all the caregivers kept an eye on them while taking care of the babies, occasionally feeding or changing them. The toddlers were soon creating a lot of problems. They were swinging the babies' swinging cots violently, slapping babies in the face as a game, and trying to take bottles away from babies. The solution the caregivers came up with was to tie a toddler to one of the beds by one of his legs, using a scarf. This way the toddler could not move around freely and would stay in one place. This, of course, caused a lot of crying. However, more importantly, it was not a very safe solution because the child was tied to a bed with a baby in it, so while he could not crawl around to cause trouble, he was within easy reach of one baby to 'play' with.

This is why small babies should be cared for in a room separate from the older children. Or, if that is not possible, create an area in the room, separated from the rest of the room by furniture or screens, where the older children are free to move around and play without putting the babies at risk. If the older children are given toys to play with and a caregiver who keeps them busy, they are less likely to cause trouble by interfering with the babies because they are occupied. While if they do not have anything to do, they will get bored and start looking around for something to do. In this case, the babies are seen as 'interesting toys'.

Precautions

Always strap babies and toddlers in when you put them in buggies, car seats or high chairs. Even if you have no intention of leaving their side. First of all, something unexpected may happen which leads to you having to 'abandon' the child you were looking after, to help out with something more urgent. Especially in a situation where there are a lot of babies and toddlers together. Secondly, your attention only needs to be distracted for a few seconds—while stirring food in a bowl with

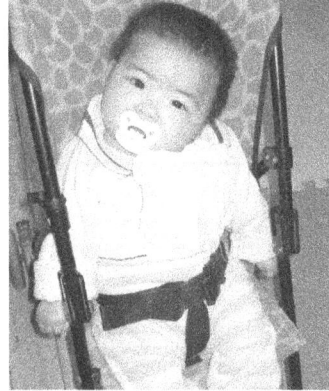

Strap children in when you put them in a buggy.

your back turned, or while very quickly walking over to the sink to grab a cup of water—for a child to suddenly fall down, head-first. This can even happen—perhaps it is even more likely to happen, because you expect it less—with a child who is usually very quiet and unadventurous.

A caregiver put a five-month-old baby in a reclining rocking seat so she could make a bottle of milk for him. The baby did not roll over yet and the chair was pretty deep, so she did not bother to close the straps. After all, she would only be gone for a minute. While the baby did not roll over, he was very angry and impatient about waiting for his milk. He was crying loudly and arching his back again and again in protest. By arching his back and getting one foot just over the edge of the chair, he started to slide out of the chair. Every time he arched, he came out of the chair a little more. When the caregiver returned to the room, she was just able to catch him, before he fell onto the floor completely.

Always place hot items such as cooking pots or cups of tea completely outside the reach of the children. Every year, many children get burned very seriously because they pull at a kettle or pan and have the boiling contents poured over them. Children who pull at tablecloths may be scalded by the contents of a teapot or have everything that stood on the table fall on them. Cups of hot tea or coffee or other hot drinks seem the most innocent, yet might do the most damage. A child pulling your arm while you were just about the take a sip might get burned when the contents of the cup spill, or a child who wanted to **imitate** you may grab your hot drink while your back is turned or while you are distracted, and either take a big gulp of a liquid that is far too hot, or be unable to manage the cup and spill the contents all over himself.

The caregiver had just made a cup of tea for herself, when she was called over to help with one of the children. She placed her cup on the windowsill and went over. A little boy of about eighteen months came over to investigate. He was just able to reach the bottom of the cup. He gave it a few pushes and then it fell down, pouring the scalding hot tea all over his belly. He needed treatment for the burns on his belly for several months.

Put something around a baby just able to sit up, to catch her when she falls.

Very interested in all the wires, tools and chemicals she found.

All of these things can cause very serious burns, which in turn can lead to dangerous infections as well as almost inevitable scarring. So even though it is inconvenient not to be able to drink a warm drink while you are holding a child, or not to be able to keep your cup within easy reaching distance, it really is worth the trouble to avoid the risks of very serious injury.

When a child sees a hoe lying on the ground, he will simply be curious as to what he might do with it. He may try to imitate the men he saw working with it earlier. He does not realise the hoe's potential of seriously injuring his legs or feet. When he tries to lift up the hoe a little, he finds it very heavy and drops it. Nor does he see the hoe's potential of seriously injuring another child–possibly cracking her skull–when he tries to raise the hoe high up to swing it over his shoulder, like he has seen adults do. Again he loses control, because of the unexpected weight, and it comes wildly clattering down from above his head. There is nothing wrong with a child being taught how to use a hoe, under supervision, and once it is clear he has a good understanding of how to use it and what the dangers are, he can use it on his own too. However, equipment like this should not be left lying around where children might pick it up unsupervised and try to figure out its use by themselves. The risks are too great for that.

A hoe left by workmen, discovered by small children.

Also make sure that the children are not able to enter the kitchen unsupervised. Small children need to be taught, under close supervision, to recognise the danger of things that are hot or that burn and things that are sharp. They should not be left to discover such things by themselves, because finding out could kill them. The same goes for matches, lighters, knives, and other dangerous utensils and tools, as well as cleaning products that could poison them. These should be stored where children cannot possibly reach them.

A child having to cross a construction site to get to his dorm.

Children allowed close to working machinery.

It is important to be aware of the limits of a child's ability to predict consequences (this will be discussed in greater detail in Part 2: 'Basic Child Psychology and Child Development'). Up to about thirteen years of age, most children are unable to predict that there is a chance of something going wrong, especially if the danger lies not so much in the initial picking up of an object, or the climbing onto something, but two or three steps further down the line.

For the holidays, all children, aged three to eighteen years old, were given a bag of fireworks to set off. The only instruction the children got was not to set them off in certain areas of the compound. The next few days were a chaos of children setting off fireworks all over the compound, mostly unsupervised. One boy got something in his eye and many children had burns to their hands and feet—mostly from grabbing a sparkler just after it had gone out, or from stepping on it with bare feet. Some of the older children emptied the powder of several pieces of fireworks into metal containers and set these off, which meant they were essentially making bombs. .

When I asked why it was organised like this, I was told that the previous year the fireworks had been set off supervised, in a large circle with the children surrounding it. But the children had said they wanted to be free to do it themselves. Of course that is what they want! But they do not oversee the consequences and dangers of handling firework. It is the role of adults to protect them by not allowing them to so. .

He is enjoying it, but does not understand the danger of standing this close to the fireworks, let alone in bare feet.

Because children's ability to predict what might be dangerous and what is safe develops over time, it is good to take their age and understanding into account when deciding who is allowed to take part in certain activities. Particularly in places where children in one dorm may have a wide variety of ages–I have seen a spread as wide as three to twelve years old for a single dorm–it is often more sensible to say 'children from age A to age B are allowed to go' rather than to say 'children from dorms X and Y are allowed to go'. Otherwise an eleven-year-old from one dorm might be left out of something that other ten-year-olds are allowed to do, just because he happens to be in a dorm with younger children.

Medical Supplies

Medication should be easily available when needed. However, it should not be within easy reach of just anyone. Children should under no circumstances have any access to medication or medical supplies. It would be very dangerous if they started playing with sharp medical instruments or if they would drink from medicine bottles. Because medication is often made very sweet, to make sure that children will drink their syrup, it can be very tempting to a child to have some more. Or a child may think that taking more medicine will make him feel better more quickly. This can lead to the child accidentally poisoning himself.

Often it is also a good idea to make sure that not all staff can access any medication. They may mean very well and want to help a child, thinking they know how to because they have seen this or that used

Medication within easy reach of the children, between their toys. Very dangerous!

before, but unless they really know what kind of medication serves what purpose, it can be very dangerous for a child to take the medication. Again, this can lead to accidental poisoning.

A toddler had a cold and a cough. His caregiver decided to give him some medicine that she still had from another time one of the children was ill. That time it had put a stop to another child's cough. However, the medication she wanted to give the boy was for a cough caused by an allergic reaction and one of the side effects of the medication is that is weakens the immune system. This means that the medicine will not only not be effective against this cough which is caused by a cold, not by allergy, but it may make the boy even sicker: his body will have less strength to fight the cold because of the medicine he is getting.

This is why it is a good idea to put all medical supplies and medical equipment in a locked cabinet, with the key available only to the people who have the knowledge to use these products properly. There should always be someone present with a key. Otherwise, at some point you might find yourself in a difficult situation.

It was the children's home's director's day off and because I was there, the medical director could also have a day off, something that she could rarely afford at this medical children's home. I was called to help by a caregiver. The colostomy bag had come off one of the babies, so it needed to be replaced.

I went to the medical supply room to get everything I needed and asked the supervisor for the keys to the supply cabinets. She was shocked. Did I not have them? Normally only the children's home director and the medical director had the keys. She went around and asked, but no one had the keys to the medical cabinets. Through the glass, I could see exactly what I needed. But I could not touch it. In the end, I found a newly arrived box of colostomy bags outside of the cabinets. So I took one and improvised. The result would stay in place for the day, but not much longer. This was rather a waste of money, because with access to the proper supplies the colostomy bag could have been used for about five days.

One more safety point is the need to keep an eye on when new medical supplies need to be bought. Usually, caregivers are the ones who find out first that you are almost out of something. Yet they usually do not tell their supervisors until they have run out completely. In some cases, this may not be a huge problem. If it is something that can be easily bought at a nearby shop and there is someone available to go and buy it immediately, it may only take half an hour, which is manageable. However, some things are not so easy to buy. They might require a journey to the next city, or may need to be ordered. Or you may even depend on donations to get this item because it is extremely expensive or has to come from abroad. In these cases, you have a big problem when you have suddenly run out of something.

Locked medical cabinets.

In the morning, the supervisor told the person in charge of supplies that she had just used the very last of the medication for the baby who had had heart surgery not long ago. She thought there was another bottle, but that was not the case. This medication had to be given three times a day, so the baby would need the next dose in eight hours. It turned out that the medicine could not be bought locally, it had to come from the capital. This would take 36 hours, under the most ideal circumstances. A dangerous situation.

To prevent situations like these, caregivers and particularly their supervisors need to be instructed to let someone know that an item needs to be bought when they *start* using the last package of it, not when they finish it. Any time something new is opened, someone should check if there is more in stock. And if there is not, this information should be passed on to the supervisor straight away. This way, there is time to arrange replacement.

Chapter 5: Essential Psychological Needs

Things like food, hygiene, shelter, sleep and safety are generally recognised as basic needs. These are things that children require to be able to survive and thrive. They are the things that people running a children's home try to provide to the best of their knowledge and ability. It is much rarer for people, anywhere in the world, to realise that affection, attention, physical contact, stimulation and **attachment** are needs that are just as basic and essential. Few people know that a child's survival can depend on these things. Researchers found that in Europe and the USA, between 70 to 100% of children in orphanages died before 1920, when they only fed and cleaned children and

The aim is to have them happy and healthy.

provided them with a roof over their heads, but did not take care of their other needs.

The problem is not really that people do not know what children need. Deep down everyone does know that. This is proven by the fact that almost all parents provide their children with what they need, without anyone explaining to them what to do. The problem lies in two other issues:

Most people are not consciously aware that the things parents do are *all* important for the child's well-being and proper development.

Because of the pressures of a very busy job, caregivers sometimes seem to forget that they work with *children*, real human beings, who have the same needs as any child in a family.

A family situation: nothing is said, but the love is clear.

In this chapter, I aim to give a better understanding of the **impact** of lacking the above mentioned things, and of what is required to provide **adequate** care in these areas. To keep things clear I will refer to what are generally recognised to be basic needs as 'practical needs' (in other words food, hygiene, shelter, sleep and safety) and to the complete set of basic needs as 'essential basic needs' (practical needs plus affection, attention, physical contact, stimulation and attachment).

The Difference between Care in a Family and Care in an Institution

What is the difference between care in a children's home and care in family, for a child? The answer seems obvious: the child misses her parents and she is not surrounded by family in a children's home. In a way, the answer really is this simple, but it becomes complicated when you start looking at the effects of not having your parents and family around.

A child in a family is surrounded by love and affection. This is very often not said in words, but it is clear from the way parents talk to their children, give them attention, touch them and look at them. In most families, there is quite a lot of physical contact, especially when children are small. Babies are held and carried around on a parent's arm or in a sling of some kind. Toddlers get to sit on a parent's lap during mealtimes and at other times during the day. Older children regularly get a hug, lean against their parents or hold their hand in the street, to be guided. Children and parents often share closeness at night too, sleeping together in the same bed or in the same room. All these things together make a child feel safe. She feels that she has someone looking out for her, and protecting her. The natural love and pride that parents feel for their children is expressed without it being consciously noticed.

> The caregiver does not pick up or hold any of the six babies and toddlers that she cares for, for any other reason than to move them in and out of bed, lift them onto the changing table or put them in their seats for dinner. On his first visit, a visitor presumes that this is because she is too busy to find the time to hold the children between cleaning, cooking, and other chores. So, when the visitor is sent outside to watch the children play, he picks up one of the smallest children from the blanket on the floor and holds her in his lap, while giving the other children attention and allowing them to lean against him. This way he feels he is able to contribute something that is usually lacking, without any cost to the caregiver. However, when after some time the caregiver sticks her head out the door to check on them, she tells the visitor sharply to put the baby down and to let the other children get on with their own play. He will only get them used to being held and getting attention, and make them difficult and demanding. The children need to learn to do without those things and then they will be fine, she claims.

Caregivers in a children's home do not have this natural bond with the children in their care, so the love does not come automatically and it is certainly not expressed unnoticed. In a children's home, caregivers are doing a job. They are usually kept busy trying to meet the child's practical needs such as making her food, keeping her clean and washing her clothes. This leaves little time for hold-

Surrounded by extended family.

ing children and giving them real attention. In a family, these things are done automatically, while in a children's home these needs are often simply forgotten. It is important to think about this and to try to do something about it consciously.

Although it is true that if, for a long time, a child received–almost–no attention and is then given some, she can become more difficult, this is not a sign of her being spoiled or of her being better off without attention. I explain this in more detail in Part 2, Chapter 6: 'Discipline' under 'Breaking the Cycle of Negative Attention Seeking'.

In a family, a child has a primary caregiver, usually her mother or grandmother. This is a person in her life whom she knows will always be there and can be relied on. If the parent goes away, the child soon learns that this is only for a short time. A bond is formed with a primary caregiver, and with other people who are always around in a child's life. For example her father, her brothers and sisters, and maybe uncles or aunts or grandparents who live in the same home or nearby. These relationships, which are formed at a very young age, unnoticed, teach the child how to form a relationship with someone and how to keep it going. These lessons are needed later in life. They are important for forming and maintaining future relationships of all kinds.

Visiting grandparents and helping on the farm.

In a children's home, there are usually few adults taking care of many children. This means that the caregivers are very busy and do not have much time to spend with each child. Plus, caregivers in children's homes quite often vary from day to day and from year to year. This can be because a caregiver leaves her job and someone else takes over, because caregivers work in shifts and are only available at certain times or because the children's home is divided into different age groups, requiring children to move from one group to another when they reach a certain age. Also, even when caregivers do live at the children's home and are available around the clock, they often look after so many children there is no time to form bonds with individual children All of this means that the child does not get the chance to learn how to form relationships because no real bonds or relationships get a chance to be formed.

In a family, children are part of a group. They have parents, maybe brothers and sisters, and other extended family around them. Seeing the daily activity around them and being a part of the group teaches children things and stimulates them. Children are allowed to play in and around the house, to explore their surroundings and learn from their explorations. They are taken along with their mother or father on **outings** to the market, the field, and to visit neighbours or relatives who live further away. Children in a family help around the house with chores that they are able to do at their age and they are taught how to do a good job at them. These children play with toys, or household items, or things they find in the road. By seeing their parents, aunts, uncles and neighbours live a regular life, children learn how the world works and what will be their role in it when they grow up. They learn about the duties and rights of men and women, of parents, and of people from their own social status. And in play, they try out their understanding of these roles by playing 'house', 'shop', and so on.

The way a children's home is run, is usually to make life easier for the caregivers. This is understandable, because often a children's home is set up more like a business than like a home. In business, best practice is to make things easier on the staff—in other words the caregivers. Mealtimes and other activities are planned at times that work well for the caregivers, and when the caregivers are all busy attending to practical things, children are expected to stay quiet and out of the way. In some places, they are simply put in their beds or locked in a room, with nothing to do. In this business model, it is forgotten that the 'goods' handled in this particular business are not objects, but human beings: children.

At 5:00 a.m. in the morning all 30 of the babies and toddlers in the home have their nappies changed and they are fed; if they are still asleep they are woken up. These are the final duties of the night shift. When they have been changed and fed, all the children are put back into their beds, to sleep or not, as they wish. The change of shift takes place, the daytime caregivers get settled in, start the laundry, feed the smallest babies once more—those under six months old get a bottle every three hours, but are never taken out of bed to play—make a start with cooking lunch, and clean the floors. At 10:00 a.m. the supervisors and management arrive and—except on holidays when supervisors do.

not work and the caregiving staff leaves the children in their bed all day apart from changing and feeding–around 10:30 a.m. children over six months old are taken out of bed, washed and changed and put on the floor to play. Sometimes three or four toys are taken from the large toy box and put on the floor with the children

At 11:30 a.m. the children get their lunch, with six adults feeding 20 children–there are ten who are not yet old enough for solids–and most children need to wait quite a while to eat. None of the children are allowed to eat by themselves, although some of them would be able to, because that would give too much of a mess. After lunch, there is a nappy change and the children go back to bed for a nap, usually around 12:30 p.m. Very few of the children sleep longer than two hours, but they are left in their beds until almost 3:30 p.m. After all, the caregivers need to have their lunch, have a rest and bring in and fold the laundry. Between 3:15 and 3:30 p.m. the children are changed again and put on mats to play. At 4:00 p.m. they all get a cup or bottle of milk and a biscuit and at 4:30 p.m. they are put back into their beds again, where they will stay until the next morning, except for another change of nappies and a meal at 9:00 p.m. in the evening, because the supervisors' shift ends at 5:00 p.m.

Being included in preparations for a festival, a rare exception on the set routine.

The routine in a children's home is usually inflexible and unchanging. Outings, or exceptions to the fixed routine, are very rare. Children in children's homes do not usually see realistic role models of adult life. Their only examples of adults are their caregivers, who are almost always women–very few men or male role models are around. And the children do not see and learn from people going about their regular lives in the way that the children do when they grow up in a family. In a children's home, what children see is people doing their job, keeping order and discipline. These people are more likely to be annoyed with difficult circumstances than to be enjoying life. This does not teach the children much about what their adult life will be like and how they should behave as adults, when the time comes. More detailed information about the role model function of caregivers will be discussed in Part 3, Chapter 4: 'The Caregiving Staff'.

✳ ─────────────

The Impact of the Difference between Family and Institution

Many people will react to this knowledge with the remark: 'Yes, that is of course unfortunate, but none of us have it all, how much worse can these let-downs be than the disappointments we all have to face?'

The answer is that it is much, much worse than the disappointments most of us have to face in life. The answer is that it can, in some cases, be fatal. So, let us now look at the effects, particularly the long-term ones, of the differences between growing up in a family and growing up in a children's home.

Receiving affection, attention, stimulation, attachment and physical contact is part of our essential basic needs, from birth onward. Especially in children's homes, these needs are often forgotten or pushed way down the priority list, as a luxury. They are not a luxury. Children who for a long time do not receive physical contact, stimulation and attention next to having their practical needs met, become emotionally scarred and in some cases even mentally handicapped, if they survive.

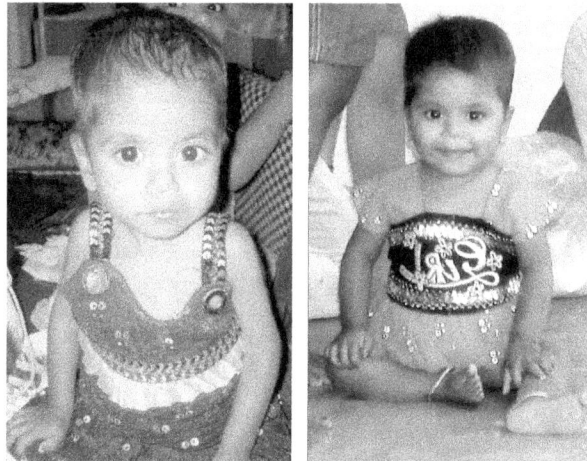

The difference after four months, with the diet still not right, but touch, attention and stimulation given.

Children show a physiological response to lacking affection, attention and affectionate physical contact. Their production of growth hormones decreases, which means that the child only grows very slowly, or may even stop growing and developing altogether. Their immune system becomes less active, and in babies it can stop working completely.

Our immune system fights bacteria and viruses in the body, to either prevent us from getting sick, or to make sure that an illness does not become too serious. The immune system needs to be strong to be able to fight off illnesses. Although we do not usually notice it, our immune system has to work very hard all the time to keep us healthy. When outside influences—such as not getting enough food, not getting enough sleep, or not getting attention and affectionate physical contact-weaken the immune system, this means that it will not have the power to properly fight off bacteria attacking the body. This means that the child will get ill much more quickly than other children. If he has a wound, the chance of it getting infected is much higher. Any illness that the child gets is almost certain to get much more serious, possibly even dangerous, than it would in a child with an immune system that works properly. In children who are HIV-positive and others who already have a weakened immune system, having it further weakened by lack of affection and a friendly touch puts them at an even greater risk of getting sick as well as of illnesses becoming life-threatening.

This explanation about the effect of a weak immune system may sound familiar to you. That is because it was also mentioned when discussing the effects of poor hygiene and malnutrition. In other words, not providing enough physical contact and attention has a similar effect to not having good hygiene and to not feeding the children properly!

A one-year-old girl was so severely malnourished and dehydrated that at the moment of intervention, there was no guarantee that she would survive. The diet at the children's home was less than ideal and it was low in certain elements, however, it was not completely inadequate. The main problem the girl faced was having to share a caregiver with more than a dozen other children and being too weak to demand attention, which led to unintentional neglect. The girl needed food and drink, but more than anything she needed physical contact, attention and affection. For her to have any chance of survival, she needed to have the undivided attention of a caregiver, to be held constantly and be offered food and drink every hour, if not more often. With all caregivers in this home looking after 15 to 20 children each, this was not possible. However, in the home there was also a fourteen-year-old girl who refused to attend school. She had expressed an interest in childcare, and already acted as a caregivers' assistant. Observing her deal with the small children, she clearly had quite a lot of insight in what they needed, as well as a lot of love for the children. So, it was decided to ask her if she would be willing to take on the little malnourished girl's care. She agreed and got to work straight away with incredible dedication. Effectively, the teenager became the little girl's foster mother, and she showed all the protectiveness and possessiveness of a real mother. Changes were also made to the diet of the small children, which brought some improvement, although it was still not an altogether balanced diet. Yet the little girl started gaining weight, growing, and catching up on her development within a few weeks' time. This showed that her need for physical contact, attention and affection was even more urgent than her need for the right food.

Even what children are capable of feeling for the rest of their lives is affected by lack of a sense of security, a result of receiving affection, attention, physical contact and secure attachment at a young age. Small babies are not able to comfort themselves. When the

Being held = feeling safe = proper development.

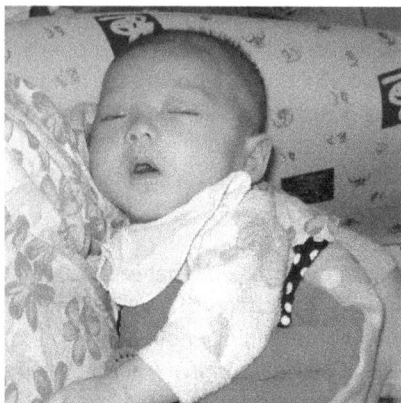

baby feels uncomfortable because her nappy is wet, because she is hungry or because she is too hot or cold, she will cry. If someone does not come soon to calm and sooth her by holding her, rocking her and fixing whatever is not right, she will cry with more and more desperation. For her this is a stressful experience, and if this happens often, or if she is left to cry for very long periods of time, it can even be traumatic.

In moments of stress, the body produces hormones that are very helpful for dealing with stressful situations for adults. These hormones evolved to help you in 'fight or flight' situations where you need to be able to act quickly and need extra strength. In occasional short bursts, these hormones will do no harm and can be of great help. However, if these hormones are active for long periods, they can cause damage to the brain and other body systems. This is the kind of damage that is for instance seen in business people who live under constant severe stress. It starts by causing all kinds of physical problems and eventually it makes people have a breakdown, unable to continue their work. This is in adults. In babies, having these hormones active for long periods will happen, for example, when a baby is left to cry for hours every day, or if a baby is often not held or soothed for long periods of time. Or when their essential basic needs are not met.

Having these hormones active for long periods of time can have two effects, both of them bad:
- Hormones stay active at high levels in the body all the time. This causes a child to become very nervous and anxious and makes her likely to overreact to anything that happens.
- Hormones in the child compensate by circulating at very low levels. These constant low levels make a child feel numb and detached from her environment, **unresponsive** to stimuli.

These effects can become permanent.

Physical Contact and Stimulation

When a child is held regularly by his caregiver, it makes him feel safe. This sense of security tells his body that all is well, and it stimulates the body to produce all the hormones needed for a normal development and for good health. When this feeling of being safe is not there for a small child, his body will stop producing these necessary hormones and his health will suffer.

In the first half of the 20th century, in many European cultures showing affection to children was seen as useless, if not indeed the cause of many problems. Harry Harlow, an American psychologist, took a different view and set about proving it. In one of his experiments (his most famous) he removed rhesus monkeys from their mothers only a few hours after birth and gave them a choice between two different 'mothers'. One was made of soft terrycloth, but did not give any food. The other was made out of wire and provided food through an attached bottle. The young monkeys showed a strong preference for the soft mother, over the wire mother that only provided food. Snuggling up to the soft 'mother' made them feel like being held.

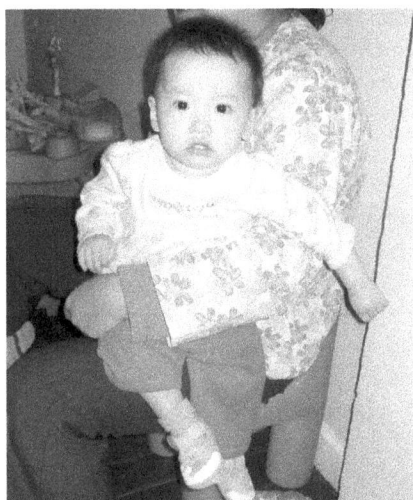

Allowing a child to sit on your lap has a great positive effect.

Not only the size of the child and his health are influenced by whether he receives enough touch and stimulation. The development of his brain is also strongly influenced by the presence or lack of touch and stimulation. There is a measurable difference in brain size between children who live in families (and are exposed to regular physical contact and freedom to play) and children who grow up in a situation with many children to few caregivers (where physical contact and freedom to play and develop is extremely limited or absent). The brains of children in these children's homes have been shown to be 20 to 30% smaller than those of children in families. So that is actual brain matter that has never developed. Various experiences such as physical contact, having the opportunity to form attachments and being talked to from a very early age, all together determine how well the brain is prepared for future learning and how well the two halves of the brain can work together to make sense of the information they are getting.

Stimulation of all kinds leads to the creation of synapses and pathways in the brain. These are the links between different parts of the brain that are needed for it to work well. Lack of stimulation–which includes being held, seeing, hearing, feeling, tasting and experiencing a variety of things–not only prevents the making of new synapses and pathways, they also lead to the destruction of existing ones. Of the connections that a child is born with only those that are regularly used are kept, others are destroyed. Young children need safety, affection, conversation and a stimulating environment to develop and keep important synapses. When a child reaches the age of ten, the phase of rapid early brain growth and the development of connections is completed, and it will stop. This means that for the foundation of the brain, what has not been created by then or what has already been lost, will not be there. So, if these things do not happen when the child is small, it is too late and the child will simply have to live without them. Research has shown that, on average, throughout the time a child spends living in a children's home, for every three months spent in the children's home, the child's development will be delayed by one month.

Attachment

The ability to form relationships–attachments–with people is also something that needs to be learned at a young age. Children who are not exposed to positive social behaviours at an early age make few connections in that area of their brains. Usually, children who live in a family do not even notice that they are learning, because they simply pick up the ability from having a role in the normal family situation and from receiving the love of their family members and having their needs met. Nobody needs to explain to a child in a family what relationships are and how to form them. In fact, it is not even possible. The child gets to experience all kinds of relationships and through these experiences he learns how to form bonds with other people.

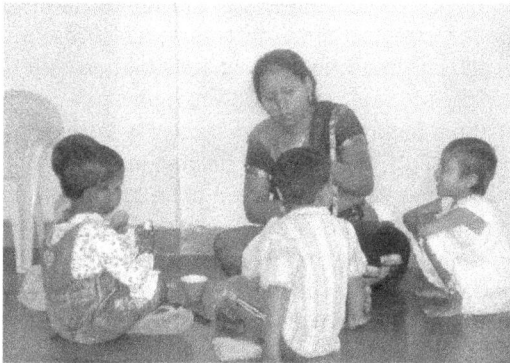

Forming a bond with the caregiver is important.

Children playing together can teach them about relationships, if the group is stable.

Children who do not get the experience of forming a special bond with a certain caregiver who is always there for them and with whom they feel completely at ease and completely safe, do not form the links in their brains that make this kind of thing happen automatically later on. This can make it difficult, or for some children even impossible, to form any kind of normal relationship later in life. Having experienced a long-term sense of security and bonding with people at an early age makes the ability come naturally to most people. But in a children's home, there are often no opportunities for a small child to form these bonds. Caregivers are not always available because they work shifts, they are too busy to give attention and affectionate touch to the child, or they do not stay in their job long enough because caregivers are regularly replaced.

Several problems are seen in children who have spent much of their childhood in a children's home. One of these problems is 'indis-

From day one, as many children as possible try to crowd around to get attention and be touched.

criminate attachment behaviour'. A child who shows indiscriminate attachment behaviour has such a great need for positive attention and affection that he will not care what risks are involved in going to strangers. He will go up to anyone and be open, trusting and affectionate, without making a difference between people he knows and strangers. Children who live in a family and who have bonded with their parents from an early age, have a resistance toward strangers from about nine months of age onwards. This mistrust of strangers is built into human beings to keep them safe, because you do not know whether a stranger can be trusted or not. For a child with indiscriminate attachment behaviour, the need for attention and affection is so much greater than the need to stay safe, that this built-in safety-mechanism is thrown aside.

During projects in children's homes, the children usually come running up to me the moment I walk in, even the very first time, when they have no idea who I am. They grab my hands, try to climb on my lap, touch my hair and lean against me.

When I go home with one of my colleagues who works at that children's home, to meet her family, her children are very curious about me and stare at me. I look different, very tall and with a different colour skin and hair. However, these children will keep their distance. They will not approach me until their parents' behaviour towards me and the way I act have reassured them that it is safe. Then they will cautiously come closer.

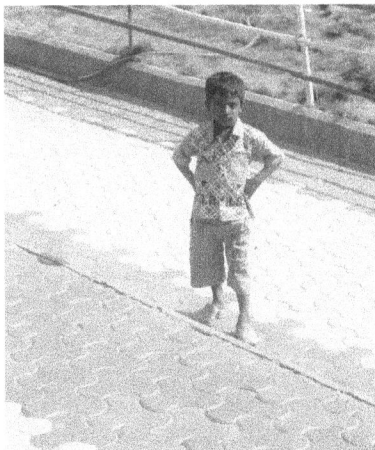

Visitors who come to a children's home often think it is wonderful, the way children flock towards them, grabbing their hands, trying to sit on their laps. Most people see this as a sign that the children are open and welcoming. In fact, it is a sign of indiscriminate attachment behaviour, a problem. Children who have had indiscriminate attachment behaviour for several years may continue to do so even after they are placed in a permanent adoptive family. Even though they now have a secure home with a primary caregiver and lots of affection and attention, they are so used to the necessity of getting attention and affection wherever you can get it, that they are just as likely to walk up to a stranger in the shop and take his hand, as they are to go to their adoptive mother.

> *During one of the projects an eighteen-month-old girl was in very poor condition. To be able to give her the one-to-one care she needed to have a hope of surviving, a teenage girl was more or less made her foster mother, under supervision. The teenager did a fantastic job taking care of the little girl and she helped her become healthy and happy. It was more than two years before I was able to visit the same project again and none of the younger children really remembered me anymore. When I arrived at the dorm where the little girl stayed, all 18 other children came out of the room to hug me and hold my hands and try to sit on my lap, even though they did not know who I was anymore. The little girl followed after them, much more slowly and kept watching me from a distance. Because she had had a chance to attach to her 'foster mother', her healthy fear of strangers was not thrown overboard and she made sure I could be trusted before approaching me, much later.*

Another problem seen is resistance to bonding. A child who shows resistance to bonding has given up hope that someone will provide him with attention and affection. Rather than risk being disappointed and rejected again, he prefers to not even try to bond with other people and he rejects their efforts to bond with him. He is convinced that even if they try to bond with him now, they will find out he is not worth it in the end and they will abandon him. So, instead, he withdraws within himself, making as little contact as possible with the outside world, to protect himself from getting hurt.

Problems with attachment can lead to a child not developing a relationship or bond with caregivers in the children's home. However, it can also lead to such a great need to form an attachment that the child will form a bond even with someone who does not take care of all his essential basic needs. It has been shown that children may sometimes even form an attachment to an abusive parent or caregiver. Attachment does not have to come from both sides. It is possible for a child to attach himself to someone who does not respond to his attachment in the way he needs. However, an attachment to a caregiver who is abusive or who does not provide everything the child needs to stay healthy and develop is likely to be a disorganised attachment. This means that while the child is attached to the caregiver and will try to stay near her whenever he can, he also knows that he cannot fully depend on her and he may show conflicting behaviour, which can include sudden aggression or withdrawal. This behaviour can continue into his adult life.

Not having the opportunity to form a secure attachment to a primary caregiver in the first three years of life has serious psychological and behavioural effects. In the course of bonding with a primary caregiver, a child learns about things like **empathy** and self-control;

it is only in a close personal relationship that he can learn about this. He learns about it through constant interaction with a trusted primary caregiver, who helps him to make sense of and to control his emotions and who explains about other people's feelings. Without empathy, a child cannot develop a conscience at a later age, and in extreme cases he might not even really see other people as people. He may not realise that he needs to take their feelings and well-being into account, because he does not understand that they have feelings. In extreme cases, he may only see people as instruments to get what he wants. Without developing empathy and self-control he is very likely to become impulsive, anxious and even aggressive or violent when he is older. This can make him a very dangerous person when he grows up. In Part 2, Chapter 3: 'How Children Think' more information is given about the development of empathy.

Vorria et al. did a study on attachment of 100 children aged between five days old and five years old in a children's home in Greece. The daily schedule of this home has the children in their beds for 17.5 hours a day; they play outside of their beds for 3.5 hours a day and the remaining 3 hours is the time it takes to feed and change them. While an earlier study of these same children showed that most children did develop some attachment, the quality of attachment had not been looked at. In this study, it was found that 66% of the children had formed disorganised attachments–which are an indication for later behavioural problems–compared to 25% of children from the comparison group of children with two parents. This result was similar to that for children of mothers who were depressed, alcoholic, mentally ill or maltreating their children.

Identity

Young children are still trying to make sense of all the things they see, hear, smell and feel around them. They need adults with whom they feel safe and whom they trust to help them interpret what all these things mean.

Showing the child that she does not need to fear the sheep.

When a baby hears a loud, sudden noise, he will startle and usually look around for someone, to find out what he should think of it. If a trusted caregiver looks like she is frightened or panicked by the sound, or if she starts soothing the child frantically repeating that all will be all right, the baby will learn that this sudden sound is a bad thing, and the next time something like this happens he is likely to be afraid and start crying. He has learned that fear is the right response to the situation. If, on the other hand, the known and trusted caregiver simply smiles and says something like 'don't worry, it is just...', the next time there is a similar sudden loud noise, the baby will still startle, but he is likely to calm himself down, because he remembers that this is nothing to be worried about.

This kind of information is constantly given to children who live in a family, throughout daily life. Most of the time, his parents are not even aware that they are helping their child make sense of the world. They are just reacting to situations the way they always do, and the baby observes this. In a children's home, this kind of information is usually lacking, because caregivers spend less time around the child than parents do. If the child does not receive information about how the world works, this can leave a great, deep confusion, as well as an inability to calm himself.

In a similar way, children depend on their parents—or a trusted caregiver with whom they have bonded—to help them develop a sense of self. In a family, the way parents act towards a child and the way they introduce him to and guide him through the world gives a child a sense of identity, self-respect, self-confidence, a feeling of belonging, of culture, and of status. In a children's home, it is much more difficult to provide a child with these things, because a children's home is usually a world of its own, cut off from the outside world. This means that children do not learn how to behave in everyday social situations such as buying things in a shop, meeting people in the street, or having family members over for a visit. Children in families pick this up from watching adults handle these situations every day. Also, caregivers are often so busy with practical matters that they do not have a lot of time to just talk to the child. In Part 3, Chapter 4: 'The Caregiving Staff', more detailed information is given about this part of the caregiver's job.

Apart from this general way in which children have trouble discovering their identity in children's homes, there is a more specific way. It is not uncommon for children living in a children's home to be completely unaware of their ethnic, cultural and religious background, particularly if they belong to a minority group in their country. Whether it is done out of an ideal to make sure the children all feel equal, out of a desire to stay away from the tensions between tribes or religions that may be present in the country, or simply because it seems easier to raise all the children with the majority culture and religion, it is never fair to the children to withhold knowledge about their identity and heritage. These things are a part of who they are and where they come from. All children should be given the opportunity to learn more about their culture, religion and background.

It has been shown that children who behave badly, have trouble learning things, have trouble paying attention, or are withdrawn and depressed, are more often those who live in a children's home than those who live in a family. This demonstrates how strong the influence of the difference in care between a family and a children's home can be.

Showing autistic traits after a long stay in poorly run orphanage.

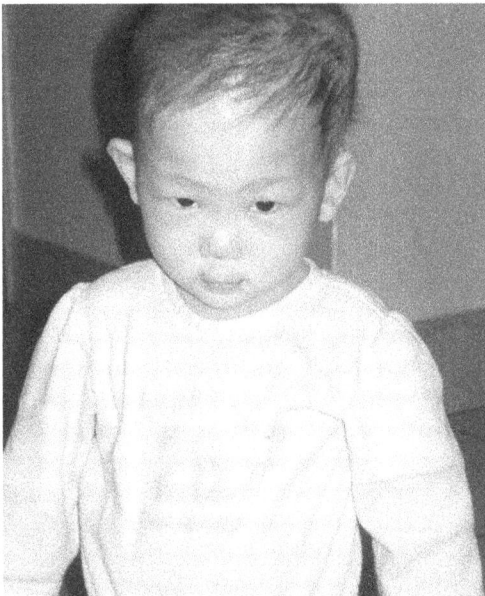

In some institutional situations, usually where staff-to-child ratios are very low and stimulation, attention given, and personal connections are little to non-existent, children may withdraw into themselves, trying to deny all the things that are lacking in the surroundings in which they live. By showing stereotypical behaviour (repetitive behaviour shown by people who try to close themselves off to the world, or look for stimulation) such as rocking or banging their heads, and sometimes pulling out their own hair, they try to provide themselves with some kind of stimulation where all other is lacking, while at the same time they try to shut out the outside world. In some cases, this even turns into 'institutional autism', a form of autism that starts in a child who used to be normal, because of a long-term lack of attention and stimulation.

The little boy was almost one year old when he was moved from an orphanage where the baby-to-caregiver ratio was over 20:1 to a children's home where there was one caregiver for every two children. Suddenly he was surrounded by affection, attention and toys. His health improved and very slowly he started occasionally making eye contact, and quite some time after that even giving a little smile now and then. However, overall, he preferred to avoid social interaction and sit by himself with a toy. He did not like to be held. After a long time, he would sometimes agree to sit on someone's lap, but only if they did not hold him. It had to be on his terms or not at all, and if he could not get up and leave the moment he wanted to, he got extremely upset. These are signs of autism. The effects of the neglect suffered in the previous home were deeply ingrained in him.

✳ ————————— *Recognising Danger Signs*

You do everything you know should be done for a child's well-being, but without meaning to, you might be missing one or two important things. This is why it is helpful to be able to recognise the danger signs of a child's development being severely affected because his essential basic needs are not being met.

Signs to look out for are:

- Weight loss and lack of growth: the child is a lot smaller than is normal for his age and/or his weight is low for his height.
- It is impossible to guess the child's age from his physical appearance.
- Not starting to speak at an age when most children do, or losing the ability to speak in a real language after he was already able to do so.
- Showing behaviour that belongs to a child who is much younger, and having no control over behaviour or emotions.
- Having a short attention and concentration span and difficulty remembering things.
- Starting to urinate and soil himself again after being potty trained, sometimes even playing with poop and urine.
- Showing a lot of repetitive behaviour, rocking, and self-stimulation.

It is very important to recognise things like these as early as possible, and to make changes in the child's care to reverse these negative developments. Because if a child who suffers from these signs is left in the same circumstances for a long time, it might not be possible to put an end to these problems anymore.

Once a child is moved from a children's home into a family, either through adoption or fostering, some of the problems that have been mentioned may improve a bit. Usually, it requires a lot of therapy, hard work and patience on the part of the new parents. However, some of the damage done is permanent and cannot be fixed anymore.

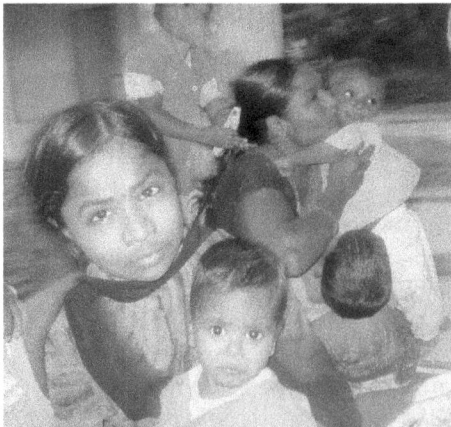

Making institutional care as family-like as possible.

This is why it is important to try to make sure that the differences between care in a family and care in your children's home become as small as possible. Because affection, attention, physical contact, stimulation, and attachment are not things that children just like. They are things the children really, really need to survive and to be able to become normal adults. Plus, since bad or difficult behaviour is one of the results of the lack of touch, attention and attachment, providing the child with these things will make him easier to handle in time, which will make the caregiver's job easier too.

I regularly get complaints, from people working in children's homes all over the world, about children who have lived in a home with many children and few caregivers for several years. The complaints are always very similar: I am told that the children are badly-behaved, ill-mannered, disobedient, disrespectful, rebellious and ungrateful. This is said as if these are somehow exceptional children, very bad ones. And they ask me how they can make the children behave better.

It always saddens me when I hear this, because the behaviour seen in these children is the natural and inevitable result of being raised without getting attention, affection, a chance to form attachments, proper stimulation and positive role models. There is nothing inherently wrong or bad in these children. Any child put in that position would either turn out that way, or not survive. As for being ungrateful, these children did not ask to be put in a place where their essential basic needs were not met, and it is easy to see how these children feel they do not have much to be grateful for, no matter how good the intentions of the people running the children's home are.

To prevent the negative side-effects of living in a children's home such as not growing well, being sick a lot, having low self-esteem, perhaps being depressed or unaware of how the world really works, our goal has to be to make the lives that children lead in children's homes as much like family life as possible. Institutional life is never going to be exactly the same for the children as it would be if they were living with their families, but we can stop to think about which elements of family life we can still provide that are missing at the moment.

UN GUIDELINES:

4. Every child and young person should live in a supportive, protective and caring environment that promotes his/her full potential. Children with inadequate or no parental care are at special risk of being denied such a nurturing environment.

100. To promote the child's sense of self-identity, a life story book comprising appropriate information, pictures, personal objects and mementoes regarding each step of the child's life should be maintained with the child's participation and made available to the child throughout his/her life.

Essential Elements of Childcare

Child-to-Caregiver Ratio

It all starts with having a good child-to-caregiver ratio. If there are too few caregivers for too many children, it is not realistic to make any of the other changes proposed here. What constitutes an adequate ratio depends on the age and circumstances of the children.

- *For babies, children up to four years old, and for children with complex medical needs, one caregiver to three children is needed, to be able to take care of both practical and emotional needs.*
- *For children of four to twelve years old, and for children with moderate medical needs and moderate to severe limitations due to handicap, six children to one caregiver is manageable.*
- *For healthy children over twelve years old, if you wish to meet their emotional and psychological needs, eight children to one caregiver is an absolute maximum.*

When you calculate what the child-to-caregiver ratio is in your children's home, make sure to only include people who spend all their time at work taking care of the children. The count should not include all the adults working in the children's home, because many of them never really take care of the children. They are busy in the office or in the kitchen or doing the washing. So only real caregivers should be counted.

When I asked how many caregivers there were for a dorm of 26 children, I was told four. That sounded pretty good. That meant a child to caregiver ratio of 6 or 7 to 1, which was appropriate for the age group. However, when I asked further about their actual duties, I found out that one of the four did all the cooking, and did not spend any time in the dorm. One of the four was responsible for all the administrative work for the dorm and would take children to hospital when needed. One of the four would spend several hours a day with the children. And only one person was with the 26 children most of the time, day and night. That is a 26 to 1 ratio, not good at all.

If you are already running a children's home and have no way to meet these ratios in the short-term, please do not give up before you have started. Begin by adding as many caregivers as you are able to, to improve the situation, and keep working on getting these ratios until you succeed. If you are planning to set up a new children's home but do not see a way of providing these kinds of ratios of caregiver to child, please do not open your children's home until you are able to provide enough caregivers.

UN GUIDELINES:

126. States should ensure that there are sufficient carers in residential care settings to allow individualized attention and to give the child, where appropriate, the opportunity to bond with a specific carer. Carers should also be deployed within the care setting in such a way as to implement effectively its aims and objectives and ensure child protection.

One adult with too many children is unable to provide care.

Primary Caregiver

Having one person take care of only a few children, instead of being in charge of 15 children or more, makes it possible to provide them with attention. Even when you have caregivers who come to work for shifts of several hours, you can still create a working roster where one particular caregiver has primary responsibility for several specific children whenever she is working her shift.

In a particular home, the division of staff results in one caregiver looking after three or four children. At the start of every shift the caregiver is told which children she will be looking after today. Sometimes the same child will be in her care more than once a week, but often she will only spend time with a particular child once in several weeks. She knows the children well enough to know which of them is likely to cause trouble and needs to be watched. Other than that, she just makes sure that everything is kept in order.

In another home one caregiver looks after three or four children. The caregiver always knows who she will be looking after, because whenever she is working, she looks after the same children. When she started working with these children she mostly made sure they were clean and fed and did not get into trouble. But over the weeks and months she began to discover that these children really are quite something. The way they trust and depend on her makes the caregiver feel important and needed, and she has really started caring for them as though they are a little bit her own. And when she sees them learning to do something new and succeeding, she cannot stop herself from feeling proud. She also notices that the children are comforted and reassured much faster by her, now that she has been there for them for a longer time.

It is extremely valuable for bonding and laying foundations for a child's ability to form relationships both through childhood and later in life, to allow relationships to form between caregivers and children and among children by avoiding constant shifts in group or dorm makeup, and allowing time to be spent together. In the short-term, it is also likely to make children feel more secure, which generally makes them easier to handle.

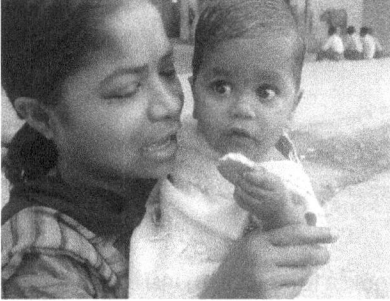

A caregiver acting like a mother.

To provide children with the opportunity to form proper bonds with their caregivers, it is helpful not only to avoid constant changes in caregivers because of shift changes, but also to provide caregivers with a contract for at least three years when they start working. This can help avoid yearly changes in caregivers and disruption of the attachment process.

Similarly, try to avoid moving children from one dorm to another, from one department to another, or even from one institution to another. These moves are usually made for the convenience of management, helping to make their logistical task simpler. However, these moves have a serious negative effect on the children. Every move disrupts a child's attachment and sense of security.

Instead of making up groups under a particular caregiver based on an age category–for example children of five to ten years old–and then making children move to another caregiver when they reach the upper age limit, it would help the child's development and ability to attach a lot to have groups grow up together, with the same caregiver. This means you assign a certain number of children of a particular age category to a caregiver. When the caregiver has as many children as she can properly take care of, stop adding more children. Then you keep that group, with that caregiver, as a set unit that will grow up together. When new, younger children arrive, you start another group, with another caregiver, in the same way.

Some people are afraid that allowing the children to grow properly attached to one or two caregivers only makes things harder on the children. Their argument is that if children are attached, they will find it very hard if the caregiver needs to leave. It is certainly true that it is hard for children to see someone they are attached to leave–whether for a short or for a long time–but this does not mean that they would be better off if they were not attached. The very serious effects of not getting the opportunity to bond have been explained earlier in this chapter. These problems are much more serious than the sadness that comes from saying goodbye to someone you have bonded with. And not allowing children to form attachments to protect them from that sadness will not do them any good.

Balancing Praise and Reprimand

In a family situation, there is a natural balance between reprimanding a child when he does something wrong and praising him when he does things well. This balance comes from the underlying, ever-present love and pride that parents feel for their children. In a children's home, the divide between children and caregivers is often much greater. When caregivers have a lot of children to look after, there is no time for forming relation-

Children do chores more willingly if they receive praise for their efforts.

ships and the caregiver's child-raising efforts concentrate mostly on correcting bad behaviour. Praising and showing gratitude for good behaviour does not seem like a very high priority. This usually means that caregivers spend most of their time reprimanding children, without praising them.

A three-year-old child lives in a children's home where he is taken care of by a caregiver together with six other children of about his age. When his caregiver pays attention to him, it is usually to tell him that he is doing something wrong. He gets told that he should eat faster, not make such a mess, and not whine just because he is tired or hungry. When he wanted to surprise his caregiver by giving her flowers, she slapped him and told him he was a bad boy for picking the flowers from the little garden in front of the office. For quite some time, he tried to do things that would make his caregiver happy. But now he just does not know how to do that anymore. These days, he often gets scared when he sees his caregiver come into the room and he gets so nervous that he makes even more mistakes. Yesterday he was not even able to stop himself from peeing in his pants, which had not happened in months. Then his caregiver became really angry with him.

Receiving praise and gratitude is not just something pleasant. It is just as important as having bad behaviour corrected. It is by receiving praise and gratitude that children will develop positive motivation (in other words, their own wish to do good things) and self-confidence, instead of negative motivation, which only leads to a child trying to avoid being caught and punished, rather than trying to do something good or well. Praise and gratitude are just as important as reprimand and discipline when it comes to helping children to become well-mannered and well-behaved.

A three-year-old child lives in a children's home where she is taken care of by a caregiver together with six other children of about her age. When she makes a drawing, or helps her caregiver by getting something she needs or tidying something up, her caregiver tells her that she did a good job, that it is nice to have her help and that she is a good girl. This makes the little girl feel very happy. When she spills her milk, or pushes one of the other children or is being impatient, her caregiver tells her that she is not supposed to do things like that, they are not nice things to do at all. It always makes the little girl feel a little sad when her caregiver tells her that she did something wrong. Once, she wanted to surprise her caregiver by giving her flowers. Her caregiver told her that is was very sweet that the little girl gave her a present, but that it was wrong to take the flowers from the little garden in front of the office, because those flowers belong to the people who work in the office, so she should not do that anymore. Because being told she is doing things well makes her feel good and being told that she is doing things wrong makes her feel sad, the little girl is determined to try to think what will make her caregiver happy and what will make her angry before she does something. She wants both herself and her caregiver to be happy all the time!

Giving Attention

Attention is not just something children like. It is something that they really need. They need it to make sure that their brain development takes place as it should, and also to make sure that they develop self-confidence and respect for themselves and for others.

In fact, children need attention so desperately that when they get no attention at all, or not enough, they will try literally anything to attract attention. This behaviour is built into all of us.

To start out with, they will try to attract positive attention by being affectionate, showing you their 'possessions', and showing off their skills. If this does not work, they will settle for negative attention because the need for attention is so deep that a child will prefer

Listening to music and clapping with the children.

any kind of attention–including physical abuse–over no attention at all. To attract negative attention a child will use bad behaviour, such as damaging objects, hurting himself or others, being extremely disruptive, or anything else he can think of to get you to pay attention to him. This will happen even when the attention he gets like this is nothing more than being shouted at or being beaten to make him stop doing what he is doing. Unless positive attention is given, there will be no end to the child's bad behaviour and ultimately, there will be no limit to what he will be prepared to do to get just a little bit of attention.

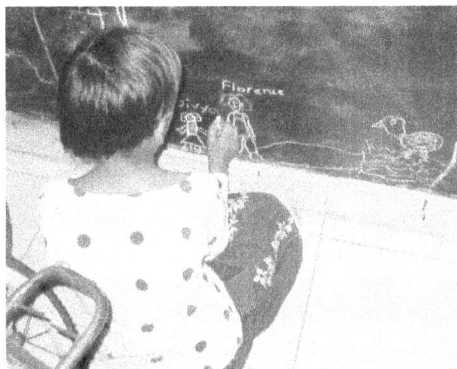

First asking for positive attention by showing off skills and endearing you.

But if pulling another child's hair is needed to get attention, that is what she will do.

In a home for mentally challenged children, one of the problems was that there were a lot of glass in the outside area where the children played. It was almost a sport for the children to find bits of glass and hide them in their pockets. Some of the children would cut themselves with the glass, to see what would happen, some would threaten others with the glass as a weapon and some would put the glass in their mouth and chew it. To improve safety, an effort was made to get rid of all the glass and any glass found on any of the children was taken away. Some of the children discovered that searching for glass and then handing it over was a good way of getting some extra attention. However, one of them was not satisfied with this, and he figured out that he could get even more attention if he showed that he had glass and then he made the caregivers chase him to take it off him and reprimand him. To put a stop to this behaviour, I gave him attention when he came to hand over the glass, but ignored him completely when he made it clear that he had the glass and that I had to come and get it. The boy was not happy with this at all; he had lost his precious attention. The solution he came up with was to stand in front of me and put the piece of glass he had to the throat of another child. He was clearly entirely willing to push it in, if that was what it took, thus forcing me to do something about the situation. Anything to get some attention.

To avoid getting into this downward spiral, or to break it, it is essential that the child receives positive attention. How to go about breaking this cycle will be explained in Part 2, Chapter 6: 'Discipline'.

If simply advising staff to spend time holding children or playing and talking to them is not effective, an option is to schedule time for

Sitting with the children and reading to them.

positive attention, holding children and playing together in the daily routine, just like there are times for getting up, having meals, and so on. Time can be scheduled for 'quality time' between children and their caregivers.

Spending 'quality time' with a child can mean playing together, reading a book out loud or talking about his experiences, without any intrusions. I would define quality time as time in which a child receives attention, is listened to, gets praise for his qualities, is held, hugged or allowed to sit right next to the adult for physical contact However, it does not need to be a separate time. Children can also receive valuable affection and attention in combination with physical contact at mealtimes, or while being involved in little chores, done together with a caregiver.

When giving a child attention, making **eye contact** with him–so looking straight into his eyes–from time to time is important. Making eye contact makes the child feel like you are connecting with him and are really seeing him. It is one of the most powerful ways to make him feel that you are there for him and to give him attention.

Physical Contact

Children have n strong need for affectionate physical contact. This is done naturally in families–babies and toddlers are carried around, older children get to sit on parents' laps or lean against them–and often (almost) absent in children's homes. Being held and receiving affectionate physical contact provides a sense of security, which stimulates the production of growth hormones, the strengthening of the immune system and brain development. Lack of physical contact is one of the reasons why most children in children's homes are smaller than

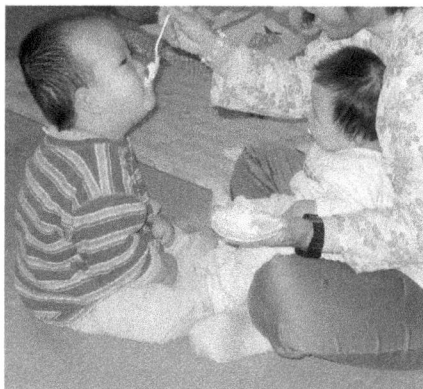

Having one child in your lap while dealing with another child still gives physical contact.

children their age who live in families, and why they get ill more often and develop more slowly. Children under three years old need to spend several hours a day being held by an adult. Older children need to have the opportunity to sit on someone's lap for a while from time to time or to hang against them or hold their hand.

Although children's need for physical contact and attention is so great that they will settle for any kind of physical contact or attention they can get, if they are generally starved of these things, this is in no way an invitation for sexual contact with children. There are no circumstances under which sexual actions towards a child or physical contact with children for personal satisfaction of the adult are acceptable! No form of sexual contact is ever in the best interest of the child. In fact, it invariably damages them psychologically and possibly physically and developmentally as well.

If you have any reason to believe that a child or a group of children is being abused in some way, either sexually or physically or by neglect, action needs to be taken. There should be someone in management whom both staff and children can go to with their suspicions and allegations and who will look into what has happened and take action if needed.

In a children's home, there was a suspicion that one of the dorms was being terrorized by the caregiver. Reasons to suspect this were that the children from that dorm were much quieter and more withdrawn than other children in the children's home. They always showed up promptly anywhere they needed to be, but always looked a bit afraid. When asked about how they were feeling or what they thought of their caregiver, the children refused to talk. And unlike children from other dorms, they did not even discuss their caregiver with other children. Also, in the growth chart, it showed that most of the children from this dorm were not growing well and that many of them lost weight all the time, even though they were getting the same food as all the other children, who were not losing weight.

A manager told me about his suspicion and I told him that something needed to be done as quickly as possible, to protect the children. The manager talked to the caregiver and gave her a warning, saying that she would be warned one more time, but if it kept happening, she would lose her job. In the weeks after that, the children from that dorm started to slowly loosen up a bit and did not seem so frightened anymore.

UN GUIDELINES:

13. Children must be treated with dignity and respect at all times and must benefit from effective protection from abuse, neglect and all forms of exploitation, whether on the part of care providers, peers or third parties, in whatever care setting they may find themselves.

46. Specific training should be provided to teachers and others working with children in order to help them to identify situations of abuse, neglect, exploitation or risk of abandonment and to refer such situations to competent bodies.

✳ ————————

Showing an Interest in the Child

Parents of families want to hear what their children have been doing, who they were playing with, where they went, all out of genuine interest in their children's lives. This seems like a small thing, but it has an enormous effect on children. It makes them feel that they are real people, **worthy** of someone who listens to them. It gives them a sense of self-confidence and identity. In Part 2, Chapter 5: 'Self-Esteem and Self-Confidence' more information will be given about the importance of self-confidence and how to build it up.

EXAMPLE

> *A thirteen-year-old boy, who never had anyone show any interest in him, was allowed to go home with a friend from school, for a visit. When they arrived at his friend's home, the friend's mother asked both of them how their day had been. The friend hardly noticed or answered the question, which was asked every day. But for the boy, this was an amazing thing. Someone was actually interested enough in HIM to ask him how his day was!*

Children who live in children's homes also need someone who will listen to what they have to say, to ask how they are, what they think about things, and to look at the small 'treasures' that they have found. This is essential both for brain development and for emotional

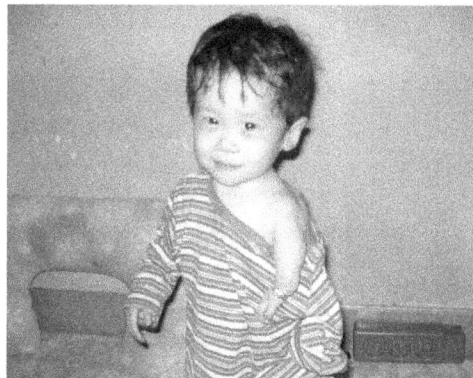

Getting to play with someone's ring is also stimulation.

well-being. Especially when a child is feeling sad, he needs someone to listen to him and to help him deal with the situation. This can be done, for example, by explaining the situation or by reassuring him.

✳ ————————

Stimulation

For children's brains to develop as they should and to prevent children from withdrawing completely into themselves, children need stimulation. Stimulation is varied input through all of their senses: hearing, vision, smell, taste, and touch. Like the need for attention, the need for stimulation, too, is so big that every child has built-in mechanisms that will start working if she does not receive what she needs, as a way of protecting herself.

A child who receives no stimulation, who is left in a single place that always looks the same, without objects to play with and without people to interact with, will start to rock herself endlessly, or even bang her head against a hard surface or pull out her own hair. All of this is done with the single purpose of feeling something, experiencing something. Without stimulation, a child will not learn anything and may even lose the skills that she already possessed.

> *"In most of the cots lie babies, or so they are called. The youngest is about a month old, but the oldest might well be two or three years old. It is very hard to say, growth and development are all stunted. Almost all are lying down, unable to sit or stand. Or, perhaps they have learned that anything other than lying quietly is undesirable. Almost all those over the age of 10 months lie rocking back and forth. Their head or their entire body. If they are not sleeping. Sores on their heads from banging against the bars of the cot. Some with their faces pressed against the bars, their neck at an uncomfortable angle. One little boy grates the paint off the bed with his teeth."*

Some examples of stimulation, all of which are needed in children's daily lives are:

- Freedom to move around and explore the surroundings
- Being talked to by other people
- Receiving affectionate physical contact
- Having a varying range of objects to play with

A stimulating environment.

Organising outings or excursions for the children from time to time is very important. It can be quite hard to do, because there are always a lot of children and usually not a lot of money. However, taking them out does not always have to be for something far away or expensive. It can also be allowing children, in varying small groups, to come along to the market to do the shopping, or to attend a religious service or festival nearby. Being allowed to go outside of the children's home, for something other than attending school or going to a doctor, is important for their general development, but particu-

When very little of interest happens, everything out of the ordinary becomes entertainment.

larly to allow them to learn about how the real world works. This is important for preparing them for life outside of the children's home, once they grow up.

It is not necessary to have expensive toys for playing. But it is necessary to have both some (safe) objects to use in play and to have the freedom to move around and make up games.

It is becoming clear to people all over the world that education is very important to give someone a chance to escape poverty and a disadvantaged background. In children's homes where school-age children and teenagers are cared for, there is usually a very strong push for children to do well in school. Children are made to spend a lot of time on their homework and study, in an effort to make sure that they get good grades. This is certainly admirable. However, it is important to remember that children, of all ages, have to learn more than just the subjects taught in school to prepare for adult life. Being allowed to play has an important role in learning about non-school things. Being given the freedom to play and explore for some time every day is essential in the learning and developing process of the child. In fact, having this freedom will almost certainly help her do better in school.

It is also useful to remember that no-one—whether we are talking about a child or an adult—is able to properly concentrate and take in knowledge for many hours in a row. You can have a child sit with a book for five hours, but that does not mean that she is able to take in information during that entire time. Making a child study for more than two hours in a row, without a break, is a waste of her time. Having her study for two hours and play for several hours and making sure she gets enough sleep, is going to lead to better grades in school than having to sit with her schoolbooks for many hours until late in the night. Even more effective would be to have her study for one hour, then play for an hour, then study another hour and then play again for the rest of the day.

✳ ———————— **Conclusion**

Understanding the big difference between the care children receive in a family and the care they get in a children's home, and the terrible consequences of that difference, makes it easier to understand why children should never be placed in a children's home if there is any way for them to be cared for in their family. In Part 3, Chapter 1 and 2, I will go into more detail about trying to keep children in families.

Even in the best children's homes, essential basic needs are never fully met. If the children in your children's home still have living family, and for some reason there really is no possibility for those family members to care for the children, you should encourage as much contact between the child and the family as possible. This can include phone calls and letters, visits from family members to the home, and also allowing the children to go stay with their family members during school holidays, whenever possible. This will help you too, in the sense that, as we have noted, families are much better at fulfilling a child's essential basic needs than children's homes are. And if at times the family can make a contribution in this,

Celebrating a birthday, like in a family.

the child's development and well-being will greatly benefit from it. It will also help him to develop his identity and his self-confidence. Despite the fact that having visited family can result in sadness on return, and sometimes some difficult behaviour, it is absolutely much better for him to have as much contact with his family as possible. The only exception to this is that he should not be allowed to visit his family if it is known that the child would not be safe in his home.

Children who do not have living family members, or whose origins are unknown, should be given extra attention and maybe certain treats or outings, at times when the children who do have families are spending time with those families. This is important to not make them feel like they are worthless.

During the two main school holidays in the year, about half of the children who live in a home for HIV-positive children, go to stay with their families for one or two weeks. For the children who do not have family to go to, activities such as sports tournaments and cooking competitions are organised. In the last week of the holidays, a bus is arranged to take those who spend their holidays at the home on a day trip to an interesting location somewhere in the state.

When the essential basic ingredients are given a place in a child's daily care, life does not only become more pleasant for the child; the benefit of developing a relationship goes both ways. Children will act up instinctively if their essential basic needs are not met;

they will try to find a way to make sure they get what they need to survive. When they find themselves in a situation where they are not lacking their essential basic necessities and where good behaviour will benefit them more than bad behaviour, they will usually become easier to deal with. Although initially after the change is made, they may temporarily be very difficult to deal with because they are unfamiliar with having their needs met and unsure whether it will be a permanent thing or not. This will be addressed in Part 2, Chapter 6: 'Discipline'.

In children's homes, the problem is always that there are many children and few adults. Money is scarce and cannot be spent twice. So, there are limits to what can be done. However, it does not make sense to accept more children into your care if it would mean that you would no longer be able to provide all of them with sufficient food and shelter. Likewise, if you do not have the resources to take on enough staff to be able to provide children with affectionate care, including physical contact and attachment opportunities, you should reduce the number of children you take in. Because if you do not, you are not doing the children any favours. Studies have shown that children who grow up in a family in extreme poverty, without education, tend to have better chances in life than children who grow up in a children's home. Even if they receive good schooling while they are in the children's home, children who grew up there are more likely to end up living in the street than living successful lives.

In a children's home, there were 85 mentally challenged children and five caregivers. At this caregiver-to-child ratio there is absolutely no way of providing proper care. The caregivers did not do much for the children. They gave them food, made them stay in a certain place and they made some of the older, smarter ones clean up the dorms. They did not see the children as human beings anymore. They even refused to physically touch them, in any way. If they needed the children to move from one place to another, they would herd them by poking them with sticks.

If you have too few caregivers to provide proper care to meet the essential basic needs, something happens in the mind of the caregiver. Being overwhelmed with too many children, who because of lack of proper care are not doing well, the caregiver will feel forced to 'take a step back' in her mind. When she gets too close to the children and too involved with them, the fact that she is not able to provide proper care for them will be too much of a psychological burden: she would become sad and frustrated all the time, would be angry with herself and would not be able to continue doing her job. The solution the mind has, in a situation like this, is to stop seeing the children as real human beings. This is called dehumanizing them.

*When too much pressure is put on the caregiver, she will
not be able to cope and care will get even worse.*

The thinking is: if they are not really human beings, then it is not
so terrible that they do not get what children need and you do not
have to worry about whether they are happy or healthy. This is not
a conscious decision taken by the caregiver, it is something the brain
does on its own, to protect the caregiver and allow her to stay in her
job. The unfortunate thing is that once a caregiver does not see the
children as human beings anymore, she is no longer motivated to
put effort into making sure the children are well. She will feel that
all she needs to do, is enough to keep her job. In other words, when
you do not have enough caregivers to provide proper care to the
children, the care they receive will get worse and worse.

Part 2:

Basic Child Psychology
and
Child Development

Chapter 1: Global Development Stages of Childhood

Children are not only smaller than adults, they are also unable to do some of the things that adults do because they do not have the motor skills and thinking processes needed to do these things. This does not mean that they do not think at all or that they cannot do *any* complicated tasks. It just means that certain ways of thinking and the ability to do *certain* things are not yet present, because a child's brain and body are not only growing, but also developing, and they have not yet reached the stage of development needed to do these things.

Both a child's body and her mind go through a series of different changes in a process that stretches over all of childhood. This process is not exactly the same for everyone, but generally speaking children learn and develop certain **abilities** within certain age groups. Having some insight into the abilities and understanding of children of various age groups can be very helpful in understanding why they act the way they do.

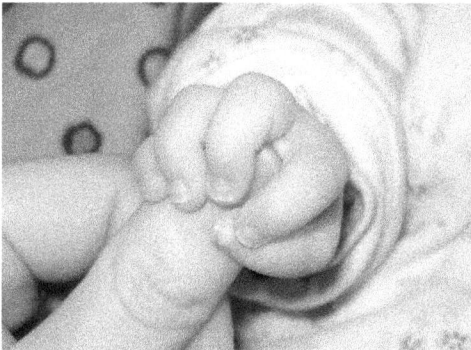

Exploring the world through touch.

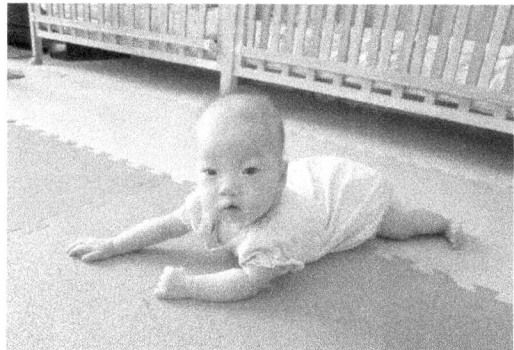

A four-month-old holding up her head while on her belly.

✳ ——————— **Birth to Eighteen Months**

Psychological   The child explores the world around him mostly by using his mouth and by touching things. The child learns to tell the difference between his primary caregiver—if he has one—and other people. Eye contact, touch and positive, affectionate care are essential for healthy development. A child who gets the care and stimulation he needs at this stage learns to trust that the world is basically okay and will develop a basic confidence in the future. If the child does not experience trust and is frustrated because his needs are not met, he may end up with deep feelings of worthlessness and mistrust of the world.

Physical   The body grows extremely fast during this stage, as does the brain. Motor development also happens quickly.

During the first eighteen months, a child will learn to:

- Keep his head and body steady and upright
- Grab, hold on to things and pass things from one hand to the other
- Roll over from his belly to his back and the other way around
- Stay sitting up when put that way and later sitting up himself without help and moving out of a sitting position
- Crawl
- Pull himself up to standing by holding on to someone or something
- Stand without help or holding on to anything
- Walk while holding on to furniture–this is called **cruising**
- Walk without help
- Pick up things between his thumb and index finger
- Feed himself using his hands
- Put things into other things and take them out again
- Smile
- Babble–this means talking without using real words
- Say his first meaningful words

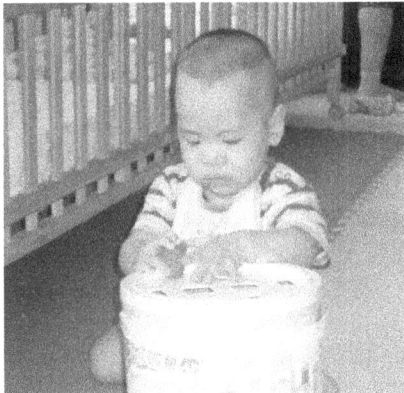

A one-year-old putting shapes through holes.

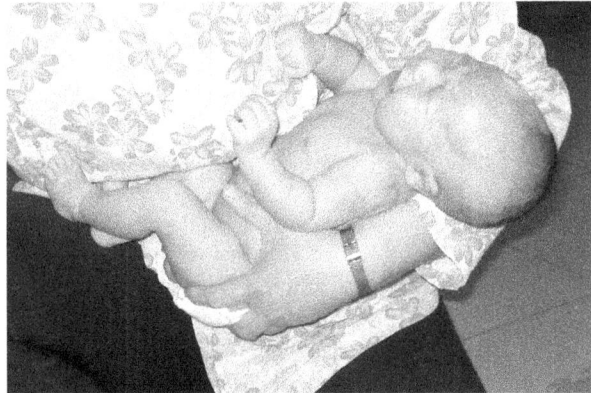

Being held is requirement for babies to do well.

Essential Needs   To make sure that a baby is able to stay healthy and develop normally in the first eighteen months of his life, a few 'care ingredients' are needed. It is very important that someone holds him for a total of several hours per day, not only while he is being fed, but also at other times to let him experience touch and attention. This allows the baby to start developing trust and a feeling of safety. These are necessary for all future development. It is also essential for good health and growth, as was explained in Part 1, Chapter 5: 'Essential Psychological Needs'.

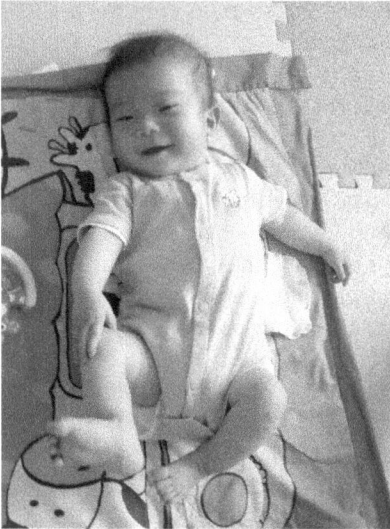

Babies need the opportunity to move their arms and legs.

To develop normally, a child needs to have eye contact with his caregiver and have someone talk to him. Babies who are left lying in their bed almost all day, with just one toy to play with or without even that, do not have the freedom of movement needed to start moving around or to sit up and are much less likely to be able to develop normally. Because there is nothing interesting in the bed to move to, he may not even want to start moving.

The first step in the motor development of a baby is to learn to bear the weight of his head and keep the head still without **wobbling**. If this is not learned, he will not learn any further skills. How will a baby who is always lying in his bed ever get the strength he needs in the muscles of his neck to hold his head still? And if he's always lying with his head on a mattress or mat, when will he have a need to start to practise keeping his head steady? It is by being taken out of the bed several times a day and held for a while, and by being allowed to play on a mat on the floor that he starts to practise these things. From one or two months old onward, while they are awake, all babies should spend at least ten to fifteen minutes a day lying on their bellies, not swaddled. This will help them learn to lift their head and strengthen their neck, upper body, and arms. From this age, a baby should also spend at the very least half an hour a day lying on a mat on the floor, on his back, not swaddled. This gives him the freedom to wave his arms and legs and strengthen them and to look around at something other than his bed. Once the baby starts trying to hold things, give him something safe to play with, so he can practise his skills with that too.

As the child starts to show signs of trying to learn a new skill such as sitting up without help or crawling, encourage him and make sure that he has room to safely practise these skills. If given enough freedom of movement and stimulation, most babies will continue to discover the world and develop their abilities by themselves. However, a baby who is left lying in his bed most of the day is more likely to get sick very often and his development will get more and more behind that of other children of his age. It is even possible for a child to lose the ability to do something that he had already learned to do, if he is always kept in his bed and does not get stimulation or attention.

✳ ─────────── Eighteen Months to Three Years

Psychological The child learns a lot of skills that lead to greater independence, such as feeding and dressing himself, and becoming toilet trained. More control over the body is gained and he starts to learn right from wrong. He discovers the meaning of the word 'no' and starts

Three-year-old boy on a potty, which is also good fun.

experimenting with using it himself. When a toddler experiments with the meaning and use of the word 'no', he can be very difficult to deal with for a while. Suddenly he goes from being very cooperative to saying 'no' to almost everything. This is not because the child is bad or because he is trying to make your life harder. He is only trying to make sense of his new understanding of the possibility of agreeing or disagreeing with things.

A two-year-old girl has learned to say 'no'. Now, when asked a question, it is always her first answer. When asked: 'Will you give him one of the blocks to play with?' she answers with a definite 'No!' About 20 seconds later, she hands the boy a block.

When he got back from hospital he latched on to the Miffy musical toy and would not let any other child go near it.

During this time, he starts building his self-esteem, meaning the idea he has of his own worth. If he builds up high self-esteem, it means that he feels he is a good person who is able to do and learn things and is worthy of other people's compliments. If he has low self-esteem, it means that he does not think he is worth much, that he does not think he is good and that he is more likely to believe people who criticise him than those who give him compliments. A child in this age group can be very vulnerable. If he is shamed in the process of toilet training or while learning other major skills, he may feel humiliated and start to doubt his abilities. This in turn will lead to low self-esteem.

A two-year-old taking off his shoes.

At this age, the beginnings of empathy start to develop. This means that the child starts to understand that other people have feelings. He begins to realise that it is possible for someone else to experience a feeling, even if he does not feel it himself. This starts with the child learning to recognise when other people are upset. He may become emotionally attached to toys or objects, for security. This can mean that he will become very upset when he is not allowed to keep a certain toy with him all the time, because he thinks he needs it to stay safe.

A two-year-old comforting a friend.

Physical
During this stage, growth of body and brain has slowed down a little, but it is still faster than during following stages. The fast growth of his body does not always take place in complete harmony, and this can sometimes cause pain. These pains are called 'growing pains'. It is not a result from playing too much as some people think, but from muscles growing faster than bones, or bones growing faster than muscles for a short while, before the other catches up. This creates a tension. This pain usually only lasts for a few hours and it is more common in the evening. Vision develops fully at this age and **attention span** becomes longer.

Up to his third birthday, a child will learn to:

- Climb stairs, up and down
- Kick a ball without losing balance
- Run
- Pick up objects from the floor while standing without falling
- Understand the order in which puzzles and other complex toys should be used
- Look through a book one page at a time
- Use the toilet or a potty to relieve himself
- Put on and take off clothes (as long as they do not have complicated buttons or ribbons)
- Express his needs in words, using two to three-word sentences

Essential Needs
To prevent the toddler from developing low self-esteem or feeling very ashamed, it is important to use a lot of praise and compliments for good behaviour, rather than focusing on punishing or shaming him for bad behaviour. Low self-esteem may seem an unimportant matter, but it can lead to the child being unable to stand up for himself when he is older, or, alternatively, to very difficult behaviour

and aggression, which arise to cover up feelings of not being good enough (more information about the importance of self-esteem is given in Part 2, Chapter 5: 'Self-Esteem and Self-Confidence'). This makes finding a balance between correcting bad behaviour and praising good behaviour very important.

> *A little boy is almost three years old. He has been using the potty for about a month now. Sometimes, he is concentrating so hard on what he is playing with, that he forgets to pay attention to whether he needs to use the potty. He only discovers that he needs to pee when it is too late, when he has already started. When this happens, his caregiver gets very angry with him, tells him he is bad and that he is making her life hard. She changes his clothes roughly and then makes him sit by himself in the corner for a long time. This never happened when he was still using a nappy. So, even though at first he was very excited about being a big boy and using the potty, and he was able to stay dry almost all the time, now he feels that maybe he just cannot do it, that he is too stupid or small, like his caregiver tells him. He thinks maybe it would be better not to try anymore, that way he might get to wear the nappy all the time again and things will be all right, like they were before.*

This also makes it important to recognise which behaviour can, in all fairness, be called bad. When a child accidentally wets his clothes, or gives the wrong answer to a question, this is unfortunate and undesirable, but it is not bad. The child did not intend to do something wrong; he did the best he could, but failed. The failure in itself is already a kind of punishment. If this is made worse by also being punished or shamed, the child might give up trying to be good, or give up trying anything at all, out of fear of making a mistake and being punished.

> *A two-year-old boy who knew me well had not seen me for a few weeks, because I had been in a different location. When I came into the children's play area, he came straight over to me. He was extremely excited. In fact, he was literally shaking, because he could not think of a way to express his joy and excitement at seeing me again. After looking at me for a moment, trying to figure out what to do, suddenly he bit me in the chest really hard, leaving a mark through my clothes.*
> *Though it was an act of aggression, and he had to be told that he could not do that, it was mostly an act of love.*

Another important part of the care of children of this age is talking to them. Spending time talking to a child and listening to what he has to say, achieves two things at the same time:

- The child gets positive attention, which makes him feel good about himself and allows him to increase his self-esteem.
- It is essential for a child's development of language and speech to talk to adults. It is through hearing adults talk to him, using correct grammar and words, and through trying to find the right way to say what he wants to say, that a child learns how to use language properly.

A child who does not get spoken to and who does not get the chance to express himself may only develop very basic speech, or may not even to try to speak at all.

The age at which they can seem big and small at once.

The development of the other skills mentioned in the list, and of skills that were not mentioned there, all depends on whether or not a child gets the opportunity to practise that skill and receives encouragement for his efforts to try to learn it well. In other words, if a child has never seen a ball in his life, he cannot learn to throw it properly. If the child has never been able to hold a book, he cannot learn how to turn the pages one by one. If he is not given the space to run and climb, he cannot develop those skills either. So, giving a child some freedom of movement to explore his surroundings and practise his skills, and giving him a variety of different objects to play with over time, are needed to allow him to develop a good set of skills. This should be combined with attention, being talked to, and being encouraged and praised in his efforts to try new things.

Physical contact is still very important at this age. Although the child is becoming more independent, taking off on his own to explore the world around him, he still has a deep need to be able to come back to you and sit on your lap. Getting this physical contact and finding this feeling of safety with you, gives him the confidence and ability to go out and try things on his own.

Three to Six Years

Psychological

The child likes to copy adult behaviour. Toys and objects are used to play out what the child understands of adult life. This is practise for her future role. She will also start to take initiative in play situations. That means that she will suggest a game to play and guide you through how it is done. This is a step beyond always waiting for you to tell her what to do and how to do it.

Around this age, the word 'why' is discovered as a way of finding out how the world works. For a while the child may react to any

The presence of things to explore

answer given by asking 'why' again, sometimes even without listening to the answer, just to ask the question. However, if you help the child discover the proper use of the word 'why'–by answering seriously when she seems to want to know the 'why' of something, and not reacting when she is only going on asking 'why' for no reason–she will find it very useful in exploring the world around her. If you do not know the answer to her question, it is all right to tell her that too.

A three-year-old boy asks me why I have no hair. I answer:
'Because I take it off every week.'
'Why?'
'Because it is more practical like this.'
'Why?'
'Because I do not get lice like this.'
'Why?'
'Because lice like to live in hair.'
'Why?'
'You would have to ask the lice that.'

If the child finds herself unable to do what she is trying to do, or if her efforts are regularly blocked–for instance because she does not have the freedom to try out things or to explore–she can get very frustrated, and may even feel guilty for trying. The child's self-esteem is mostly influenced by how the important people in her life treat her and what they tell her she is worth. In other words, a child of this age who gets reprimanded a lot and does not get any praise will have low self-esteem, while a child who receives a good balance between being corrected and praised will have a much higher self-esteem.

Physical During this stage a child is physically very active. Although she can sit still and pay attention to something for some time now, it is still quite difficult for her to do for more than about half an hour at a time. Again, growth has slowed somewhat, but is still impressive. Up to her sixth birthday, a child will learn to:

- Skip, hop and jump with good balance
- Balance while standing on one foot, after some time even with her eyes closed
- Cut out pictures with scissors

- Tie her own shoelaces
- Use cutlery, other simple tools, and pens and pencils
- Learn and sing songs
- Count to 10
- Name colours
- Speak in sentences and use the past tense

Essential Needs   Like in the previous stage, getting positive attention, encouragement and room to play and explore are essential for healthy development in this stage. At this age, a child moves from learning the basic structures of her language to learning to speak in a more subtle way, by using different tenses and expressions for example. A child who does not get spoken to and who does not get the chance to express herself may only develop very basic speech, or may not be inclined to try to speak at all.

The development of the other skills mentioned, and of skills that were not, all depends on whether or not a child gets the opportunity to practise the particular skill and receives encouragement of her efforts to try to master the skill. In other words, if a child has never held scissors in her life, she cannot learn to neatly cut out a picture with them. If the child has never heard a song, she cannot learn how to sing the song herself. And if she is not given the space to skip and hop, she cannot develop those skills either. So, giving a child some freedom of movement to explore her surroundings and practise her skills, and giving her a variety of different objects to play with over time, are needed to allow a child to develop a range of skills. This should be combined with attention, being talked to, and being encouraged and praised for her efforts to try new things.

Impressive climbers, who may not know any fear.

Eating by himself, with a spoon without making a mess.

Exploring friendships and forming little gangs.

Physical contact is still important. While the child may spend a long time playing by herself or exploring things, she will come back to experience the comfort of sitting on the lap of a trusted adult. Having the opportunity to do this will make her feel more secure, which will both help increase her independence and her health and development.

Six to Twelve Years

Psychological

The child starts to become more and more involved with children of her own age, and less dependent on her caregivers. She starts to find out how relationships work by building friendships with people her own age. If the child has low self-esteem or feels she is worth less than her classmates or friends, this can lead to very deep feelings of worthlessness and self-hate. The child needs to be helped in the process of making friends if she has trouble doing it on her own. She needs to be encouraged and stimulated to feel good about herself, which you can do by praising her when she does things well. She should also be explained that not everything that goes wrong is her fault.

A child this age forgives the people she loves easily and finds excuses for them, even if they have clearly done something wrong. However, she is very ready to look for blame in herself, even for things that are completely out of her control. In the song 'Family Portrait' the singer P!nk describes the reasoning of a young girl whose parents are fighting a lot and are getting divorced. This part is where the girl pleads with her father not to leave: "I'll be so much better, I'll tell my brother/ Oh, I won't spill the milk at dinner/ I'll be so much better, I'll do everything right/ I'll be your little girl forever/ I'll go to sleep at night" Of course, the parents' fights have nothing to do with her spilling milk or not going to sleep straight away, but the reasoning of a child of this age will almost always go towards finding blame in herself, for all circumstances.

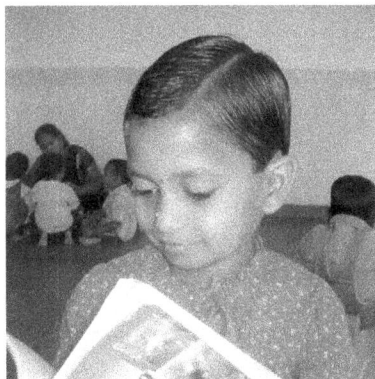

At this age, the child develops an ability to learn, create, and accomplish many new things. She starts to discover what she likes doing best and how to go about doing those things. By learning new things and becoming able to perform tasks and chores she will feel she is contributing to the world. This gives her

Learning to read and write.

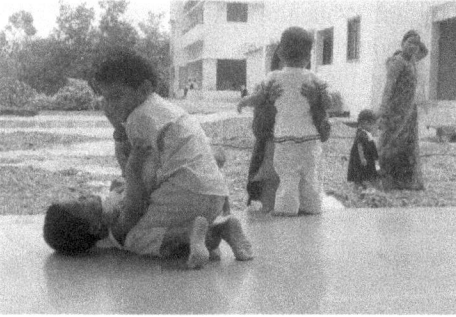

Fighting your own battles.

the satisfaction of doing something productive and useful. Allowing a child to explore this and praising her accomplishments and attempts to help are important at this time to stimulate this feeling of satisfaction.

Physical
During this stage, skills that were learned before are improved and new ones tried out.
A child usually learns to:

- Read and write
- Do arithmetic
- Use language to really **communicate,** not just to express wishes
- Understand and deal with rules–in the early stages without room for exceptions, later with more flexibility
- Understand concepts of space, time, and dimension
- Understand how her behaviour affects others

Essential Needs Like in the previous stage, receiving positive attention, encouragement and room to play and explore are essential for healthy development. At this age a, child starts to discover things such as hidden meanings in metaphors and expressions. She starts to realise that language can be used to present your point of view in a certain way. A child who does not get spoken to and who does not get the chance to experiment with these extra layers of language, may only develop very basic speech, or may not be inclined to try to speak at all.

Toys are not a must, tables can be interesting too.

Leading younger children in a project.

The development of the other skills mentioned, and of skills that were not, all depends on whether or not a child gets the opportunity to practise that particular skill and receives encouragement for her efforts to try to master the skill. In other words, if a child never goes to school or is never tutored in some other way to learn to read, write and do arithmetic, she is not likely to learn how to do these things. If the rules she lives with are random or not consistently applied, she will not find it easy to learn the true meaning of rules. And if no one explains to her, gradually, how her behaviour affects other people, she may not be able to understand it.

Physical contact still has a role at this age. Becoming more and more independent, at times the pre-teen might reject physical contact started by the caregiver. This is a way for her to show how big she is, and it should be respected. However, this does not mean that all physical contact is unwanted. Gradually the child will start to take the initiative to show what kind of physical contact she wants and when she wants it. Very occasionally a larger child might still want to sit on your lap. Generally, though, physical contact will shift to holding hands or her sitting or standing next to you and leaning against you. Even though the amount of physical contact needed has become less, it is still very important for children of this age to receive some physical contact from caregivers.

Twelve to Eighteen Years

Psychological

At about twelve years old, what is known as 'the teenage years' begin. This is a period in which both the child's body and his mind take the step from childhood to adulthood. This process can be quite difficult, both for the child and for the people around him. The changes taking place are so great that they can cause a lot of confusion in the child. When at times he does not know how to deal with the changes, or how to control the things that are happening in his body and mind, he may suddenly behave very badly, which confuses his caregiver, because he never behaved like that before.

> *A fourteen-year-old girl had won some money in a sports competition. She decided, on her own, to use most of the money to buy oranges. She was able to buy enough so that all the children in the children's home she lived in could have half an orange. This was a rare treat in this particular children's home. And the girl beamed with happiness at the joy of her friends thanks to her treat.*

At this stage, the child starts to become even more independent. How he feels and what he does no longer mostly depends on what other people decide for him or tell him. He is more strongly influenced by what his friends think of him than by what his caregivers think of him. Life is now getting more complex for the child. He starts searching for his own identity, separate from the people who raised him. He also works on understanding his interactions with other people and how to behave in these interactions. He develops his own ideas on what is right and what is wrong. The child searches for a philosophy of life at this age and usually thinks in easy rounded ideas without contradictions or doubts, rather than in terms of experience or reality.

To start forming his own identity and own ideas, the child feels the need to distance himself from his caregiver –this happens in families as well as in children's homes. He is less likely to take things said by authority figures as automatically true, because he wants to think it through for himself and make up his own mind. This can lead to heated discussions and arguments. Caregivers

A teenager mothering a toddler.

may feel this is simple stubbornness on the part of the child, when in fact it is his attempt to take his life into his own hands, rather than

She is capable of helping out with a lot of practical things, but still in need of guidance and support.

depend on support. The situation is complicated by the fact that teenagers almost always feel they are more mature and more in control than they really are. This makes them resent any attempt on the part of their caregivers to protect them or hold them back a little, while it may still be very much necessary to do so at times. Many children withdraw from responsibilities at this stage. A child may leave his room/living area messy, not do the chores he is expected to do, and refuse to give anything consideration except for what he wants to do. It can drive his caregivers to despair. While it is important to remind him of his responsibilities, it is also important to realise that this is just a phase that will pass again. It is not badness of the child.

A teenager needs to be given both the opportunity and space to discover who he is, and still receive support and guidance and the opportunity to talk to about his worries and insecurities. If he does not have this, it can lead to a lot of confusion and anxiety. And this can make his final step into adulthood, when it is time for him to take care of himself, very difficult and problematic.

Teenagers are still more likely to blame themselves than to blame others when difficult situations happen.

A teenage girl had been made the 'foster mother'–under supervision–of an eighteen-month-old girl who was severely malnourished due to neglect, in a children's home where there were not enough adult caregivers to give the little girl the intensive attention and care that she needed to have a chance of survival. The teenage girl did an excellent job. She took the little girl with her wherever she went, gave her small amounts of food and drink very often and gave her lots of attention. The little girl started improving very quickly. However, after this arrangement had been in place for about three weeks, I was called to have a look at the little girl. She had developed a fever and diarrhoea, two things that were very dangerous for her at this stage. We could not be certain that she would survive this. I looked at the little girl and gave some instructions for her care. And then I asked the care supervisor, who was there with me, to please translate for me and tell the teenage girl that this was not her fault. The supervisor did not understand and asked me angrily who had said that the teenage girl was to blame. I answered that no one had said such a thing, but that the girl would think it anyway. The supervisor thought this rather ridiculous, but eventually I managed to convince him to tell the girl. The moment he said it, the girl burst out in tears and said 'But I was the one who gave her all the food, and it has made her sick!'

I explained to the girl that she had done nothing wrong, that I had been the one who had made the decisions about what the little girl should be getting, she had only followed my advice, and that it was no one's fault that the little girl got sick now, it happened because she was still very weak. I emphasised that she had done an excellent job taking care of the little girl. The supervisor looked very surprised at the girl's reaction and asked how I had known. To him, I explained that a girl of that age will almost always blame herself for bad things happening, whether she had any influence over them or not.

Physical While for some time the child had been growing a little slower than when he was very small, suddenly he will have a growth spurt again for a year or two. With girls, this usually happens somewhere between the ages of eleven and fourteen years old, with boys usually between the ages of thirteen and sixteen. This growth spurt can make a child seem quite clumsy, because he will hardly have time to adjust to the changes in his strength and size before his body changes again.

Apart from just getting taller, their bodies also change from children's bodies into the bodies of men and women. If children have not been given any information about the changes that will be taking place and what they mean, they can become quite worried

Going from boy to man.

about them, and even ashamed or very scared.

It is a good idea to give thought to providing sex education to children of twelve years and older. The topic of sex is taboo in many cultures, even in rich countries. Many adults seem to think that children will remain childlike and innocent until someone tells them about sex, and that at that moment suddenly the idea, which was not there before, is put into their head. These adults seem to have forgotten what happened when they were that age. The fact is that a teenager need never be told or shown anything to do with sex at all to become curious about it. The teenagers' body and his hormones will direct him in this exploration. So, not talking about it is not going to keep his innocence safe. And while at the moment I am using 'him' and 'he' to talk about a teenager, this goes just as much for girls as it does for boys.

What the teenager's body will not tell him, is what all the feelings and urges he gets mean. It will not tell him what the cultural rules surrounding sexuality are. And it will not tell him what the health risks connected to sex are. These are things that he cannot know about unless someone explains them to him.

> In this particular children's home, about half the children were teenagers and sex was not something that was discussed with them. The boys' dorms were on a different floor from the girls' dorms, but despite this, one night, one of the girls was found in a dark room on the ground floor together with one of the boys. Both children were severely punished. And the manager of the children's home was trying to think of a way to keep the boys and the girls apart more effectively. Her first suggestion was to put a gate at the staircase of the top floor, where the boys slept, and to lock it at night, so that they could not get down to the girls. I had to remind her that with a locked gate at the only exit, if a fire were to break out, none of the boys could hope to get out alive.

This is especially relevant if the teenager himself carries the HIV virus and might start spreading it around without knowing it. Or if the teenager lives in an area where sexual contact puts him at high risk of being infected with HIV or other serious illnesses. Giving sex education is suddenly no longer just about making sure local morals are upheld. It turns into something that might save lives. So it is worth giving some careful thought to whether or not you provide sex education to teenagers.

With the changing appearance of their bodies, which they are not used to, and the new smells their bodies suddenly produce, teenagers can be very insecure about their bodies and about how they look. Many teenagers are convinced that they are not good-looking, no matter what others think or say. This is one of the reasons why many girls, and boys as well, can become very preoccupied with things that they *can* control about their appearance, such as hairstyles, clothes, and accessories such as caps and jewellery. Some teenagers can become completely obsessed with personal hygiene, wanting

Self-conscious about an unfamiliar, changing body.

to shower or wash several times a day and use all kinds of fragrances. This is usually because they are afraid that the smells produced by their body, which were not there when they were children, mean that they are dirty or that other people will think they are dirty. Reassuring the teenager that this is normal and that the process is the same for all children his age—who will not seem as 'dirty' to him as he does to himself—will help him overcome his fears and doubts.

Although a teenager's size is starting to approach adult standard, with all the growth and changes going on in his body, he still needs more sleep than the average adult. Most teenagers need eight to ten hours of sleep per night to have enough energy to grow, to stay healthy and to concentrate and do well in school.

Mental During their teenage years, from the age of about twelve, children start to develop new ways of thinking:

- Hypothetical thinking: this means thinking about what might happen if this or that would be done; thinking through the possible outcomes of something that has not actually happened.
- Logical thinking: this means thinking while using only the rational parts of your brain, not allowing feelings to get in the way of a decision you make.
- Abstract thinking: this means thinking about things that have no real shape or structure; they are more concepts, such as 'love', 'hostility' or 'dedication'.

EXAMPLE

> *I do not need to jump off a roof to know that that is going to end badly and that I will more than likely break several bones if I do. A nine-year-old will not think about any possible danger at all, he will just be fascinated with what it will feel like to 'fly through the air'. And if, by some miracle, he jumps off a roof and does not get seriously hurt, he will take that as proof that it is safe to jump off roofs. It is only after the age of twelve that children slowly start developing this kind of insight that considers danger, and this development is only completed around age twenty-five.*

These ways of thinking were not possible when the teenager was younger. He needed concrete examples to be able to understand things. Emotions and rationality were a mixture in his head that he could not separate. It was too hard for him to predict what would happen if he had not already experienced something. During the teenage years, these new ways of thinking are slowly learned. This is not something that happens from one moment to the next. The child will go through periods of not being able to keep emotion out of any of his thoughts or decisions, while at other times he will be able to make logical decisions. Thinking abstractly and theoretically are also things that are learned gradually, through a lot of trial and error.

Essential Needs At this stage, the child tries to make sense of his own identity, the complexity of the world around him, and the idea that quite soon, he will be forced to take the step from being cared for to taking responsibility for his own life. This thought can be exciting and terrifying at the same time. The process is made more difficult by the fact that the child's body is changing and he has to deal with all kinds of new things happening to him over which he has little control. Hormones can cause him to suddenly–and temporarily–become very emotional or over-sensitive, while at other times a previously unknown wave of aggression may wash over him, which he may find difficult to deal with or to control. It is important for caregivers to be aware that these things will happen in any teenager's life, and to provide guidance about how to deal with it.

Learning by experimenting.

Teenagers need a certain amount of freedom to make their own choices, under guidance, so that they can learn how to make their own choices in a safe environment. This will make it a lot easier for them to take the step of going out into the world and taking care of themselves. If they have to go from always having to do what they are told to having to decide everything themselves in one step, they are likely to make a lot of mistakes during the learning process.

Teenagers too need someone to depend on through their growing independence.

It can have big consequences when they are fully dependent on their own decisions while still learning how to make them.

The things mentioned so far, go for all teenagers, whether they live in families or in children's homes. However, there are certain challenges that only children in children's homes face. As was explained in Part 1, Chapter 5: 'Essential Psychological Needs', children in a children's home do not usually automatically get prepared for their role in life through observation and taking part in family life. Plus, while children in families do have to eventually leave home to go study, or start a job elsewhere, or to get married, in most cases they will not be thrown out to take care of themselves from one moment to the next on their eighteenth birthday. For many children in children's homes, that is the reality they have to face. In most children's homes, children 'age out' at eighteen years old. In fact, in some countries children's homes are not even allowed to keep children anymore once they turn eighteen.

Because children are expected to take care of themselves from one moment to the next without a family network to fall back on while they are still quite young, it is extremely important to make sure they are prepared for this situation as much as possible. It is not something to tackle in the last few weeks before they leave, it is something that should be part of everyday life for several years. This preparation involves all the things that a teenager is usually taught in a family, such as cooking, washing clothes, keeping the living area clean, buying things in the market, the value of money, fixing small problems and so on. While it is very important to allow teenagers to learn how to do these things and to practise them, there is a very fine line between giving a learning opportunity and having children help out–like they do in any family–and exploiting them by having them do all the work. In Part 3, Chapter 2: '**Ethics** in Running a Children's Home' this will be discussed in more detail.

This children's home cares for a lot of teenagers. The dining hall kitchen is run by cooking staff, but all girls are taught to cook as well. At times cooking competitions are held, between the girls. And occasionally the girls cook lunch on a Sunday, to show off their skills. As they reach the age of eighteen, the children's home gives the girls a choice. If they want to pursue a college education, they arrange for funding to make this possible, as well as safe boarding houses for the girls. If a girl indicates that she would like to get married, the children's home arranges a marriage for her (as is common practice in this country) and provides her with a wedding.

Developing specialist skills.

Teenagers need some freedom to keep certain thoughts to themselves. On the other hand, they need to know that there is a responsible adult available to talk to, who will listen to them, keep their issues confidential, and offer advice, rather than judgement. If such a person is not available, chances are that the child will try to get information in less reliable places, become misinformed, or even just go ahead on his own because no one warned him.

So, the teenage years are not an easy time, but helping a teenager grow into an responsible adult certainly has its rewards.

UN GUIDELINES:

94. All carers should promote and encourage children and young people to develop and exercise informed choices, taking account of acceptable risks and the child's age, and according to his/her evolving capacities.

131. Agencies and facilities should have a clear policy and should carry out agreed procedures relating to the planned and unplanned conclusion of their work with children to ensure appropriate aftercare and/or follow-up. Throughout the period of care, they should systematically aim at preparing children to assume self-reliance and to integrate fully in the community, notably through the acquisition of social and life skills, which are fostered by participation in the life of the local community.

132. The process of transition from care to aftercare should take into consideration children's gender, age, maturity and particular circumstances and include counselling and support, notably to avoid exploitation. Children leaving care should be encouraged to take part in the planning of aftercare life. Children with special needs, such as disabilities, should benefit from an appropriate support system, ensuring, inter alia, avoidance of unnecessary institutionalization.
Both the public and the private sectors should be encouraged, including through incentives, to employ children from different care services, particularly children with special needs.

133. Special efforts should be made to allocate to each child, whenever possible, a specialized person who can facilitate his/her independence when leaving care.

134. Aftercare should be prepared as early as possible in the placement and, in any case, well before the child leaves the care setting.

135. Ongoing educational and vocational training opportunities should be imparted as part of life skills education to young people leaving care in order to help them to become financially independent and generate their own income.

136. Access to social, legal and health services, together with appropriate financial support, should also be provided to young people leaving care and during aftercare.

Chapter 2: Motor Development

Developmental Milestones from Birth to Four Years Old

The previous chapter gave a very brief overview of some of the things that children learn to do at various ages. This chapter gives more detailed information about what you can expect children up to four years old to learn, and at what age. This is not to say that all, or even most children achieve these milestones at exactly these ages; these are averages. The older they get, the larger the range is within which children reach a certain milestone.

> *For instance, walking: Among children who do not suffer from any physical disability, or lack of stimulation, the age of starting to walk without support ranges from about ten months to about fourteen months.*

What can be said, however, is that the younger babies are, the smaller the acceptable range within which they should reach milestones. For example, while with walking the acceptable range is four months or even more, it is different when it comes to one of the first motor development milestones: lifting the head off the surface while lying on the belly. If this has not been achieved by three months of age, so only a month and a half 'late' (though you could also say half a lifetime), this is a serious delay, which will have an inevitable domino effect on future milestones. Because without head control, the baby cannot start building upper body control, cannot start to roll over, cannot start to sit up, and so on.

I do not go into motor development milestones after four years old, because first of all the range of when children learn things becomes wider and wider. Secondly, the older a child becomes, the more her skillset will depend on the opportunities that she is given to learn things. So, it becomes harder to make general predictions about what a child will be able to do.

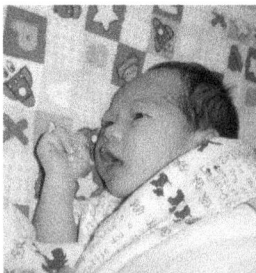

One month
- The baby lifts his head slightly for a moment when he is on his belly
- Hands grasp tightly
- Looks at things and follows them to his **midline**
- Is alert to sounds

Looking around him.

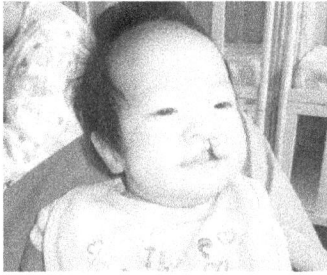

Social smile.

Two months
- The baby is able to lift her head to 45 degrees when on her belly
- Stretches her arms and legs a bit more when on her belly
- Holds her head in line with her body when held upright
- No longer clenches her fists tightly
- Looks at things and follows them past her midline
- Recognises her primary caregiver
- Smiles socially (after being touched or talked to)
- Coos (=makes small sounds)

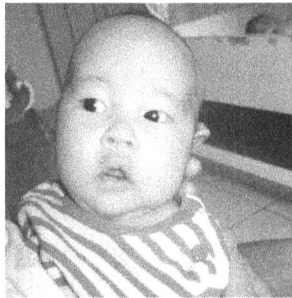

Sustained social contact.

Three months
- The baby is able to lift his head and chest off the surface when lying on his belly, supported on his forearms
- Holds hands open at rest
- Reaches for objects and misses
- Recognises signs that he will be fed soon
- Sustains social contact (keeps it going over a long period of time)
- Says aah or naah and vocalises with pleasure

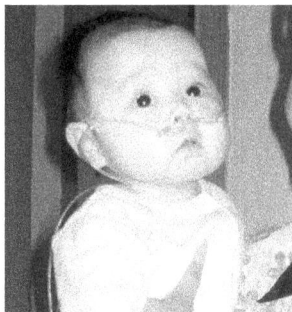

Holds her head steady held in sitting position.

Four months
- The baby starts trying to roll over
- Holds her head steady when held in sitting position
- Is able to sit straight if propped up
- Is able to grab a rattle with both hands
- Is able to bring things to her mouth
- Brings her hands together in the midline and plays with them
- Pulls her dress over her face
- Laughs out loud
- Turns her head to a sound at the same level

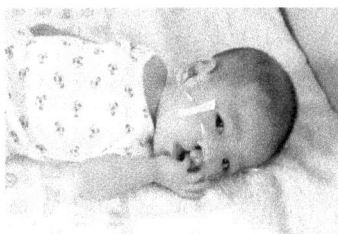

Puts hands and things in his mouth.

Five months
- The baby has full head control
- Is able to grab objects deliberately
- Plays with toys
- Smiles at himself in the mirror
- Looks to see where his toy has fallen when he drops it
- Turns his head to a sound below his level

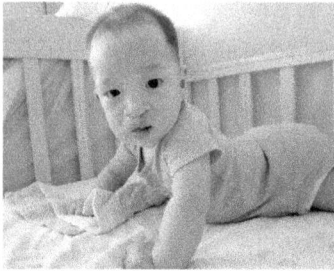

Lifts his chest off the surface, weight on the hands.

Six months
- The baby is able to lift her head and chest off the surface, supporting her weight on her hands
- Is able to sit unsupported
- Puts her feet in her mouth when lying on her back
- Is able to grab objects with one hand
- Passes objects from one hand to the other
- Babbles–talks without using real words
- Tries to get her toy back when she drops it
- Laughs when her head is hidden under a cloth, playing a peek-a-boo game
- Recognises when someone is a stranger

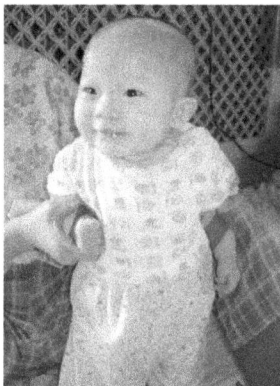

Briefly bears weight on his legs when he is held.

Seven months
- The baby rolls over from back to belly
- Bears his weight on his legs briefly and may bounce when held in standing position
- Can bear his weight on one hand while reaching out with the other hand, when lying on his belly
- Will hold on to a toy in his hand, even if another one is offered
- Resists if a toy is pulled from his hand
- Bangs objects on the table or floor
- Puts all objects into his mouth
- Is able to eat a biscuit by himself
- Makes sounds of more than one syllable, such as mama, baba, and dada
- May have a preference for a certain caregiver

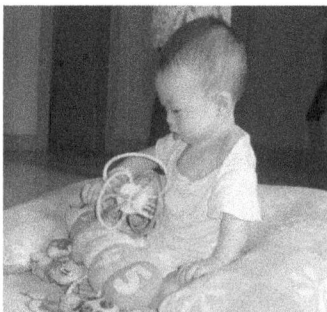

Sits alone with a straight back.

Eight months
- The baby sits alone with a straight back
- Is able to let herself be pulled to a standing position
- Grabs objects between her thumb and index finger
- Uncovers hidden toys
- Responds to her name
- Is able to wave bye-bye
- Reaches for toys out of reach without giving up
- Responds to 'no'

Tries to crawl.

Nine months

- The baby can pull himself up and stand holding on to furniture
- Can lean forward and turn around while sitting
- May move backwards when trying to crawl
- Uses **pincer grip** (=picking up tiny objects, like crumbs, between thumb and forefinger)
- Probes things with his index finger
- Throws or shakes objects
- Plays gesture games (pat-a-cake)
- Puts his arm in front of his face to prevent washing his face
- Says mama without meaning a specific person
- May be scared of being left alone

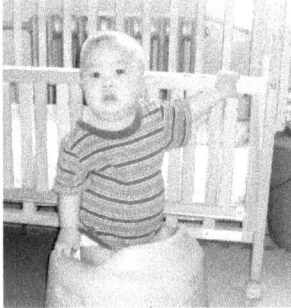

Climbs on the seat backwards and sits like that.

Ten months

- The baby can get to sitting position by herself
- Crawls with abdomen on surface
- Lets objects drop on purpose
- Can understand the meaning of some words

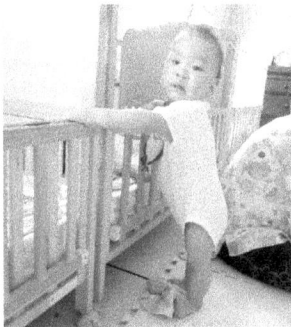

Cruises

Eleven months

- The baby crawls with his belly off the ground
- Is able to lean sideways and turn around when sitting
- Walks with two hands held
- Cruises
- Says one word with meaning
- Likes repetitive games

Puts shapes through holes.

Twelve months

- The baby walks with one hand held
- Lets go of an object to let another person take it, when asked
- Imitates actions
- Comes when called
- Cooperates with dressing
- Uses two words with meaning, other than mama, dada
- Points to pictures in a book when asked 'where is…?'

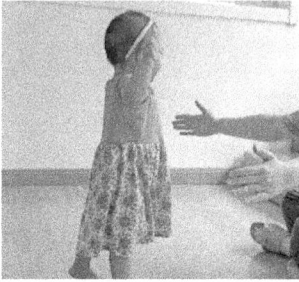

Walks alone.

Twelve to fifteen months
- The toddler walks alone
- Is able to stand without support
- Is able to climb stairs on knees
- Makes a tower of two blocks
- Draws a line with a crayon
- Takes off shoes
- Feeds herself with a spoon
- Follows simple commands
- Indicates some needs by pointing

Copies adults.

Fifteen to eighteen months
- The toddler runs stiffly
- Throws objects while standing without falling
- Is able to walk upstairs, with one hand held
- Make a tower of four blocks
- Uses seven to ten words on average
- Knows five body parts
- Copies adults in tasks
- Feeds himself

Not thrown off-balance by holding something over her head.

Eighteen to twenty-one months
- The toddler is able to walk backwards
- Picks up objects from the floor while standing without falling
- Is able to walk upstairs with two feet per step
- Makes a tower of six blocks
- Asks for food or drink
- Obeys three simple orders

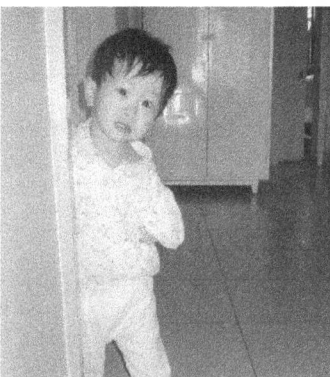

Opens doors.

Twenty-one to twenty-four months/two years
- The toddler runs well
- Is able to walk up–and down–the stairs one step at a time, with two feet per step
- Opens doors
- Jumps
- Makes a tower of seven blocks
- Turns pages one at a time
- Washes and dries hands
- Follows two-step commands
- Uses 50 words correctly
- Uses two-word sentences
- Helps to undress
- Listens to stories with pictures

Plays with others.

Two to three years

- The toddler is able to pedal a tricycle
- Can alternate feet when going up steps
- Is able to balance on one foot for a moment
- Undresses completely
- Dresses partially
- Makes a tower of ten blocks
- Shares toys
- Takes turns
- Plays with others
- Knows his full name, age, and **gender**
- Uses a minimum of 250 words
- Uses three-word sentences
- Has daytime control over bladder and bowel function

Tries to be independent.

Three to four years

- The child hops and skips
- Alternates feet going down steps
- Dresses completely
- Buttons clothing
- Catches a ball
- Knows colours
- Says a song or poem from memory
- Asks questions
- Makes up stories
- Tries to be independent

✳ ——————————

Providing Opportunities for Development

For all milestones at any age goes: the child cannot possibly attain a milestone if he is not given the chance to develop the muscle strength and the skills needed. In normal, healthy children this is not a very complicated thing to do. In fact, parents all over the world for the most part manage to give just the right stimulation to make sure that their child is able to develop normally, without any special education. The problem is that in a children's home there are always many children and few caregivers. There are always many things to do and there is little time. That is why in many institutions a lot of the things that people know need to be done, things that they do themselves at home with their own children, are pushed

Plays a clapping game.

aside as not important. It even seems like caregivers forget to make the link between children they know in their family and the children they care for at work, thereby forgetting that all these children are essentially the same and all have the same needs.

Has belly-time to strengthen muscles.

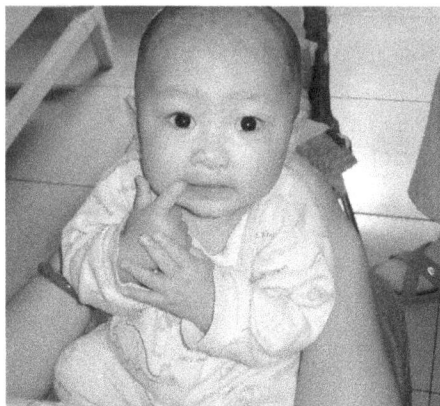

Is held upright with support for practice.

We are talking about things as simple as sitting down and hold-ing a baby; talking to a child; singing to a child; listening to a child; encouraging a child in play; assisting a child in what they are trying to do; and providing the child with enough objects and attention to stimulate him to develop. Of course, there are many other things that need to be done, but that does not mean that there is no time at all for this essential part of the children's care. There is time to sit down with the children in-between other chores and to simply pay attention to them and hold them.

How is a small baby supposed to develop the muscle strength he needs to hold his head steady, when he is always lying down on his back, with his head resting on a mattress or mat? When you hold a baby, even though you support him fully with your hands, you still make his neck work, slowly building up muscle strength, allowing him to develop head control. When the neck muscles have devel-oped enough, the muscles of his upper body will start to develop, and so on. Also, he should not always be lying on his back. From two months old, at the very latest, every baby should spend at least ten minutes a day on his belly while he is awake so that he can practise lifting his head. When he is able to lift up his head, he will start try-ing to lift his head up higher and support himself with his forearms, making his arms stronger. When he can do that, his arms will con-tinue to become stronger and he will slowly become able to support his weight on his hands. Then he will move on to strengthening his legs and learning to roll over and crawl. The baby himself knows he needs to do all those things. All he needs is to be given the opportu-nity to do them.

When a baby is able to hold his head upright, you can start holding him in a sitting position on your lap more and more, giving him the opportunity to practise using the muscles he will need for sitting up. Again, over time, you will notice that he gets more and more capa-ble of holding himself steady longer and longer.

In one location, I noticed that there were several babies of four months old, and some older, who were not yet able to hold their head steady. Then I was asked to look at a six-month-old baby who, when he was put in a baby seat, would let his–rather big–head fall all the way to the side, almost resting on his shoulder. They were afraid there might be something wrong with the boy. I checked the boy and looked around at how the caregivers–who did spend quite a bit of time holding babies–held babies. It was clear to me straight away that there was nothing wrong with little boy, other than that he was not used to using his neck muscles, and with his head being quite big, this was giving him trouble. Looking around, the 'why' behind this was immediately solved too: any baby who was not making a physical effort to be upright, was held in a newborn position. The caregivers continued to hold the babies like this because they had not developed head control, and the babies did not develop head control because they were always held like this. A self-sustaining cycle.

Once I had pointed out ways of holding babies upright while providing them with the support they needed, the babies' development progressed all around.

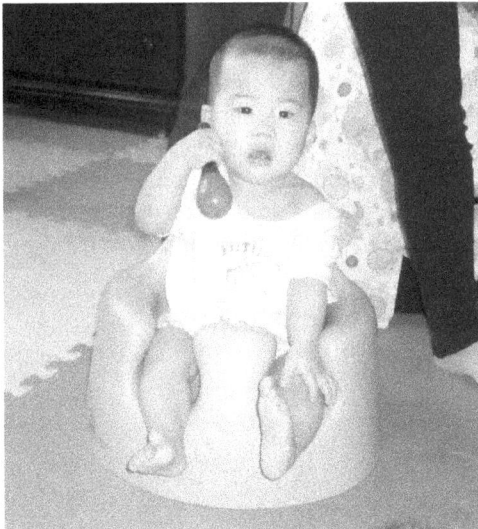

A Bumbo seat gives support for sitting.

When you look through the lists, the same goes for every new milestone. If a child is given the opportunity to build the muscles and skills needed, he will do so. But, of course, if a child has never seen blocks or a tricycle in his life, how will he learn to build a tower of ten blocks or to ride a tricycle by the time he is around three years old? This is not to say that it is essential for all children to learn to ride a tricycle. It just means that if you expect a child to learn a skill, you need to give him the opportunity to do so.

So, giving stimulation and attention is very important. And in fact, in the end it will make your work easier: if you end up with a twelve-month-old who is unable to crawl or walk through lack of stimulation, it means that *you* will be carrying him to and from the changing table, instead of being able to let him go over there himself. It will also save having to invest in expensive physiotherapy or developmental therapy to help the child catch up, later in life.

In some places people use Bumbo® seats (photo), which are great for allowing children who are not able to sit without support prac-

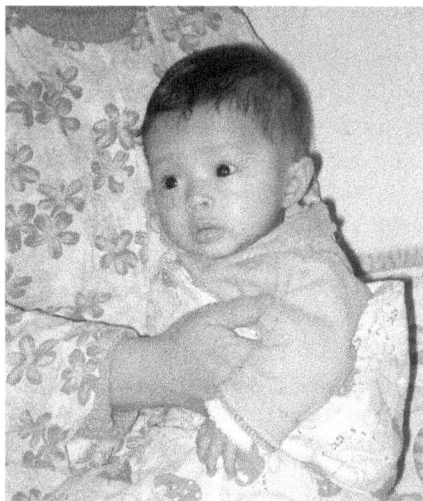

Unable to sit alone, but held in a sitting position.

tise sitting without needing to be held all the time. However, children should not be put in these seats–or in exercise saucers or similar things–until they are able to keep their own head upright without wobbling, and until they do not slump to a side almost immediately while sitting in the seat. If this happens, the child is not yet ready for such a seat, and putting him in it can cause damage to his spine and neck.

It is important to try to find out whether a baby or toddler is delayed because of lack of stimulation–in which case they catch up quite quickly once the situation improves–or if it is because of other problems–in which case they will probably need therapy to help their development. When you are not sure if a baby is suffering from a lack of stimulation and attention, first look if he seems to have any physical disabilities. If he does not and he shows a combination of some of the following signs, then it is likely that he is suffering from lack of stimulation and attention:

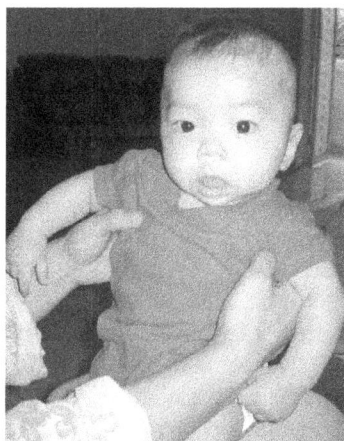

Prevent unnecessary developmental delay in spastic children by giving stimulation.

- Delayed **fine and gross motor skills**
- Low muscle tone: this means a baby is quite floppy
- Language and speech delays
- Passive, withdrawn, unresponsive to others
- Lacks curiosity
- Self-stimulation–rocking, head-banging

If he does have physical problems such as very low or very high muscle tone, which makes it harder for him to learn different motor skills, there are exercises that can be done with him every day to help him continue to develop. However, it is best to have a doctor, a physiotherapist, or an occupational therapist advise you on what would be best to do in his specific case.

Chapter 3:   How Children Think

How children think varies greatly, from child to child and from age to age. It is not possible to look into a child's head and know exactly what is going on in there, any more than with an adult. However, some things are known about the different developmental stages of children's thought processes. At different ages, children become able to understand different things. This changes their view of

Hard to know what goes on in his mind.

the world, and the way they deal with it. It is important that anyone who works closely with children has some idea of the different stages a child goes through during her development, because this gives an idea of what you can expect her to understand, as well as the most effective way of communicating with her. Especially with babies, who are not yet able to tell you what they think, it is very helpful to have some understanding of the developmental reasons behind their behaviour.

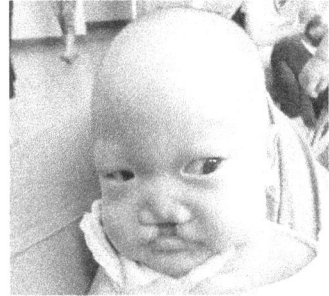

When trying to get a feeling for what very young children under-stand and why they react the way they do, it is important to remem-ber that they usually think very literally and that most of the time they are not fully informed when drawing their conclusions. The lack of information can come either from not being given certain information or from not understanding the information that they have been given.

When I first started taking care of small children, as a babysitter, it became clear to me that in the eyes of some toddlers, I caused trou-ble. They did not know that I only came after their parents called me. And they did not know that, as a fourteen or fifteen-year-old, I had no authority over their adult parents. They saw me as 'really big!' All they knew was what they could see: every time I arrived at the door, their parents would leave the house within 15 minutes and stay away for hours. So, clearly I had chased their parents away!

In this chapter, I will explain some of the thought processes that you usually see in children of certain ages, as well as explain the con-sequences that are the most likely result of common situations in children's homes. It is important to realise that what applies to the thinking processes of a child of any given age—be it six months, two years, or seven years old—also applies to children and adults of all ages who are mentally retarded and whose mental age is the same as the given age.

A large man in his twenties with cerebral palsy had an inner ear infection. He reacted exactly the same as a baby of eight months old–roughly his mental age–might do, by rocking his head violently from side to side against the headrest, to try to do something about the pain and the itching in his head, while crying loudly. He wanted someone to make it go away.

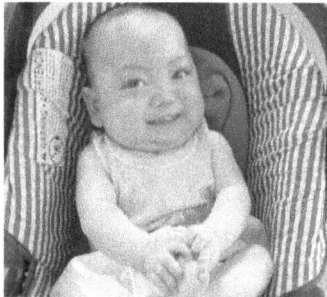

Enjoying life despite a serious heart defect.

Everyone starts out living entirely in the present. Babies (most babies until up to about nine to eighteen months old, some children with mental handicaps for longer or for the rest of their lives) are unable to think about the past or to have expectations about the future. Babies are not able to think in solutions. For a long time, babies have no understanding of the possibility of solutions or change. All they know is that they are uncomfortable now and they cry to give voice to their discomfort. The first few months of their lives they do not even expect anything to come from the crying, it is just a way to express pain, discomfort or frustration. During this stage, it is impossible to spoil a baby, because they have no concept of 'cause and effect': no idea of the possibility to make something happen.

Understanding Cause and Effect

This usually changes around six months of age. I believe the beginning of a consciousness of cause and effect begins more or less when the baby starts rolling over on purpose. The first few attempts at rolling over succeed by accident. The baby reaches over to try to grab something, and suddenly finds herself on her belly, looking around confused, trying to figure out what happened to the world, which suddenly looks very different. After a while, however, she starts noticing that this is something she can make happen. I believe that this realisation is the seed of understanding cause and effect: if I make certain movements, I turn over... and I can grab the toy.

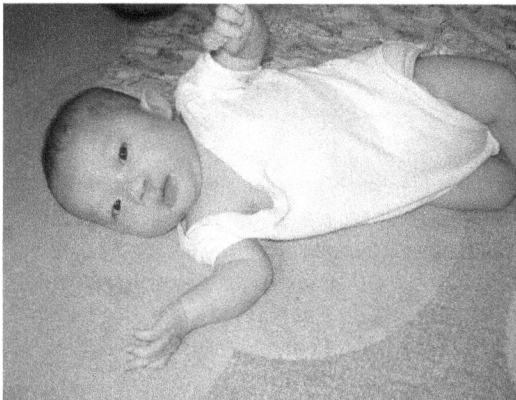

Rolling over on purpose brings understanding of cause and effect.

Once the concept of cause and effect spreads in the baby's mind, she starts to apply it to more situations. One of them being: if I cry, someone will come and pick me up. In other words, from now on, it *is* possible to spoil the baby, because she has figured out that it is possible to manipulate situations; it will not take her long to find out how to do this. That does not mean that you should never do what she asks, or that every time she cries she is trying to manipulate you. However, this is the age from which you can start setting limits, something that will be discussed later, in Part 2, Chapter 6: 'Discipline'.

Fear of Strangers and Abandonment

At a certain age, usually around eight or nine months, varying from child to child, most (but not all) normally developing children become shy or even hysterical when held or touched by people they do not know well. This is an indication that they are able to remember and recognise faces and distinguish between people they know and people they do not know.

If a baby does not become afraid of strangers, it does not mean that anything is wrong. She may just have a very social nature. However, at this age, even babies who do not make a problem of being with a stranger should smile and 'chat' more easily with someone they know than with someone they do not know. The most well-known reaction of a baby during this stage is to start crying when someone she does not know comes too close, sometimes even to the extent that no one apart from one or two primary caregivers are accepted. Though, as has been mentioned before, this preference for certain caregivers will only happen if there is an opportunity to bond with a caregiver.

The baby can also become clingy, not wanting to let her caregiver out of her sight. When she discovers the caregiver has left, she starts crying and may take some time to be consoled. Sometimes, she might also find it hard to go asleep, left alone in a room.

What happens is that the baby develops an understanding of the primary caregiver as a person separate from herself, an understanding she did not have before. Plus, she has developed a certain amount of memory. Before, she would just have been very happy to see the primary

Not too sure about the stranger with the camera, usually they are all smiles.

caregiver, but was not able to remember that the caregiver existed when she was not there. Now she also realises it when the person is not there. A memory of someone who is not present is developing. What makes things difficult is that while a sense of absence or missing has developed, the idea that 'this person will be right back' does not make any sense to her yet, so absence is thought to be permanent, until the person returns.

A girl of about one year old with a complicated heart defect had recently been abandoned by her parents when she arrived at the children's home. From the very start, she would start to cry heartbreakingly whenever anyone left the room, clearly expecting them not to come back again and leaving her alone for good. Not long after her arrival at the children's home in a remote location, she was brought to a different children's home, run by the same organisation, in the capital city where there was access to better hospitals, to find out what could be done for her. She spent several months in the capital and slowly started to become less fearful. After this time, it was felt that she could go back to the children's home that had originally taken her in, so that there would be room for other children needing medical care in the capital. Since I happened to be traveling from the capital to the remote location at that time, I would take her with me. In the remote location, the girl had known me, but this was a long time ago to her, and now she saw me as a stranger. So, she screamed when I picked her up and brought her to the car that would take us to the train station. On the way to the train station, the little girl realised that no one she knew was going to 'rescue' her, so she moved her trust to me, temporarily. For the entire eight-hour journey on the train she clung to my body, with her arms wrapped around my neck as if her life depended on it–she probably thought it did. When we got to the remote children's home, where the caregiving staff wear the same uniform as in the capital, she immediately abandoned me to cling to one of the caregivers. During her time in the capital she had learned to put her trust in the uniform, rather than in the individuals in them, who changed with every shift. For several weeks, the girl became absolutely terrified whenever I entered the room. She was afraid that I might take her on another horrible, scary trip to who knows where, away from what she knew.

It is important to provide support during the period when the baby experiences fear of abandonment, which is quite difficult on the child. However, it is equally important not to go too far. Even though the baby does not yet understand that you will be coming back, it is still important for you to tell her so, every single time, so she can learn. Giving in to her desire to have you not leave her at all or to stay longer will not help her overcome this fear.

The most important and most difficult thing to do, is to always warn the child when you are leaving–but do not wake her up for it; when you know the baby or toddler is going to be asleep when you leave, it is a good idea to let her know that you will not be there when she gets up before she goes to bed. This is something that most people try to avoid. A common method is to try to sneak out while the baby is distracted, to avoid a **tantrum**. This does not work. It may avoid you seeing the tantrum, but the tantrum will still take place as soon as she discovers you have left. At this age, children

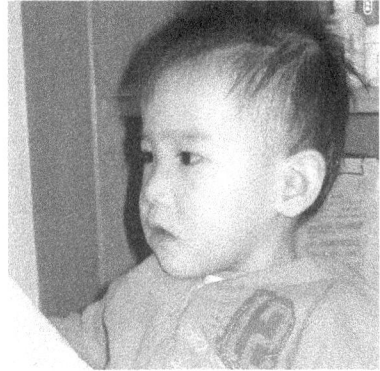

Anxious she will be left, even while she is being held.

are usually very watchful, so it will most likely not take her long to find out that you have gone.

What is worse, however, is the effect on the child of you disappearing without warning. For you it might seem perfectly predictable that you are going, because it is the end of your shift, the same time you leave every day. For the child, these things are not as predictable. She does not know what time it is, nor can she recognise many of the signs of something that is about to happen. This is too complicated to oversee for a small child. So, for her, your leaving comes as a complete surprise.

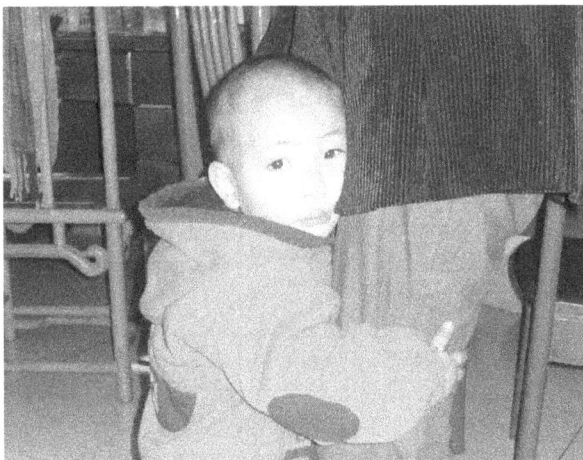

If not handled well clinginess can continue for months.

If you regularly leave unannounced, this will make the child extremely insecure and more and more clingy with every time it happens. Because in her eyes, after a few times, your unpredictable disappearance could happen, without warning, at any given moment! There is no way to make sure she is safe from this 'catastrophe' happening, except to stay with you and make sure you are never, ever out of her sight.

While if she always gets a warning before you leave, and it is explained to her again and again that you will be coming back and that in the meantime there are all these other great things to be done and people to take care of her, after a while she will start to relax. Because, slowly, the concept of 'people who leave, come back again' will start to sink in. At least, as long as you make sure you never tell her someone will be coming back when you know they will not. This I will cover in more detail under the section 'Lying to Children' in Part 2, Chapter 4: 'Interaction with Children'.

So, despite the annoyance of having to go through some crying every time you leave, for a while, if you give warning every time, in the end you are doing both yourself and the child a favour. Once the child realises that there will always be a warning; that all the crying in the world will not stop you from going out when you have announced that you will go; and that eventually you will come back again, life will become a lot easier for both of you.

Power Struggles

Once a toddler approaches about two years of age, he starts to find out a lot of things about the world and about how he can make things happen. He has a good understanding of the cause and effect principle by now, and experiments with how to use it to his advantage. At times, it can seem like he is trying to make your life difficult. He gets himself from one spot of trouble into the next, at an amazing rate, barely giving you the time to keep up with cleaning up after him. Actually, what he is doing is not aimed at you. He is simply trying to explore the world and to find out how things work through trial and lots of error.

Convinced they can take on the world by themselves.

Toddlers are also known for their ability to be very stubborn and to confront their caregivers. They have discovered their ability to say 'no' and are very curious to see how much power this gives them. While adults do not like to admit it, it does give them a lot of power. It is entirely possible for a caregiver to pick a child up and put him somewhere else, to prevent him from doing what he would like to do and to deny him things he wants. However, when you think about it, when it comes down to it, if a toddler *really* refuses, you cannot force him to eat, drink, sleep, walk, stand, sit, pick something up, and so on. As an adult, a caregiver has a great ability to convince and manipulate a child, but if the child decides to take it all the way, he can go limp and there is nothing you can do about it. He can refuse to swallow and if you force him to by closing off his nose, he can throw everything back up. One of a caregiver's top-priorities is making sure that children never find out how much power they really hold.

A caregiver should never get into a power struggle with a child. First of all, if you find yourself in a power struggle, you have lost already. There is no way to get out of a power struggle gracefully: generally, all parties end up losing. Secondly, when he really goes head to head with an adult, the average child digs his heels in so deep that he may get a glimpse of the relative powerlessness of his caregiver.

Power struggles are almost always born out of a deep frustration on the part of the caregiver when trying to get through to a child about something. In these situations, it is very hard to keep a cool head and continue to think reasonably, while that is exactly what is needed in such a situation, more than at any other time. When thinking clearly, you will see that you may stand a much greater chance of 'winning' if you use your adult abilities to convince and manipulate than if you enter a full-on head to head struggle. Or, if manipulation does not work, you can simply let the child experience the consequences of his 'no'–always provided this is a safe option of course–and let him learn that way.

The caregiver announces that it is naptime and the almost two-year-old girl says 'No' in a determined way. She looks ready for a fight. Instead of entering into this fight, the caregiver moves the subject. She asks the girl: 'Do you want me to put you to bed, or do you want Anna to do it?' 'Anna!' the girl says triumphantly, feeling that she had been able to make her own decisions and that she has not given in to the caregiver. Anna picks her up and she goes to bed quietly.

When your own mind is made up about what is going to happen, there is no point in entering a discussion or an argument with a child. This is almost certain to spiral out of control, into a power struggle. When there is still room for input and change of plans, discuss it with the children and see what they have to say about it. This makes them feel valued. But if the course has been set, you simply explain what you want to happen and why it needs to happen, and leave it at that.

Mealtime is one of the main areas of struggle in many places. It becomes a problem at some point in any place where a young child lives. Trying to force a child to eat is useless. He either will eat or he will not. All the shouting, screaming and crying–on one or both sides–surrounding it simply become part of the process. When a child feels he needs more attention, he may even create a fight over eating, simply to get the negative attention that he can provoke here.

Usually children are willing to obey reasonable demands.

Instead of forcing a child, give him a choice and let him experience what that choice brings. For instance, a child who will not eat can be offered to be spoon-fed, to be allowed to eat by himself, or to not eat. This last option is seen as a non-option by many caregivers, but that is not true. Missing one meal will not kill any healthy child, nor will not eating for a day or even very little for several days. A power struggle would have to have escalated to an enormous extreme before a child will truly not eat, once he is hungry. If the child chooses not to eat, respect that.

Halfway through the meal and just before taking everyone's plates or bowls away, check again–friendly and casually–if the child is sure he does not want anything. Explain that not eating the meal will also mean no desert and no snacks until the next meal. If the child insists that he does not want to eat, accept this and leave it at that. During the meal at which the child does not eat, he does have to remain in his seat until everyone else is done. If he starts screaming or crying, throwing a tantrum, ignore it. Ask him once if he is trying to tell you that he does want to eat. If he says 'no', leave it at that. 'Not eating' should not be rewarded with attention–positive or negative.

If the child complains of hunger or asks for snacks before the next meal, explain to him that he is hungry because he did not eat at the last meal and that if he eats again at the next meal he will be fine, but that he will not get anything until then. Usually, one skipped meal is enough to make the point–unless not eating brought a lot of attention, or hunger was quickly resolved afterwards by snacks and treats, which are preferred to meals. If the child chooses to skip another meal at some future point, remind him that he got hungry and unhappy about it the last time he skipped a meal, but if he insists, respect his choice again.

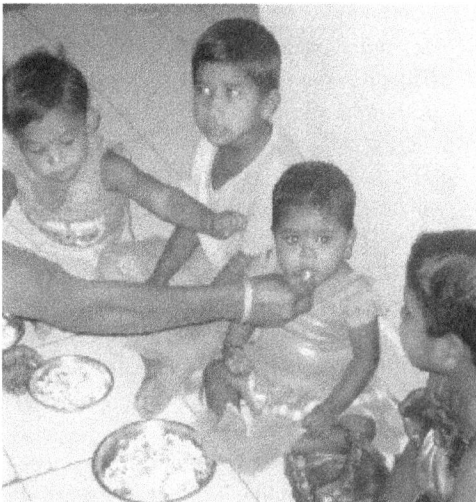

Trying to MAKE a child eat.

The only children with whom this will not work, are children who cannot feel hunger because of a physiological condition. However, this is very, very rare, even with children who have severe brain damage. If a child finds out that he will not get attention, or snacks, by not eating at mealtimes, the problem is usually gone within a few days. Though it is possible that he will try to test you from time to time, to see if there is anything to be gained from starting a fight.

While power struggles are particularly common with toddlers, that does not mean that they do not happen with older children. One of the things that is important to be aware of, is that while tantrums (a child screaming and crying, and possibly throwing himself on the floor) are usually a passing thing–a period when the child is two to three years old and is trying to discover how solid the rules are and how much power he has to bend them. If they are rewarded, tantrums can become a set feature in daily life for many, many years. A tantrum is rewarded if you provoke a power struggle–which provides attention, even if most of it is negative–, if you allow something after first saying 'no' several times, if you **postpone** going away or if you give the child something he likes to make up for not getting exactly what he wants. Rewarding tantrums in any of these ways will teach the child that it is useful to scream and cry, and it will encourage him to do it more often.

Do not give room for a fight, let them decide.

Lack of Empathy

Before they have learned that it is not acceptable to hit other people, all toddlers hit others for some time. Some toddlers do it more and longer than others, but they all hit people occasionally. Initially hitting is not a deliberate action, it is more of a motor exercise: moving your hand and arm around and bringing it into contact with something–or someone–else. It is part of exploring the world. It gets him attention from caregivers, even if it is only negative attention. Most importantly, however, he is likely to figure out quite soon that it is his action that provokes a reaction. That realisation is very interesting to many toddlers, and they want to explore it further. After some more time–and experimenting–the toddler usually starts to realise that others do not like being hit, so apparently hitting is an effective way to get revenge when you are not pleased about something.

Up to three to four years old, most toddlers have no ability to empathise with other people. They are also unable to make the connection between what they experience under certain circumstances and what someone else might experience under the same circumstances. A toddler's thinking roughly is: 'If I hit you, that is funny. If you hit me, it hurts, so that is not funny at all.' He cannot understand that you feel the same thing when he hits you, as he does when he is hit by someone, because he does not feel pain when he hits you.

When children hit caregivers, you usually see one of three responses:

- Allowing the child to continue hitting, because he does not understand that he is doing something wrong. Doing this can cause the situation to get out of control eventually, because while being hit by a two-year-old is not likely to really hurt you, if you allow him to continue, by the time he is eight he will hurt you and it will be harder to stop him.
- Getting very angry with the child from the first time he hits, telling him he is bad for hitting you and possibly punishing him for it. This will confuse him very much, because he did not intend to do anything wrong and he is not sure what it is that he did wrong.
- Hitting the child back, thinking it will teach him what it is like to be hit. However, it does not work that way, because as explained, until three or four years old, a child is not able to make the connection between what you feel when you are hit and what he feels when he is hit. Another side effect is that if you hit him, you show him hitting is acceptable behaviour. So you are actually encouraging him to hit people.

Getting ready to take the toy away from him, she has no empathy yet, so she does not know he will get upset.

If you want to stop a child from hitting—and it is a good idea to do so—it is more effective to take a middle road. Stop him from hitting you by holding his hand or wrist, and without getting angry but making it clear that you are serious, explain to him that he is not allowed to hit because it hurts you. To start with, he will not really understand why he is not allowed to hit, but he will know that it is not allowed. If you continue to stop him every time and explain to him why, he will slowly start to learn and begin to understand. He still will not truly realise that you might be hurt until he is about three or four years old, because he cannot feel it himself. But telling him that you are hurt can help this understanding to begin. And in any case, he will understand that hitting is unacceptable behaviour. The same thing goes for biting, pinching, scratching and other aggressive behaviour.

With children older than four, it is useful to talk to them when they are violent or aggressive. Ask them why they did what they did and help them think about whether violence is the best approach when they are frustrated or angry. Asking the child how he would feel if someone else did the same to him, can help him understand that there is a link between his feelings and the feelings of other people.

Empathy is not only about understanding that someone else can feel physical pain at a moment when you do not. It is also about understanding that other people have emotions and that your actions can influence those emotions. It is extremely important that children get help in developing an understanding of other people's emotions and how their actions affect those emotions. If a child does not develop this understanding, he can grow up believing that while he is a real person with thoughts and feelings, the people around him are like robots, only there to help him and entertain him. If he does not real-ise that other people have feelings, he will not feel the need to take their feelings into account when he does something. This can lead to very severe behavioural problems and to behaviour that is very cruel, dishonest and dangerous.

You can help a child to develop this understanding by not only explaining when what he does physically hurts you, but also when what he does makes you sad, angry, happy or proud. Give him words for these emotions and help him put words to his own emotions when he feels them. When he interacts with other children, you can make a point of letting him know that he scared another child or that he made another child very happy.

Stubborn Independence

As a toddler becomes able to do more things, she often also gets more determined to do things by herself. She wants to explore her freedom and abilities and may refuse all help. This can be dur-ing play, getting dressed, eating, and so on. It is very good for her to practise doing these things herself, but at times it can be very time-consuming.

Children should be given the op-portunity to do things for them-selves. It is not always possible to give the toddler half an hour or more to dress herself: sometimes you are in a hurry and need to be on time for something. How-

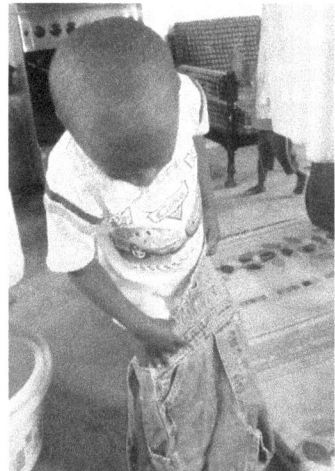

Allowing a child to attempt dressing himself, while you help another.

ever, often it *is* possible to give her an opportunity to try things for herself.

If the child is allowed to sometimes try to do things for herself, she is more likely to be willing to compromise at times when there is no time for her to do things on her own. When you explain to her that today she needs to get dressed quickly, so this time you will help her, and next time she will be allowed to do it herself, she is more likely to cooperate—if she knows from experience that the promise for next time is true—than if she is never allowed to try to dress herself.

When you have several children to dress in the morning, you can start by giving the child who insists on doing things herself her clothes and let her try, while you continue dressing the other children. When all the other children are dressed, you can go back to her and help her finish, or if she is almost done already, allow her to finish by herself and just straighten her clothes afterwards. Praising success will help her become more confident.

With a toddler's sudden drive towards independence, there can also be a lot of frustration when she is not able to do something. The average toddler does not have a lot of patience. When she first starts trying out new skills such as dressing herself or building something with her toys, she may get very upset when it does not go right the first or second time. She does not realise that these things need practice. Nor does she know that there are some things that are still too difficult for her, because her motor skills have not yet developed enough.

Although some children may accept help when they are unable to do something alone, many toddlers will become even more determined to refuse help when they get frustrated. And after several failures—or only partially successful attempts—she may give up completely, screaming that it is impossible. It is a delicate situation. If you come and say, 'let me do it for you', the toddler is likely to either start screaming even harder in frustration, or to simply walk away, feeling defeated.

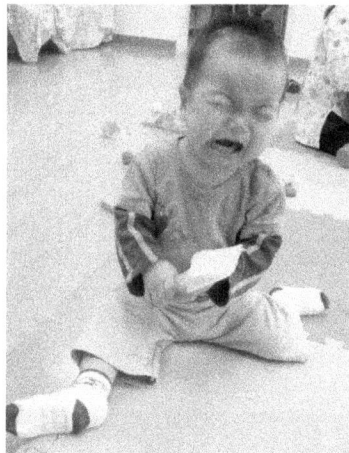

Frustration when the game does not go as he feels it should.

You can start by saying from a small distance, 'but it is going really well', and naming the parts of the process that the child has done successfully. There are almost always some things that were done well, even if the end result is not what it should be. Then say, 'this step is just a little difficult, let's do that together'. And then you gently come forward and help her through the next step—rather than doing it for her—while praising her efforts. This approach is more likely to get her cooperation, as well as being more likely to help her improve her skills and teach her to keep trying until she is able to do something.

Another period of fierce independence is likely to start when the child becomes a teenager. Most teenagers feel like they understand and know more than they actually do. The teenager feels like she is practically an adult already and may resent any attempt at help or guidance. Again, it is usually helpful to think about what kind of compromise is possible, allowing the teenager a certain amount of independence and freedom to do or decide things for herself, while at the same time keeping her safe. If a teenager is involved in deciding on the rules she has to follow, she is more likely to actually follow them.

A five-year-old girl with a bag full of fireworks. She sees this as interesting and fun, not aware of any danger.

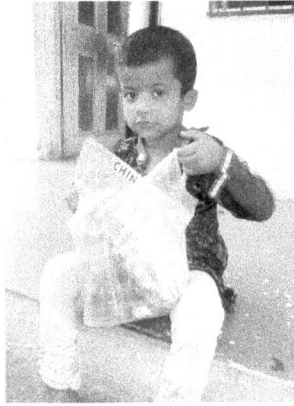

Predicting Consequences

Young children have no ability to predict the consequences of their actions. Especially if they are about to do something that they have never done before–in other words, things they have not yet experienced.

> When a baby crawls straight over another baby, putting a knee in her face along the way, he does not know that what he is doing is very dangerous. All he knows is that he is trying to get to the other side of the room and that this is the most direct route.

> When a young child puts a small chair on the table and then puts a stool on top of the chair and then starts climbing this unstable tower, she does not know that she will likely end up going to hospital for stitches, at the very least. All she knows is that she wants to look out of the window, and like this she might be able to reach it..

The kind of thing that will give you a big fright, but is not fair to punish if he has not been told he is not allowed to be up there.

Seeing, for example, a child climbing up a self-made tower gives adults a big scare. The first reaction is usually to get very, very angry with the child, while the child is confused about what she has done wrong. It is very important to stop these children from doing dangerous things, because they are putting themselves or others at risk. You should explain to the child that he cannot do this again, and why. However, it is not fair to punish him for the scare he did not know he was giving you.

> *A four-year-old girl has learned a new song and wants to show her ability to her caregiver. While she is singing, the caregiver is looking away from the girl, at other children who look like they might get into trouble. While she is singing the song, the little girl pulls a wooden pallet towards the radiator and leans it upright against it. Still singing, she starts to climb the 'ladder' that she made. Then the pallet slides down and lands flat on the ground. The little girl falls with her face on the radiator, leading to several loose teeth and a lot of blood.*

The fact that young children are not able to predict consequences or judge situations makes it very important that the adults looking after them are always alert and nearby to make sure that they do not get themselves into very dangerous situations. Part 1, Chapter 4:'Safety' gives more information about this.

Taking on Blame

As mentioned briefly in Part 2, Chapter 1: 'Global Developmental Milestones', children from about five years old are very quick to take the blame for things that happen. Even when the things happening are completely out of their control, or when for an adult it is obvious that someone else is responsible for what has happened, the child will find excuses for other people and take the blame themselves. Particularly when the other people involved are people she loves, the child prefers not to acknowledge that they could be part of a situation or a result that she does not like. So, she will reason that they did not know what was going on, or that they had no choice but to do what they did, or even that it only seems like they were involved, but really they were not.

Likely to feel bad and blaming themselves even about things that are outside their control.

At the same time, she will also come up with—often very unlikely—ways in which she was responsible for what happened. This can even take the form of thinking that a person she loves was hurt in a car accident because she did not make her bed in the morning after being told by a caregiver to do so. To an adult this sounds like complete nonsense, but in a child's head these thoughts can become fact and she can be torn apart by guilt and self-blame. This leads to very low self-esteem, something that will be explained further in Part 2, Chapter 5: 'Self-Esteem and Self-Confidence'.

Whenever I say goodbye to children when I leave after a visit to a children's home, I make a point of telling them that my leaving is not because they have done anything wrong. I explain that I love them very much and that I will miss them, but that I need to go home, or that I need to go visit another home with children who want to see me too. If there is a particular child who has been a bit troublesome in the last days before I leave, I make sure I talk to him or her separately and tell them, once again, that I am not leaving because he did not eat his food, or because she did not listen to her caregiver, and that I hope to see them again on another visit.

To prevent children from taking on unnecessary blame and suffering, it helps to make a point of telling the child that whatever happened is not her fault. If you know more about the cause of what happened, you can explain this to her. For example, you can tell her that someone falling off a ladder was simply an accident, which was no one's fault, and that it had nothing to do with her walking by on the other side of the road. Or that the car accident was caused by the other driver being very drunk and driving carelessly, not by the child.

Apart from taking the blame for things that happen in their day-to-day lives, children who live in children's homes very often also burden themselves with the blame for their parents abandoning them or for their parents passing away. This is a terrible burden to carry, and it is one of the reasons why counselling should be available to all children in children's homes.

Private Possessions

Children in children's homes are almost always very careless with their clothes, books and toys. This leads to great frustration among caregivers. Caregivers of individual children's homes are not aware that this is the case almost everywhere, and they usually feel that the children in their care are particularly destructive and ungrateful.

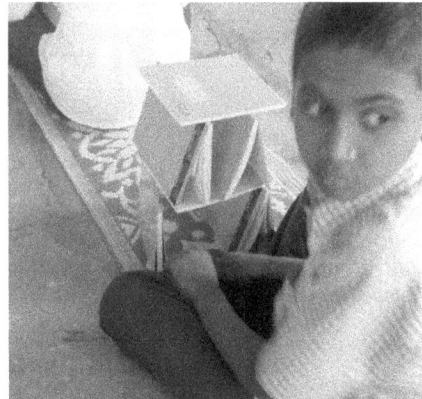

Using things in ways they are not meant to be used, which will end up damaging them.

Toys and books are received with great enthusiasm. They are played with vigorously, passed from hand to hand, ripped away from smaller hands, taken apart and in the end, destroyed. This gives the impression of ingratitude. This seems like a valid complaint.

However, it is not quite fair on the children. The reality is that it is very rare for children who live in a children's home to have any experience with private possessions. Everything is there for everyone. Even if someone says 'this is yours', their experience is that this will only be temporary. Sooner or later one of the other children is going to get their hands on it—either by force or by taking it when it is lying somewhere—and *if* it ever gets seen again, it probably will be broken or torn. These children have never had the experience that when you have something for yourself and you take good care of it, it will last longer and you will be able to enjoy it longer. Their experience is that one way or another, it is going to be destroyed by the end of the week, so what is the point of being careful with it?

On day 1, I saw that the youngest children had been given a yellow bus, which would ride by itself if you pushed it in a certain way. The children were looking at the bus on all sides and pushing it between them. On day 2, I saw one of the bigger boys pulling the yellow bus along by a piece of string that he had tied to the bus's bumper; the bus would not ride on its own anymore, but the older children were having fun pulling it around. On day 3, I did not see the bus. On day 4, I saw two pieces of yellow plastic that had belonged to the bus. That was all that was left.

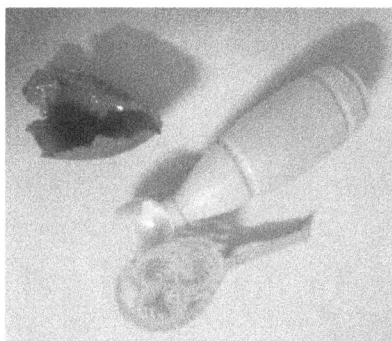

The remains of some toys that have been thoroughly enjoyed for a brief time.

Much of what seems like careless destruction on the surface is in fact only curiosity and exploration. Taking something apart to find out what is inside it and how it works, and then finding out that you are not able to put it back together again. Or using something in a way that it was not made for and finding out that this will break it. Or, quite simply, the continuous use of dozens of pairs of hands for hours and days, which more or less equals the use of one pair of hands for a year or more.

Children cannot be expected to know how to value possessions when they have never had the opportunity to have anything for themselves and keep it whole for a long time. Children in families also need to learn this. Toddlers are never careful with their toys or clothes. As they grow up, children in families learn to take care of possessions and they learn that if you take care of them, you have something and you can enjoy it for a long time. If you do not take care of it, you do not have anything anymore.

If you want the children in your children's home to learn this lesson too, you will have to invest some time—and possessions—into teaching them. For children to learn to take care of their clothes and books and toys, they need to be in a situation where they have clothes and books and toys of their own. Caregivers will need to support this by making sure children do not take something that belongs to another child without asking the owner for permission. The child should be encouraged to take care of his possessions, explaining that if he breaks, rips or dirties them, he will have to go on with it broken, ripped or dirty and he will not get a replacement until it is time for everyone to get something again. It will take time for children to learn this, and the older they are when they start, the harder they will find it to learn to respect other people's things. All staff needs to be absolutely consistent in not allowing children to spoil the possessions of others. To help children learn about having private possessions and taking care of their things, the very least they will need to have is a small box that can be locked and to which only the child has the key. Without that, the child has no way of keeping his possessions safe and he will not learn to care for them.

You do not have to teach the children about possessions. It is a lesson that is not relevant in all cultures. It is just important to realise that if children have never had the opportunity to learn about caring for possessions, they cannot be blamed for carelessness or ingratitude when it comes to keeping their clothes and books and toys in order.

✱ ———————————— **Favouritism**

Most caregivers have their favourites, once they have been in a children's home for a while. These are children with whom they have a

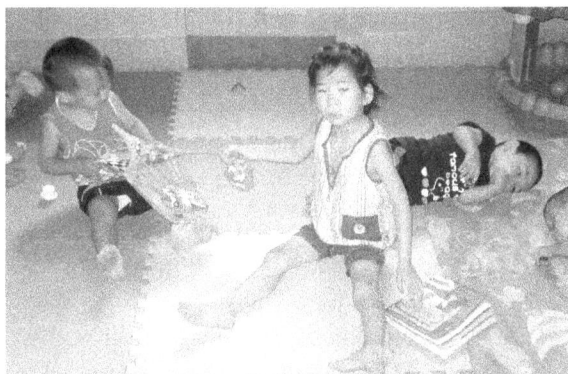

special bond. In itself, there is nothing wrong with this, particularly because, if there are enough caregivers around, different people will have different favourites so more or less every child will be a favourite. But it is important not express this special fondness by always taking 'your' child's side against others in arguments or by giving 'your' child lots of extras—no matter if it is food, gifts, or attention—that the other children do not get. This kind of favour-

Though younger, the boy feels more entitled than the newly-arrived girl.

itism has several unfortunate effects that are not intentional, but that are still real.

One effect is that the other children will feel left out. In this case, it is more than just a feeling of disappointment. Children living in a children's home generally already have very low self-esteem and feel like they are probably there because they are not good enough— even if they will not say it out loud and may laugh loudly if you suggest it to them. Seeing that another child is clearly liked more than them will make these negative feelings stronger. They may see it as proof that they are not good enough, that they are not lovable. Because look, you chose the other child over them! That must have a reason. More information about the importance of self-esteem can be found in Part 2, Chapter 5: 'Self-Esteem and Self-Confidence'.

The children's home director of a home that was particularly strug-gling to get enough funds to feed the children properly had one big favourite among the children. It was a four-year-old boy, who had arrived as a tiny baby who seemed unlikely to survive for a long time. She had helped save his life, by personally caring for him in his early days, even letting him sleep with her. This bond had stayed intact. While the other children were expected to be grateful for what they were given, this boy was always given more attention, as well as special snacks. One of the older children would be given money—from the director's own pocket—to go buy a snack for the boy. When the child got back, the snack was given to the boy and all the other children in the room would watch him eat it, almost drooling as they did so. This little boy did not have any friends among the other children.

Another unintended effect can be that when you give your favourite child extra treats, this can make the other children very resentful and jealous. At moments when you are not there, or when you are not watching, the other children may turn against your favourite, taking revenge for the way they were excluded. So, in effect you made your little favourite the target of anything from being exclud-ed from the group to having his treats taken from him, to bullying, to beatings. This was never your intention, but it is something that you need to be careful of.

In some places, very small children's homes are set up by families who have their own biological children as well as the children from outside whom they care for. It is logical that the parents' bond with their own children is stronger than that with the other children, and that their protectiveness is stronger for their own children. Howev-er, in some places the divide between the kind of care given to the biological children and that given to the other children is so great that it causes a lot of unnecessary suffering.

It is, of course, a positive thing that you have opened your home to these disadvantaged children. But if living with you means that they have to watch your children eat large amounts of good food while they only get the bare minimum, if they have to watch your children sitting on your lap and being sung to while they never get any physical contact and only get shouted at, and if your children are allowed—and in some places even encouraged—to show off their greater privilege and power in front of the other children, then you are only adding to their suffering. In cases like these, the children would probably have been better off living in the street.

Giving one child a little more attention than the others is fine. Giving one child a little extra on one occasion, if it is not very noticeable, is also not the end of the world. But for the sake of all of the children, including your favourite, please do not be obvious in giving extra attention and extra treats to just one or two children.

This particular children's home mostly took care of babies and most children only stayed there for a few months before they went into foster care. However, there were four children between eighteen months and three years old. One of these children was three years old and he had been at the children's home since he was very small. The office staff had known him for a long time and was particularly fond of him. So, several times a week, this boy was allowed to come into the office and watch TV there for a while. Sometimes he was given extra treats and at times he was taken along when someone had to go out to buy things. The other toddlers looked longingly at the door whenever he was taken out of the room and the older ones would cry at being left out. The little boy himself was becoming more difficult to handle, because he knew that the office staff particularly liked him and that if he threw a tantrum, he would usually either get what he wanted, or get something else to make up for not getting what he wanted.

Trouble Learning

Most children's homes put great importance on the children in their care getting a good education. In some cases, more money is put toward school fees and the buying of books and school uniforms than toward feeding the children. With all these efforts made, the disappointment is great if a child ends up not doing well in school. In many places, a child who does not do well in school is quickly called 'lazy' and is blamed for not trying hard enough or not putting in enough work to do well. There may be cases when this is true, but in the vast majority of cases, there is a different reason why the child is not doing well.

Some of the reasons that I have come across quite regularly are:
- Essential basic needs not being met: if these are not met, brain development is unable to take place normally and this can affect the child's ability to learn; Part 1, Chapter 5: 'Essential Psychological Needs' gives more information about this.
- Problems with vision/hearing: if a child is not able to hear or see well, he may not be able to understand everything that is said in class or he may not be able to read the blackboard or his books, which makes it very hard for him to study properly. If there is any sign of a child not hearing or seeing well, he should be tested, so that something might be done to help him.

- Mental Retardation: some children have mild forms of mental retardation that are not very obvious, but that do make it harder for him to learn.
- Dyslexia or dyscalculia: these are conditions, the first to do with letters and the second to do with numbers, where a child is perfectly able to read individual letters or numbers, but when they are put together into words or bigger numbers, in his mind the letters and number seem to change places. This makes it very hard for him to read correctly. It is possible to help a child who has this problem by allowing him to say things out loud or to have questions read out to him, rather than having to write and read himself.
- Sleep deprivation: in many places, children do not get enough sleep, often because they are made to do homework or study until late at night. This makes it much harder for the child to concentrate and to absorb the knowledge he is supposed to learn. In Part 1, Chapter 3: 'Sleeping', there is an overview of how much sleep children need to be well-rested.
- Difficulty concentrating in a noisy environment: when a lot of children are studying in the same room, particularly if all of them are reading out loud or if smaller children are playing in the same room, it can be very hard for a child to concentrate on his own work. Some children have

All these children are saying their lessons out loud, making it hard to concentrate.

no problem learning in such circumstances, but for other children it is almost impossible.
- Fear of punishment: if a child is regularly punished for not doing well enough in school, the stress caused by the fear of punishment can make it impossible for him to focus on his studies. This is a situation that keeps getting worse and worse: if he cannot focus, he will do badly again, he will be punished more often and he will become even more scared of punishment and less able to learn.
- Giving up: if a child has been told over and over again that he is too stupid to learn things, or if despite his very best efforts to do well in school, he keeps getting very poor grades, a child may decide to give up on school work completely. Because in his mind there is no point in trying, and he lacks the encouragement and praise needed to make him keep trying.
- No opportunities to ask questions: if a child is trying his best on his school work, but gets stuck because he does not understand something; he might be able to go on and do well if there is someone he can ask for help. However, if that is not possible, either at school or

at the children's home, he is likely to stay stuck and he may give up.

- Behavioural problems: there can be many reasons why a child might have behavioural problems or be depressed, such as a traumatic experience in his past, a medical condition or not having his essential basic needs met. Whatever the reason for behavioural problems, once a child has them, it can become extremely difficult for him to focus on his school work.
- All work, no play: if the whole day is devoted to either chores or schoolwork, with no free time to play and relax, the child will not only lose his motivation to do well in school, he will also slowly lose his ability to concentrate properly. To take in information and do well in school, it is necessary to relax and be free from time to time.
- Too many hours behind a book: if you spend more than 1.5 to 2 hours at one time behind a book, trying to take in the information, you will not be able to take in any information anymore. Your concentration will be gone completely. You can, of course, stay seated behind the book for another few hours, but it will be more like staring at the page than like learning: breaks are important.

So, instead of blaming the child straight away, it is a good idea to consider whether any of the issues mentioned in this list are relevant to a child who is not doing well in school. If you have identified an issue that seems relevant, you can think of how you can help the child to do better.

UN GUIDELINES:

85. Children should have access to formal, non-formal and vocational education in accordance with their rights, to the maximum extent possible in educational facilities in the local community.

✳ ————————— **Survival of the Fittest**

In places where there are many children over the age of four and very few caregivers, management is often surprised and shocked by the chaos, the violence and the aggression that is seen among the children. Often the presumption is that there is something wrong with these children, that they have a bad nature. Because why else would they be acting like that?

The answer is that they are acting like this in an attempt to survive. First of all, as explained in Part 1 Chapter 5 'Essential Psychological Needs', when a child's essential basic needs are not met—and with too few caregivers, it is not possible to meet those needs—the child's brain has been programmed to try to fight for what she needs, and if she does not succeed in getting it, her brain structure will change.

Secondly, apart from needs not being met, with fewer than one caregiver for eight children at the very most, there is going to be a lack of supervision. When there are too many children, it is quite simply not possible to keep your eyes on all children most of the time. No one would be able to do that.

Without supervision or guidance, children will find their own way of dealing with things.

In a situation where children are left on their own, without supervision and guidance, most of the time they become aware that they have to solve situations by themselves and they will do that in their own way. Because children are still learning about culturally and socially acceptable behaviour and do not know or understand the rules yet, they do not yet have a proper sense of morality–this means an understanding of what is acceptable and 'proper'. They are not immoral–which means a perverted or deranged sense of what is wrong or right–but they are amoral–they do not have a sense of what is morally wrong or right. Their decision-making is not based on what is culturally or socially acceptable, and most children do not yet have an impulse to help and support those weaker than them. The most important motivation for their decisions is their own self-interest and survival–in other words: what do I want or need?

This means that a group of children who are largely unsupervised and unguided will enter into a mode of survival of the fittest. Through physical fights and bullying they will determine who is strongest and who has the biggest say. Once this hierarchy is established, the children at the bottom of the hierarchy can expect to be bullied, abused in various ways and to lead a life of fear.

This is the natural consequence of the situation in which these children grow up: not having their essential basic needs met and having no supervision and guidance. There is no inborn difference between these children and the children you know in your family. If you were to switch the children in your family–who are considered gentle and well-mannered–with children in the children's home and you kept them in their switched positions for several years, you would find that the children from the children's home who were raised in your family (provided they were treated the same as the family's own children would be) are growing up into gentle, well-mannered people and the children from your family appear to suddenly be rebellious, ungrateful, aggressive and depressed. The conditions in which they live influence these children's behaviour. The more extreme the living conditions, the greater the influence on behaviour.

Chapter 4:   Interaction With Children

✱ —————————— **Why Talking to Children Is Important**

It is very important to communicate with children of all ages, even newborns. Even when they cannot talk or communicate themselves, talking to children and explaining things to them serves several purposes. First of all, talking to a child is giving him attention. This fulfils some of the essential basic need for attention that all children have.

Secondly, to develop thinking processes, children need to develop a language to think in, and this development starts with being talked to. It does not make a lot of difference whether this is spoken language or sign language, as long as they are offered a language in which they can develop their thought processes.

Talking, singing, playing games: they all help development.

Thirdly, it is quite true that when they start out, babies do not understand language. They do not know what your words mean. But they do have an instinctive understanding of the general meaning of what you are saying; they can sense it. They learn the meaning of words by repeatedly being told and explained things in similar situations. By talking and explaining, you slowly provide the baby with both the rules of language, the rules of behaviour, and an understanding of the way the world works. By starting to use words like 'no' and 'well done' even before they are able to understand the words themselves, you help them get familiar with the words' meanings. Every time 'no' is said, the baby is picked up and placed somewhere else or otherwise stopped from doing the same thing again, and adults are displeased. Every time 'well done' is said, adults are smiling and the baby is encouraged to do the same thing again. These are principles that slowly take hold in the baby's brain.

Understanding will slowly grow when you give more information such as: 'No, you can't do that, because it hurts me' or 'No, you can't do that, because you will fall and hurt yourself'. When these kinds of messages are combined repeatedly over time with the experience of falling, getting hurt and then being asked 'Did you fall? Did you hurt yourself?' for example, a connection will form very gradually between the theoretical 'you will fall' and the actually experience of falling and it hurting.

Once toddlers start to understand what you are telling them, explaining things to them serves another purpose, which is to make them feel more safe and secure. If difficult or big things always come as a complete surprise, it gives a child the feeling of helplessness and vulnerability. If many unexpected things happen in a relatively short period of time, he is likely to become very stressed and nervous. After all, if there is no warning or way of predicting that unpleasant things will happen, they could happen at any moment. Maybe even right now... or now... or now! The child becomes very tense, ready to deal with the impact of anything that might happen at any time. This is not a

Anxious, expecting nasty surprises.

healthy way to live, and can cause health problems as well as behavioural problems.

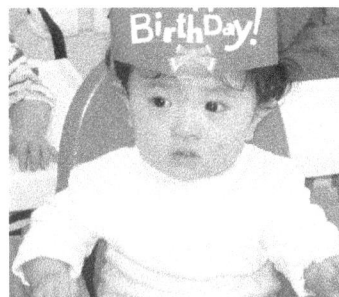

Of course, life throws difficult things at everyone out of nowhere from time to time and we have to deal with that. However, there are often some warning signs that help us prepare for what might be coming. There are also signs that indicate quite reliably that nothing big is likely to happen for a while. Especially in the life of a small child, there is not very much that cannot be predicted by the adults around him. It is just that many adults, whether they are parents or caregivers, do not warn the child. Either because, in their eyes, it is obvious what is coming, because they cannot be bothered to explain it, or because they expect crying or a tantrum and prefer to postpone having to deal with it until it becomes inescapable.

A two-year-old boy calls out to his caregiver many, many times every hour. And every time she does not answer immediately, he starts crying and goes into a panic. The caregiver is getting very tired of this and she impatiently answers him, saying 'I'm right here, why do you need to keep calling out all the time, I'm HERE!' The reality is that if she needs to leave, she sneaks out without warning the boy, because if he knew she was going, he would scream and cry. This means that in the boy's experience, he regularly calls out for her, only to find that she is not there. This is why he feels the need to check whether she is still there or not many times an hour: he knows that she can disappear, without warning, at any time.

The long-term benefit of a child who does not feel like life is waiting to surprise him in unpleasant ways all the time far outweighs the short-term inconvenience of having to deal with a child who is crying about something he does not want to happen. Plus, if you make a habit of explaining things to a baby from the start, before you can even be sure he understands what you are telling him, he is likely to already feel more secure and trusting once he reaches the toddler stage, meaning there will be fewer tantrums.

Older children are a little better at predicting things that will happen, so it may not be as necessary to warn them about every little thing. However, it is helpful to make sure that they are told about big events in advance, whenever possible. This goes both for happy events, such as a festival, a celebration or an outing, and for events they will not be happy about, such as a caregiver leaving her job, or an upcoming doctor's visit. Just like with telling toddlers that you are leaving to help them develop a sense of trust that you will not be leaving if you have not warned them, it will help older children feel more secure if they know that they will be told in advance when something big is happening and that it is very rare for big things to come as a complete surprise. Being told in advance allows the child to prepare for what is coming. And it helps build his trust in you.

UN GUIDELINES:
68. The child should be prepared for all changes of care setting resulting from the planning and review processes.

Lying to Children

Caregivers and parents all over the world lie to children. The aim is usually not to deceive them; the adult simply tells the child what he thinks she wants to hear, to prevent crying or tantrums. The problem with not telling children the truth is that, in the long run, there are a lot of consequences that are often not considered. First of all, if you lie to children, they learn from your clear example that it is acceptable to lie, and they will follow your example and start to lie as well.

Secondly, telling a child something that is not true or making a promise you have either no intention of keeping or cannot be certain you will be able to keep may prevent or put an end to the crying at that moment. However, once the child realises the truth, and usually they do figure it out eventually, this discovery will bring on the tears or tantrum anyway. In other words, the lie did not get rid of the issue: it only postponed it.

A child was being quite difficult and to make him cooperate, someone from management told him that if he did what he was told, he would be allowed a ride on a helicopter–something he had wanted to do for a very long time. This was, of course, a crazy promise that was impossible to be kept. So, at that moment, the boy immediately did what was asked of him. Then he asked to be taken to the helicopter. He was told that he could go tomorrow. For many weeks, the boy kept bothering all caregivers and management staff several times a day, asking to be taken on the helicopter, as promised. As it became clear to him that it might not happen, he became more difficult to deal with and very uncooperative

Thirdly, as children start to realise that what you say is often not true, they eventually learn that you cannot be trusted: what you say does not need to be taken seriously, because you will apparently say anything at all. By regularly making promises that you do not keep–and it does not matter whether this is because you were never going to, or because you did not think through whether it was possible–children will learn to only believe things when they happen, and will not be so easily calmed down or bribed with promises anymore, even when a promise was sincere and would have been seen through.

If you threaten with things that you have no intention of doing to make something happen–such as taking away or destroying toys, leaving the child behind alone in the street, or getting other people to punish her–this will very soon become clear to the child as well. Once the child realises that the warnings you give are nothing more than empty threats, she will push you to prove yourself. Any further threats you make will become a joke, and it will be your own fault.

EXAMPLE

At a train station, a child was being very difficult and refused to listen to his father. This even led to dangerous situations, such as him running away into a large crowd of people to get to the escalator. After a while his father had had enough and threatened to call the police if the boy would not listen. The boy still did not listen and the father pretended to call the police on his mobile phone, saying they could come to get a little boy who would not listen to his father. This did not have much effect either. A few moments later, a police officer happened to pass by while patrolling the station. The father pointed and warned the boy that the police had come. No effect. Then the father took the boy by the arm and dragged him towards the police officer, who ignored them completely and walked on. The father was left to deal with his son by himself, and with the result of having made too many empty threats in the past.

Empty threats can cause more problems than just a loss of believability of the person who makes them. For instance, in a medical situation I often hear caregivers, and also doctors and nurses, make threats such as: 'if you don't stop crying, I will give you an injection'. Apart from being untrue, this also worsens the child's fear of doctors and needles. This makes it likely that the child will become even more uncooperative at the next doctor's visit.

Lying about dangers–something that happens very often–is particularly dangerous. Even though it is usually done to protect the child, the risk is too great to take.

The child will learn from experience that your warnings need to be taken with a large pinch of salt. Therefore, she is more likely to ignore a future warning and plunge head first into danger. So she is at greater risk after your warning than she was before being lied to, despite good intentions.

There is a hot stove in the room; the children need to stay away from it. The caregivers always tell a child that the stove is hot, even if it is not at that moment. This is done to make sure the child always stays away from it, which seems like the safest thing to do. How-

Exposed hot stove.

ever, one day the little girl decides to find out for herself what 'hot' means and if it will really hurt if she touches the stove. The moment she decides to try this out, it is summer and the stove is completely cold. She goes to the stove very carefully, expecting something to start hurting at any moment. But, since nothing happens, she comes closer and closer, until she puts both her hands on the stove and it still does not hurt. Suddenly, she is discovered by a caregiver and taken away from the stove quickly, while being told 'do not touch the stove, it is hot, you will hurt yourself'. This is very confusing to the girl, because she has not hurt herself at all.

Several months later, this little girl makes her way over to the stove again while her caregiver is not watching. This time she is not careful, because she already knows that nothing happens when you touch the stove: she tried it before. Just before she reaches the stove, her caregiver screams that she has to get away from the stove or she will burn herself. That is what she was told last time and nothing happened, so the little girl confidently puts both her hands on the stove anyway. She lets out an enormous scream. When her caregiver reaches her, she has to pull at her hands to release them from the burning stove, some of the skin comes off her hands, and straight away both the palms of her hands start to cover with big blisters.

Instead, you might tell the child that sometimes the stove is hot, and that it is dangerous to touch it at any time, because you cannot see from the outside if it is hot or not. This can be demonstrated by asking the child if she can tell if the stove is hot or not from a distance, at a time when it is hot. She cannot. You can carefully approach the stove together with the child, and allow her to experience the radiating heat, without going close enough to burn her. This way she learns how to assess the danger herself, while continuing to trust you.

Pain is another issue about which caregivers rarely tell the truth to children. Caregivers are often confused when a child starts crying when a doctor wants to listen to their lungs and heart with a stethoscope. After all, it does not hurt, and they told the child. In this case, what they said to the child happens to be true. But how is the child supposed to know that? After having been told that getting an injection and having a broken leg set would not hurt, how can they know that you are telling the truth about the stethoscope?

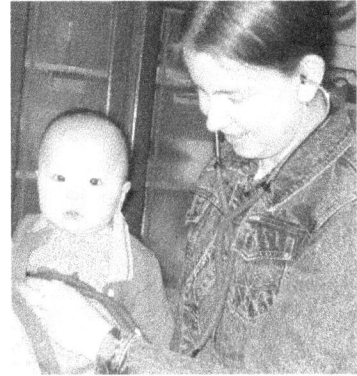

When the child knows he can trust you, he stays calmer.

In a particular medical children's home, the standard practice was that when a child was well enough and no longer needed specialist care, he or she would go into local foster care until an adoptive family had been found for the child. A week before adoption would take place, the child would be removed from the foster family and sent to stay at the children's home. This was done to allow the child some time to grieve over the loss of his foster-parents, before having to make the next big adjustment: settling into a permanent new family. Most of the children would cry most of the time for three or four days and then they would start to come to terms with the situation. It was heart-breaking to see a child so sad and at times the caregivers would say literally anything to try to cheer the child up a little and to make him stop crying. Though it was done with the best of intentions, it sometimes went too far. Caregivers would try to comfort the child by telling him that his mother would be coming back soon–meaning the foster mother, the only mother the child could remember. The child would, in fact, never see this mother again.

Now ask yourself: when this child has been adopted, is starting to bond with his new family and cries when the adoptive mother goes out for some shopping and the adoptive father tells the child: 'Your mother will be coming back soon', what is the child likely to think?

Instead of telling the child that his mother will be back soon just to stop the crying, you help the child a lot more if you explain the real situation, even if it will not put an end to his tears straight away. It will help him deal with the difficult transition from the foster-family that he knows and loves to the adoptive family who are complete strangers to him–and who in many cases look and sound weird.

> You could say to him: 'Your (foster-)mummy and daddy did not want you to go either. They love you very much and they are very sad that you are not living with them anymore. But they cannot take care of you their whole lives. The reason why they have let you go is that they know that there are a mummy and daddy who are able to take care of you their entire life. They want to take care of you and love you so much, that they are coming all the way over here to make you their little boy. Your (foster-)mummy knows that even though right now it is very sad, letting you go with this new mummy and daddy will make you the happiest for the rest of your life. On Thursday, your new mummy and daddy are coming. They have been waiting for a long time to finally meet you and give you a hug. They are so happy that you will become their little boy.'

Thinking of what might help children deal best with the difficult things they need to go through and learn is a more sensible strategy than to only think about how to make your life easier right now at this minute. In the end, making your life easier right now will end up making your life—or that of the next caregiver—a lot harder, regardless of what it will do to the child . Caring for the child can become harder if what you say causes more crying and tantrums, more clinginess and more dangerous accidents that need to be dealt with in the future.

✱ ——————————— **Lying Children**

Even if a child has never been lied to by her caregivers, and so has not been taught to lie by her role models, it is almost certain that she will lie to you at some point. This is not a sign that the child is bad or dishonest by nature. Lying is a part of children's natural development. To start with, it is part of their language development to find out that it is possible

As children start discovering the world, lying is part of discovering how language works.

to say something that is not true. Then they find out that saying something that is not true can be used to get yourself out of trouble or that you can get someone else into trouble by lying—as a kind of revenge. At this point, lying becomes part of the child's survival techniques. Only later will she start to learn that lying is not socially acceptable and that there are negative consequences to lying a lot and being considered untrustworthy or even deceitful.

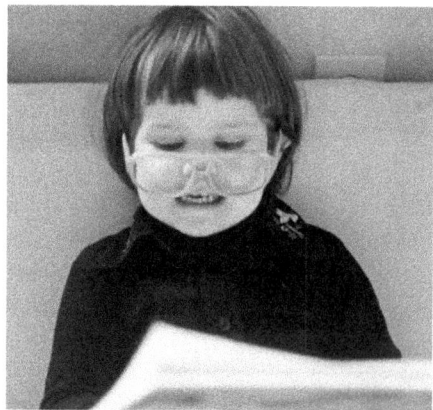

How much a child will lie depends on several things:

- Whether the adults around her lie very much.
- Whether lying is necessary for self-protection–for example if small mistakes usually receive very severe, painful or humiliating punishments, this will motivate the child to lie to escape the punishment.
- Whether the child is taught that it is not acceptable to lie: if it is not explained to her that and why lying is a bad thing, she has no way of knowing.

One way of encouraging children to tell the truth is to reward honesty. So, for example, to give a lighter punishment to a child who has honestly confessed to having done something wrong, than to a child who lied about it before you found out she did it.

It is important to be aware that children will sometimes lie and that they cannot always be trusted at their word. Being aware of this helps you make sure that you try to get more information, from various sources, about any serious matter. However, on the other hand, you should not be too quick to jump to the conclusion that a child is lying simply because you do not like the answer you get. Both taking a child's word as true unconditionally and taking a child for a liar unconditionally can have very serious consequences.

In a children's home, there was a suspicion that a sixteen-year-old boy was doing some bad things. This was confirmed, to a certain extent, when they searched the dorm he shared with other boys. However, based on the things they had found, the management came to some pretty extreme conclusions. That evening, the boy was called into the office in front of the manager and the director of the children's home–I was asked to be there too. The boy was questioned and he admitted to some minor offenses, but he denied the more extreme accusation and gave an explanation for the things that had been found–which quite frankly sounded much more reasonable than what the manager was proposing. Other children were called in, one by one, to give their view on parts of the story told by the boy, and for the most part all these stories–independently–supported what the boy said. However, at the end of it all, the manager and the director were convinced that everyone had been lying and that their conclusion was still the right one. The boy was thrown out of the children's home, 'for the safety of the children'.

If a child feels that no matter what she says, caregivers are going to think she is lying, she has no reason to be honest anymore. No one will believe what she says, so she may as well lie.

Being Taken Seriously

Many caregivers–and parents–feel that the children in their care do not listen to them when they tell them something. At times, they are right. However, a lot of the time it has much to do with the way in which they tell children something.

> A boy, who is almost three years old, is playing with his caregiver and several other children. After a few minutes, he slaps his caregiver on the arm. She tells him not to hit her, with a smile, and then tickles him. Not long after, he hits her again. With a smile, she wags her finger at him and says, 'No, no, no!' in a song-like voice. This happens several times. Eventually, almost immediately after being told 'no' again, the boy slaps her face, while expectantly looking her straight in the eye. Now the caregiver gets very angry with him, she shouts at him for being bad, for not listening and for being so bold as to look her in the eye while hitting her. The boy looks very confused for a moment and then starts crying. He thought they were playing a game!

When you play games with children you often joke that they should not do something, to provoke them into doing it. For example, you may tell him not to grab something from your hand, or not to climb onto something, to make him do just that. This is said with a smile and doing these things is rewarded with praise, attention and fun. If you use the same sort of voice and expression, a young child is not able to tell the difference between these situations and situations in which you tell him not to do something because he is not allowed to.

If you want a child to take you seriously, you need to appear serious. There is no need to get angry or threatening straight away, but it does make a big difference if you use a serious or even stern voice and look at the child without smiling. Make it very clear that you are not

If you want to be taken seriously, your face and tone of voice should show that you are serious.

joking and that you expect to be listened to at these moments. Once this message has arrived, you can go back to smiling and playing with him.

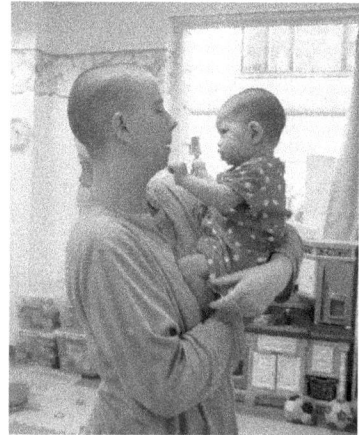

Whether children take you seriously will also depend on whether you take any action to stop them from doing something you told them they could not do, or to make sure they do the things you told them to do. If all you do is tell them and then warn them again and again and again without further consequences if they continue to do what they want, children are not likely to take you seriously. In Part 2, Chapter 6: 'Discipline', you can find more information about this.

✱ ——————————— **How Children Learn**

We often think that most of what children know comes from what we tell them and what they read about in books. It is certainly true that children learn a lot from what we explain to them and from the reading material they get. However, most of what a child knows and is able to do, she has learned through observing the behaviour of other people, particularly the adults around her, and through her own experience.

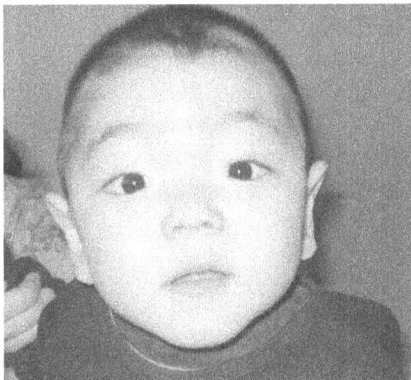

A toddler closely studying an adult.

Watching real life through the window, from a distance.

'Do as I say, not as I do' is the wish of many people who are raising children. They feel that it is okay to use rude behaviour, for example, and think that if they just tell the children not to act like that, all will be well. But children observe adult behaviour very closely, thinking that what they see is what it means to be an adult. They are not yet able to tell what is a good role model and what is a bad role model. They try to copy any behaviour they see in adults around them, trying to get every detail of it right, so that they can be just like the adults they know best. In this process, children pay much more attention to what they see adults do than to what they are told. Being a role model is what it means to be a caregiver. The children in your care will do all they can to copy your behaviour. So, maybe it is a good idea to think about the role model that you present with your behaviour, not with your words. Compare this to how the children around you behave; generally speaking, you will see the two are quite alike. In Part 3, Chapter 4: 'Caregiving Staff' there will be more information about your function of role model.

Children who grow up in a family get to observe the roles that men and women have in the world, in the community and in a family, from the day they are born. They see how men and women interact amongst themselves and between the sexes. They see how elders are treated. They see how people with a different status to their own are treated, relative to their own position in society. Children get to see all these things day in, day out. They take in this information, and slowly they will start to act like the adults around them as much as possible.

Children who grow up in a children's home are cut off from society. Until they reach school age, their world is the grounds of the children's home. Even when they do go to school, where they meet teachers and classmates, they still have not come into contact with the concept of family, or with their place in society outside of the classroom and the children's home.

The caregivers and role models of these children usually mean well, but they are more concerned with keeping the home running smoothly than with the child's emotional development or wellbeing. The caregivers usually have much the same role as a teacher: someone who is to be respected and obeyed, at a distance from the child, rather than the caring and nurturing role models that children in families have. In other words, while the world view of a child who grows up in a family holds both people who provide support, love and safety, and people who are authority figures, to be respected and obeyed, the world view of a child in a children's home is much narrower, because it only contains people from the last category.

All caregivers and educators have more or less the same goal in mind for the children: to provide them with good social and moral standards, as well as good practical care. The goal is not the problem. What is sometimes more difficult is to know how to reach it.

Teaching Values
It is possible to teach children what is right and what is wrong by explaining things to them. You can teach them about justice by giving examples and explaining why something is or is not fair. However, as I said before, however well you are able to put these things into words, your actions will speak much louder to the child. If your behaviour does not match what you say, the children may learn from your behaviour that justice does not exist.

Values can only be taught by example. Telling a child about the virtues of this or that is not going to have any effect if she never sees you acting in line with your words. One area that is very important in this respect is religion. In a lot of children's homes, it is considered very important to raise children as good, spiritual people, within the teachings of a particular religion–which religion we are talking about in individual homes is not relevant here. Caregivers and management are often disappointed in the lack of piety or religious feeling in the children.

When adults do not show any sign of taking things like prayer assembly seriously, how can the children learn?

A particular children's home has a board that is largely Hindu. However, it prides itself in the fact that it does not turn away any children, Hindu or not. While the majority of the children in the home are Hindu, there are also quite a few Muslim children there as well as some Christian children. As proof that they are open to all religions, the management proudly announce to me that aside from Diwali, they also celebrate Christmas. This is nice to hear. But it does then surprise me that when I am at the children's home at the end of Ramadan and Eid comes around–which could be called the Muslim equivalent to Diwali and Christmas when it comes to importance–there is a day off school, as it is a national holiday, but there are no celebrations whatsoever. Some of the Muslim children pointed out to me that this was their big day, but there is no festival for them. This experience spoke louder than words of being welcoming to all religions.

However, in most cases, it is not hard to see where this comes from. Very often children, are told stories and teachings from their religion, they are taught to pray and to observe other religious rules, but in many cases the caregivers are not particularly good role models when it comes to integrating the religious teachings into daily life. If a child is constantly reprimanded and made to do chores without receiving gratitude, how is she going to understand the principles of respecting and loving others?

EXAMPLE

In a children's home, a daily prayer assembly is held before dinner. The children sit down in lines, boys on one side, girls on the other side. Everyone prays together, out loud. Adults patrol the lines to make sure they are completely straight, to make sure the children close their eyes at the right times and that they hold their hands in the correct position. Corrections are not done discreetly, but rather they tend to disrupt the prayers. The adults sitting in the front, facing the children, generally do not have their eyes closed. They tend to sit or stand there with a bored expression on their face, as if they are waiting for it to be over. Usually, one or more of them will be checking their phone, some may even take a phone call. Some adults are talking with each other.

The caregivers are very annoyed that children are not doing things right, that they are not taking the prayer assembly seriously and that they even whisper together during prayer. I explained to them that even though I know the meaning and the importance of the prayer assembly, if I had to learn about this from the adults–the role models–who attend it, I would not get the impression that it is something to be taken seriously either. If the adults cannot be bothered to seriously take part in the prayers for 15 to 20 minutes, how can you expect the children to do better?

Chapter 5:   Self-Esteem and Self-Confidence

Self-esteem is how much you feel you are worth. Someone with low self-esteem feels that he is worth very little or even nothing, someone with high self-esteem feels that he has worth and value. If you believe that you are not worth much, it makes you less likely to protest when someone treats you very badly, because you feel that you probably deserve it. If you have high self-esteem, you are able to stand up for yourself and say: I do not deserve to be treated this way, stop it! It is easier to have some self-confidence if you have enough self-esteem. Without feeling you are worth something, it becomes hard to believe that you are able to do things. Having low self-esteem and low self-confidence can lead to shy and withdrawn behaviour. Or it can lead to a child acting very aggressively, to try to hide that he feels worthless.

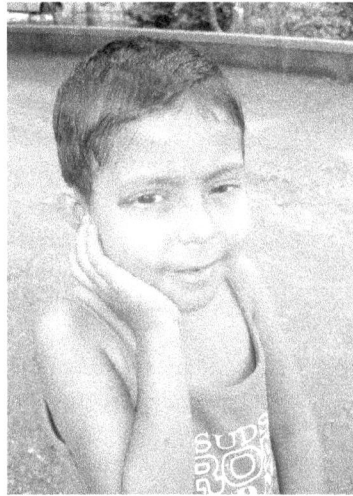

Extreme shyness is a sign of lack of self-confidence.

Self-confidence is a belief in yourself and your own abilities. When you have self-confidence you are able to listen to people criticising you and decide for yourself whether you think they are right or not. If you think they are right, you try to improve yourself and do better. If you do not think that what they say is fair, you let them talk and ignore what they are saying. A self-confident person will not allow people to make him feel bad about himself when he knows there is no reason for it.

> *"I have never tried that before, so I think I should definitely be able to do that."*
>
> *Pippi Longstocking by Astrid Lindgren*

Self-confidence is very important for anyone to have, because it gives a person inner strength. Believing that you are a good person who is able to do and learn things, will make you try harder at those things, instead of giving up when something is difficult. It will help you enjoy life more and it will help you not to break down every time something goes wrong, thinking that this is what you deserve and that it will always be like this. Self-confidence is also what helps you stand up for yourself and make your own decisions. If someone with self-confidence is asked or told to do something that he does not agree with, because he knows it is wrong or that it is bad for him, he is able to say 'no'. While when someone tells a person with low self-confidence that, for instance, she should try using drugs, or she should allow someone to have sex with her, because that will make people like her better, this person will not have the strength to say no. She will go ahead with it, even though she might not want to.

Self-confidence is something everyone can build, though it does take some work. The work involved in building self-confidence mostly has to do with daring to look at yourself very honestly and getting to know yourself completely, both the good parts and the parts you are not so happy about. The first step towards building self-confidence is realising that there are no 'bad' parts in you. You are *good*! Sometimes, you behave badly; everyone behaves badly from time to time. But it is important to always remember that while what you *do* may sometimes be bad or wrong, you *are* not bad! This also goes for the children in your care. While a child might be mischievous or naughty, it is his behaviour that is bad, not the child himself.

No one gets self-confidence automatically. We all have to build it for ourselves. For some people this is harder than for others. It becomes especially hard to feel good about yourself and build your self-confidence when you do not receive praise or encouragement, and when you are often told that you do things wrong and that you are bad. Being told very often that you are bad or useless will make you believe it. You may think that if everyone says so, it must be true. When this happens, instead of building self-confidence, you will be breaking it down and with it you break down your self-esteem too: you will start feeling that you are worth less and less.

As mentioned before, without high self-esteem, it is harder to build up self-confidence. In this respect, children living in a children's home are at a disadvantage. As we saw in Part 2, Chapter 1 and Chapter 3, children often blame themselves for bad circumstances or bad events, even if it was something that was completely out of their control. Children in a children's home all live away from their family, and almost all of them will blame themselves for that to some extent. If a child's parents have passed away, he may feel that he should have done something to prevent that, that he should have looked after them better or—if his mother died in child birth—that he should never have been born. If parents or other family members are known to still be alive, or if nothing is known about his family because the child was abandoned, the child will feel that he must have done something to deserve to be rejected. All these thoughts will leave the child with less and less self-esteem, feeling that he is worthless and terrible. That is a very difficult point from which to start building your self-esteem and self-confidence.

It is very important to be aware of this, because it works the same way for all people, children and adults alike. When you deal with the children in your care, be aware that how you talk to them can do a lot to either help them build their self-confidence, or to make sure they start feeling like they are worthless, or even more worthless than they already think they are. Small children do not yet have an opinion about themselves. They are waiting for important adults in their lives to tell them if they should think well of themselves or if they should think badly of themselves. You are one of those important adults in the life of the children in your care.

Being excluded and ignored breaks down self-confidence.

What Breaks Down Self-Confidence and Self-Esteem

- Regularly telling a child that he is bad, instead of saying that his behaviour or what he has done is bad.
- Ignoring the child, not listening to what he tells you most of the time, not looking at what he wants to show you most of the time, and not giving more than minimal attention; this will make the child feel he is not important enough to be noticed, so really, he is worth nothing.
- Regularly taking over something that the child is doing while showing impatience, because it will be done better and faster if you do it yourself; often it is true that something would go better and faster if it is done by the caregiver, but the child also needs to be given the opportunity to practise and learn. If you regularly take over, complaining about the quality and speed of the work done by the child, the child will start to think that he is probably not able to learn to do it properly anyway, otherwise he would surely have been given the chance to do so. As a result, he will feel useless and stupid.
- Comparing the achievements of the child to those of someone who did better. This makes the child feel that nothing he does is good enough and that you do not think he ever does a good job.

- Shaming or humiliating a child in front of other people. Being shamed in front of other people makes a child feel very small, inferior and worthless, and if it happens regularly he will be convinced that this is only because he really is small and worthless.

Two visitors came to the children's home and the children's home director sat and talked with them, surrounded by playing children. She told them the story of a girl who was now six years old, who had been severely beaten by her family before she came to live at the children's home. Then the child was called and made to show her scars to the visitors. The visitors showed a lot of compassion and made a nice donation. The girl looked thoroughly humiliated.

We were waiting outside the dining hall for the bell to ring to indicate that dinner was ready and a teenage girl who had recently arrived at the children's home was hanging on my arm. A manager joined us and asked me if I knew the girl's history. Since I had been working with this manager for quite some time already, I was able to answer: 'No, and you are not going to tell me while she is standing right here, even if she does not speak English'. The manager smiled and nodded.

Children who live in an institutional situation, for whatever reason, by definition have had to live through psychologically difficult experiences. If they are generally mostly healthy, they are there because they have lost their parents through—possibly violent—death, through abandonment, because the parents are in prison, or because they have been removed from their families by the state for reasons of neglect or abuse. If they are seriously ill or handicapped, they are there because their parents are unable to take care of them full-time, or even part-time, and they have to deal with the limitations that their condition imposes on them. Whether or not they are consciously aware of their situation and history does not change the fact that it does have an effect on them.

Self-confidence and self-esteem are formed from the time we are babies, and they are very fragile. It is not very hard to cause low self-esteem for life in children. Especially in those who already feel like they have been rejected by their parents and therefore feel they are worthless. Low self-esteem does not only dictate how assertive and independent a child is, it can also have a big impact on health and ultimately even the will to live. A person of any age does not need to commit suicide to end his life: if he genuinely loses all will to live, he will simply waste away and die.

A boy of about nine years old was living in a children's home where care was severely lacking in all respects. The only thing the children in this home received was three meals a day, clothes and a blanket to roll themselves in at night. First, the boy stopped showing any interest in what was happening around him: even if someone would approach him and give him attention, he would not react. Then he stopped eating. Very soon he was no more than skin and bones and he lost his sight. A caregiver told me that he had brought nice food in, from home, to try to get the boy to eat, but he would not take it. The boy was not ill, he just did not see the point of going on the way things were. After a few weeks, he died.

Saying 'thank you for helping' helps build up her self-confidence, while only saying 'you forgot something' will make her feel bad.

The importance of helping a child maintain or boost his self-esteem does not mean that you should only praise him, and it does not mean that he should not be told when he has done something wrong. It just means that you need to be conscious of how you say things, to not make a child doubt his own worth unnecessarily. It is simply a question of degrees, but a tiny difference has a big impact. The difference lies between telling a child that he *is* bad and telling him that he *has done* something bad.

Similarly, caregivers—or anyone else—should not speak with contempt about children in their presence, and not pass judgement on the child's family background when he is within hearing range. This should not be done out of hearing range either, but caregivers are only human. Even if you think he will not understand, or that he is not listening, you can never be entirely sure that this is true. Often it is even worse when children only understand certain bits of what is said, because they have a lively imagination that will fill in the blanks, which ends up creating a picture even worse than reality. Hearing themselves or their parents spoken ill of, will damage the self-esteem of most children.

All the children from the children's home were assembled to listen to the introduction and the speeches of two people who had just made very big donations for a new building to be put up. The children had been instructed to listen attentively, to smile and to applaud. What they had to listen to was a speech about the amazing work done by the children's home, and how it had plucked these children out of the gutter. How these children came from nothing, were nothing. And now, living in the children's home and with the help of generous donors like them, they had a life and a future ahead of them. Several children's heads hung down by the end of a long speech that repeated their worthlessness again and again.

I always want to ask people who do this why they cannot simply say that with their money the children's lives will be even better, rather than pounding on and on about the children 'being nothing and having nothing'.

> To 'buy' his cooperation, one of the managers told a teenage boy that if he did what she asked, she would arrange for him to go back to his family again soon. The boy eagerly cooperated and was very excited at the prospect of leaving the children's home. This excitement lasted a few weeks. But every time he asked when he would be going home, he was told to go away. Slowly he started to realise that he would not really be allowed to leave. He became very depressed when he realised the truth. It was almost impossible to get him to do anything anymore, even to make him get up and move somewhere, and he ate almost nothing for quite a long time.

Speculations about the child leaving the institution soon should never be discussed within hearing of the child, as this will raise and afterwards often crush hope, which does not help the child. Once it is certain if, how and when the child will be leaving, this should be explained to him directly, in a way that he understands. If a departure is uncertain, it should not be discussed when there is any possibility that the child—or any of the other children—might be able to overhear the conversation.

When a child has done something unacceptable, dangerous or destructive, have one caregiver take care of this. Talk to the child, explain that his behaviour—not he himself—is bad and why, and that it should not happen again. Do not gang up on a child by calling on other adults to witness and comment on what has been done wrong. This will make a child feel very, very small and severely damage his self-esteem. The aim of correcting or disciplining a child is not to make him feel small, but to make him understand why this behaviour is unwanted and should not be repeated. Aiming to make a child feel small or hurt is childish and cruel.

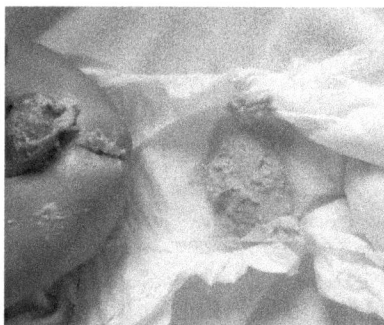

If you cannot deal with this, you are in the wrong job.

If a caregiver talks about her dislike of vomit, poop and urine all the time, this has a negative effect on the child's self-esteem. Most people are not particularly fond of having to deal with these substances, but if you really have a problem doing so, you are in the wrong job. A child does not vomit because he likes it so much or to make a mess. Small children are supposed to produce a poop-filled nappy at least once and often more than once a day. Telling a baby or an older child who is unable to control his bowels because of a physical disability 'you're disgusting, pooping so much all the time' can greatly damage his self-esteem and can cause insecurity to the extent that it may stand in the way of progress in toilet training, because of anxiety about bodily functions. I want to emphasise that I did not include this example as a theoretical situation: I have seen this happen.

Young children and people with the mental age of young children do not have any shame about showing off their body or acting like a fool. This is because shame is tied in with cultural and social rules of dignity and pro-priety. Once these cultural and social rules have been learned, breaking them causes shame in most people. Young children still have to learn these rules, and people

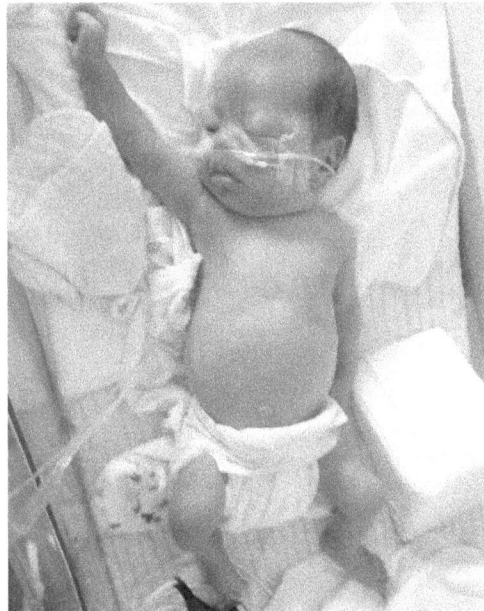

Babies have not learned to feel shame about an exposed body yet.

who are severely mentally handicapped do not always have the ability to learn them. Most cultures make an exception for babies and toddlers when it comes to social and cultural rules. They are for the most part excused from the rules of propriety until they are between three to six years old.

However, it is important to preserve the dignity of all people, no matter their age. Especially those who have adult bodies but the mental age of a child, who are not aware of social rules about modesty. Take these children to a separate room if they need to have any part of their body uncovered that should be kept covered in public according to the rules of propriety. This can be for a medical exam or a nappy or clothes change for example. This preservation of dignity can be linked to a child's self-confidence. Because while he does not feel that exposing his body is humiliating, he may be aware of the ridicule or disapproval of other people present and feel humiliated by that.

✳ ———————————— **What Helps Build Self-Confidence and Self-Esteem**

- Praising a child when she has done something well.
- Giving a child attention regularly and listening to her when she tells you something.
- When something that a child is trying to do takes too long or is not going very well, praise the effort she has been making and suggest that you continue doing it together. This way, you help her improve her skills and give her the feeling that she is able to learn things.
- Complimenting a child in front of other people.
- Trying to give praise and encouragement if you know that the child was really doing her best to do well, even if the results are not what you would have hoped. You can praise the effort that has been made, for instance, or you can point out that it might not be entirely right yet, but it is already a lot better than the last time.
- Allowing the child to have a say in certain decisions.
- Giving the child small responsibilities within her abilities; this is also called helping a child 'experience success', which will drive her to try to do well at other things too.

Having someone cheer when you succeed.

To help children build self-esteem and self-confidence, it is very important to not tell them that they are bad, difficult or worthless. However, there is more to it than not putting them down. It is equally important to **validate** them, meaning to praise them when they do something right, to let them know that they are wanted, and to make them feel that they are taken seriously. No matter how young a child is, she needs to feel that someone is listening and doing their best to understand her when she is trying to communicate something. It does not matter whether she tries this through nothing but crying and smiling, through crooked speech or hand gestures, or through endless tales with a point hidden in them somewhere.

One way to validate a child is to acknowledge her feelings. Let her know by telling her that you understand that she is sad or angry or excited, even if you have no way or no intention of changing this. Acknowledging the fact that you realise she feels this way already makes a big difference. And not only when you happen to pick up on a child's mood: acknowledging feelings is particularly important in situations of conflict.

What often happens when a young child is told she cannot do or has to do something is that she starts crying in anger or frustration and the caregiver then shouts at her to stop crying because it annoys her.

This is likely to quickly turn into a vicious cycle with the caregiver yelling and the child crying harder and harder–not only out of the original anger now, but also because she is being yelled at. Instead, acknowledge that the child has the right to be angry at you–after all, we adults are often angry or frustrated about things we are told we have to or cannot do, we just do not express it by crying anymore– and allow her to cry for a while, to get it out of her system.

Almost all children are interested in the feeling and taste of sand in their mouth at some point.

EXAMPLE

It often happens that the child is told 'Yes, you do want it', not because the caregiver thinks it is true, but because she wants it to be true. This does not serve any purpose, except for making the child feel misunderstood. Instead, say 'I understand you do not want it, and you do not have to want it, but you will have to do it anyway.' Or 'I understand that you are angry with me over this, and that is all right, but we still have to do it.' This explains that there is no choice in the matter, but the child's feelings are validated.

It is an interesting phenomenon when caregivers tell children what they are thinking or feeling, when they know it is not true. This is seen all over the world. Statements such as, 'It does not hurt', 'You don't want that' or 'Sand tastes bad' only make the child feel the caregiver knows nothing about her, because she feels it does hurt, she does want it, and the sand actually tastes kind of nice; at least nice enough to try it again. It almost implies a kind of magical thinking on the part of the adult that is usually only seen in children under eight or nine years old, where they assume that if they say something is so, it will be so. More reasonable behaviour is to try to put yourself in the child's shoes and show sympathy, even if your decision will not be changed by tears or tantrums.

If you have made a definite decision that something will be done, it is best to tell the children this as a statement, rather than as a suggestion or a question.

EXAMPLE

For example: 'We are going outside now, go and get your shoes' instead of 'Shall we go outside?'. This seems like an insignificant difference, but in fact it is not. If you ask the child 'Shall we go out-side?' you are suggesting that the child has a choice. It is possible that the child will be excited and shout 'yes!' However, it is also pos-sible that for whatever reason he does not feel like going outside right now and answers, 'no'. What will you do then?

If you simply want to go for a walk or to let the child have some time outside, it does not matter much. If the child really has a choice, it is good to allow him make the decision from time to time; this is very validating. However, if you were planning to go outside and to take him with you because of something that has to be done right now, there is no choice. If you put it to the child as a choice and the child gives a 'wrong' answer, you have a problem. Of course, you are able to have things your way and drag the child out with you. How-ever, you are likely to have to deal with a very uncooperative child. Plus, the child is given to understand that even though you gave him a choice, you put no value in his answer: you simply ignored it.

A father wearing the decorations made by his children to show his pride in them.

So, in other words, only ask something as a question if you are willing to accept any answer from the child.

It helps if you occasionally show enthusiasm for things they are excited about. No matter how trivial or nonsensical they may be: endless sto-ries, a tower of three blocks stacked on top of each other or a drawing that consists of nothing but scratches. Praise the child for these things and show enthusiasm. It makes her feel like you are taking a real inter-est in her, and thereby that she is someone worth taking an interest in. It also gives her the experience of sharing something with an adult. It makes the child feel like she is good and interesting enough to count for something.

One of the teenage girls came to sit on my bunk bed in the dorm that I shared with six other girls in the children's home. We talked for a while and then she became quite emotional. 'You are really here with us,' she said. 'Other volunteers come to visit, but they do not want to live with us. You are here, just like us.' She had tears in her eyes. I had not done anything in particular with or for this girl, but just by sharing their dorm and eating the same food as them, I had apparently made her feel valued.

Chapter 6:   Discipline

In this chapter, discipline will be discussed from various perspectives. Not only by looking at effective ways of punishing, but also at why it is necessary to set limits and have rules. I will show how bad behaviour can be reduced by breaking the cycle of negative attention seeking and by making sure that the children clearly know what is expected of them.

She just wants to play with the funny door and the buttons on top. She does not know the unfortunate effects of cutting off another child's oxygen supply.

In many places, any undesirable or unacceptable behaviour from a child is seen as badness and something that needs to be punished. However, it is important to try to understand why a child does what he does. Not all undesirable results come from a child's intention of doing something bad. For example, in some cases a child does not know that something is not allowed because he has never been told. So, when he ends up doing what is not allowed, it is not because he is trying to break the rules, but simply because he did not know about them. Many times, children get themselves into trouble when they are exploring their surroundings and trying to find out how the world works, without understanding the consequences of what they are doing. In some cases, the child may have been trying to do the right thing, but may have made a mistake along the way or failed to do what he wanted to do. Again, this is not an attempt to break rules or to defy you, it is simply falling short of what he hoped to do.

As was mentioned in Part 1, Chapter 5: 'Essential Psychological Needs' and Part 2, Chapter 1: 'Global Developmental Milestones', if a child's essential basic needs are not met, this can lead to serious behaviour problems and negative attention seeking. Again, this is not the child's fault. The child is simply fighting for his well-being. The bad behaviour seen is the natural and inevitable consequence of what is lacking in the care he receives. This is not something that should receive punishment on top of the–possibly permanent–damage already caused. So, look at why a child behaves the way he does and whether disciplining him is reasonable and likely to be effective, given the circumstances.

✳ ——————————   Setting Limits

Children explore the world and try to figure out how it works. As part of this exploration they are search for limits, to get an idea of the framework within which their existence can take place. Some people find it very hard to set limits for children, because they feel the child's freedom will be reduced, or because they feel the poor

Next time she may try to put her finger through it when it is on.

child has already been through so much difficulty that she should be allowed a little extra freedom. They are also held back because children tend to rebel against new limits. The tantrum is taken as a sign that the limits are unfair or unbearable.

In fact, the screaming and crying is done to test how solid and dependable the newly discovered limits are. Of course, like people of any age, children also try to see if they can win a little more than what is offered. However, that does not mean that they do not want the limits or that they want them to keep shifting. If the child succeeds in pushing the boundary a little bit further every time she tries, that is a scary experience for her. It means she cannot find a solid framework within which to feel free and safe. Every time the child wants and needs to lean on something, it is like the wall moves a little bit further away. So there is nothing secure and dependable for her to lean on. Children need and want to have limits, however much they act like they do not. Without limits, they do not feel secure.

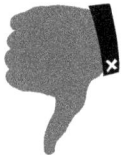

The caregiver of a two-year-old boy provided the children in her care with random rules: what would be allowed one day, would be 'strictly' forbidden the next and the other way around. This way, she tried to assert her authority over the children. 'Strictly' only applied in so far as none of the children protested. If a tantrum was thrown, she would sternly say 'no' another few times and then give in. The little boy knew this very well and he played her, very clearly.

One day, he had a complete meltdown and interestingly enough this was not in protest against something he was not allowed. His entire manner and behaviour made it clear that, through his screaming, he was practically begging for limits to be set. He was screaming in desperation, looking very confused. He was demanding things he did not even want and would then scream even more, no matter if the answer was yes or no. He did not want to win from his caregiver; he very clearly wanted to be stopped. He kept making more and more outrageous demands in the hope that somehow he would finally cross the line and would run into something solid to hold onto. Unfortunately, his caregiver did not see it that way, she just saw it as behaviour typical for the child and continued her random approach.

Total freedom brings with it total responsibility. Set rules tell you what you cannot do and thereby provide the framework within which you know you can move freely and safely. If no adult will clearly indicate what you can and cannot do, or the rules are changed as soon as you give an indication that you would rather they did not exist—in short, with nothing to stop you—the decision of what to do and what not to lies on your shoulders. Children's shoulders are far too small to bear this kind of responsibility. Even more so when you consider that they do not even yet have full knowledge of what is dangerous or not. That is why they are by definition unable to make informed decisions.

A boy of two and a half years old has lived in a particular children's home since he was one month old. The transition from treating him like a baby—trying to give him what he wants—to treating him like a toddler—setting limits and giving him clear rules—has only partly taken place. He is smart and curious. He likes to pick up objects that adults use, to study them and try to use them. The problem is that this is sometimes very dangerous because some of the objects regularly used by adults are sharp, or contain medication for one of the other children, which could poison him if he would taste it—and he certainly tries to do that. If it is noticed that he has picked up something like this, he is told angrily not to touch these things. The caregivers ask him why he is so bad, they have told him again and again not to touch these things and he still does it. The little boy begins to cry and one of the caregivers picks him up to comfort him.

This is a smart little boy. Although he does like to look at the things he is not allowed to touch, he has discovered that if he is 'bad' and gets told so and then starts to cry, the caregiver—who is usually too busy to spend much time with him because she has other, smaller, children to look after—will pick him up and hold him until he decides to stop crying. The reward for touching things that you are not allowed to touch is much too great to stop doing it. Especially since the little boy does not understand that what he does can be dangerous.

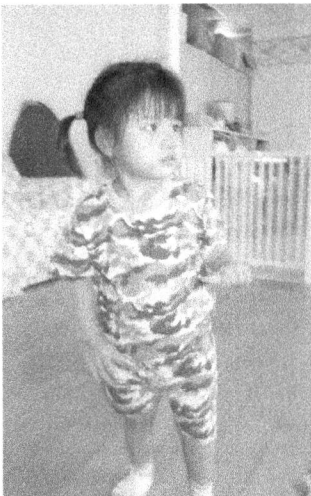

While failure to set limits can lead to worse behaviour in all children, especially if they have innate (=part of a person's essential being, which he is born with) problems with self-control and aggression, it is especially dangerous in one specific group: children with a significant mental handicap. Unfortunately, this group of children usually has even fewer rules and limits than other children. This is often because of the perception that 'the poor children' already have so much going against them that they deserve 'a bit of freedom'. This is a particularly great problem with children who are cared for by their parents, but occasionally it is also seen with children in **institutional care**. Another reason is that a lot of people seem to think that a mental handicap means that the child is unable to learn anything.

At this age she is still easy to stop, but it will not stay that way if she does not learn that there are limits.

After lunch, the mentally retarded teenagers are all taken away from the area where they ate, so that it can be cleaned before they are allowed to play there again. While they used to be able to sneak back in to search for scraps of food from the floor, we decided to put a stop to that once and for all, for hygienic reasons. Some of the severely retarded boys need to be physically stopped. One boy was particularly persistent: he needed to be held, which required all the strength I had. It would usually take 20 to 30 minutes before the area was clean and the boys could be allowed back. On the third day from the start of our new policy, this particular boy was still making attempts to escape and he had to be held securely. However, because he was starting to notice that I was not going to let him get away no matter how hard he tried, he was already fighting with less energy and force than he had before. Every day he put in less effort to try to get away: this is the result of consistency.

However, on that third day, I had been holding him back for about ten minutes, when a caregiver–who had been informed of what was going on–brought the boy a plate with some food. I had no choice but to let go of him, since the food was right in front of him. And I walked away, because I did not want the boy to associate me with the reward he had just received for fighting me. The staff had felt sorry for me, seeing how much effort it cost to keep the boy from escaping, and had wanted to make things easier for me. I was not happy at all. I knew that the boy had found out that there was a chance of a reward for putting up a fight, and now he would be much harder to restrain for several days. And I was right.

In a child of two to three years old, running wild, destroying things and hurting people is mostly seen as cute. The hitting does not really hurt yet and the destruction only takes place on a small scale. From about four years up to the age of about twelve it becomes annoying. After that, it can become dangerous.

A teenager with all the size and force of an adult but a mental age of three years old or less, has no understanding of danger, value, or the fact that you can hurt or injure someone. At seven years old, it is still possible to pick a child up and drag her away from a dangerous place or if she is about to destroy something valuable or important; or to restrain her when she is really hurting you or someone else. Good luck trying to do that with a mentally retarded seventeen-year-old. If the seventeen-year-old has not learned to obey and accept certain limitations from an early age, she will be a real and great danger to herself and her surroundings. With no idea of her own strength and without having been taught how to control her aggression, she may, accidentally, seriously injure someone or even beat him to death, without knowing what she is doing.

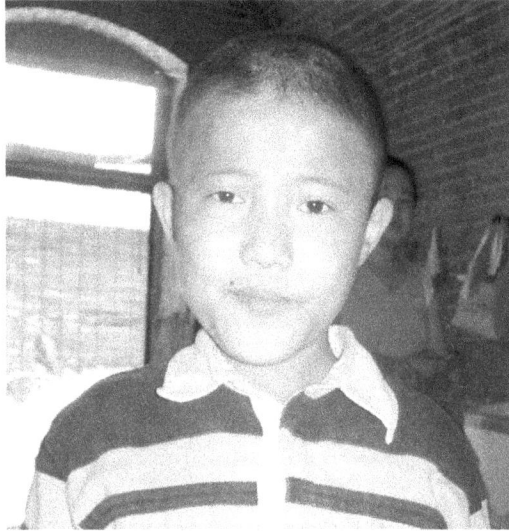

This boy, autistic and intellectually disabled, is usually very sweet, but if he is not taught clear limits, his occasional outbursts will become dangerous to himself and his surroundings.

It usually takes me less than five minutes to recognise a problem with lack of limits when I see a primary caregiver and a child together. In many cases, the problems caused by a lack of limits are much greater and make life much harder than all the other problems that may come from a child's handicap put together. A caregiver, however, may think that is almost impossible.

> *A mother visits the paediatrician with her six-year-old, multiply disabled son. She complains that he will not eat anything and she is very worried about him. She does not understand why her son simply will not take any food at meals and she wants the doctor to help her. While she explains this, her son starts making a slight whining noise and the mother takes her bag, pulls out an enormous bag of crisps and gives it to the child. The paediatrician's eyes widen and he suggests that maybe she could start by not giving the child lots of snacks. That way he is more likely to be hungry at mealtimes. The mother's reaction is very angry: 'But he wants it, if I don't give them to him, he cries!'*

'She wants it. If I don't give it, she will start screaming and hitting me' is something a lot of people say. This is exactly my point. You have not taught her that wanting something and not getting it is an option. So, of course she will not easily accept it as a possibility after so many years of being shown that this is how the world works. By always giving in when she cries/screams/hits you, you have taught her that crying/screaming/hitting is an acceptable way of making sure she gets what she wants. She rules you. That is to be expected, because you have taught her that is a good thing to do. Common sense is important for anyone involved in childcare.

The later you start setting limits, the harder it will be. If you think it will be hard to break the pattern now, just try to imagine what the situation will be like in five years...

A particular institution houses between 70 and 80 boys aged between twelve and twenty-one with varying degrees of mental retardation. These boys have not been taught any rules–or anything else–because they are seen as too stupid to learn anything. Sometimes, when the caregivers have suddenly had enough, they will beat one of the boys, but otherwise they are left to do what they want. This means that boys beat–or bite, or kick, or whatever seems most appropriate at the time–each other a lot. The smarter boys steal food and objects from the ones who are more handicapped–and from visitors when they can get away with it–and sexual harassment is part of the weaker boys' daily reality.

When the initiative was taken to introduce rules and discipline among the boys, this was greeted with extreme scepticism by the caregivers. The start was very difficult, because boys with the size and strength of adult men needed to be physically kept from things they were not supposed to be doing, put in 'time-out' to make them realise that they did something they were not allowed to do, and any objects that they used as weapons had to be confiscated. However, through being very consistent, soon the boys started to understand what was unacceptable. Balancing reprimands with praise when they behaved well helped them understand what they should be doing instead of the unacceptable behaviour. When a regular visitor came to the home again after a two-week absence, she noticed the enormous change. Not only were the boys much better behaved and easier to handle, many of them also seemed happier to her.

Breaking the Cycle of Negative Attention Seeking

In situations where there are few adults looking after many children, there is little attention for individual children. It does not take the average child very long to find out that while positive attention is hard to get, you can always get negative attention if you know what to do. Every time you break something, get yourself stuck, or hurt another child, a caregiver is sure to come over and yell at you. Of course, negative attention is not very nice, but a child's need for attention is so great that negative attention is a lot better than no attention at all.

Generally, this situation very quickly spirals into a vicious cycle. Bad behaviour and tantrums demand so much negative attention and cause such irritation that both the time available and the will to give positive attention to this particular child will disappear fast. The child feels powerful on the one hand–because he can control his caregiver to a certain extent–but he has very low self-worth on the other hand, because he is constantly told he is bad.

Escaping this vicious cycle is entirely possible, but not at all easy. The caregiver needs to become conscious of the situation that has developed and make a determined effort to change it. The way to change the situation is to show the child that good behaviour is more rewarding than bad behaviour.

Step 1:   Introduce positive attention and praise. This is not an easy thing to do, especially if the situation has been spiralling downward for some time. You will need to actively search for something that you can praise the child for and reward him with a few moments of positive attention every time. To start with, what you are looking for are not exceptional accomplishments, but simply behaviour that is not bad. If he has been playing for five minutes without hitting anyone, breaking anything or screaming, you praise him. Tell him you think he is playing very well and that you like to see him doing it. If he has spent a few minutes eating without throwing his drink all over the table or his food on the ground, praise him. If he does anything only remotely 'special' in a tiny way– handing a toy over to another child, holding out his arm or leg so that you can more easily dress him, anything at all–praise him. At the very beginning, if things are already rather out of control, you generally need to look very hard to find something to praise, and you need to constantly remind yourself to do it. However, if you do manage to praise him regularly and keep doing it for some time, it will pay off.

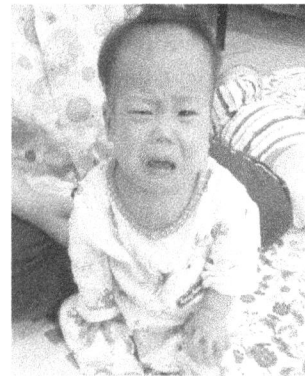

Ignore screaming and crying.

At the start, this is a scary thing to do. You do not want to interrupt the few moments during which the child is not causing trouble and draw attention to yourself. Because to start out with, this is almost guaranteed to set him off: he will use bad behaviour again, to try to keep your attention. Still, it is very important to praise him anyway. If he starts with bad behaviour again, gently–as friendly as you can–tell him that you liked it better when he was doing so well, and move on to step 2.

Step 2:   Ignore bad behaviour as much as possible. Unless it causes a danger to himself or others around him, ignore it completely. Even if that means having to put up with a lot of noise or some destruction. If there is danger involved, keep the attention to an absolute minimum. Take the dangerous object away from him and explain to him why he cannot play with it. Or pick him up and put him down somewhere else where he cannot continue to hurt another child or possibly hurt himself, again explaining to him why. Other than that, ignore him, his crying, screaming and the whole situation. Pretend to be busy with another child or another chore—while, obviously, keeping an eye on the situation discreetly to make sure the toddler does not get himself into danger again. If negative behaviour and tantrums consistently do not bring the desired attention, while it becomes clear that there *is* attention to be gained with positive behaviour, the child will realise this quite soon and start changing his behaviour.

Step 3: Make time for happy playtime together every day, for several minutes at the very least. This means giving the child your complete and undivided attention, at a moment when he is well-behaved. This can consist of him sitting on your lap and you reading to him, playing with a toy on the floor or at the table together, singing or playing games together, or whatever works for the two of you. If the child becomes difficult during this playtime, explain to him that you would like to play with him, but not if he behaves like this. If he does not improve his behaviour, say you are sorry, but if he does not want to play nicely with you, you will go and do something else and walk away. In this case, if at all possible, you should try to initiate another playtime on the same day, when the child is well-behaved again, to show that there is no **resentment**.

Using this system, the problematic situation will not resolve itself from one moment to the next. As I have mentioned already, it is not easy to do. But it does work. For an outsider who is consistent, it usually takes little more than a day to break through the pattern. For the caregiver and child who have been in the vicious cycle together for some time already, it is likely to take at least a week. It will only work if the caregiver is completely committed to making the change and is completely consistent in her approach to making it happen.

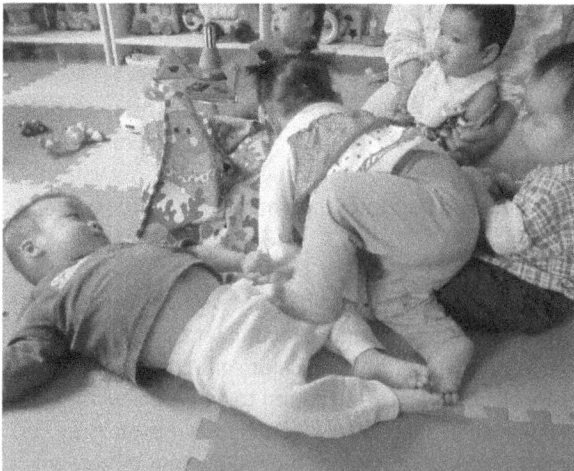

Quite regularly, the situation escalates to a point where it becomes very hard to see that there is still a way out, and that it is almost always a question of bad behaviour and not of bad character.

Children need to learn that what they do can be dangerous or inappropriate.

I met a caregiver and a two-and-a-half-year-old stuck in a cycle of negative attention seeking. She was completely convinced that there was nothing that could be done, because in her eyes it was simply a question of the little boy's nature. So much so, that she refused to change anything about her own approach to him or to believe that anything could possibly change. During the two weeks that she was away and I took charge in her place, the boy was no trouble at all after the first day or two. But this was a coincidence, according to her. To me, it was quite clear that once she returned, the boy was almost impossible to deal with whenever she was there, while he remained quite easy-going with me when she was out of sight.

While there is usually a difficult transition period, giving positive attention will almost always reduce negative attention seeking behaviour. Just do not expect the difficult child to turn into a model child– this is too much to ask of anyone. And make sure that you continue to offer positive attention after the change has taken place. Because even when the cycle has been broken, every child still needs attention, and if no positive attention is available, he will again do what it takes to get any kind of attention at all.

The Purpose of Rules

Rules should be kept simple. There should be as few as possible, just enough to keep the child safe and guide him towards socially acceptable behaviour. This will provide more than enough restrictions on a child's life. Inventing rules for no other reason than to assert authority only means that you end up sounding like a monster shouting and reprimanding almost non-stop. This will not make you more respected by the children. It will probably make you less respected, in fact. It is amazing how quickly and flawlessly children see through an authoritarian front and lose respect for the person hiding behind it. Just like it is quite astonishing how quickly they realise that they have got no chance of overstepping certain marks with someone who is truly consistent and who follows through on what they say, but has never said a harsh word.

Rules and authority should be kept as limited as possible. We will start by having a look at what sort of rules are useful to have:

- Keeping the child safe from serious physical harm: Children are often not aware of the risks of walking along the edge of a cliff, crossing a busy road, going near an open fire, or playing with sharp objects. So, activities that have a high likelihood of ending in serious physical harm are generally forbidden if there is no adult supervision. The reason for this is to prevent the child from seriously hurting himself. It is, however, important to note the word 'seriously'. Accidents will happen, children will fall, scrape themselves, and get minor cuts and bruises. All of this is part of growing up, learning and living. If you try to prevent all of these things, you essentially prevent the child from having a life, which is harmful to the child's psychological and even motor skill development.

She does not see the risk of the drop.

- Keeping the child from harming others: Especially young children do not yet understand that if they hit someone, they hurt that person. They do not understand this because the child who does the hitting does not feel the pain. They understand the possibility of causing injuries even less. So, they are given rules to stop them from being aggressive towards other people to prevent them from causing injury or pain.
- Keeping the child from causing destruction: Young children are not yet aware that if they take something apart or break it, it may not always be possible to put it back together or to replace it. So, until they start to develop an awareness that stops them from destruction, they are given rules about not destroying things. However, it is good to allow them, from time to time, to take apart items that are cheap or beyond use, to allow them to learn from this experience and from their attempts to put it back together again.
- Older children are sometimes overwhelmed by feelings of aggression or frustration, which they need to let out somehow, and occasionally they choose to destroy things to do this, even though they are aware of the meaning of destruction. These children, too, should be given rules about destroying objects, while at the same time they need to be offered other ways to let out their pent-up energy. This can sometimes be done effectively by doing sports.
- Teaching the child socially and culturally appropriate behaviour: Every culture and social situation has its own rules for what is appropriate to do and what is not. The knowledge of these proprieties is not present at birth. The rules need to be learned over the course of childhood. So, as children grow older, they should be taught more and more rules about appropriate behaviour when dealing with elders, with family and strangers, with people from the opposite sex, and how to behave in various settings and on various occasions. As children learn these rules, they become well-mannered people.
- Aiding the child's development: Rules such as having to tidy away toys, helping out with chores, and washing hands before eating, are all designed to teach children something about living and

taking care of themselves and about helping others. These rules benefit the child's development and prepare them for their adult life.

Not the Purpose of Rules

If there are too many rules, if punishment is extremely severe or if rules have no valid reason, the chance of children following the rules becomes smaller. In most cases, their goal will move from obeying the rules to avoiding getting caught breaking them. In this, they are likely to make no distinction between rules that are there to protect them and other rules, often because they are unable to tell the difference between the two. So they may put themselves or others at serious risk.

That is why it is important to be aware of the following two categories of rules, which do not help a child's development or well-being, though they are widely used by both caregivers and parents. Being consciously aware of the existence of these two categories may help you to avoid them.

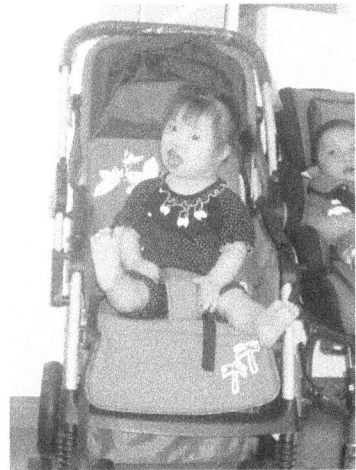

Keeping her in a buggy because it is more work to let her move around.

- Rules for the sake for authority: They are the 'because I say so'-rules. They are rules that do not help the protection or development of the child, but only serve to make the adult feel powerful. Randomly saying, 'you cannot play with your favourite toy today', can be enforced and may make the adult feel powerful. However, if random punishments such as this happen often, the child will not take any of the rules issued by this person seriously any more. Nor will he learn anything about fairness this way.
- Rules to improve the caregiver's life: While there is nothing wrong with a rule like 'no screaming in the house', to protect the caregiver's ears and that of the other children, which teaches a child proper behaviour, in some cases these kinds of rules go too far and are no longer about keeping the child safe and advancing his development, but about making the caregiver's life more comfortable.

It has to be remembered that while taking care of children is very hard work, in the end it is the caregiver who is employed and paid to give the children pleasant lives, not the other way around.

These are some examples of situations I witnessed in which caregivers tried to make their own life easier in a way that crossed a boundary.

A rule such as, 'between meals you are to sit on the sofa and not make a sound', makes the caregiver's life a lot easier: there is no noise, the children do not need a great deal of supervising and no mess is made, nor do they become dirty. However, the children will lack exercise, fresh air, and opportunities for learning through experience, stimulation, language development and social skills. In other words, this may be convenient for the caregiver, but it is very bad for the children's development. Plus, it invites bad behaviour, because small children are quite simply not capable of sitting still without anything to do for more than a minute or two.

A group home consisted of babies, toddlers in the age up to two and a half years old, and, due to circumstances, one five-year-old. This five-year-old was not allowed to play around the house with the toddlers, because the caregiver felt that he was too rowdy and that meant she would have to keep a constant eye on all the children playing together–something I consider to be a good idea anyway when there is a group of toddlers running around. He was also not allowed to interact with the older boys from the other group home on the compound, because the caregiver felt that they would be a bad influence on him, which would only get him into trouble. So instead, the whole time that he was not in school. he was only allowed to play in the little park–within the compound and within view of the house–on his own, mostly watching groups of younger and older children playing from a distance. Except for the times that he was eating his meals or sleeping, he was kept in complete isolation. This is not an acceptable situation. The five-year-old was not treated as a little boy, but as a nuisance that should be kept out of the way.

Another example, which is a little more common than the previous one, is when very small children are given a bath, dressed up in fine clothing, and then made to sit on chairs for hours without being allowed to play or basically move. This is done to prevent them from getting dirty before going to a religious service, or receiving important visitors, or something like that. If it is really important that a small child is spotless for something, the only reasonable way to make sure that happens is to wash and dress him only minutes before the event.

So, we have established that it is important both for the caregiver and for the child that limits and rules are set and that they are maintained. Now, how does one make sure these limits become clear to the child and that they are obeyed?

Imposing and Enforcing Rules

The most important thing is to be clear and consistent about what the rules are, to follow through on what you say, and to be fair about the rules. Explaining to a child why you do not allow something, or why you make him do something, will help him learn. Once a child starts to understand the reasons behind the rules, he is much more likely to obey them than when he is always simply told 'because I say so'.

A fourteen-year-old boy has a mental age of about nine and he has cerebral palsy with severe contractures. He is able to move around, but only slowly. When daily bathing was introduced at this children's home, at first someone would usually carry the boy into the bathroom, so that he could be washed. I would not allow them to do that anymore, because it was important for the boy to move by himself as much as he could. Because he moved so slowly, the boy would be called to go to the bathroom right at the start of bathing time, and would usually arrive just before the last of the children were done. He liked being washed, both because he liked being clean and because it offered extra attention. However, after a few days, he discovered that there was another way to get more attention. When he was called to go to the bathroom, he would make two or three shuffling steps and then he would stop until someone came to tell him to go to the bathroom again, or at later stages, came to tell him to hurry up. Each time someone came to tell him to go, he would take two or three more steps and then he would wait for more attention. He was smiling broadly throughout this whole process. In the end, there was usually not enough time left to allow him to move the whole way by himself, so someone would come to carry him, saving him the effort of walking the whole way as well as getting attention. When I discovered his game, I talked to the caregivers, telling them not to carry him and not to encourage him. I asked them to just call him once, at the start, and then ignore the whole situation and if he was not at the bathroom door in time, he would not get washed that day. Then I went to the boy and I told him the same thing: If you do not go to the bathroom, you will not be washed and will have to wait until tomorrow.

The first day the boy decided to test me and did his normal three steps and then stayed where he was. I only went past him once and reminded him that he would not get a bath if he did not go to the bathroom. Then he was left alone. He did not get a bath that day.

> *The second day, he moved to within three metres of the door of the bathroom and stopped, hoping for more attention. Again, just before the last remaining child was given a bath, the boy was reminded that if he was not in the bathroom on time, he would not get a bath. Then he was ignored. Again, he did not have a bath. From day three onward, he was in the bathroom on time, without any problems. He had tested the system and made his decision.*

Just like in a game, in life children are more likely to follow rules if they are clear, fair and consistent.

The importance of consistency cannot be overstated. Children learn mostly from having the same thing repeated over and over again, in exactly the same way or with a slight variation. Bit by bit, they begin to recognise how that particular thing works. This goes for limits and rules as much as for anything else. Constantly changing the rules is very confusing and unsettling for children. It deprives them of their sense of stability and security. In the end, it does not really matter whether you let them drink/have something/do something or not. What is important is not to say 'no' five times first, and then give in. If you do this only once, it will inevitably lead to a period with lots of tantrums, because the child has learned that crying or protesting can get him what he wants. Plus, as I explained earlier, while the child might be very pleased with having 'won' the one extra cookie—or whatever he got—if this happens a lot, it will be very unsettling for him.

Following through means making sure something does or does not happen, as you have told the child. If you say 'you cannot play with that', but then let him play with it and only shout at him for not listening much later, you show the child that you do not need to be taken seriously when you say things. Instead, if the child continues to play with it, you could give one more warning: 'I told you cannot play with that, if you do not put it down, I will take it off you.' Give the child a moment to do what you said, and if he does not do it, take the thing away from him. This shows him that you are serious when you say something like this.

A teenage boy with a mental age of about three years old was in the habit of taking food from the plates of the children sitting beside him during meals. He also got up halfway through the meal and walked around, grabbing handfuls of food from other plates, rather than finishing the food still left on his own plate. When I started to work at teaching him to eat from his own plate and not that of others, the staff told me not to bother: the boy was too stupid to learn. I continued anyway. At every meal I stood beside him and stopped him from putting his hands into plates other than his own, again, and again. When he tried to get up, I made him sit down again and told him that he could eat from his own plate, not from that of others. If he really insisted on getting up, I reminded him that if he left his plate, the meal was over and he would not get any more food until the next meal. Then I would keep myself between him and other children's food until everyone finished eating, to prevent him from stealing food. Gradually, the message got through. After a month, someone still needed to stand beside him to discourage him from grabbing or getting up. But when someone was there, he would simply eat his own food and stay seated until he was full.

When a child does something he is not supposed to do for the first time, he should get a warning and an explanation of why it is not allowed. Toddlers, and in some cases older children too, do not have the insight or the ability to think of the consequences that might be connected to their actions. They only see as far as, 'hey, my finger fits into that hole', or, 'that's a funny sound when I whack this toy on the floor, what would happen if I whacked it on that girl's head?' So, while you might get a tremendous shock or scare from something a child does, it is not fair on the child to punish him when he does not know that what he did is wrong. Punishing in this case is nothing more than taking out your fear on someone much smaller than you. The first time, warn the child very sternly not to do it again, and explain as plainly as possible why. Then, if he does it again, he can be reprimanded for doing something he has been told not to do—not for causing danger, because he still will not truly understand that.

Every time a child does something that is not allowed, there are three steps:
- Tell the child not to do it and explain why, then give him 10 to 15 seconds to think about what you have said and to react.
- If he continues to do what you told him not to do, tell him again to stop. This time, warn him about what will happen if he contin-

ues—so you state the punishment or consequence of his actions in advance. Again, give him 10 to 15 seconds to start reacting.

- If he still continues, you stop him yourself, while explaining again why he should not do what he is doing. Then you follow through with the punishment or consequence that you have announced.

A caregiver complained that a group of three toddlers never listened to her. She would tell them to sit down to start their meal and they would still run around. After they had started to eat, they would get up again and run around some more. She felt that they were very badly behaved children. What I saw was that the children were told to sit down to eat and then ignored. After another ten minutes of playing, another request would be made for them to sit down. The same thing happened when they got up while they were eating. They were allowed to run around, come back for more food, and run around some more. They would get shouted at a little, but nothing else would happen. The children did not have the impression that the shouting was all that serious, because nothing happened after it. So there was no reason for them not to enjoy themselves and play.

When I was in charge of these three children on the caregiver's day off, I told them to sit down to eat and made them sit down straight away. If they got up, I would put them back behind their plate, again, and again, and again. Towards the end of the meal I would warn them that if they got up from behind their plate, they would be done with the meal and the food would be taken away. Every time they wanted to get up I asked them if they were done eating and if not to sit down again. And if they left their plate, I made sure to take away the food immediately. If they came back for more, I reminded them that I had told them to stay seated to eat and that they could have food again at their next meal. The next week, when I covered the day off, the three toddlers would come almost immediately when I called them to dinner and they made fewer attempts to get up. The week after was even better. They knew I was going to follow through on what I said, so they saved themselves the energy of trying to go against it without getting anything out of that. Meanwhile, with their caregiver, the situation was still the same.

When rules or a new form of discipline are first introduced and are still quite new to the children, with most children you will have to go through all three steps a few times in the first week or two. However, if you prove to them that you are consistent and that you will always follow through on what you say, pretty soon children will start to take you more seriously and you will only rarely need to go any further than step 2. In other words, most of the time it is enough to just tell the child what to do or what to stop doing, possibly followed by a warning, and that is it.

Once they knew I would follow through, getting them to sit down and eat until they were done was no problem.

So to the most important things to make disciplining effective are:

- *Be clear about the rules and your expectations.*
- *Make sure the rules are fair.*
- *Be consistent in applying the rules.*
- *Follow through on what you say.*

Doing these things is more important for making disciplining effective than the actual punishments you use. To many people, particularly those who mostly use beatings as punishment, this sounds ridiculous and weak. However, these are the methods I have always used and I have not yet met a group of children with whom they are not effective.

Her wrist is held to stop her from tearing the flowers apart.

Discipline Strategies

For babies, discipline becomes relevant around five to six months of age, when they start to reach out around them to explore the world. At this age, babies do not yet have the ability or need to learn social rules, but they do need to be kept safe and to start learning what behaviour is 'wrong' because it brings them into danger. Setting limits and disciplining at this age simply consists of preventing the baby from doing something dangerous. The first method used is usually to pick the baby up and put him somewhere else, out of reach of the danger, or out of reach of the other child he was hurting. While moving him away, explain that he cannot do that and why this is so, even if he is at an age where he is not likely to fully understand. The repeated explanations will start the development of understanding.

Once a baby starts moving around by himself, this method is no longer always effective. If the activity that he is prevented from doing is interesting enough, he will do what he can to make his way back to where he was to continue what he was doing. If moving him is not effective in stopping him from going back to where he is not supposed to go after two or three tries, the most effective method is to block his way. Either put yourself between where the baby is and where you do not want him to go, or put something else in his way that he is unable to get under, over or around.

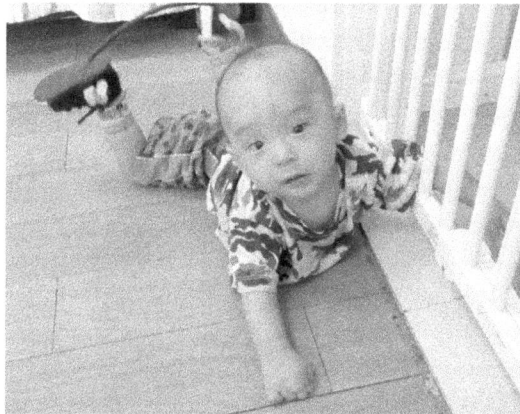

He needed to be removed repeatedly, before he gave up.

At this stage, holding his hand—or both his hands—away from where he wants to use it by gently, but firmly, grabbing his arm by the wrist, is effective after it has been repeated several times. Hold the hand long enough—usually about a minute or two—that he does not think it is a funny game anymore and becomes annoyed at not being able to use his hand. While holding the hand, explain what he is not allowed to do and why. This technique can be effectively used with children of all ages—basically until they become stronger than you—to stop them hitting other children or yourself, and to keep them from grabbing something. If you start using this technique at a young age, once the child becomes older there is usually no need for it anymore: just explaining that hitting is not allowed because it hurts someone will be enough, sometimes combined with a warning of consequences if the child continues.

As a child moves out of the baby stage into toddlerhood, he becomes more inventive in ways to explore the world. He is able to get himself into more trouble. He begins to have a greater understanding of the world around him and of social rules. So, step by step, he does not only need to be kept away from things that are dangerous, he also needs to start learning some of the social rules that are part of his culture. From this time onward, he can start learning more from what is explained to him, in addition to what he learns from his experiences.

A child put in time-out, away from the rest of the group and facing away. An adult is nearby to make sure she stays where she is, without giving her attention.

'Punishments' or consequences from this age onwards should ideally be as close as possible to natural consequences. This will help teach the child about the way the world works and why what he does is not allowed. There is no point in punishing a child by not giving him food or sending him to bed several hours earlier than normal. Nor is it effective to punish a small child who has broken something in the morning, by not allowing him to go on an outing in the afternoon. These kinds of things hold no connection, not in the natural order of things, nor in the mind of the child. When the two-year-old is crying over not being allowed to go out with the other children in the afternoon, he will not remember what happened that morning, and telling him will not really bring back the memory. To the child this will seem like an unpredictable, random act, which to him is more like favouritism than like discipline.

If natural consequences are impossible or too dangerous to be experienced by a child–for example paying for the damage done to a car or letting him injure another child –giving him a time-out is a good alternative. Time-out is a period during which the child sits on his own–in a safe place, preferably not his bed, because this can cause negative feeling about being put in the bed–and does not receive any attention. When the child is put in this spot, it should be explained to him why he is there. For example: 'You are not allowed to hit Mary. If you hit someone, you have sit here until I come and get you, to learn that you cannot do that.' Say nothing more than that, in a calm voice. If you continue to reprimand him while he is sitting there, you are giving him attention. For almost all children, negative attention is still better than no attention at all, making the time-out more of a reward than a punishment.

If the child starts screaming and crying, ignore him. If he gets up from the spot where you have told him to stay, simply pick him up and put him back without saying anything to him and without making eye contact. Put him back as many times as he gets up and leaves. The time-out period starts from the last time he has sat down: if he keeps getting up, the clock keeps resetting.
Time-out should last a reasonable time, according to a child's age. One minute per year of their life is a good guideline. So two minutes for a two-year-old, six minutes for a six-year-old. Leaving a young child in time-out for 15 minutes to half an hour is not helpful and

can even be counterproductive. After a few minutes, the child will have forgotten why he is there, and will only have a vague memory that he is supposed to stay there. So, in effect, it invites more 'bad' behaviour. The child will not remember what he is doing on the step or the stool, he will get bored because he is 'isolated', and he will start looking around for something to do, usually finding something you do not want him to do. To us, two or three minutes do not seem like a very long time, but to a toddler, it is half an eternity. Time-out is effective to use up to about twelve years of age.

Natural consequences:
In the case of a child who will not stop throwing toys–across the room/at other children/out the window/onto the roof–after being warned not to, an effective and understandable way to show natural consequences would be to let him play without toys for half an hour. Explain why this is so, and in the set period calmly take away any toys from him. Every time you take away the toys, calmly explain that no, he cannot play with toys right now. Because if you throw toys, you are left with nothing. Also tell him that later on he will be allowed to play with toys again, and then he can show whether he is able to play without throwing them.

Do not keep accusing him. There is no need to raise your voice to the child, nor do you need to bring the subject up again, unless he attempts to grab a toy before the time is up. Keep an eye on the clock and after the agreed time–do not let it go on longer than the period which you have stated to him–let him know that he can play with the toys again now, if he wants, but that he is not allowed to throw them anymore. If he plays with the toys without throwing, that is the end of the 'episode'. If he starts throwing toys again, whether it is straight away or later, treat it as a new incident: still without raising your voice, give one warning and if it happens again, take the toys away again for half an hour.

Keep an eye on the clock!

Keep an eye on the clock to make sure that the child is not left in time-out longer than he is supposed to be. When the time is up, go and get him. Before letting him go off to play, explain to him again why you put him in time-out. Tell him he can go and play now, but 'don't [...] again, all right?' And with that, the issue has to be left behind you. There is no need to bring it up again.

With somewhat older children, you can teach them to tell you they are sorry for what they did and that they will not do it again, before they go off to play again. With toddlers, it is possible to teach them to say this, but it would be very naïve to think that they will have spent their time-out thinking about what they have done, regretting it afterwards. They simply do not understand enough about the situation for that to happen.

Time-out had just been introduced as a new form of punishment for disruptive behaviour. A seven-year-old boy had been teasing other children and grabbing their toys and he continued doing this even when he was told to stop and warned that if he continued he would have to sit on his own for a while. So, the caregiver took him by the arm and had him sit down in a quiet spot, away from where the other children were playing. She explained that he had to sit there for a while until she told him he could play again, because he had been taking toys from other children and was not listening to her. The boy was very angry and resentful, and sat in the corner crying. Once, he tried to get up and run away, but the caregiver grabbed him and put him back in the same spot. When he had been there for seven minutes, starting the second time he was put there, the caregiver went to him and told him that he was free to go play with the children again, but that he could not take toys from other children. If he wanted a toy from another child, he had to ask for it, instead of grabbing it. The boy was still angry and did not say anything. Despite the caregiver's invitation to go join the other children, the boy stubbornly stayed where he was. The caregiver told him that that was fine too. Whenever he was ready to go play again, he was free to go. If he wanted to stay where he was, that was no problem either.

If a child refuses to join the activities after time-out, usually because he resents you for having punished him or because he feels humiliated, accept this. It is not a good idea to spend a lot of time trying to convince him to join the other children, because it will become a new source of attention that all children will be quick to make use of. Instead, you might go to the child every five to ten minutes to remind him that he is free to come play again whenever he wants, and leave it at that.

Do not hold a grudge. After a child has been disciplined, life goes on as if nothing happened–when you allow him to join the normal activities again, remind the child once more not to do whatever he was being punished for, and leave it at that. It is not always easy, but it is important to remember that your memory stretches back a lot further than theirs.

As children grow older, natural consequences become more effective than other forms of punishment. Usually natural consequences are very easy and straightforward. Examples of natural consequences are:
- If you disrupt the activity that you are a part of, you can no longer take part.
- If you sabotage the attempts of other children to take part in an activity, you are no longer allowed to take part.

- If you abuse the privileged position you were given—such as eating some of the food that you are supposed to hand out or bullying children when you are supposed to supervise and help them—you will lose your privileged position.
- If you destroy someone else's property, you will have to get them a replacement—this can be in the form of having to buy a new one, having to make a new one, or having to hand over your own.

In the dining hall, more than 100 children aged four to eighteen years old have their lunch. There are two places where the children can form a queue to be served. Some of the older children feel that they are too important to have to wait long, so they cut in front of the line. The younger children in particular are afraid to say anything about it, because they are intimidated by the older children. When I saw one of the 'cool' teenage boys cut in front of a long line, I went over and told him that he needed to join the end of the queue. He refused. I told him again, and when he still did not move, I took him by the arm and put him at the end of the queue. As I walked away, I noticed the boy going back to the front of the queue. I went over again, took the boy by the arm, and this time, I stood with him by the wall, waiting until everyone in the dining hall was either in one of the queues or sitting down with their food, before I led him to the end of one of the queues, where I stayed with him until it was his turn to be served. The boy was very indignant: he had to wait much longer now than he would have had to wait if he had taken his original place in the queue. I let him know that that was my point exactly: if you try to cut in front, you end up waiting longer, so you are better off just joining the queue. From then on, whenever someone tried to cut in front of the line, they would get elbowed by their friends, who pointed in my direction, and then the attempt was abandoned straight away.

How you make disciplining ineffective:

- *Not explaining why you are punishing a child.*
- *Punishing randomly.*
- *Giving attention while punishment is going on.*
- *Letting punishment go on for too long.*
- *Allowing other children to crowd around when you punish a child: this kind of audience can provide some children with the kind of attention that makes them proud of being considered 'bad'*
- *Awarding fight or flight: giving up on punishment if the child runs from you or tries to hit you.*
- *Letting the child keep the 'reward': if a child has stolen something and is allowed to enjoy it, or cuts in front of the line and is told off, but not put to the back of the line, this is a motivation to do it again.*

Teaching children to wait for their turn at mealtimes.

In a children's home with mostly babies, there were a few toddlers, who were allowed to do as they pleased in the play area. Two of the toddlers usually found any toy that another child was playing with most interesting and they would go over and pull the toy out of the other child's hand. I started to put a stop to this. Whenever one of the children took a toy from another child, I would ask them to give it back and if they did not, I took it from them and gave it back to the first child while explaining that that child was playing with it and that no one is allowed to take a toy from someone else. At first, the boy would start crying very loudly whenever he was stopped from grabbing a toy from someone. I would ignore this and focus my attention on another child until he stopped crying. After a few days, I had taken a toy from the boy to give back to the child who had it first, put him out of reach so he could not grab the toy again and turned around to ignore him. The boy stayed quiet and played with the toy I had given him. The caregivers were very surprised: 'He normally always cries!' they cried out. I explained that he had learned that it was pointless to cry because I would not give him any attention for it, so he had learned to save himself the trouble.

Physical Punishment

There are several issues associated with physical punishment that a lot of people are not aware of, the most important one being that it is not an effective way to encourage obedience in children. These are some of the drawbacks of using physical punishment:

• It is quite simply not effective. Inflicting pain will never instil respect in the person you hurt. It only makes them scared. In a limited sense, fear can be a strong motivator, and if you are feared enough it is likely to lead to obedience in your presence. What you need to ask yourself, however, is: what is fear a motivator for? The answer is that it is not a motivator for doing the right thing or for pleasing you. It is only a motivator for making sure that you do not find out about anything you do not approve of.

- Because people—children as much as anyone else—who are ruled by pain and fear feel humiliated, they become *less* motivated to do what the person using physical punishment wants. In fact, they become more motivated to do things that person does not want—while making sure not to get caught—to save some of their honour and dignity. In other words, however obedient and sub-servient the children who fear you are in your presence, they are by definition not to be trusted when you are not looking. When your back is turned, they will do what they can to get away with as many 'forbidden' things as possible, even if this means putting themselves in danger. Because in a situation where someone is ruled by fear, he develops a strong need to rebel—even if only in very small ways or at personal cost—to affirm his own identity and humanity to himself.

- Making children understand that they are not allowed to hit oth-er people is high on any caregiver's priority list. This is true even for caregivers who themselves use hitting, slapping or spanking children to discipline them. It is very important to realise that if a caregiver uses hitting to correct children, they are teaching those children in the clearest possible way that hitting is an acceptable way to let someone know you are unhappy with their actions or behaviour. 'Do as I say, not as I do', as mentioned before, is a command that most caregivers would like to see followed, but that is not the way it works. Ultimately, children learn by follow-ing examples, and if the caregiver hits, that must be the right thing to do.

- Using physical punish-ment shows your weak-ness, rather than you power or strength. This is something not every-one realises. In human nature, violence is a last resort. When we are completely desper-ate and feel thoroughly powerless, what re-mains is to use violence to try to escape from the situation we are in. If this last resort, this tool of desperation, is the first thing someone uses when they disci-pline children, they are

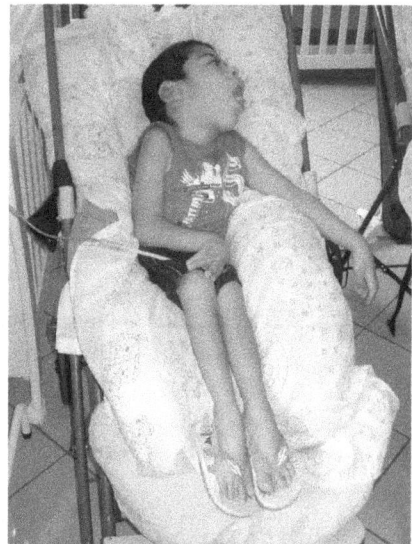

A child can end up like this for life as a result of a beating gotten out of hand.

showing their weakness. They are making clear that it is all they have. They apparently do not have any other ways to deal with the situation. This is not really the position of power they might have thought they were displaying.

- There is a risk of accidentally going too far: frustration and anger can blind you and lead to much unintended damage. I have come across two children so far whose severe cerebral palsy was known to have been caused by beatings from their caregivers.
- Something I am often told is: 'It is the way things are done here, my parents and my teachers beat me, and I'm fine.' Okay, so you were beaten yourself. That is useful: think back to a moment when you were given a proper beating and remember what you were feeling when that happened. And then remember that when you beat someone to discipline them, they will feel the same about you. Is that what you want to achieve?

In a home for mentally retarded children the staff beat the children with sticks, saying it was the only way to keep them under control. Even when they threatened with the sticks–or actually used them–the staff often struggled to get the children to do what they wanted them to do. When I gave a training about the disciplining methods discussed in this chapter, I was almost laughed out of the room. They thought it was extremely naïve of me to think that something like that would work with children like these. I then started implementing what I had taught, on my own– I was the only one to set down rules and enforce them in a non-violent way–with 85 children. It was a difficult start, of course, because this was something completely new to the children and it took a while before they started to understand what was expected of them and why they were regularly put in time-out. However, after about a month and a half, a great change was visible. The children were calmer and better behaved and I only needed to discipline on average one child out of 85 once a day or once every other day. What amazed the staff more than anything, was that if I saw two children at the opposite side of the inner court–about 20 metres away–do something they should not be doing, and I shouted 'HEY!' across the court, more often than not they would stop. This was something they had never managed, with all their threatening to beat the children up. The caregivers did not understand how I could have that much control over these children. In their mind, it could not possibly be explained by the weak story I had given them during the training, there had to be some other, secret, ingredient. But there really was not. I had told them how to do it, I had shown them that it worked, and they still did not believe it.

So, my arguments against using physical punishment do not come from a fear of hurting someone. They are quite simply based on the clear fact that, essentially, physical punishment does not work. I have been told numerous times 'but he won't listen unless I beat him!' I know the people who say this sincerely believe it, but time and time again I have shown that once I took sole charge of the child, established clear, consistent and fair rules that were followed through and used 'non-violent' disciplining, the child was more obedient with me than with the caregiver who beat him or her.

Using the methods of discipline I have provided here will not be the complete and utter end of bad behaviour or disobedience. There is no way to accomplish that. Practice and history have shown that even when you impose the death penalty for the smallest crime, it will not put a complete stop to all crimes. However, the methods discussed in this chapter have been proven to help bring about more good behaviour. And think about it for a moment, if beating is so much more effective than what I suggest, are you saying that you only needed to beat the child once and then he never did anything wrong again?

UN GUIDELINE:

96. All disciplinary measures and behaviour management constitution torture, cruel, inhuman or degrading treatment, including closed or solitary confinement or any other forms of physical or psychological violence that are likely to compromise the physical or mental health of the child, must be strictly prohibited in conformity with international human rights law. States must take all necessary measures to prevent such practices and ensure that they are punishable by law. Restriction of contact with members of the child's family and other persons of special importance to the child should never be used as a sanction.

Part 3:
Running a
Childcare Institution

Chapter 1:   Different Kinds of Caring Setups

At this point I would like to say that although I work to improve conditions in children's homes, I am aware that institutional care is *never* good for children, no matter how well it is organised. Institutional childcare has been around for several centuries. For a long, long time the state and religious or other idealistic groups have taken it upon themselves to care for orphaned or abandoned children who cannot be taken in by their extended families, as well as children who appear to be at risk of harm from abuse, neglect, poverty or **stigma** in their own families. Often, it was even thought to be better for children to live in a 'properly run' children's home than to live with their families. The intention behind institutionalisation has always been good. However, over the past 50 years, extensive research has shown that institutionalisation is almost never in the children's best interest, because various essential basic needs cannot be sufficiently met in an institution.

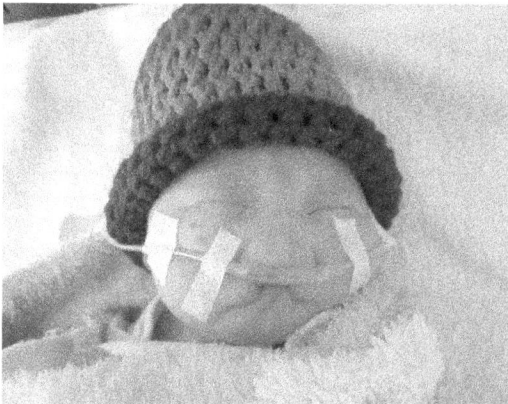

This baby has different needs...   *... than this baby.*

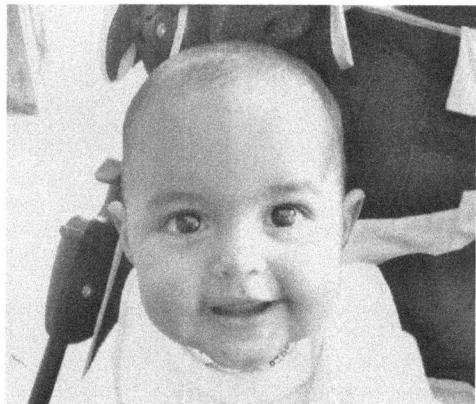

It has been shown that even children who live in terrible poverty in a family—with not enough to eat and little opportunity for schooling—have better chances in life than children who have been raised in a children's home. Children raised in a children's home have a greater chance of ending up living in the street, even if they were fed every day and received an education, because they are not prepared for normal life and their brain is not able to develop normally because many of their essential needs were not met. In Part 3, Chapter 2: 'Ethics in Running a Children's Home' this will be discussed in more detail.

So, I would like to ask all people involved in children's homes to do whatever they can to find ways for the children in their care to live more normal lives in family situations. Ideally, this would be done by reuniting them with their family or by trying to get them adopted, since that is a permanent solution. Or, if that is not possible, by finding long-term foster families for them, with or without continued guidance from the home. The first priority should always be to find a way to allow a child to live in a family situation. The second priority is to make sure that, if it is not possible for the child to live in a family, the care she receives resembles care in a family as closely as possible.

A particular children's home mainly cared for children who were HIV-positive. Some of the children really had no one to care for them, but many of them still had family or even living parents. They had been sent to the children's home because their family was struggling to deal with their health problems. Meanwhile the children's home was struggling to find people willing to work as caregivers to HIV-positive children, because of the stigma attached to HIV. This meant that on average 16 to 22 children were looked after by a single person, which did not improve their health and well-being.

A plan was put forward to start little centres in the communities these children came from. At these centres, the children would be able to get their ART medication twice a day–so the family did not need to worry about that–and one hour after receiving the ART medication in the evening, they would also get dinner. This ensured that everyone would have at least one good meal a day and also that the meal did not interfere with the medication. Both the child and the rest of the family would still have access to the free school that was part of the children's home and to the free hospital that was there. This way the child would get the advantages of the services provided by the children's home and the advantages of living with their family. And it turned out that helping the children this way would be much cheaper and easier to organise than running a children's home.

The advice I give about institutional care is meant for places where there is no viable alternative to a children's home because of complicated caring needs, a lack of resources, or a stigma placed on the child by the cultural or social attitude of the community.

There are different reasons children end up in children's homes. Usually a combination of the situation of the child and the situation of the people running the children's home determines the best kind of care for the child and how to give it.

A state-run orphanage is state-funded and obliged to accept all children that arrive on its doorstep. It has a different set of needs and resources than a children's home run by an NGO in an attempt to improve the quality of life of children of a certain background that is

They cannot be left to care for themselves

funded by donations and able to say 'full is full'. Another option is a children's home for displaced, unaccompanied, children in a refugee camp during or after a war or a disaster. A home for displaced children will have little resources and will not have the luxury of asking if there are more beds—and more importantly if there is more food—available for another child. They take in all who come to them. They do what they can with what is there, and there are always too many mouths and not enough resources to feed them.

In situations that allow it, however, it is very important that people who run a children's home ask themselves the question: how many children can we take good care of? This is an incredibly difficult thing to do, because your feeling tells you that even if you end up overstretching your staff and resources, at least the children will be better off than if they were dying in the streets. However, this may not always be true. There is a breaking point: once that point is reached, it becomes questionable whether the children really are better off in a children's home, when they receive too little care and too little food.

> *I once visited an orphanage where the situation was so bad that instead of going down a long road of suffering at the orphanage, it is possible that the children would have been better off dying by the side of the street. In most cases, the situation in the orphanage led to death anyway. This was a slow death, not a mercifully fast one as it would have been by the side of the road. In this case, it was disinterest in the well-being of the children that led to inadequate care. But in the end, if you keep taking in children beyond your capacity, any place might end up the same. A caregiver works 24/7 on two-week shifts, and has the responsibility for between 15 and 20 children aged newborn to about three years old. It is not humanly possible to provide even remotely decent care under circumstances like these.*

Caregiver-to-child ratios needed for good care:

• Newborn to three years old and older children with complicated special needs	1-3
• Healthy children aged four to twelve years	1-6
• Healthy teenagers	1-8

With fewer caregivers than that, children will suffer. Not just at that time, but with long-term or permanent consequences. It might be acceptable as an emergency short-term solution from time to time, but not as a permanent care system. It is also important to remember that when you make one caregiver look after too many children or if you make her work too many hours, it will not only affect the children's well-being. Caregivers will get overworked and will become more likely to leave, if this is a permanent situation.

In a particular medical children's home, caregivers work 12-hour shifts, either dayshifts or waking nightshifts. Officially they rotate on a two days on, two days off work roster. Normally, two to three children are assigned to the care of each caregiver. Over a certain period, more babies than usual were accepted because they were all in particularly poor condition and did not seem likely to survive if they did not get the care provided in the home. Attempts were made to hire more staff, but no suitable candidates were found who were willing to work in the remote location. This meant that caregivers now had to take care of three to four babies each and that they were made to work a lot of extra shifts. In practice, this came down to most caregivers working six 12-hour shifts per week.

Initially the caregivers were happy to help out. However, after a few months the situation had not changed and the staff was getting exhausted. More and more regularly, caregivers would call in sick at the start of their shift and stay away for several days–meaning someone else had to work an extra shift to cover theirs–or announcing that they were taking unpaid leave for a week or longer. There was also more and more talk of people wanting to quit.

At this point I stepped in. At that moment, 34 babies with complicated special needs were taken care of in the home. I asked the children's home director to calculate how many children the home was able to take care of with the staff that was there, without anyone working extra shifts and with no one taking care of more than three children. The answer turned out to be 18 babies. No wonder the caregivers were overworked and unhappy!

I pointed out that although it is extremely hard to say 'no' to any baby, under the current circumstances it looked likely that within three months most the staff would walk out and the home would have to close down, because there would not be enough staff left to take care of the babies. That would leave the 34 babies in the home without care, as well as all the babies that could not be accepted in the future. The point was taken and a stop was put on accepting babies until either the number of babies had dropped to a manageable number–as their health improved and they moved into foster care–or until enough new caregivers had been found, trained and settled in. This considerably improved the motivation and goodwill among the caregivers.

Some children's homes have a large turnover: new children constantly come in, but they also leave again. How they leave depends

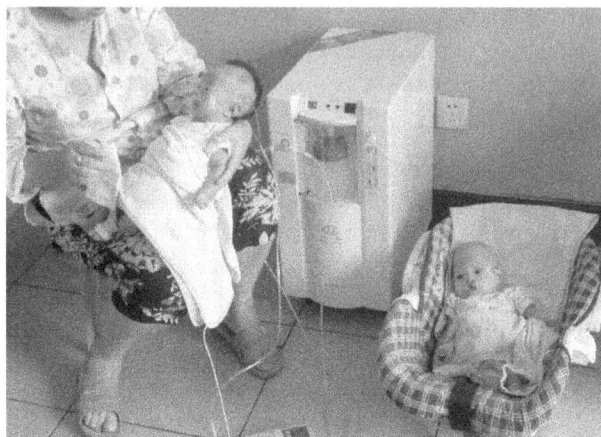

The kind of care that cannot be given in a family home.

on the kind of home. Some children's homes manage to find adoptive families or foster families within a few months. In a home where children are placed who have been removed from their families by the state, they might leave again soon. Either because the home situation has improved or because the state has made permanent arrangements for the child. In a **hospice**, children usually only have a limited time left to live. In medical children's homes, the child's medical needs may be met within a few months, so that she can move on to a different location. In these situations, providing stability and high-standard care are still very important. However, these are not the places where the child has to learn everything needed to become a well-functioning adult.

Other kinds of children's homes provide a home for children until they reach adulthood and are able to look after themselves. Or, in the case of long-term care facilities for people with mental and/or physical handicaps, they may even provide life-long care. In a home where this kind of long-term care is given, it is very important to be aware that your children's home provides the only childhood these children will ever know. When we talk about care for a few months, as long as practical needs are met, damage done by some needs that have fallen by the wayside may still be 'fixed' once the child moves on to his new environment. When we talk about care for years, or for life, needs that are not met and damage that is done will leave a permanent mark on the children in your care. It is also important to become aware that some of a child's needs quite simply cannot be met in a 'traditional orphanage' setup.

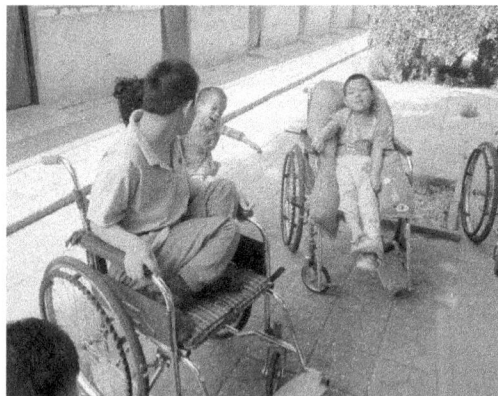

These three will need lifelong care.

Responsible for sixteen children, and for hand-washing their clothes.

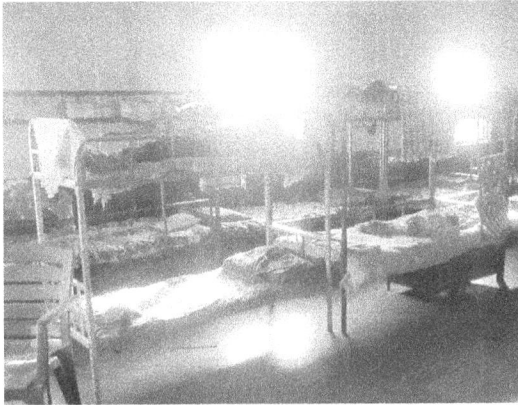

Traditional orphanage dorm.

The traditional orphanage setup with large dorms, few caregivers and a regimental approach is the least ideal for children's well-being. In cases where most children are expected to live in the home until they reach adulthood, this old-fashioned style orphanage setup is not at all recommended. The low number of caregivers, the lack of steady role models, and the complete lack of opportunities to form attachments or to learn from natural social situations are, in many cases, severely damaging both developmentally and psychologically. So, if there is any way to do it, placing these children in group homes–which are discussed later in this chapter–would be a big positive step.

It is emotionally and psychologically damaging for children to permanently live in a large group as one small person, with many, changing caregivers who mostly focus their attention on practical matters such as feeding, cleaning and keeping order. This damage is permanent. In Part 1, Chapter 5: 'Essential Psychological Needs', some of the effects this situation can cause were explained. For this reason, I recommend that all children's homes consider the possibility of finding foster families where children are allowed to experience a more normal family life. Or, if that is impossible, to create a setup with group homes, which is more beneficial to children's social and emotional development.

Remember, children's essential basic needs are:

- *Food and drink*
- *Shelter*
- *Sleep*
- *Hygiene*
- *Safety*
- *Affection and attention*
- *Attachment*
- *Physical contact*
- *Stimulation*

Interestingly, various studies have shown that the options that are preferable for the healthy development of children–having them live in foster families or in group homes in order of preference–are also the ones that cost the least money overall. This is an important thing to keep in mind. Letting a child live in a family-like situation does not only serve the child's well-being, it is also cheaper. The traditional orphanage setup is actually the most expensive option. In fact, research has shown that 'residential care' (meaning care in a children's home) is 5 to 20 times as expensive as foster care or kinship care (members of a child's extended family receiving support to take care of the child).

The basic principle of any children's home is always the same: children are cared for by caregivers who are not their parents, in a situation where more children with a similar background are cared for. However, the form in which this care is provided can differ quite a bit. In this chapter, I will provide an overview of the most common forms of institutional childcare, and I will point out some of the features and requirements specific to each of them.

UN GUIDELINES:

3. The family being the fundamental group of society and the natural environment for the growth, well-being and protection of children, efforts should primarily be directed to enabling the child to remain in or return to the care of his/her parents, or when appropriate, other close family members. The State should ensure that families have access to forms of support in the caregiving role.

11. All decisions concerning alternative care should take full account of the desirability, in principle, of maintaining the child as close as possible to his/her habitual place of residence, in order to facilitate contact and potential reintegration with his/her family and to minimize disruption of his/her educational, cultural and social life.

12. Decisions regarding children in alternative care, including those in informal care, should have due regard for the importance of ensuring children a stable home and of meeting their basic need for safe and continuous attachment to their caregivers, with permanency generally being a key goal.

22. In accordance with the predominant opinion of experts, alternative care for young children, especially those under the age of 3 years, should be provided in family-based settings. Exceptions to this principle may be warranted in order to prevent the separation of siblings and in cases where the placement is of an emergency nature or is for a predetermined and very limited duration, with planned family reintegration or other appropriate long-term care solution as its outcome.

60. Frequent changes in care setting are detrimental to the child's development and ability to form attachments, and should be avoided. Short-term placements should aim at enabling an appropriate permanent solution to be arranged. Permanency for the child should be secured without undue delay through reintegration in his/her nuclear or extended family or, if this is not possible, in an alternative stable family setting or, where paragraph 21 applies, in stable appropriate residential care.

87. The specific safety, health, nutritional, developmental and other needs of babies and young children, including those with special needs, should be catered for in all care settings, including ensuring their on-going attachment to a specific carer.

88. Children should be allowed to satisfy the needs of their religious and spiritual life, including by receiving visits from a qualified representative of their religion, and to freely decide whether or not to participate in religious services, religious education or counselling. The child's own religious back-

ground should be respected, and no child should be encouraged or persuaded to change his/her religion or belief during a care placement.

93. All alternative care settings should provide adequate protection to children from abduction, trafficking, sale and all other forms of exploitation. Any consequent constraints on their liberty and conduct should be no more than strictly necessary to ensure their effective protection from such acts.

123. Facilities providing residential care should be small and be organised around the rights and needs of the child, in a setting as close as possible to a family or small group situation. Their objective should generally be to provide temporary care and to contribute actively to the child's family reintegration or, if this is not possible, to secure his/her stable care in an alternative family setting, including through adoption or kafala of Islamic law, where appropriate.

153. The present Guidelines should continue to apply in situations of emergency arising from natural and man-made disasters, including international and non-international armed conflicts, as well as foreign occupation. Individuals and organizations wishing to work on behalf of children without parental care in emergency situations are strongly encouraged to operate in accordance with the Guidelines.

158. Care within a child's own community, including fostering, should be encouraged, as it provides continuity in socialisation and development.

161. Should family reintegration prove impossible within an appropriate period or be deemed contrary to the best interests of the child, stable and definitive solutions, such as adoption or kafala of Islamic law, should be envisaged; failing this, other long-term options should be considered, such as foster care or appropriate residential care, including group homes and other supervised living arrangements.

✱ ——————————— **Children's Homes**

The most widely used institutional childcare setup is the traditional orphanage setup, which I shall here call the 'children's home'. In

places like these, the rooms in which children up to about three years old are cared for often look a lot like a hospital ward: a room with rows of cots in which babies and toddlers are lying, sitting, or standing. The living arrangements for older children look a lot like a boarding school: the children sleep in dorms with many bunk beds, where everyone may have a little shelf space or a locker for their personal belongings. There are usually a few caregivers taking care of a large group of children. This kind of setup is most often used in state-run orphanages.

Babies in rows of cots.

261

Something on the floor to let babies play there.

Some children's homes will have a kind of living room or play area where babies and children can sit and play, so they do not need to spend all their time in their beds. In warmer climates, there may be a playing area outside where it is safe for children to play and explore. Every children's home should have such a room or area.

Especially babies and toddlers are made to spend their entire day in their beds in many places, being taken out only to have their nappies changed and sometimes–not everywhere–to be fed. This is an unacceptable situation, which will certainly lead to developmental delays and may also cause severe psychological harm and behavioural problems. It is important to make sure that all children are taken out of their beds for several hours a day and given the opportunity to play on mats on the floor and to be held. If there is a living room or play area–inside or outside–it is a good idea to have a rule stating that children can only be in their bedrooms for sleep time. When they are not asleep, they should be taken to another space to allow them to play, to move around and to explore things. Just like in families where children only spend time in bed for sleep and rest.

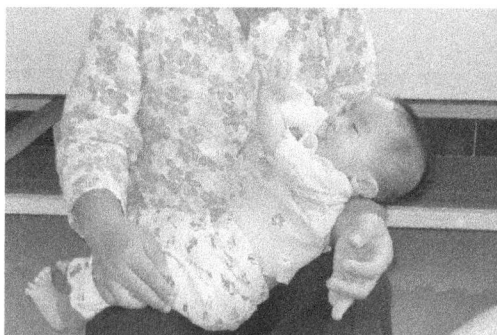

Uniform example: blouse.

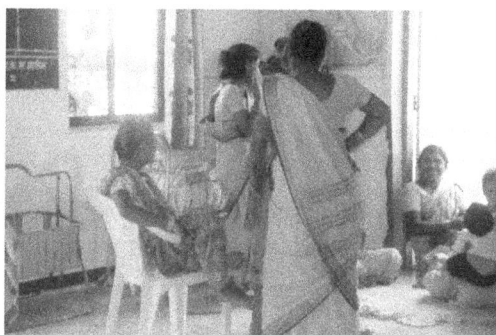

Uniform example: sari.

If caregivers work different shifts, it can be a good idea to have some kind of uniform. It can be as simple as a shirt that is worn over regular clothes, or an apron. Such a shirt has the double advantage of protecting the caregiver's own clothes and making her recognisable as a caregiver. Having caregivers dress alike, gives the children a sense of continuity and security. Even if they do not have a primary caregiver to attach to, at least they can form an attachment to a certain appearance. In Part 2, Chapter 3, under 'Fear of Abandonment and Strangers', there is an example of a little girl who showed a clear attachment to the uniform worn by her caregivers, even though they were different people in different locations.

Reducing Large Crowds

With an eye on the children's well-being rather than business-like efficiency, it is important to try to make sure the children do not have the constant feeling that they are just a drop in a sea of children. This can be done quite easily. For example, it makes a very big difference if a child shares a dorm with 5 other children or with 19 other children. With 5 other children, the child is part of an intimate group. With 19 other children, the child becomes part of a crowd.

> *In the evening the bell is rung for dinner, usually a little after 7 p.m. About ten minutes later the children start to come into the dining hall, which can hold about 150 people. About half an hour after the bell has rung, the dining hall has filled up completely, but food is not yet handed out. The talking and shouting is getting louder and louder among the children aged three to nineteen, who are all hungry and bored. Some of the children start fighting. Supervisors get very angry, shout, give lectures and tell everyone to be completely quiet. About 45 minutes after the bell has rung, the chaos among the children is complete. Then the pails of food are brought in from the kitchen and the food is handed out along the lines. It takes 15 to 20 minutes for everyone to be served. A prayer of thanks is said and then the children are allowed to eat. Food is never hot anymore by the time they start eating.*

When a hundred or more children have their meals in a great hall, sitting in long rows, the feeling of being meaningless and small becomes very strong. And because usually everyone has to wait until everyone is served, no one ever gets warm food. To reduce this negative feeling, you can divide the mealtimes over a period of two and a half hours (if you have more than a hundred children to feed, otherwise, less time will be enough) and have smaller groups come in at set times. Instead of lining the children up in rows, you could have them sit in groups with their caregiver, or two groups with their two caregivers together, in a family-like situation. This will also take care of the issue of supervising many children at the same time. Most importantly, it will give the children a more natural, family-like experience at mealtimes.

Meals happen in a large dining hall, sitting in rows.

Homework is also done in large groups.

Avoiding an assembly of all children on all but very important occasions is also a way to reduce the sense of only being a drop in the sea. During large assemblies, a child's identity disappears, as he only exists as part of the crowd. There is nothing wrong with this if it only happens now and then. However, when it is part of daily life, and it is combined with sleeping in very large dorms and eating in a large dining hall, very little room is left for the child to feel that he is someone in his own right, and that he has a value. It will undermine his self-esteem–more information about the consequences of this is given in Part 2, Chapter 5: 'Self-Esteem and Self-Confidence'. If he does not feel like he counts as a person, it will also make him feel less responsible for his actions and the results that come from them. This can lead to more difficult behaviour.

Around 250 children live in a certain children's home. The children live in dorms of about 20 children, sometimes more, under the supervision of one caregiver. They all eat together, in rows, in the dining hall. They all pray together, in rows, during daily prayer assembly. They live their lives as one in a big group. When a volunteer comes to spend a few weeks at the children's home, the children will introduce themselves on the first meeting. At EVERY meeting after that, they will ask the volunteer if he knows their name. They desperately want the reassurance that they have been remembered and that they are recognised as a real person.

Assemblies are often held for reasons of convenience for management or even for show, rather than because they are necessary. There are even some assemblies where nothing of any interest is said. They are just held to keep up the routine of regular assembly. In some places, children are expected to assemble once or twice every day. There are occasions when it really *is* necessary to gather all children and to make sure that they all get certain information at the same time, from the same person. However, in practice this may only be needed once or twice a month. Many announcements made at assemblies could just as easily have been made by informing the caregivers and having them pass on the message to 'their children'.

UN GUIDELINES:

86. Carers should ensure that the right of every child, including children with disabilities, living with or affected by HIV/AIDS or having other special needs, to develop through play and leisure activities is respected and that opportunities for such activities are created within and outside the care setting. Contact with the children and others in the local community should be encouraged and facilitated.

89. All adults responsible for children should respect and promote the right to privacy, including appropriate facilities for hygiene and sanitary needs, respecting gender differences and interaction, and adequate, secure and accessible storage space for personal possessions.

98. Children in care should be offered access to a person of trust in whom they may confide in total confidentiality. This person should be designated by the competent authority with the agreement of the child concerned. The child should be informed that legal or ethical standards may require breaching confidentiality under certain circumstances.

99. Children in care should have access to a known, effective and impartial mechanism whereby they can notify complaints or concerns regarding their treatment or conditions of placement. Such mechanisms should include initial consultation, feedback, implementation and further consultation. Young people with previous care experience should be involved in this process, due weight being given to their opinions. This process should be conducted by competent persons trained to work with children and young people.

✳ ———————————— **Group homes**

A group home setup is far preferable to the traditional orphanage setup. It offers many more possibilities to meet all the children's essential basic needs. And it will prepare them more effectively for adult life, by giving children a better chance to experience how real life works. This is true both for children with and without mental retardation.

Biological sisters placed in one group home.

The idea of a group home is to create a family-like situation for children who do not have families of their own to take care of them, and who cannot be placed in foster families. Instead of having children live as a tiny part of a big crowd, as is the case in the traditional orphanage setup, they become a significant member of a 'family'. There are different ways in which you can choose to structure your group homes—which I will go into later in this chapter—but the basic outline is the same in all cases: Two adults live together with up to seven children, and in this setting, parental, child and sibling roles are effectively recreated. If some of the children are really siblings, it is usually a great comfort for them to be able to live together, in the same group home.

The two adults who take care of the children may or may not be a married couple. If it is possible to find couples willing to become (paid) 'foster parents' to a group home that would be ideal, because the existing bond between the 'parents' will be a great support to them. Plus, usually people are more likely to stay on for several years, if not permanently, if they are together as a couple than if their work keeps them away from their partner or family. However, if a couple is not available to head a group home, it can also be headed by two caregivers working together, as long as the two who live in the same house get along with each other and are willing to commit to staying in the job for several years.

> School-aged children with moderate to severe physical handicaps and some with mild mental retardation are cared for in a cross between a group home and a foster home. Each group home has up to five children who are cared for by a married couple, living together like a family. The couples are mostly in their forties and fifties, their own children have grown up and left home and now the parents are raising another family. Sometimes, the parents' biological children come to visit or stay the night and the families are mixed. Several of these group homes are spread throughout a regular neighbourhood. All of the group home parents and children visit each other and play together regularly. They are all provided with support and training from group home managers, who have their office in the same neighbourhood.

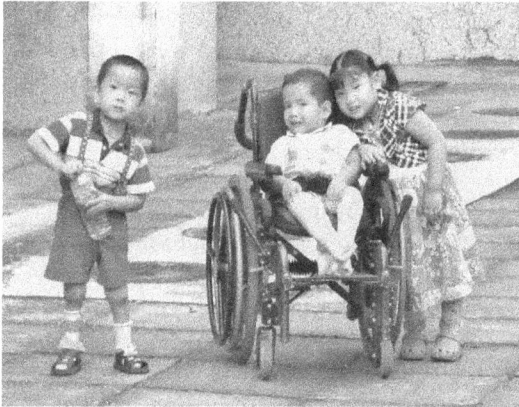

Group home siblings outside their home.

In the group home setting a family situation is created as much as possible. Children should help in the home, according to their age and ability, just like children in normal families do. Caregivers should take an interest in what the children do, stimulate and support them, and give them attention. This does not always have to be sitting on the floor to play. It can just as well be the 'mother' chatting with the 'daughters' and giving them guidance while they are helping to prepare dinner.

In such a situation, where a few children are always around each other like siblings, and caregivers are there for the children like parents, children will start to feel safer and more confident, and their health and growth is likely to improve. The ability to bond with 'siblings' and 'parents' will lay the foundation for the ability to form relationships of all sorts, later on in life. Obviously, neither the 'parents' nor the children will be locked up in their homes. Children from different group homes will play together, they may all go to school together, and the 'parents' can find support and assistance from their neighbours, just like in a regular community. If you house a number of group homes together on a separate compound, like most children's homes, it will still be somewhat cut off from the world. In that case, the group home 'families' will make up their own community together. It is also possible—and preferable—to house the group homes in regular neighbourhoods or communities. When that is the case, children and caregivers can interact, play and develop relationships not only between the different group homes, but also with other adults and children in the community. The group home parents may take their children to the market, the park, and so on, just like regular parents do.

The make-up of a group home should be stable. Children should not be moved around from one group home to the next. If a space opens up because a child is reunited with her family, has been adopted or passes away, a new sibling can be introduced, but otherwise no change should be made.

In a medical children's home, they decided to start a group home system they called the 'mother care system' for the medically stable toddlers. While the babies who were weaker had caregivers work in shifts to keep an eye on them day and night, twelve toddlers were cared for by four caregivers around the clock. Each caregiver had three children assigned to her. During the day, all twelve children would play together in a large play room and for their afternoon nap and at night, each caregiver had a room with a bed for her and three cots for the toddlers in her care. The idea was to make sure that the children would have an opportunity to form bonds with caregivers this way. However, in the early months of the new system, any time there was a change–for example a child who had to go into hospital, came out of hospital or was a new arrival at the home–all the children would be divided up again, meaning that they would sometimes end up with a different caregiver after all. It had to be explained that this took away the opportunity to form attachments and security with the caregivers.

How to Make Up Group Homes

There are several different ways in which you can distribute children over group homes. The choices you make about this are entirely down to personal preference and what is culturally appropriate.

Some options in no particular order:

- Normal family structure: A mixture of different ages and sexes, of healthy children and those with special needs, where the older children help take care of the younger and the healthier help the less able.
- **Segregation** of sexes but mixture of ages: Homes with either all boys or all girls but with a variety of different ages.
- Segregation of sexes and specific age groups: Homes with all boys or all girls who are of more or less the same age.
- Mixture of sexes and specific age groups: Homes with both boys and girls who are of more or less the same age (this should only be done if the children are under five when they first start to live together; if they grow up together from a young age, they will see each other as brothers and sisters, but if they are only put together for the first time at a later age, attractions can develop between children of different sexes).

Some things to keep in mind:

- If special needs children are segregated, their group home should have no more than an absolute maximum of six children with two adults. This is because these children will place a much greater demand on their caregivers' time, if proper care is provided. By blending one or two special needs children in with otherwise healthy children, the burden is divided. This choice should be made by management.
- Segregation of HIV-positive children is done in certain places, because of the stigma attached to the condition. However, it is not necessary for the safety of the children because HIV does not spread very easily. As long as non-infected children are made aware that they should never touch the blood of their affected 'sibling', chances of infection are very small: for infection to be possible both children would need fairly large, fresh wounds to come into direct contact with each other.

In a particular children's home, children who are HIV-positive sleep in separate dorms, in a different part of the compound, away from children who are HIV-negative. During the day, the two groups of children play together, eat together and go to school together, but they live in separate parts of the grounds. When I asked the management why this was the case, they said that they are not worried that the HIV-negative children will get infected with HIV. However, they said that HIV-positive children often have an opportunistic skin infection, chest infections and tuberculosis and they did not want to expose the HIV-negative children to the risk of being infected with these.

I explained that opportunistic infections by definition are infections that are unlikely to make healthy children ill because the bacteria are too weak. They only make HIV-positive children ill because their immune system is failing, so separating them is not likely to make any change in the health of children who are not infected with HIV.

Setting Up/Transforming to Group Homes

When you start a new children's home, it should not be too complicated to set it up divided into group homes. Especially if you are building the accommodation yourself. You can build small living units for each group, instead of big buildings with large halls and dorms. Or, as mentioned before, you can build, rent or buy flats, houses or huts in the community to have group homes there, giving children a better chance of being part of the community.

If you are changing your organisation from a traditional orphanage setup to a group home model, this may raise some problems. You will have all the structures in place to care for the children in large groups, but there are no small living areas suitable for 'families'.

Still, even in this case it can be done without tearing everything down and starting all over. The way the buildings are divided up will need to be adjusted somewhat. Placing simple thin walls–made of plywood to start with, or even curtains, if nothing else is available or affordable–can help to make separate 'homes' without too much cost or construction trouble. As a first measure, just dividing the existing halls into separate living areas is a good start. Over time, as construction for either expansion or maintenance is necessary anyway, you can start building custom-built flats or huts for your group homes.

A very large children's home, caring for close to 300 children, was considering changing to a group home system. While discussions were going on about how this change could take place, I was given a tour of the campus. One of the things that was pointed out to me was a big building site. An enormous hole had been dug in the ground and the first work on the foundations of the new building had started. I was told that this was to become the new dining hall, which would be big enough to allow all the children to eat at the same time, instead of in groups as was happening at that moment. And above the dining hall would be a floor of offices and a floor of large dorms. At the next meeting, I brought up the fact that this was a perfect opportunity. Because a large building project was already taking place, and they were only just getting started with the foundations, there was still time to make adjustments. This meant that we could redesign the building to contain a lot of purpose-built living spaces for group homes. With a group home system in place, there would be no need for a large dining hall and kitchen, because all children would be eating with their 'family', so that space could be used for living spaces. The floor of dorms could also be transformed into living spaces, and with the old dorms becoming empty when the children moved into their group homes, it would be quite easy to change the old dorms into offices, so the office floor could also be turned into living spaces. That would create 'homes' for 25 to 30 group homes, meaning that we would only have to create living spaces in the old dorm buildings–a more complicated process– for the group home of a relatively small group of children.

The management said they would consider it. However, when I next visited the project, I was shown around the shiny new dining hall, the offices above it and the floor of large dorms above that. The opportunity had slipped by and the transition to a group home system was delayed because of the logistical complications of creating living spaces. The management said they would consider it.

The transformation will not be easy. It is complicated in the practical sense of figuring out how to create living spaces and how do divide up groups and train caregivers. And to start with it will be difficult for the children–which automatically means it will also be difficult for the caregivers having to deal with them–in an emotional sense, because it is a big change for them. Children who are no longer used to close personal relationships are likely to be quite difficult in the first months after the transformation has taken place. This is something to be prepared for, but it helps if you realise that initial difficult behaviour from the children does not indicate the failure of the transformation. What causes the difficult behaviour is that the children are trying to adjust to having their essential basic needs met, something they did not expect to ever experience again. To start with, they will not be sure if they can trust the positive change to be permanent, because they have never been able to rely on positive changes before. Most of the children will have experienced short moments when they were suddenly cared for much better, for example when volunteers came to help out, or when there was an important official person visiting, but it was always only temporary. They have learned not to trust that these kinds of improvements will stay, and they are afraid to hope. So, it is understandable that they will be uncertain and unsettled for some time.

If I prevented you from eating anything at all for two days, or even longer, and then I put a plate of food in front of you, you would be happy and relieved and you would start eating. If when you had eaten about half of the food on the plate, while still feeling hungry, I took the plate away from you because there is only a limited amount of food and other people need to eat too, what would you do? You would get angry and you would fight me.

Does this mean that you are a bad person or that you were being spoiled by the food I put in front of you? Would it have been better if I had not given you that food, even if it was less than you would have wished? No! What it means is that you are fighting for your survival: you need the food and you need more of it, so you demand it. Also, having experienced a situation where I was able to keep food from you for two days, you feel unsure whether this might happen again and whether you might get the next meal or not.

Now, having had this experience and being starved for food once more for several days before I bring you food again, this time you expect me to take the food away from you before you are done. So you will eat faster, guard the food closely and be extremely aggressive whenever I make any move at all. It does not matter that I am not going to take away the food from you this time and tell you so, because you feel you cannot be sure of that. The same is true for children who are starved for attention, attachment and stability.

*When new buildings are built, make sure they are suitable
for group homes.*

Changing the setup of a children's home from a traditional orphanage model to group homes is not going to be the end of all
problems. However, it is a big step in the direction of improvement
for both children and caregivers. For a caregiver, it is much easier
and more enjoyable to provide good care for children with whom
she can bond, with a workload that does not overstretch her. In a
traditional orphanage setup, it is quite simply impossible to provide
children with the care they need. Even in the best run children's
home, where the traditional orphanage set-up is used, essential basic needs are never all met, while the group home set-up allows you
to create the same kind of circumstances and conditions that exist in
real families. This at least give you a chance at being able to provide
adequate care and meeting the children's essential basic needs.

The more the caregivers at the head of a group home start to see
themselves and feel like the parents of the children they care for,
the more likely they are to really fulfil all of the children's needs.
Plus, the more they feel like the children's parents, the less their job
will feel like hard work, because a lot of the most important things–
such as giving children attention, forming attachments, giving physical contact and showing an interest in them–will start to happen
automatically, without conscious thought or effort. When that point
is reached, you know that your group homes are a success and that
the children are likely to thrive in them.

Another advantage of using a group home system, is having the children in small groups rather than large ones. This is particularly great

when caring for children with mental retardation. There is a variety of reasons why this is an advantage:

- A child is more likely to pay attention to what you are trying to tell or teach him without the distraction of many people around.
- A child who easily gets overwhelmed or upset by a lot of noise or many things happening at once, will be calmer and easier to deal with when he is surrounded by fewer people, in a quieter place.
- A child who gets very overexcited or upset, screaming and crying, can 'infect' the children around him, making them upset too. If there are 50 children around, it can affect 50 children; if there are only five other children around, it will not affect more than those five. You may even be able to prevent those five being affected because you have a stronger bond with them, so will be able to comfort them more effectively.
- A child usually likes to copy the behaviour of others, and when he is part of a big group there will often be someone misbehaving, while in a small group this will happen less often and is more easily controlled.
- A child will have more opportunities to interact on a one-to-one basis in a small group. This will increase his chances of being able to learn new skills and aspects of self-care, making it easier to care for him in the long run.
- A child is better able to learn what will be expected of him out in the real world if he has the opportunity to see normal human relations and interactions—the way children in families do all the time—instead of only seeing caregivers going about their jobs.
- So by living in a small group in a family-like situation in a group home, he will be better prepared for what life is really about.

So, in short, caring for children in a group home setup provides much better chances of giving the children a good quality of life, as well as improving their future possibilities. And it will make the caregivers' jobs easier and more enjoyable.

UN GUIDELINES:

17. Siblings with existing bonds should in principle not be separated by placements in alternative care unless there is a clear risk of abuse or other justification in the best interest of the child, in any case, every effort should be made to enable siblings to maintain contact with each other, unless this is against their wishes or interests.

✱ ——————— Medical Children's Home
Some children's homes specialise in giving care to children who have medical conditions or who are in poor health. This adds considerable responsibilities and challenges; how these take shape depends on the kinds of issues the children in your care have. In some places, only children with one particular problem are cared for. For

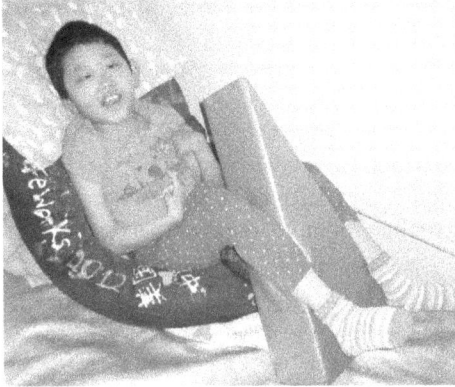

Children with cerebral palsy need help with positioning.

example, there may be a home for children with cerebral palsy, a home for children infected with HIV/AIDS, a home for blind children, or a home for children who were orphaned and injured in armed conflict. In these cases, the children in your care have a very specific set of special needs that you can specialise in.

For example, when dealing with children with cerebral palsy, you will require assistance—or at least training—from physiotherapists, occupational therapists, and most likely also speech therapists, to deal with the required exercises, positioning and different aids for the children. Aside from that, you will need a nutritionist to help provide a balanced diet for the children who may not be able to eat regular adult food. When dealing with children who are blind but otherwise healthy, however, only minor adjustments are needed to make it easier for them to find their way around safely and learn to live independent lives.

With children infected with HIV/AIDS, it is important to have medical assistance close at hand to monitor the children's health and to treat infections. And it is essential to have mealtimes at set times that never change, to make sure that ART medication can be taken at the same time every day and in the right manner. However, other than that, these children can and should lead normal everyday lives with a just slightly greater emphasis on hygiene and healthy eating to prevent opportunistic infections.

At 6:00 p.m. every evening the children were assembled for prayer. After prayer, at 6:30 p.m. ART medication was taken and dinner was at 7:30 p.m., to allow the stomach to stay empty apart from the medication for an hour.

The holidays were coming up, and one evening several visitors arrived at the end of prayer. When the ART had been handed out, the children were all told to sit back in their rows. The visitors started handing out goody bags full of sweets and other snacks, as well as a little candle. As soon as all of the children had gotten their bag and had thanked the visitors, they opened the bags and started eating the snacks, and no one stopped them. Having a snack 15 minutes after taking the particular kind of ART medicine that most of the children here were taking, has the same effect as skipping the dose.

There are also children's homes that provide care to children with all kinds of problems and medical conditions. These homes are especially found in countries where children are sometimes abandoned because either the parents have been given a diagnosis with a pessimistic outlook, or they do not have the money to get the care that the child needs to survive. Such places can operate almost like children's hospitals, only with caregivers instead of parents looking after the regular practical and emotional needs of the children. Here, medical assistance as well as a good relationship with the local hospital(s) is extremely important. Generally, places like these also need a certain amount of equipment, such as machines that provide children with oxygen or to suction them, to improve their chances of survival.

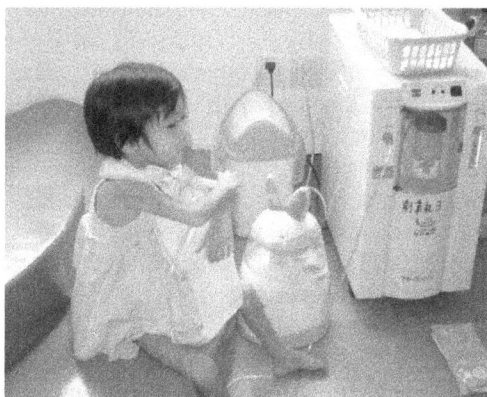

Needing oxygen, nebulisation and suctioning often.

Enjoying life, even though they live with HIV.

Then there are regular children's homes that take in any child that arrives on their doorstep, with or without medical problems. In such a situation, it is important to have someone in the home who is able to do a check-up as soon as the child arrives or to take the child to a doctor on the day of arrival to see if he has any special requirements or needs medical attention. It is good for children with and without special needs to live and play together. Children should only be kept apart in situations where a child has a very contagious disease that could put other children at risk–this does not include HIV/AIDS since children are extremely unlikely to be infected simply from living alongside infected children–or if a child's condition is so weak that contact with other children endangers his health–for example if catching a cold from another child is likely to turn into something serious, like pneumonia, for him.

In any kind of medical children's home, it is important to remember that although the children in your care have special needs, in the end they are just like other children. They may not be able to do everything quite in the same way as other children of their age do, but they still need to be given the opportunity to live, develop, and enjoy life. They need to receive physical contact, attention, stimulation and the opportunity to form attachments. They need to be allowed to take care of themselves, to the extent that they are able to, to explore their surroundings as best they can, and to play with toys and with each other.

A four-month-old baby arrived at a children's home with scabies. She had clearly had it for some time already, because there was barely any part of her skin that was not affected. Not wanting to risk infecting all the other children and caring staff, the girl was never taken inside the children's home. As soon it was discovered that she had scabies, she was moved to an empty room in the storage building together with a caregiver. The room was turned into a bedroom, and disposable nappies and old clothes that could be thrown away when she had used them were brought in. Both the girl and the caregiver were treated for scabies. They lived in the storage building for a week, and the medical manager came to check on them every day. When both had received the full course of treatment and the scabies was gone, the little girl was allowed to go into the children's home and join the other babies.

In the book *Sick Children Everywhere. Book 2: Basic Medical Care for Children in Institutions*, you will find more information on how to deal with various medical conditions and about the basic necessities of providing care for children who are ill or have a medical condition in children's homes.

UN GUIDELINES:

97. Use of force and restraints of whatever nature should not be authorised unless strictly necessary for safeguarding the child's or others' physical or psychological integrity, in conformity with the law and in a reasonable and proportionate manner and with respect for the fundamental rights of the child. Restraint by means of drugs and medication should be based on therapeutic needs and should never be employed without evaluation and prescription by a specialist.

Children's Hospice

A children's hospice takes care of children with terminal illnesses or conditions. These are children for whom doctors are not able to do more to help them live longer. The reason why children end up here may be because they have been abandoned by their parents when a diagnosis was made that nothing more could be done for the child. However, it is also possible that the parents do still come to visit the child, but are unable to take care of him at home. Parents may bring a child to a hospice because they prefer that the child does not die in hospital, although they recognise that he needs more complicated care than they are able to give him at home.

Children in hospice care may not be acutely dying the moment they are admitted—in fact, some of them may surprise you and continue living for months or even years beyond their life expectancy against all odds—however, they will not grow up to be adults.

A little boy–abandoned–arrived at the hospice when he had just turned one year old. He had a severe heart condition that could not be fixed. His heart condition gave him a purple colour and his body was quite weak. He was not able to sit up yet. He was not expected to live very long: in his condition, catching a cold would probably kill him.

When he was four years old he got chicken pox, something that someone in his condition could not possibly survive, but he did. He was walking around now, looking a lot more purple, and he had become a bit of a menace. The reason for this was that, with the constant expectation that he would not live very much longer, no one had taught him rules or set limits. Now he was at times a danger to himself and to the children around him. Although it still seemed unlikely that he would live long, he was placed in a foster family, to give him a more normal life for the time that was left. When he was six years old, he got very bad headaches. He was diagnosed with cysts in his brain and got surgery to remove them. Unfortunately, the surgery led to a serious infection in his brain. His condition was critical and he was placed in the hospice again. With his heart condition, he could not possibly pull through, but he did. However, either the surgery or the infection had caused so much damage to his brain that he was now in a vegetative state. His body continued to live on against all odds, but his mind was gone.

Sometimes unusual things are tried to ensure comfort.

Having fun despite inoperable heart defects.

In effect, a hospice is a lot like a medical children's home, with the difference that the children are not expected to get better. This has consequences for the treatments they receive. While for most children you do whatever can be done to make sure they get better, with a terminally ill child a switch is made to what is called 'palliative

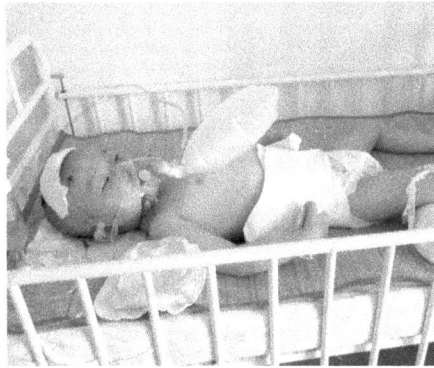

A little boy in hospice care, kept as comfortable as possible.

care'. This is care aimed at making the child as comfortable as possible and to make sure he is not in pain, rather than trying to make him better.

Not everyone is suited to work in a home like this. So, special care should be taken when selecting caregivers. It should be explained to staff, very clearly, what kind of children they will be dealing with and that the children are not expected to survive. People working here need to be able to accept death as the almost inevitable outcome, while still allowing the child to live a life that is as normal as possible under the given circumstances.

In the end, terminally ill children are also just children. At moments when they are not too weak or in too much discomfort to have an interest in anything at all, they need to be allowed to play, to learn, to explore. Let a toddler take his first steps, let a child explore the garden and have his quarrels with the children around him. If children want to, they can continue their education as long as they are able to. Do not end the child's life before it is over. Allow him to live whatever life is still left to him.

In the book *Sick Children Everywhere. Book 2: Basic Medical Care for Children in Institutions*, Part 3, Chapter 5: 'Palliative Care', you will find more information about providing palliative care for children in children's homes.

UN GUIDELINES:

117. Agencies and facilities should ensure that, wherever appropriate, carers are prepared to respond to children with special needs, notably those living with HIV/AIDS or other chronic physical or mental illnesses, and children with physical or mental disabilities.

✳ ——————————— **Respite Care Facility**
Instead of running a children's home for children with special needs, running a **respite care** home is a great way of both helping families and the community, and allowing more children to live with their families. For children with mental or physical handicaps, it can be a way to have the best of both worlds. A respite care facility usually provides day care for children–or adults–with complicated special needs. The children cared for in a respite care facility almost always

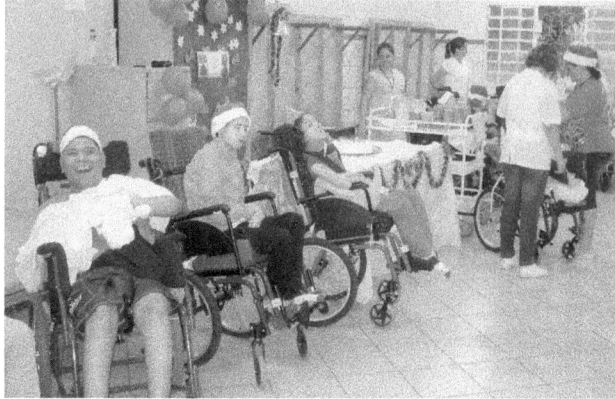

A Christmas celebration at a respite home for children with cerebral palsy.

have families and live with them. However, they have serious health issues, severe physical handicaps or mental retardation, which makes it very hard for their parents or extended family to cope with their care on their own. It may also be difficult for families to find someone to look after their child with special needs when they need to go out to work to earn money for the family. Being able to leave their child in the safe care of a respite care facility can solve this problem without the need of abandoning the child. A respite care facility can also take the form of a special education school, where education is provided to children with mental retardation who are unable to attend regular schools. This education might be combined with things like providing therapy and teaching life skills.

> *A church group has started a respite care centre for 35 children with severe cerebral palsy. In the morning, all the children are picked up from home in specially adapted vans. Once all the children have arrived and are in their usual groups, they eat breakfast that has been specially prepared for their individual needs under the supervision of a nutritionist. The same goes for their lunch. Through the course of the day, each child is bathed and most of the children need several nappy changes. Aside from the caregivers, the centre has a physiotherapist, an occupational therapist, a speech therapist, a psychologist and a nurse. The nurse gives medication when needed and she monitors the children's health. The other professionals take each of the children to their therapy room once or twice a week and they work on their exercises and on developing their abilities. There are also two special educators, who do arts and crafts and vocational activities with the children. And sometimes volunteers come to sing with the children or do activities with them. At 4:00 p.m. the children are put in the vans again and are dropped off at home.*

Usually, children are dropped off at the facility in the morning, or picked up at home with a bus of some kind, and they go home again in the late afternoon or early evening. They usually spend their evenings, weekends and holidays at home, with their families.

Because these children receive the love, attention and opportunities to form attachments they need at home, the focus in the respite care facility can be on specialist care. Children get the therapy they need, as well as medical check-ups. This means that medical and paramedical (= therapists) staff are needed to provide good respite care. The more difficult or physically heavy aspects of daily care such as bathing and wound care are often taken care of here as well.

Children are provided with the meals appropriate for the hours of their stay at the facility. This can be breakfast, lunch and dinner, or sometimes only one or two of those meals. The children are given stimulation in the form of activities and events. Children who have the mental age and ability for structured education may be given schooling as well. This might be at a nearby school, with guidance from the respite care home, or by teachers employed at the home. A respite care facility can also have an important role in educating both the parents and the wider community about the special needs of the child, as well as her abilities and potential.

After having taken her daughter with cerebral palsy for a doctor's appointment, a mother brings her back to the respite home. She hands her daughter over to the caregivers and then goes to the nurse's office. There, the nurse and the mother discuss what the doctor has said and the nurse explains what this means for the girl's care at home and at the respite home.

Anyone considering starting a children's home for children with special needs should consider whether starting a respite home would be more beneficial to the children and the community. In many cases, parents feel forced to abandon their child with special needs because they are unable to cope with the daily care, or because they are unable to pay for the various therapies and aids that the child needs. When there are no options for help other than for 'orphans', abandoning the child seems like the only way to help her. With the availability of free respite care that makes the burden less heavy, many families are very happy to keep their child with them. So, while opening a children's home of children with complex special needs may encourage abandonment of children out of desperation, the opening of a respite home may help decrease the number of abandoned children.

A particular medical children's home specialises in care for children with heart defects. They have 30 beds for 'orphans', but they also have space for up to five families. When a family is too poor to pay for the costs of the surgeries needed, they can come to this children's home. There, they will receive help with the funding of the surgeries,

but also with making complicated medical decisions. The family is given training on how to take care of their child's daily medical needs. Once the surgery is over and the child is doing well again, the family takes the child home.

While most respite homes are set up to care for people with complex special needs, that does not mean that is the only kind of respite home that is acceptable. In areas of extreme poverty, you might also help avoid child-abandonment—or recruitment of children in exploitive situations—by opening a respite home that acts as a kind of free day care for all village children, providing one or two good meals a day, providing the children with toys and other stimulation to help their development and by, for example, providing homework guidance after school, while allowing the children to continue to live with their families and experience regular life. These options are not only much more beneficial for the children and the community. They are also more **ethical** and much cheaper than running a children's home around the clock.

Guided Foster Care

Normally, foster care is where a child's experience with institutional care ends. However, I have come across a transitional form of foster care that I want to mention. In this particular case, the care in the

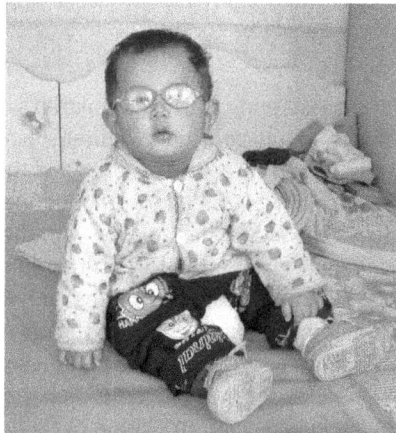

A little boy in his foster home.

foster home was more closely linked to the care previously given in the children's home than is normally the case.

In this case, the children's home was a medical home, where all children had medical conditions. Once they had received the necessary operations and special care and they were strong and healthy enough the children went into local foster care. On average, most children would only spend between three and nine months in the children's home. The foster families were screened and trained in basic childcare by foster care coordinators attached to the children's home, before a child was assigned to them.

At least one family member would then spend a day in the children's home with their prospective foster child. To get to know her, but also to learn about the special care she needed. They could practise any special care needs under guidance and decide whether they could deal with taking care of these things at home every day. If all went well, the child would be placed in the family. The children's home would provide the family with a small mat and blanket for the child to sleep on, clothes, formula, bottles, some toys and any medication or special devices needed for the care of the child. The family also received a modest wage, which meant that they were effectively working for the children's home and knew they were expected to follow all instructions given concerning the care of the child. If necessary, additional training would be given to the family later on.

A girl in her foster home, playing.

Two older girls sitting outside their foster home.

The foster family would receive weekly visits from the foster care coordinators, to make sure that everything was going all right and to check up on the child. During such visits, the foster parents could also ask questions or raise concerns. New supplies of formula and clothes–of gradually bigger sizes and appropriate for the season–were delivered on these visits, as needed. Once a month, the children would be measured and weighed, to keep track of their growth. If there were ever any medical issues–ranging from the child catching a cold to their condition relapsing meaning there was need for new surgery–the family would contact the foster care coordinators, who would accompany them on any doctor's or hospital visits– paid for by the children's home–and would afterwards provide them with new care instructions.

This system allowed them to minimise the time spent in an institution for children who were well enough to do without constant specialised care, but not well enough to do without close monitoring. These children could experience family life while early detection of problems and help were still easily available.

For most of these children, adoption papers were prepared around the time they went into foster care, and many of them were adopted internationally after living with their foster family for about a year.

One night, a fire broke out in a house where a baby was fostered. The family all got out unhurt (including the foster baby), but they had lost everything they had and needed to live with relatives. The foster care coordinator went to visit the family the morning after the fire. Among other things, he offered to take the foster child back to the children's home, now that the family was in such a difficult situation. The family would not hear of it. The foster child was part of their family now and they said it would make the situation even worse to lose him as well as all their possessions.

When deciding how much money to pay the foster parents, a very careful balance needs to be found. On the one hand, you need to give enough to make the foster parents feel they are getting a fair reward for their troubles and to cover any expenses they may have to make. This way it will become affordable for them to take care of a child and it will motivate them. On the other hand, you do not want t o give so much that some people might start taking in foster children purely for the money, because this is not likely to lead to good care for the child. So it has to be enough to help motivate foster parents, but little enough to make sure only people with a real interest in and heart for children will be tempted by it.

UN GUIDELINES:
118. The competent authority or agency should devise a system, and should train concerned staff accordingly, to assess and match the needs of the child with the abilities and resources of potential foster carers and to prepare all concerned for the placement.

119. A pool of accredited foster carers should be identified in each locality who can provide children with care and protection while maintaining ties to family, community and cultural group.

120. Special preparation, support and counselling services for foster carers should be developed and made available to carers at regular intervals, before, during and after the placement.

Chapter 2:   The Ethics of Running a Children's Home

The first thought is: how can someone who has opened their home to underprivileged children and spends their life feeding them be doing anything other than a good thing? Unfortunately, the answer is not 'of course they are doing a good thing!' There are many children's homes around the world where children are *not* better off than they would be in an alternative situation. Sometimes this is despite the best intentions, because of lack of knowledge or resources. Sometimes it is because of lack of good faith, and the children or their situation are exploited in some way.

No child should live in a children's home if there is anyone who can take care of them.

There are a lot of ethical issues involved in running a children's home. This means issues that make it necessary to look closely at a child's situation and ask yourself: is what we are doing really right and in the best interest of the child? If the answer to this question is 'no', you should think about how the situation could be changed.

In this chapter, we will look at different situations in which the children's well-being is not central to the decision-making process, or where incomplete knowledge about the consequences of certain situations lead to unfortunate circumstances. These are all situations that I have come across in different places. They are things you should keep in mind if you are running a children's home, to see whether a change is needed. They should definitely be thought about long and hard if you are considering setting up a new children's home, to make sure your children's home is started in the children's best interest.

Should These Children Be in a Children's Home?

For a long time it was believed that children would do just as well, if not better, when they were raised in a children's home as when they were raised in a family. The thinking was that people who had received training were far more qualified to raise children than parents who did not have any training. During the twentieth century, this belief started to change. But some of it still remains to this day. It is now widely accepted that children are better off growing up with their parents if they have two living parents who are moderately wealthy and able to provide them with an education. However, the belief still exists in many places that if one or both parents are dead,

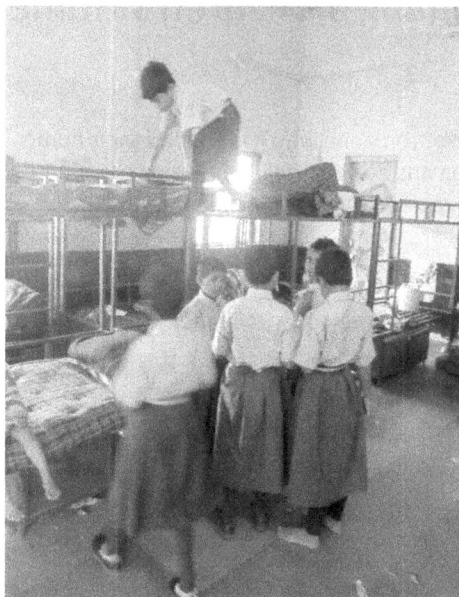

Even if you provide them with better education, they are still better off in a family.

if the parents are very poor, or if the child does not have access to formal education, she will be better off in a children's home. In some cases, the same belief exists with regards to religion: the thought is that getting a more thorough religious upbringing, particularly if it is a minority religion, will give the child a better life. No matter how persistent these beliefs about the benefits of institutional care for children are, they are not true.

Research has shown again and again that even if a child gets an education in a children's home, one which she might not have gotten with her family, she is unlikely to be successful in life and runs a very high risk of ending up living in the streets. This is particularly unfortunate because many children's homes are opened to keep children *off* the streets. It has been shown that even if a child lives in severe poverty with her family and receives little or no education, her chances in life are better than those of a child who was raised in a children's home with an education. The main reason for this is most likely that her essential basic needs were met by her family, giving her body and her brain a better chance of developing normally, something that almost never happens in a children's home.

A study of young adults who had grown up in children's homes found that they were:

- 10 times more likely to be involved in prostitution as adults
- 40 times more likely to have a criminal record
- 500 times more likely to commit suicide

There is a surprisingly large number of so-called 'orphanages' around the world where the children actually have living relatives, or even parents. It is estimated by the UN that about 8 million children live in children's homes around the world. About 80 to 90% of them have at least one living parent. Most children in these places have families who sent them there in good faith, believing they are giving their children better chances. Some people who run children's homes will even go around convincing parents to let them take the children with them, to live in the children's home and be educated there. This sounds like a wonderful proposal to the family, because many people still think that living in a children's home can be a good solution. However, neither the children nor the family will be better off in this arrangement.

It was explained to me that while the children from this children's home had living relatives, they came from the poorest area of the country, where there was hardly any education or healthcare available and, in many places, not even electricity. So, the children were taken into a children's home in the big city to provide them with education. The reality, however, is that the school-aged children live in a house in the city with the person who set up the 'orphanage' (and sometimes some of his extended family). They are removed from the family, the village and the life they know to the completely different life of the city. They receive food, clothes, schooling and tuition and when they are not in school they are expected to behave well and take care of chores like cleaning, cooking and generally serving the founder and his guests. Attention, affection, and concern for the children's emotional well-being are rarely seen.

When I asked whether these children ever get to visit their families, the answer was 'no' in all cases. When I asked whether these children are in contact with their family at all, the answer was only 'yes' in some cases. I was told that it was too difficult, because of the great distance, the great cost and the difficulty of reaching the remote villages that these children come from. I was told that if they were allowed to visit their family, they might not want to come back again. They told me that as long as the children were in school, they would live in the children's homes; when they finish their studies–in four, eight, or twelve years' time–they are free to go back if they wish. But after so much time without any contact with their family, having lived in a city and not being used to rural life anymore, why would they want to go back?

If you want to help children who are poor or live in remote locations to get an education, it is much cheaper, more effective and more beneficial to the children and the community to set up a school in their village, rather than to take them out of their village and away from their family.

You may have children in your care who do still have family members, but whose family is completely unable to care for them, for whatever reason. In this case, it is important to help the child stay in contact with her family and to encourage visits both from the family to the child, and from the child to the family. If it is possible for the child to spend her school holidays staying with her family members, this should also be encouraged. The reason why this is important, is that having time with her family will help to make sure some of the child's essential basic needs are met, that are not met in a children's home. It will help her learn about her identity and help her prepare for adult life. And if the child does not return after the holidays but stays with her family, that is good news, not bad, as it was said to be in the last example. Being with her family is what is best for her. The children's home is there to do what is best for the child, the child is not there to give the children's home an excuse for existing.

> In a particular children's home, a lot of the children still had family members, many of them even had living parents. They were living in the children's home to get a proper education and in some cases also because their family had trouble dealing with their medical conditions. At times, the families would come to the home to visit their child. When I visited, the school holidays were coming up and I asked if the children with families would be going home. I was told that management had decided not to let the children go to their families this time, because previously they had been very difficult to handle when they came back.

It is entirely possible that a child may be a little more difficult, or may find it hard to readjust to the children's home after a stay with her family. However, this is not a sign that it is better not to let her go, nor is it a sign that the child is bad. It is a sign that the child has experienced what it is like to have all her essential basic needs met and that she is now fighting for that to continue. As I mentioned before, this is simply a survival instinct, not a sign that you are spoiling her or that things like this should not be allowed. Letting a child have as much contact as possible with her family is very important for her development and well-being.

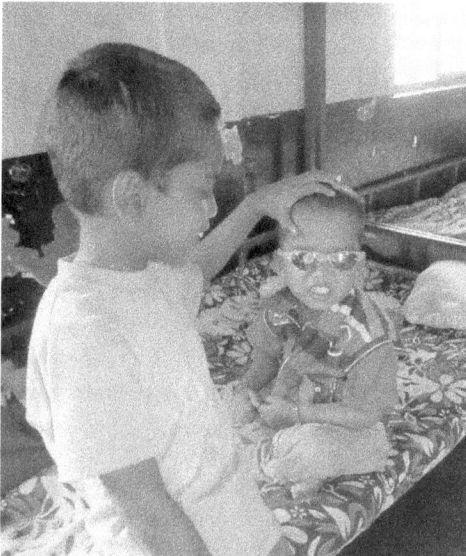

Doing what you can to reunite them with their family should be a priority.

If you are running a children's home that takes in children who lived on the street, or who were brought by the police because they got lost or because they were rescued from human trafficking, aside from providing these children with a roof over their head and food to eat, you should make every effort to find out more about the child. As much information as the child is able to give you about her name, the names of relatives, where she is from and anything else that might help, should be gathered. With this information, every effort should be made to find the child's family and to bring them back together. Reuniting families is a much greater help to the child than having her grow up in a children's home, no matter how good the intentions are.

So, in short, a children's home is only an acceptable solution if there is no other solution. Only if the child has *no one* who is able and willing to take care of her, or if she is at severe risk of neglect or abuse by her family, is she likely to be better off in a children's home than outside of one. And then, the children's home should make every effort to find a family-like solution for her as quickly as possible, by finding adoptive or foster families or by structuring itself into group homes. This, in a very practical sense, means that most of the children who are living in children's homes around the world, should not be there.

As mentioned in Part 3, Chapter 1: 'Different Kinds of Caring Setups', you could also consider opening a respite home, rather than a children's home, to help children and their families cope with difficult situations without forcing them apart.

UN Guidelines:
14. Removal of a child from the care of the family should be seen as a measure of last resort and should, whenever possible, be temporary and for the shortest possible duration. Removal decisions should be regularly reviewed and the child's return to parental care, once the original causes of removal have been resolved or have disappeared, should be in the best interests of the child, in keeping with the assessment foreseen in paragraph 49 below.

15. Financial and material poverty, or conditions directly and uniquely imputable to such poverty, should never be the only justification for the removal of a child from parental care, for receiving a child into alternative care, or for preventing his/her reintegration, but should be seen as a signal for the need to provide appropriate support to the family.

20. The provision of alternative care should never be undertaken with a prime purpose of furthering the political, religious or economic goals of the providers.

21. The use of residential care should be limited to cases where such a setting is specifically appropriate, necessary and constructive for the individual child concerned and in his/her best interests.

51. Regular and appropriate contact between the child and his/her family specifically for the purpose of reintegration should be developed, supported and monitored by the competent body.

81. When a child is placed in alternative care, contact with his/her family, as well as with other persons close to him or her, such as friends, neighbours and previous carers, should be encouraged and facilitated, in keeping with the child's protection and best interests. The child should have access to information on the situation of his/her family members in the absence of contact with them.

155. Organizations and authorities should make every effort to prevent them, separation of children from their parents or primary caregivers, unless the best interests of the child so require, and ensure that their actions do not inadvertently encourage family separation by providing services and benefits to children alone rather than to families.

166. The validity of relationships and the confirmation of the willingness of the child and family members to be reunited must be verified for every child. No action should be taken that may hinder eventual family reintegration, such as adoption, change of name or movement to places far from the family's likely location, until all tracing efforts have been exhausted.

Taking Responsibility

Opening a children's home means taking on a tremendous responsibility. Taking in the children makes you responsible for their safety and well-being. Not just today and tomorrow, but for as long as they are with you, and after that you will be responsible for the children who come after them and so on. This is something you need to think about. It is not just about making sure there is a roof over their head and a place for them to sleep. Most people take the responsibility very seriously, but not everyone is aware of how big the responsibility they have taken upon themselves really is.

'God will provide' is something I have heard many times. This is a beautiful sentiment and it is admirable to put your trust in God and pray for what you need. However, when you have several dozen hungry mouths to feed, you are not taking your responsibility seriously if *all* you do is to pray and wait for God to deliver what you need. Some effort on your side, to help God to provide, is needed too.

> A former volunteer who still made regular donations to cover children's school fees wrote an email to the children's home. In it, she mentioned that she had heard that the diet and hygiene standards at the home still were not great. She wrote that she was disappointed by this. The care manager of the home was very angry about this email. She said: 'In December we had no money, NOTHING to feed the children. And did she send more money for food when we needed it?! Then how can she complain?'

If you feel that your job is done with providing the children with a roof over their head, and it is up to the outside world to feed the children and take care of them without your interference, you are not honouring the burden of responsibility that you suggested you would be taking on by opening a children's home. In the end, it is the children who will end up suffering. They are the ones who go hungry because you refuse to keep your end of the bargain. If you will not

They need more than just a roof over their head, and they only have you to provide what they need.

provide complete care, the children are better off not living in your children's home, regardless of what the alternative is.

Responsibility also includes making yourself aware of whether the children's needs are being met. Pretty much any children's home manager around the world will tell you that her job is to care for the children in the children's home. This is true, that is her job. However, that is not always what really happens. Over the many years that I have spent visiting dozens of children's homes, I have gradually become aware of the difference between 'keep' versus 'care'. These are two very different things.

'Keep' can be compared to what is done for animals in a zoo: the lion is given a cage, the cage is occasionally cleaned, the keeper makes sure the lion cannot get out and cause harm and from time to time he throws a piece of meat to the lion, to eat. With that his job is done, he is considered an excellent keeper of the lion.

> *A children's home houses close to 250 children aged three to eighteen years old. The children sleep in dorms, are provided with clothes from the donations they receive and they are fed. They are also given an education. There are a total of 12 caregivers to keep an eye on the children. There is no time for individual attention, the children live as groups. The main priorities are to keep them safe, fed and healthy. Much like animals in a zoo.*

'Care', on the other hand, means more than just taking care of a child's practical needs, it means to form a bond and to take care of all the essential basic needs. Not just making sure that the child behaves acceptably and is fed, but making sure that she develops properly, that she learns to build up self-esteem and self-confidence and that she becomes a good person.

> *I had been involved with a certain children's home for several years already. However, despite my repeated remarks that there were not nearly enough caregivers to take proper care of the children, recently the number of caregivers had gone down, instead of up. So I had to let the management know that it did not seem to make much sense for me to hold training sessions for the caregivers. Because now that they were each responsible for 20 to 25 children, there was simply no way they could possibly provide the children with what they needed, even if I told them what that was. I emphasised that if I, the expert, would be in charge of 20 to 25 children, I would not be able to meet their needs, even though I know exactly what the needs are and how to go about meeting them. It is just not possible.*

'Care' is something that cannot be given if one caregiver takes care of more than six to eight children. As a single person, it is simply not humanly possible to fulfil the essential basic needs of more children than that. This means that in most places children's homes do not actually provide 'care', they are unable to do so with the low staff numbers they have. They merely 'keep' the children.

So, taking responsibility also includes making a conscious decision about whether you are going to provide 'keep' or 'care' and to make sure you have the people needed for that. And if you are only planning on providing keep, I advise you: please do not open a children's home, for the sake of the children.

The Fine Line Between Helping Development and Exploitation
There is a large grey area when it comes to dealing with children in a children's home and deciding whether the situation benefits their well-being or whether it is closer to exploitation. It is not always easy to be certain whether something is more good than bad or more bad than good. I want to mention a few issues that I have come across that are in the darker part of the grey area, or that are in some cases very clearly not in the children's interest.

In recent years, it has become popular among people in rich countries to make donations to 'orphanages', to sponsor a child without parents or to volunteer in a children's home. These donations can sometimes be quite big and some people have discovered a market in the running of 'orphanages'. It has become a source of income, in some cases. This is exploitation of the children, their families, and the emotions that the concept of 'orphans' stirs up. While this does not always mean getting a lot of money out of foreigners' pockets—simply sharing in the housing and the food for the children paid for by foreign donations and maybe inflating the monthly cost by a dollar or two provides a comfortable living in many places—it is still a form of exploitation. Some of these places may be run out of a certain sense of idealism: to give children an education or a better religious upbringing. However, there is still a motive of profit as well.

The manager of a children's home–which he called 'orphanage', though all the children had families–told me about the poor and remote conditions of the village from which he came, and from which he had brought the children to the capital to get an education. He emphasised how bad everything was over there and that there were no opportunities for the children. He explained that he was sacrificing his life and career opportunities to make sure that these children would have an education. He regularly asked me if I had friends who might want to visit or donate to his children's home.

Later that week I happened to see an announcement that UNICEF was planning to open schools and clinics in the remote area that the children's home manager had told me about. So when I visited him again, I mentioned this news and asked him if that was not wonderful. His face did not look like he thought it was wonderful news at all.

Most children's homes struggle to get enough money and donations to feed the children and keep everything going. This, of course, is a great problem. However, that does not mean that any means are acceptable to solve it. Sending out children to beg for food or money is going too far. Even if it is in a religious context.

Adult Buddhist monks make the decision to live without possessions and to live only off what is given to them. This is an admirable way of life. It is also wonderful that Buddhist monasteries take in children who have no one else to take care of them, and raise those children in their midst. However, sending these children out to go beg for food to be fed, may be somewhat less admirable.

I once received an email from a children's home asking if I could give advice on how they could have their children bring in more income. I wrote back that I do not give advice on that area of childcare.

Allowing children to help, working alongside an adult and receiving praise, is fine.

Making children do all the work, with adults only looking on, is going too far.

While there are examples of outright child labour or the trafficking of children from children's homes, in most cases the question of whether or not a child is exploited is much harder to answer. This is because there is large grey area between helping a child prepare for life by teaching her to take care of herself and others, and child labour.

It is important to give children the opportunity to learn to cook, to wash their clothes, to fix things and to keep a house clean. To learn this, they need to have a chance to try it out and to practise. These are things that children in families are also expected to help with, and as they help, they learn. However, it is another matter to make the children fully responsible for doing all the work. In that case, you are talking about child labour and exploitation. Where exactly you cross over from one area to the other is not always easy to say. As an indicator, it is useful to think how much you would expect a child of the same age in your family to take on.

A children's home was built on a very large compound, stretching over several acres. Certain teenagers were expected to keep the compound clean and tidy. They spent a lot of time sweeping the large stretches of ground every day. During a training session with the staff I brought this up and asked the caregivers if they made their own children, of roughly the same age, fully responsible for keeping the entire grounds around their home clean. The answer was 'no'. They were only expected to help with that. They were expected to keep their own bed and the space by it tidy, and otherwise help their parents with chores. So, I asked, if you feel it is not reasonable to ask your children to take full responsibility for the small area around your house, how do you feel about what is asked of the children here?

In a small children's home for 12 children, the person running the home says he wants to give the children an opportunity to learn and develop a creative mind. So, he gives them money and allows them to buy whatever they want with it at the market and to cook it how they want. He will eat whatever comes out of that, together with the children, without complaining. This sounds admirable. However, the reality is that a fourteen-year-old girl spends all the time she is not in school in the kitchen, cooking three meals a day for 16 people. She only comes out when she needs to serve the adults, or is ordered to do more chores.

So, it is important to find a middle road where children are able to learn and help, but are not expected to take the burden of full responsibility for everything that needs to be done. Making sure to thank children for their efforts when they help out and to praise them for a good result also help chores to feel less like a burden.

In a children's home, the teenagers cook the Sunday lunch once a month. They do this under supervision of adults, and as they work, they learn to cook new dishes. They have a lot of fun together while cooking. And when the other children enjoy the food they have made, they feel quite proud of their accomplishments.

UN Guidelines:

108. The forms of financing care provision should never be such as to encourage a child's unnecessary placement or prolonged stay in care arrangements organized or provided by an agency or facility.

More children is not better, just harder to provide proper care for.

Expanding

It seems that some people still think that bigger is better. Certainly in the case of children's homes, this is not true when it comes to the well-being of the children. In fact, the smaller the children's home, the greater the chances that essential basic needs are met, to some extent. There are people who want their children's home to be as big as possible, not so much because they think it will be better for the children, but because it will give them a better reputation. They hope to be seen as even more noble, self-sacrificing and wonderful if they take care of more children. While it may be true that some people will admire you for it, I am sure I am not the only one who does not. Anyone who knows what is involved in caring for children properly, knows that in children's homes where more than 50 to 60 children are cared for, children generally only have their practical needs met, if that. Why the threshold is at that number is not clear to me, but I have noticed it repeatedly over the past ten years: children's homes with more than 60 children never provide the care needed by the children.

> *I regularly get emails asking me to send money to orphanages, to help them out. The emails are designed to make people cry and pull out their wallet. However, when I received an email that said that the home was caring for 60 children and that those children regularly went to bed hungry, it did not make me want to pull out my wallet. It made me want to scream at the computer: 'Then why did you take in 60 children, if you do not know how to feed them!'*

When I see a brochure of a children's home currently caring for 50 children—and struggling to provide them with food—saying that they aim to care for 300 children within five years, this does not make me admire them. It makes me wonder if they care for the children in their home at all. Those kinds of expansion can only happen at the cost of the children in your care.

If you want to build up a name or income over the back of something or someone else, please do not do it in childcare. The children have suffered enough.

Chapter 3 : Setting Up a Children's Home

Hopefully the first step you will take when deciding to open a children's home, will be to consider the issues mentioned in Part 3, Chapter 2: 'Ethics of Running a Children's Home', to determine if the plans you have for the home are in the best interest of the children. Next, you can take a look at some of the practical and organisational issues. Different setups of children's homes and other caring systems lead to different needs and areas of focus. However, there are also several issues that are fundamental to taking responsibility for the lives and well-being of children. Issues that will be present in any children's home. In this chapter, I explain several of these issues, both ones that are sometimes overlooked and ones that can lead to problems.

The First Steps

When a new children's home is being planned and set up, the focus is usually on how to get things like money, suitable accommodation, and how to find staff. These are practical, concrete needs: giving the children a roof over their head, food to eat and clothes to wear as soon as they arrive. Long-term logistics and management structures seem irrelevant—and quite frankly boring—compared to the excitement of being about to make a real practical difference in the lives of these poor children.

This is not enough to start a children's home with.

Boring and annoying as they may seem, management structures are very important. While different caring setups will require different management setups that are more or less complex, it is essential to give the matter some thought from the very start. In practice, this issue is often postponed and the person—or people—setting up the home ends up becoming seriously overworked surprisingly quickly.

A hospice for babies and toddlers was opened. At the time of opening they had the staff and facilities to care for six babies. Later, this would be expanded. It was a momentous occasion when the first four babies were brought in. They had varying conditions: severe epilepsy, inoperable heart condition, spina bifida, and hydrocephalus.

A few hours later, the little girl who had the heart condition had to be brought back to the children's home she came from—thankfully this was not very far—because the oxygen concentrator that was supposed to provide her with the oxygen she needed so badly, had not been delivered yet. A few days later, when things were in order, she was able to come back.

People setting up a children's home without thinking about setting up a management structure become overworked because they have to manage contact with sponsors, suppliers, volunteers, recruiting agencies, and curious visitors, as well as select and train new staff, paint the walls, go out to buy essential items that were forgotten, spend endless time at government or police offices waiting to get all the required documents, signatures and permissions, *and* work shifts caring for the children because there is not enough staff. When you see it written out like that, it suddenly makes sense that this is far too much for one person to manage. Yet very often it

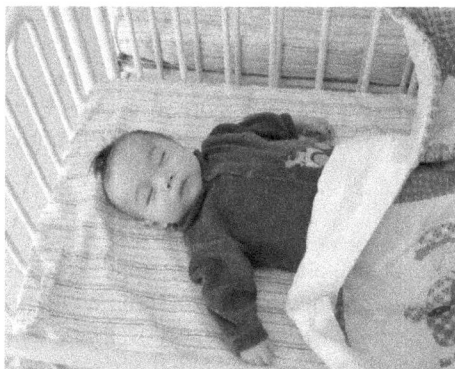

is what happens, because people do not think ahead. They just take things as they come. If you do that, you will become overwhelmed by all the things that come your way demanding to be done and may start feeling as if they are trying to bury you. Sometimes, this goes on for months, and almost no one is able to keep this up very long without either despairing or physically breaking down.

Just arrived in a newly opened home, time for a rest.

I want to warn you about what to expect, so that you can prepare for it and stand a better chance of success—and survival. To a certain extent, chaos and surprises cannot be prevented. The first months are going to be hectic, with lots of running around and stepping in wherever a gap suddenly appears. However, if you give some extra thought to what is needed right from the start before you begin, you are more likely to take a more realistic approach than: 'We have the building and the beds, so let's bring in the children. I am sure we will find staff soon, and until then we can take care of them ourselves.'

To save yourself a lot of unnecessary stress:

- Make sure you have hired and trained enough staff to cover all the shifts and take care of the number of children that you are going to accept initially, before bringing in the children.
- Keep the number of children you take in below the ratio that your staff can cope with; *first* hire and train new staff, *then* accept more children.
- From the very start, preferably even before you take in children, make sure you have (hired) one or two 'office' people, meaning people who will not care for the children, but who will take care of the buying of necessary items, maintain contact with various organisations and people, and, if possible, do the administration too.
- If you intend to leave the daily running of the children's home to someone else, make sure this person is involved with the home from as early on as possible, so that you can work together and get to know each other's ways of working and thinking. And

make sure you actually allow this person to assume her responsibilities.

This may sound like handing everything to others and leaving nothing for you to do, but do not worry. I promise, you will still extremely busy trying to make sure that everything works somewhat smoothly during the first period of time. Having the above list taken care of will make the tasks that remain to you slightly more manageable. Even when these issues are dealt with, and arranged well, there will still be plenty of surprises waiting for you.

✳ ——————————— **Accommodation**

Visit different children's homes in the region where you want to establish yours, if you have any way to do so. See how they are divided, what kinds of solutions they have for various problems, and determine what works and what does not according to you. Based on what you have seen and what you know to be roughly possible, work out what you think would be your ideal setup. Then look for a building that fits your wishes as much as possible.

Through the generous donation of a group of volunteers and visitors, the money was found to add two floors on top of the existing building, housing 40 children. The floors were designed to contain dorms for the children, toilet areas and a play room, with a staircase linking everything. However, the staircase that was built was not very safe when it was used by a large group of children pushing each other along the way–not to mention the toddlers who fell down them regularly. And lack of detailed finishing lead to even more dangerous situations.

It is also important to get local information about how the water and electricity supply are arranged:

Water cuts are frequent, so water is stored.

- Is it possible to get running water?
- What is the alternative?
- Is the well where water is fetched far away?
- Are water and power cuts frequent?
- How long do they usually last?
- What are the possibilities for backup?
- What does that cost?
- Where can you get safe drinking water?

I urge you to go for smaller living spaces, rather than large halls and dorms, whenever you can choose. This is to allow the children to have as much of a family-like life as is possible, in Part 1, Chapter 5: 'Essential Psychological Needs' there is more information about why it is important to aim for this.

UN GUIDELINES:

91. Accommodation in all alternative care settings should meet the requirements of health and safety.

* ——————————— **Management Structure**

If you do not let one or two people take care of absolutely everything this means you need more people. And if you have several people on your management team, it makes sense to divide tasks instead of having everyone do a little of everything. This will get things done more efficiently and more thoroughly, with fewer tasks forgotten because people thought someone else was going to take care of them.

The following is a list of areas that need to be looked after to have a children's home run smoothly. Whether a separate person is hired for each of these areas, or whether a single person's job description can include two or more of these areas without this person being severely overworked, depends on what kind of home you run, how big it is, and which issues are major and which ones are minor.

- Staff: someone should be in charge of finding, interviewing, and training new staff, as well as making up rosters for shifts (if applicable) and holidays, finding replacement in case of illness or absence and keeping in contact with all staff members. This person should make sure staff is kept up to date on changes in the system, listen to their complaints, and see if anything can be done to improve things. She should hold occasional meetings with all staff–though never all at the same time, because that would leave the children without supervision–to keep them up to date of developments and listen to their issues, possibly bringing up general complaints from the management side about the level of care provided. This person is also in charge of firing staff whose work is consistently not good enough, despite previous warnings and chances to improve.

- Children: someone should personally know *all* children who live in the children's home and be aware of their general circumstances–name, age, background, health, education, and other problems or accomplishments. She should not necessarily know every detail of every child by heart, but certainly the general outline plus the knowledge of where to find the details. This person should regularly spend time with all children, listen to them and see if improvements can be made (if complaints are reasonable), be in close con-

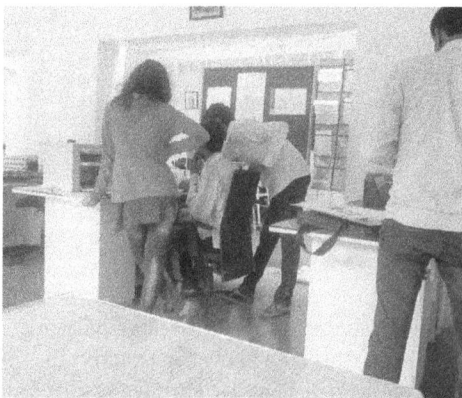

Various people working together to manage a children's home.

tact with the medical 'head', both giving and receiving information, and, if at all possible, always be present when a new child arrives at the home so she can get to know him straight away and become familiar with his story and his situation.

- Medical 'head': every children's home should have one person in charge of the children's overall health. How big and complicated this task is depends on the kind of children's home and the state of health of the children in it. This role can be taken on by a doctor, a nurse, or simply someone who has a lot of knowledge from experience of the medical issues that regularly come up in your home. This person should be well acquainted with the medical situation of every child, and she should regularly visit all children, to pick up on early warning signs of illnesses or conditions. This person should always be notified if there is a clear change to a child's health and would ideally also accompany children on doctor's or hospital visits as the one to communicate with doctors to stay fully up to date. Although in a medical children's home it is usually preferable to have a separate person appointed for this, because in that situation it will be a full-time job. This person should be given the right to make health decisions for the children (sometimes within certain limits, such as having to check whether money is available for an expensive procedure).

A children's home had been running for many years already before they gave someone the job of 'health coordinator'. One of the children was in a lot of pain and was taken to hospital. She was diagnosed with having large kidney stones. When the health coordinator looked back through her records, he discovered that eight years earlier this girl had already been diagnosed with very small kidney stones, and nothing had been done about it. This showed how important it was to have someone do his job.

- Volunteer Coordinator: volunteers can be a lot of help, but they also require a lot of guidance, support, and training—in other words, work. If you receive a lot of volunteers, it is a good idea to have someone who takes charge of the volunteers, which can include communicating with them before arrival, providing them with information, agreeing on the time and duration of the volunteer's stay, organising a pick-up and drop-off at the airport, train or bus station, providing guidance during the stay, and being the 'face' of the children's home for the volunteers. It is very helpful if this person speaks reasonably good English, especially if a lot of the visiting volunteers are foreigners. More information about dealing with volunteers can be found in Part 3, Chapter 6: 'Day-to-Day Issues'.
- Accounting: someone needs to take care of the children's home's bookkeeping, keeping constant track of how much money is currently available, how much money is going out, and whether

this is for necessary expenses or whether money is being wasted. This person should consider how money can be saved without compromising the children's well-being and be aware, at all times, how many months' worth of operating budget is still available before everything runs out in case there is no more funding.

> *I was rather surprised at the Annual Board Meeting to hear the proud announcement that the children's home had only used 70% of its budget in the past year. It is good to save money. However, in a place that had less than half the caregivers needed to provide proper care for the number of children in the home, and where the children's diet was still not great, I would have liked to have seen a little less saving. Putting the remaining 30% of the budget to good use might have made an enormous difference in the lives of the children.*

Someone needs to keep the storeroom stocked and organised.

- Supplies: someone should have an inventory list–which is regularly checked and updated–of all supplies (which can include food, clothes, bedding, products for personal hygiene, necessary equipment, medical supplies, and office supplies). This inventory should be kept up to date and used to ask for re-stocking when items run low. The buying may or may not be the responsibility of the person in charge of the inventory lists, but this person should be the one requesting the buying of new stock. This person should also be made aware, by other management staff, if there are new items–previously not kept in stock or used–that need to be bought, explaining why.
- Accommodation: someone needs to be in charge of the maintenance of the children's home including the terrain and buildings. This person should be (made) aware of problems, breakdowns, and leaks. She should also take care of the upkeep–such as painting or replacing things that are worn–either fixing these problems herself, or getting someone (from inside or outside) to take care of it. She may also be put in charge of organising and supervising new building projects on the grounds.
- Contact with officials: it is often beneficial to have a single person in charge of dealing with authorities and other official bodies, because this person will get to know the people she is dealing with and the ways to get around obstacles on the usual 'tracks'. Aside from that, the people this person deals with will become familiar with her and trust her more, meaning more may be accomplished. This person should be consulted by other management staff when a plan will require negotiations with officials, and in turn this person should bring the relevant people within the children's home up to date on the issues that have been resolved (or not) in their contact with officials.

A children's home manager was attending an appointment with a state official from the Child Protection Department. Before she had a chance to start talking about the issue for which she had come, the official asked, with much irritation: 'And who are you, now? Every time you people send someone else, and you never tell me what is going on!' This meeting was not off to a good start, and did not end well either.

- Fund-Raiser: if your children's home is mostly financed through private or corporate donations, it requires a lot of time and work to make sure that enough funds keep coming in. Someone who takes charge of this can be very helpful and can raise the budget of the children's home. What exactly this job involves depends on where most of your funds come from and what target groups you wish to reach. It can include things like creating and updating a website, keeping a blog about the home (always emphasising the great things achieved and how they could be even better if...), writing and sending emails or newsletters to people who might donate, keeping up contact with people who have previously donated money or visited the home and might be inclined to give more, and organising events to raise money and/or awareness for your cause.

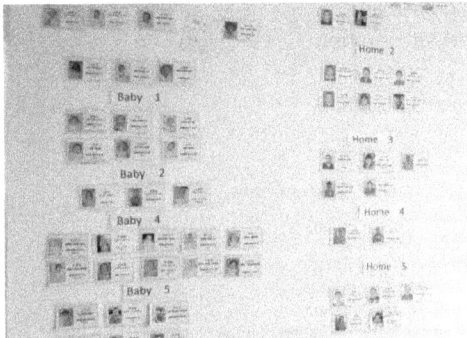

With many children in your care, a quick overview in the office can help.

The important thing is that all the issues mentioned are taken care of by someone who is able to pay proper attention to them, so someone who is not overworked. Aside from all these separate tasks, which need to be divided over several people, there also needs to be one person who has the overview if you are looking after more than 20 children in total. This person does not necessarily have to take care of issues herself, but she does need to be kept aware of everything that is going on in the home, to make sure that communication between the different people is adequate and that issues (and sometimes even children) are not being overlooked. Everyone needs to have a clear idea of whom they answer to and whom they should go to with a particular problem. It does not matter whether the setup is hierarchical or not. It is essential that everyone knows who has what function. That way, staff do not need to waste time asking others who might be able to help with this or that problem.

Keeping this overview can be done by all different departments sending regular reports to the person who has the overview, or by weekly meetings in which everything is discussed. These meetings can be one-to-one or with the whole management staff. The person with the overview should also try to regularly spend time working alongside the people taking care of the different areas of management, to keep a feel for what those jobs involve and whether the system still works well.

Reporting

In a hierarchical structure, an efficient way to make sure information is passed on is to have everyone send weekly reports directly to the person they answer to. Reports can be simply written, describing the events that have taken place, or they can be templates (a prewritten form, in which only certain words or numbers need to be filled in) that must be filled in, for example:

> *This week ..... new children were accepted.*
> *This week ..... children were ill.*
> *Name..... ..... , problem ....*

Reporting is a minimum requirement for good communication, but record-keeping is also essential to run a children's home effectively and safely. When a new child arrives, a new file should be started for this child straight away. This file should include the following information:

- Name
- Date of birth or approximate age
- Any known background information
- Health information
- Any official documents available

As time passes, all important documents about the child's health, education, legal status, and any evaluations or incident reports should be added to this file. It is also wise to monitor a child's growth and weight regularly to make sure that there are no delays or other problems, and to add that

Files should be kept on all children.

information to the file. If at all possible, it is a good idea to also keep a digital version of the file on a computer that is frequently backed up.

This file should be freely accessible to the medical 'head' and the manager in charge of children, to allow them to effectively do their job. Access by anyone else should be restricted and, if access is granted, it should only be under supervision in cases where it is judged to be safe and in the child's best interest to share the information with a particular person. This is to protect the child's privacy.

The person in charge of staff should also have a file on all staff members currently working at the children's home with:

- Name
- Contact details
- Date of start of employment
- Any notes about their quality of work
- Their current job description
- Current wage entitlement
- Any other relevant information

The only person who should be allowed to access this file should be the person who is in charge of staff. Also, it is generally a good idea to give staff members the right to view their records.

UN GUIDELINES:

109. Comprehensive and up-to-date records should be maintained regarding the administration of alternative care services, including detailed files on all children in their care, staff employed and financial transactions.

110. The records on children in care should be complete, up to date, confidential and secure, and should include information on their admission and departure and the form, content and details of the care placement of each child, together with any appropriate identity documents and other personal information. Information on the child's family should be included in the child's file as well as in the reports based on regular evaluations. This record should follow the child throughout the alternative care period and be consulted by duly authorized professionals responsible for his/her current care.

111. The above-mentioned records could be made available to the child, as well as to the parents or guardians, within the limits of the child's right to privacy and confidentiality, as appropriate. Appropriate counselling should be provided before, during and after consultation of the record.

112. All alternative care services should have a clear policy on maintaining the confidentiality of information pertaining to each child, which all carers are aware of and adhere to.

164. The confidential nature of the information collected should be respected and systems put in place for safe forwarding and storage of information. Information should only be shared among duly mandated agencies for the purpose of tracing, family reintegration and care.

✳ ─────────────── **Suggestions for Caring Rules**
Particularly if you have a large caregiving staff, you need to make sure that a certain standard of care is given by everyone, to all the children. To effectively run a children's home, it is essential that you have clear rules about how you think the home should be run and

what standard of care you require. These rules should cover everything involved in the care given at your children's home. This includes the routines to be followed, the rights and duties of staff and children, holidays and pay for staff, and rules regarding behaviour, hygiene, and discipline. All staff should be made aware of the rules and standards

早产儿房间 1
Preemie Room 1

微弱早产儿 谢绝参观
Fragile   Preemies   No
Visitors! Thank You!

For example: rules about who is allowed to be where.

that you expect them to uphold, as part of their training when starting the job. Over time, these rules may be changed or adjusted. Staff should be told in advance about changes and receive a clear explanation of the new situation and why the change was made. This is will improve their cooperation.

> *Because the medical children's home needed to be fully staffed 24 hours a day, seven days a week, all year long, to be able to provide proper care for the children, an agreement was made with staff before they started their job. While it was permitted to ask for time off up to a certain number of days per year, this had to be done at least a month in advance so that it could be taken into consideration when making the roster. The agreement also said that, because most people would have to work through holidays and because otherwise there would be big fights and rushes every year, caregiving staff were not allowed to ask for time off for major holidays. If your day off falls on a holiday, you are lucky, and every effort will be made to make sure everyone gets a day off during one of the holidays, but extra leave is not permitted during this time. Because this was clear from the start, there were almost never any issues over this.*

Without formulating these rules for yourself and clearly passing them on to the staff, you cannot expect the home to run smoothly. Nor can you blame staff for not living up to standards that exist only in your head.

Ideally, the rules for you children's home and staff should also explicitly state any situation that could lead to the instant firing of staff. This warns them and lets them know what they can expect. This can include things like 'sleeping on a waking night shift', 'any proof of sexual misconduct towards children or other staff', 'causing harm to children intentionally or through neglect' or 'showing up drunk or intoxicated for work'. Stating these kinds of rules clearly helps remove any confusion in the future.

EXAMPLE

The list I am giving here is not meant to be 'the list of rules' for your children's home. It is only an example of possible rules, which may inspire you to create a rule about a certain issue, even if you do not agree with the one I have given here.

- *Children of age group X should have at least Y hours of sleep per night.*
- *Children need to be bathed, dressed, and ready in time to leave for school.*
- *Children should brush their teeth twice a day.*
- *Children should have three meals a day, plus milk twice, and fruit once.*
- *Children should do their homework every day.*
- *Children whose grades are below X are required to attend tuition.*
- *Children should help with chores and be taught how to do them well (and receive praise and gratitude for doing them).*
- *Watching TV should be limited to X time per day.*
- *Children should have time to play/relax every day.*
- *Children should receive positive attention from their caregiver every day.*
- *Babies should be held by their caregiver every day.*
- *Babies should spend time playing on the floor every day.*
- *Children are/are not allowed to eat sweets.*
- *If you do not know how to handle a situation, ask for help.*

UN Guidelines:

106. All agencies and facilities should have written policy and practice statements, consistent with the present Guidelines, setting out clearly their aims, policies, methods and the standards applied for the recruitment, monitoring, supervision and evaluation of qualified and suitable carers to ensure that those aims are met.

107. All agencies and facilities should develop a staff code of conduct, consistent with the present Guidelines, that defines the role of each professional and of the carers in particular and includes clear reporting procedures on allegations of misconduct by any team member.

✱ ——————

Money

Finding the funds to set up a children's home and to keep it running is never an easy thing to do. This too is something that needs a lot of thought from as early on as possible. You will need to calculate how much money you will need for

your monthly expenses. These expenses include the staff salary, possibly the rent of–or mortgage on–the property, food and other consumable materials (such as soap, nappies, cleaning products or bottled water), utility bills (gas, water, electricity, and possibly wood to burn), office supplies, and internet connection. These may also include expenses such as taxes. You need to find out as exactly as possible what all these things are going to cost you every month.

If you have not yet started your children's home, it would be a good idea not to do so before you have found a way to more or less guarantee (when it comes to donations there is no such thing as a solid guarantee, unfortunately) that the amount of money needed will actually be coming in every month. This is also the case if your children's home is already up and running and you want to expand. First, determine by how much an expansion will make your monthly expenses go up and how you are going to cover this. Only *then* go ahead with the expansion.

Making sure you can cover your monthly bills is not the end of the story. Money–or donations in kind–also needs to be found to cover start-up expenses: beds, covers, mats, clothes, bottles, cups, plates, furniture, toiletries, toys, cooking necessities, laundry necessities, school materials, and so on. If you are taking care of special needs children, the list will be much longer.

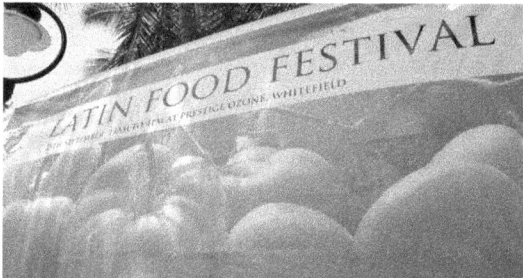

Fundraising events can take many forms.

Having covered that, you are still not there: you also need to be able to cover **incidental** expenses, which, though individually incidental, usually amount to a considerable monthly expense all together. This includes things like repairs and the replacement of appliances that are not working anymore–because usually items that are made for household use are burdened with industrial use in a children's home, they have a much shorter life than you might expect–doctor's bills, medication, and necessary new investments.

How you are going to get this money and what you need to do for it depends on many things. Among other things, it depends on whether or not you:

- Receive government grants
- Get money from corporate sponsors or from private donations
- Mostly get (or want) one-time donations
- Have a sponsorship system with people paying set amounts at set times, long-term
- Mostly receive local donations, or mostly international ones
- Have a specific ideological or religious background

It also depends on your ability, or the ability of the people you hire, to take care of funding. Are you willing and able to:

- Organise big fundraising events?
- Manage a website and/or blog or mobilise (social) media?
- Get access to a few people able to make very substantial donations?
- Apply for grants given out by foundations?

All these things are possible, but different people have different strengths and different contacts, making certain options more realistic than others.

In a way, a charity is just like a business: it has a group of people who are willing to 'buy' what you offer, meaning they are willing to donate and feel good about having helped you to help children on their behalf. However, certain people are only willing to donate money for certain causes. First of all, you need to target people who are willing to help out with childcare, as opposed to people who would prefer to donate money to save endangered animals, to support the arts, or to cure cancer.

A child with donation, a photo for a donor.

You are selling something, and you need to be aware of what *exactly* you are selling; you are selling the fact that you take care of the children on behalf of the donor. Selling the statement, 'with your money these children are no longer living on the streets' is different from, 'your money has paid for the operation that saved this child's life', which is different from, 'your money helps this terminally ill child live out the rest of her life surrounded by affection and comfort'. There may be people who are sensitive to all three and willing to donate to all three, but there will not be many people like that. Most people have a special place in their heart for a specific cause. So, to be get people to donate effectively, it is helpful to think out very carefully what *exactly* it is that you are doing and to find the group of people most interested in supporting that.

Whatever the background of your organisation and that of your donors, it is very important to make sure that the money does not dry up. You can do that by keeping people who donate money updated on what is happening. This can be done through a newsletter on paper or by email, through social media like Facebook and Twitter, through a website and/or a blog, through personal visits to people, or through lecture tours. If people never hear what their money is used for, they are unlikely to want to continue to support you.

It is entirely possible to depend on a certain set of donors–people who are loyal and committed to financially supporting the work you do–for a long time. Finding such people is a huge blessing that takes away a lot of stress. At the same time, you need to be careful that you do not become too dependent on certain people, because that can put you in a vulnerable and weak position instead of a position of strength and ownership of your children's home. Plus, it is import-ant not to become blinded by the long-term loyalty of these donors. However long they have been supporting you, it is always possible for them to change their minds and withdraw their money. Or even if they do not wish to abandon you, their financial situation may change and it may not be possible for them to continue making the generous donations they always made.

A photoshoot to keep contributors happy.

So, you always need to remain aware that even if funding seems to be steady and secure, it can disappear at any moment. For this reason, it is important to always be aware of your financial reserves and of how far that money would stretch if major donors were to suddenly fall away. In other words, you need to know how many months of operating budget–money that covers all expenses–your organisation has if nothing is added to it.

If you only have as much money coming in as money going out–so no reserves or buffers–the moment a major donation stops will be the moment you have to close your children's home, because you will not be able to pay for staff, rent, food, and so on. The same situation occurs if you do not start calculating what you have and what you need until you notice that there is practically no money left after one or more major donations stop: the moment you find out you cannot pay the bills anymore, is the moment you children's home will be closed.

On the other hand, if you make sure that you do have some reserves and you make sure that every month a calculation is made of how much money there is and how long that money can last with the current expenses, you will have some time if donations suddenly stop. If at the moment you hear that a large part of your donations will stop, you know that you still have a reserve that will cover your costs for two to three months, you will have two to three months to do everything you can to find new donors or sponsors. There is no guarantee that you will succeed and that the children's home will be able to stay open, but it does give you a fair chance of finding money to be able to continue.

Donations

The first instinctive thought of anyone running a charity and struggling to get enough money to keep things going is that any and all donations are welcome. 'As long as money keeps coming in, we will find a way to make it work.' However, some donations come with so many strings attached that you might be in danger of getting strangled by them. You need to ask yourself if it is worth accepting these donations.

There are various ways in which donations–and most of all the people giving them–can make you feel despair. The reasons are often cultural. In some countries, there is a strong feeling that if I provide you with what you need to continue your work, then you are indebted to me and you need to do what I want.

In this particular country, it is a custom to donate food to the underprivileged. Doing this provides status and esteem. At mealtimes the family who donated food for the large group of children personally serves the food out to the children, which takes a lot of time. Then the children all have to rise and sing a national song, and then a song of gratitude and blessing for the family, who stand together looking on. The family feels good about themselves, having helped the poor, unfortunate children, and receiving their gratitude. The children are allowed to sit down and start eating. They feel somewhat humiliated having to accept their food as a hand-out in such an obvious way. And their food is completely cold by the time they are allowed to touch it.

It can also be a matter of character or suspicion when a donor wants to see certain 'improvements' (which may or may not be of real benefit to the children) before committing to give money. A donor may be afraid that their money will end up in someone's pocket and demand an opportunity to keep a very close eye on what the money is used for.

A foreign lady offered to make a very big donation after she had taken a tour of the children's home and asked many critical questions. A specific sum was promised. However, she demanded to be told what would be bought with it before she gave it. With so many nappies and clothes to wash, the children's home was in need of a new washing machine. They found a company who offered them a very interesting deal: if they bought two washing machines, the second one would only cost a fraction of the normal price. The two washing machines could

be bought with the money promised by the lady. This way they could also send a washing machine to the children's home that the organisation had in another city. The person who had done the research contacted the lady and proposed this. The lady refused: the other city was too far away, she would not be able to go there to check if the washing machine was used responsibly. When the children's home director was told about this, her reaction was: 'Let her keep her money!'

Not every donation is worth meeting the donor's demands.

While most of the suggestions or demands made by donors are made with good intentions, the fact is that the donors do not have the whole picture. They may want to change something that is done a certain way for a very good reason. Many donors may make demands about small things, which together add up to quite a lot. Sometimes the demands made by different donors are complete opposites of each other. If you go along with them, it would probably cause your care system to get worse and that would not help the children. For this reason, it is sometimes wiser to draw a line and sometimes even decline the offer of a donation under certain conditions. Donors who make a lot of demands are almost always going to cause you a lot of trouble. Of course, it is up to you whether you take all donations or whether you set up conditions for them. But it is a good idea to at least give the situation some thought.

You can choose to allow your donors to make a donation for a certain expense or for a certain child. For example, you can set up a system where a donor can pay all the expenses involved in the care of a particular child. If you do this, the donor has every right–and should be given the opportunity–to check that their money is really being used to take care of that child. You can also tell donors that all the money that comes in becomes part of the overall budget and will be distributed as needed, and assure the donor that the particular child who caught his eye will, of course, be benefitting from the money as well.

In a children's home with more than 200 children, a foreign visitor was very touched by two or three children and announced that she wanted to sponsor them. This had to be refused, because the children's home did not have a system in place for sponsoring individual children. Having two or three out of 200 children sponsored would mean providing these children with nice food, new clothes and new school materials, while all the other children had to look on jealously. That would be cruel.

While it is important to have a certain business-like attitude to the way you get money to keep things going and when making decisions about what to spend money on and what not, it is essential that you do not lose sight of the fact that, in the end, it is about helping as many children as you can, as best you can.

This particular children's home acts as the medical centre of an organisation. When children with medical problems arrive in any of the orphanages connected to this organisation, they are sent to the medical children's home where they receive specialised care. The children spend some time here while they wait for a bed to open up in the hospital where they will have surgery, or while they gain enough weight to be able to have surgery. When the children are discharged from hospital, they spend a few more days in the children's home and then they are sent back to their original orphanage.

The organisation 'sells' its care to donors by letting them know how many life-saving or life-improving operations were paid for by generous contributors, which makes people feel good. They send the children back to the original orphanages soon after their surgery because that frees up beds for other children, which means that greater numbers of children can pass through the medical children's home. Fundraising is very successful here. The numbers look great!

What they do not tell people is that many of the children who are sent back to their original orphanages are still medically fragile and need a kind of care that their own orphanage is unable to provide. They do not mention that although the children have received life-saving surgery, not all of them survive, because of infections and other complications that would have been much less likely to happen if they had spent more time recovering and gaining strength at the medical children's home. If children were allowed to stay at the medical home longer after surgery, the numbers might look less impressive to donors, but more children would live.

Medical Help

Anyone who takes care of a large group of children is inevitably going to be confronted with medical care. Children get ill, they fall or fight and hurt themselves, and so on. Since you know this from the start, it helps to get an idea of what kind of medical help is available near the location of your children's home at an early stage. If you wait until you have a child who needs a doctor 'right now', you may lose so much time looking for a doctor that help may come too late. If you already know where to go when a child needs a doctor, you will save time and possibly a life.

It can also be helpful to go and visit a doctor or a hospital and see if

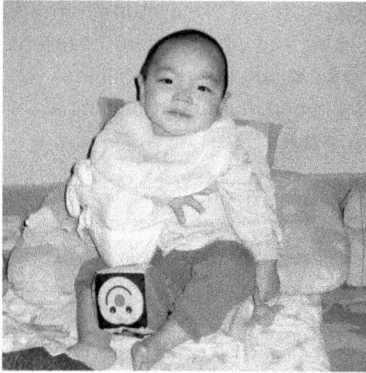

A broken arm can happen anywhere.

you can start a friendly relationship with the medical staff. In some places, you can find a doctor who is willing to donate some of his time to visit your children's home–for example once a week–to check up on children who show any signs of illness. Or, in other places, you might be able to strike a deal with a doctor or a hospital to reduce the medical bills for the treatment of 'your' children, as a contribution to your children's home.

You should also look into the possibility of arranging vaccinations, either by going to a nearby clinic or by having healthcare workers visit your children's home. This will be a lot more convenient than having to transport all the children to a healthcare centre or a hospital to have them vaccinated. It is extremely important to be vaccinated, particularly for children in a children's home. Because with many children together, any one of them getting one of the childhood illnesses will immediately turn into an epidemic. This will not only put a lot of stress on the caregivers because it means more work for them. Several of the children are also likely to become very seriously ill because their immune system is not as strong as that of children who live in a family. Children with a weak immune system are much more likely to get a more serious version of a disease, possibly with dangerous complications.

> *A six-year-old HIV-positive boy who lives in a children's home is diagnosed with SSPE. This is a rare complication of measles that often does not appear until years after the child seems to have recovered perfectly from the measles. The disease essentially breaks down the brain and there is no cure for it. First you notice behavioural changes, then clumsiness and muscle weakness, then the child will go into a coma and then his brain will stop working and he will die. On average, you can survive for about a year and a half when you get SSPE. The only way to prevent death by SSPE is by vaccinating against measles.*

You can find more information about dealing with medical problems in a children's home in *Sick Children Everywhere. Book 2: Basic Medical Care for Children in Institutions.*

UN GUIDELINES:

84. Carers should promote the health of the children for whom they are responsible and make arrangements to ensure that medical care, counselling and support are made available as required.

✳ ———————————

Conclusion

It is important to realise that, in essence, setting up a children's home is a process that never ends, at least not for a good quality home. Of course, after the initial most chaotic period–which can easily last up to a year–things will become a little bit more stable and calm down. However, if you want to provide good quality childcare, the most important characteristic you need is flexibility and a willingness to continue to change and improve.

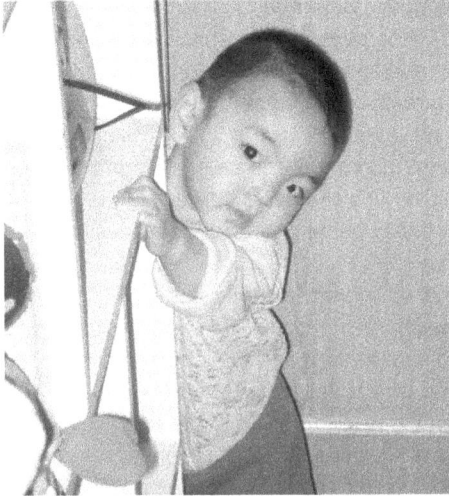

There is no such thing as perfect childcare. There is always room for improvement. And the greatest mark of quality in any children's home is a willingness to keep learning how to do things better and to find ways to improve. This does not mean that you cannot stand by your convictions or that you should change according to the recommendations of anyone who visits. But it does mean that you should seriously listen to recommendations and think carefully about how much value they have for your home. In some cases, you will conclude that the recommendation will not be of help, or might even make things worse. However, in some cases, you will realise that a recommendation is valuable and could make a change for the better. Occasionally, you may even have a sudden insight: 'Of course! This is the solution we have been looking for.'

Surprises will appear around corners.

Chapter 4:   The Caregiving Staff

What Is a Caregiver?

It seems like a strange and unnecessary question: What is a caregiver? It is obvious, is it not? A caregiver is someone who takes care of other people. This is true and a valid short version of the answer. However, ask yourself if you *really* know what it means to be a caregiver. To try to keep things as simple as possible, I will not go in to at all the things a caregiver 'in general' can be. I will concentrate on the main roles of a caregiver in a children's home. You may be surprised at the number of things being a caregiver includes.

The Roles of the Caregiver in a Children's Home:

- A provider of practical necessities: the caregiver makes sure that children are fed, clothed and washed and that the living environment is kept clean and tidy. If there are things the children need, part of the caregiver's task is to try to make sure they are there–by letting the relevant person in management know what is lacking, or if she is authorised to do so, by buying the things herself.

- A trusted support: children need to have the chance to talk to someone about the things they like and do not like, about the things they hope for and the things they fear, and quite

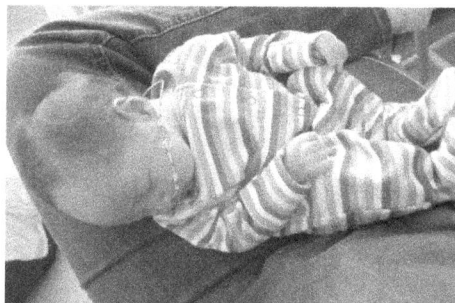
Providing a safe little nest.

simply about how their day has been. One of a caregiver's tasks is to regularly spend time with each child in her care and listen to what the child has to say, reacting to it seriously. This helps her win the trust of the children in her care by being a constant, affectionate presence who is there to help her children when they need support. If she manages to do this, she will give her children a deep feeling of safety and well-being, which allows them to develop well and explore the world around them.

- A builder of self-confidence: self-confidence is a belief in yourself and in your abilities. Having self-confidence is very important to be able to function well in society. Self-confidence has to be built by the child, and this process is helped along by the caregiver, who gives the child the feeling that she is important as an individual. The caregiver can do this by dealing with the child fairly and respectfully and by praising her achievements and encouraging her to believe people when they praise her achievements. More information about building self-confidence can be found in

Part 2, Chapter 5 'Self-Esteem and Self-Confidence'.

- An educator in life skills and a role model: in school, children are taught knowledge from books; at home—a children's home just as much as a family home—they should learn the things they need to know to be able to take care of themselves and of their own family when they grow up. For instance: personal hygiene, keeping the living space clean and tidy, preparing food, washing clothes, helping others, and behaviour towards others. These things are taught by showing the child how they are done, and when she reaches an age where she is able to start doing it herself, by explaining how and why they need to be done and by encouraging the child to do these things herself. The caregiver helps children grow up into well-behaved, good people by guiding them through a combination of explaining things—using a careful balance between correcting bad behaviour and praising good behaviour—and setting the right example.
- A supervisor: as children grow up, they are not yet aware of all the risks and possible consequences of their actions, so they need someone to watch over them. Someone who will stop them if what they do is likely to damage or endanger themselves, other people or property.

The lid to cover the keys of the piano was always kept open to prevent children from being able to lift it up, with the risk of it crashing down on their fingers. Standing in front of the piano, the toddlers were not able to reach the lid. However, a little girl of almost two years old decided to try if she might be able to reach the lid from the side. She succeeded. The lid fell closed on the tip of her finger and chopped it off. The girl had to be rushed to hospital. After this incident the lid was duct-taped to the body of the piano to prevent further danger.

- A substitute parent: children who do not grow up in a family still need someone to give them affection and attention, someone to hold them when they need it. Their caregiver is the only person in the world they can turn to so their needs will be met.

If you want to make sure that your caregivers are able to spend enough time giving the children in their care attention and stimulation, it is a good idea to relieve them from some domestic duties. This is true especially for caregivers of babies and very small children, and for those who are expected to look so many children that it becomes difficult to balance taking care of the children with doing household chores. I can only hope that this last category only exists in the early transition period, while you are recruiting more caregivers to bring down the child-to-caregiver ratio.

Two very time-consuming activities that most caregivers need

Cooking takes up a lot of time.

to attend to, aside from spending time with their children, are cooking and (hand) washing clothes. With so many children together, it takes almost the entire day just to take care of these two things. So, in the interest of providing the caregivers with time to meet their children's essential basic needs, it helps to hire someone to take care of the laundry, and maybe also the cooking. One person could take over the laundry for several caregivers, resulting in greater efficiency and making better care for the children possible. If taking on an extra person to take care of the washing is out of the question, then at the very least the purchase of a washing machine should be considered. Of course, if you have a group home system where the group homes function like family-units and the number of children per caregiver is kept low, the caregivers should be able to take care of these things themselves, just like any mother does.

As mentioned in Part 3, Chapter 2: 'Ethics of Running a Children's Home', it is useful and good to have older children help with chores around the house, to help them learn to take care of these things and to take some responsibility for their own care. However, there is a fine line between having the children help and making them do all the work.

> In a home for mentally retarded children, the few caregivers who were there mostly took on the role of supervisors and not much else. Apart from the cooking–with which the children only had to help–the teenagers were expected to do all the work at the home: sweeping and washing the floors, washing the dishes, washing the clothes, hanging them to dry and bringing them in again. Aside from that, they also had to take care of any heavy lifting and carrying that needed to be done. The teenagers would be called out of their classroom or out of activities to do the work. They never received praise or gratitude. They did not receive instruction or guidance on how to do something properly. They only received reprimands or beatings if they did something wrong.

UN GUIDELINES:

71. Special attention should be paid to the quality of alternative care provision, both in residential and in family-based care, in particular with regard to the professional skills, selection, training and supervision of carers. Their role and functions should be clearly defined and clarified with respect to those of the child's parents or legal guardians.

90. Carers should understand the importance of their role in developing positive, safe and nurturing relationships with children, and should be able to do so.

✱ ——————————

Selecting Caregivers

When you hire staff to work as caregivers, it is very important to select them very carefully. Childcare is not the same as an office job or work in a factory. In childcare, you need people who really care about the children. They are not required to love them as their own, but they do need to be genuinely concerned about their happiness and well-being. It is important that they do not get upset by the messier or noisier parts of the job such as nappy changing, dealing with children who throw up, and at times lots of crying.

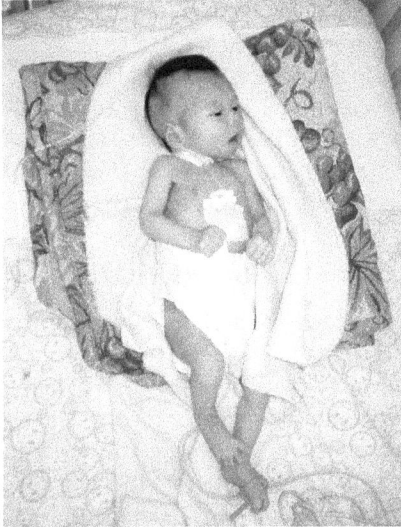

Not everyone can deal with this. Surprising them will not help.

For this reason, it is important that you not only read candidates' CVs, but that you also meet them. Ideally, if you think they might be suitable, you should observe them interacting with children. For example, when you give a tour of the home, allow some time for them to sit with some of the children and see if they are eager to interact with them or if they keep their distance, or want to hand a baby back at the first sign of tears. This is harder to do when you hire staff before the children's home opens. In that case, you will need to trust your intuition about the person, and if possible get references. A trial period to make sure the person is suitable for the job is a good idea.

A children's home wants to make sure they have good quality staff. This is why they look for people with a degree in Social Work or in Psychology. They feel that these people have had proper training in how to protect vulnerable children. However, in practice, people with a degree do not end up staying in their job as a caregiver very long. This was not the kind of work they had in mind when they went to university and pretty soon they find out that there is not much chance of advancement or for building a career as a caregiver. So, they keep looking around for other opportunities and they leave the job as soon as they find something else.

Make sure that candidates are given a clear and honest idea of the kind of children they will be asked to care for. Not everyone is willing or able to work with handicapped, sick, or terminally ill children. Candidates should be informed about what they can expect and what will be expected of them. If you do not do this, there is a chance that they will leave once they complete their training and have only just started their jobs. You will have wasted time and effort. The background of the children should be explained to candidates as well. Are they orphans, abandoned children, children in respite or palliative care with parents? Where do they come from? Also explain why the children are cared for in a particular way, if it is important that this continues to happen.

A particular children's home houses close to 300 children of all age groups. These are children of commercial sex-workers and about half of them are HIV-positive. It is very hard to find staff to take care of these children, because of the stigma attached to both their family background and their HIV status. In this home, more than half of the caregivers are men, because an unmarried woman who comes to work here will not be able to find a husband anymore. And a married woman will not get permission from her husband to come. All HIV-positive children are cared for by HIV-positive caregivers, since no one else will work closely with them.

Previous experience with children, either professionally or as a mother and grandmother, can be a great advantage for a caregiver. However, sometimes, someone who has raised five children of her own and regularly helps with her grandchildren, or someone who has worked several years at another children's home, is so convinced she knows everything there is to know about childcare that she is unwilling to take instructions. These people can sometimes be almost impossible to train. In an interview, find out how willing the person is to learn new ways of doing things. If you have someone who is experienced *and* willing to receive training and do things your way, she is likely to be a great addition to your staff. It is usually well worth listening to her input and suggestions as well. She may have valuable things to teach you.

To make sure that children get an opportunity to form attachments with caregivers, it is helpful to do what you can to make sure caregivers intend to stay in their job for as long as possible. One way of doing this could be to ask a new caregiver to sign a contract for two or three years after their trial period, with provisions for firing them if they do not follow your rules for the care of children. More information on setting down these rules was given in Part 3, Chapter 3: 'Setting Up a Children's Home'.

For the safety of the children, it is wise to do a background check on candidates for jobs in your children's home. This includes checking out the references they bring, as well as enquiring with the police if there is anything known about the candidate that makes them unsuitable to work with vulnerable children. Particularly a history of violent or sexual offenses could put the children in danger.

In some places, a children's home does not stand on its own but it is part of a bigger organisation. An organisation that rescues people of all ages who live on the streets, for example, or an organisation that takes in women and children who were rescued from human trafficking situations. When this is the case, it is often decided that instead of going through the trouble for finding caregivers for the children, some of the women who stay in a different department can be asked to take care of the children. In itself, it is not a bad idea to offer these women—paid—job opportunities once they have fully recovered from their traumatic experiences. However, 'fully recovered' means more than not having any more bruises or wounds. Whether they were previously forced to be prostitutes or to beg, or whether they were living on the streets for a long time, these women are all severely traumatised. They need a lot of professional counselling, and a lot of time—usually years—and help from the people around them to start to be able to let go of that trauma and to start to function normally again. Until they have reached that point, they are not suitable as caregivers. Someone who is severely traumatised needs someone to take care of her, she is not able to take care of someone else. And the flashbacks and survival instincts that are still present while the woman is traumatised, can make her—unintentionally—violent towards children. So an organisation like that is not a good place to look for caregivers.

In a centre for people rescued from the streets, women who are physically recovered from their experiences are asked to volunteer to take care of the children in the children's department. Both the women and the children still have their survival skills and their 'every person for himself' attitude from their days on the streets at the front of their mind. The result is that when a donor comes and hands out packets of biscuits to the children, as soon as the visitors have left, the women try to take the packets from the children to eat the biscuits themselves. Both the women and the children are very aggressive towards each other and amongst themselves, and no one is inclined to help anyone else. So in this situation, although the children are no longer living on the streets, they still have to fend for themselves and fight for their survival in the children's home.

Having grown up in a children's home does not make her a great candidate for a caregiver job.

Another group from which caregivers are regularly recruited are girls who grew up in the children's home and are now adults. This is seen as a way to help out the girls when they become too old to stay in care, by providing them with a job in an environment they know. Aside from that, it is seen as an easy way to find caregivers who are already familiar with the system. This sounds like a good plan. However, there are some problems with it. In Part 1, Chapter 5: 'Essential Psychological Needs' and Part 2, Chapter 4: 'Interacting with Children', I have explained that children learn how to behave when they are adults, from watching the adults around them. It was also explained that children in children's homes do not have realistic role models and that not all their essential basic needs are met. A girl who has grown up without having her essential basic needs met, has not had the opportunity to learn how to meet someone else's essential basic needs. This means that people who have grown up in a children's home are among the least suitable people to become caregivers. It is great if you decide to offer the children jobs when they become adults, but make sure they are jobs that do not involve the actual care for the children. Instead, they might come work in the kitchen, wash the laundry, or become a driver or a gardener for example.

> In a particular children's home, all girls are offered a chance to stay there and work as caregivers when they become adults. Many of the girls take up this offer, because they do not know much about the outside world and going out there scares them. This means that, in contrast to most children's homes in the region, this children's home has a very good caregiver-to-child ratio. However, when you see these caregivers in action, it does not look so great anymore. While there are always a lot of caregivers around, they almost never give any attention to the children. Not because they are too busy, but because they are more interested in talking and laughing amongst themselves. They go through the motions of the practical parts of care, nothing else. After all, they were never taught that anything else should be done, and now they are teaching the same to the little girls who will be caregivers in the future.

UN GUIDELINES:

113. As a matter of good practice, all agencies should systematically ensure that, prior to employment, carers and other staff in direct contact with children undergo an appropriate and comprehensive assessment of their suitability to work with children.

Training Staff

Even if you hire staff experienced in childcare, even if they have degrees in things like psychology or social work, it is very important that you—or someone you have hired for this purpose—give all staff basic training before they start working with your children. There are two reasons for this.

The first reason is that providing all your staff with the same information is the only way to make sure that they all have the same level of knowledge, on all relevant subjects. Even experienced or qualified people may never have encountered a particular situation that you know will occur in your children's home. It would cost you much more time to find out what a caregiver does not know about and teach her those things, person by person, than it does to just have everyone go through basic training. This way, after making a mistake, the caregiver cannot say: 'But how could I know?' Now you can say: 'I told you about this in training, that is how you were supposed to know.'

The second reason to train all your staff before putting them to work, is that many parts of childcare can be done in many different ways. The people you have hired for the job may have changed hundreds of nappies and bathed dozens of children, but you may want them to do it in a different way than they are used to. For example, knowing about the risks of feeding a baby while she is lying flat, you will want all babies to be held while they are fed. This may not be the way the caregivers did it in their previous jobs. So, by providing them with training, you do not only make sure the staff has the information they need to do a good job, but also that they do things in the way that you believe is best for the children.

In a children's home for HIV-positive children there were very strict rules about children not being allowed to eat for an hour before they received their medicine and for half an hour after they had taken it. This was because if they did eat during that time, the medication would not be effective and the child would get very sick. One evening, I saw a new caregiver, who had only been there two or three weeks, hand out biscuits to children only ten minutes after they had taken their medication. She had not received training. Although she was trying to do something very nice, she was putting the children's health at risk, because no one had told her about the rule.

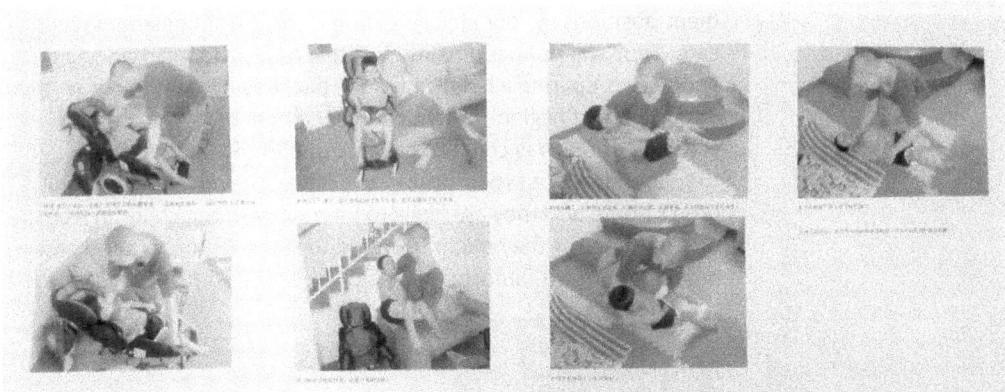

Some training may be needed to help keep your staff healthy and safe.

It will be helpful to train caregiving staff to create awareness of the importance of affection, attention, physical contact, and bonding to the well-being and health of children. When caregivers are aware of the reasons behind the rules laid down by management and of the impact of their actions on the children–both positive and negative–

the chances of caregivers following the rules will increase, and they may feel more motivated to accomplish things with the children. Often, the problems institutionalised children have to face are not down to malice or disinterest on the part of the caregivers, but simply due to a lack of knowledge or understanding of the essential basic needs of a child.

Instead of only saying: 'You have to wash your hands and change your clothes as soon as you arrive and before you start work,' explain that the babies in the home have a weak health, and if they come in contact with things from outside the home, they could get very ill. Tell them that even being infected with a minor cold could lead to life-threatening pneumonia and being infected with what is only minor diarrhoea to an adult can lead to severe diarrhoea and maybe even dehydration and death in the baby.

Hygiene standards were very good in a particular baby home. All caregivers would wash their hands very regularly, when they came in and between handling different babies. However, whenever someone working in the office came upstairs to the baby home to tell someone something or to get information, they would not wash their hands, while they would often still touch a baby's hand or pinch a little cheek. The management regularly reminded the caregivers of the importance of hand washing, but seemed to think that when you work in the office, bacteria will not pass from you to a baby.

Aside from the caregivers and their supervisors, it is a good idea also to give the people who are to work in administrative and management positions in your children's home some training about childcare. They will not need to know all the details about changing a nappy or preparing a balanced meal, but they do need to know the importance of hygiene, and it can help if they have some understanding of the way children develop and think. Because, although they spend most of their time in the office, they do work in a children's home and they are likely to interact with the children from time to time. Or they might be asked to show visitors around and provide them with information.

It is useful to do a refresher training at least once a year.

It is helpful to remind your staff of their training from time to time. Although a lot of the things you taught them at the start will be used on an almost daily basis, certain parts covered by the training may not occur for long periods of time and the knowledge of how to deal with them may fade. There is a chance that certain things that are (supposed to be) done every day will start to be taken for granted and will be done less consistently. Constant washing of hands is one of these things. Most people need to be reminded once in a while that the fact that you washed your hands very thoroughly and very frequently last month is not going to prevent infections this month. This is why it can be helpful to go over the basic training again to refresh the staff's memories, in small groups, at least once a year.

Together with the caregiver, I was cooling down a girl with a high fever and tried to make her as comfortable as possible. She was stripped down to her underwear, and we were using damp cloths to cool her down. Then, a group of more than ten people appeared in the doorway of the dorm. They were being given a tour of the children's home by someone from management, and he did nothing to stop the group. I positioned myself so that I mostly blocked their view of the girl, with my back to the door. After a minute or two, two of the people came into the dorm, to get a better look at the girl. I turned around and pointed out that we do not usually enter the dorm with shoes on. Then I told them that I would be happy to come outside the room to talk to them, but that this girl was feeling miserable enough without an audience. There were nods, but no one moved. I got up and left the room, the group reluctantly followed and started asking me questions. The person who was guiding the tour had still not said anything and was apparently not aware of the children's home's policy to allow children their privacy and dignity.

A children's home had only 1/3 of the caregivers needed to have any hope of meeting the children's essential basic needs. I provided training to the caregivers and the management about what children's essential basic needs are and how they can be met in a children's home. However, I reminded the management that with the current caregiver-to-child ratio, there was no possibility of the caregivers actually giving the children in their care the attention and stimulation they needed. Various times I reminded the management that finding more caregivers had to be a priority, before other changes could be made. Trying to find new staff was a very slow process, and even after a few years, there had not been much progress. However, the management did provide refresher training to the caregivers every year. I remarked that this was rather a waste of time when there was no hope of staff actually doing what they were being reminded off at every training.

Over time, you will gain more knowledge about dealing with difficult situations by seeing examples and receiving recommendations. As your knowledge and insight increase, you can adapt your basic training. The new information will be passed on to everyone during the yearly basic refresher training to all the staff. One thing that remains very important to keep in mind, is that for caregivers to be able to meet the children's essential basic needs, the caregiver-to-child ratio needs to be reasonable. Workable caregiver-to-child ratios are given in Part 3, Chapter 1:'Different Kinds of Caring Setup'. If one caregiver has to care for too many children, no amount of training is going to help her to meet the children's needs because it is not humanly possible to make use of the training in such a situation.

> *A children's home with over sixty children had one manager, a cook and one caregiver. Older children were expected to help younger children and they were not believed to need help or guidance. The children ran wild. There was a lot of violence and behavioural problems. The adults blamed the children, calling them ungrateful and bad.*

Please feel free to use parts—or all—of this manual and the other manuals in the *Children Everywhere* series for training your staff. You can photocopy, translate, and distribute it. As long as you do not sell the whole manual or parts of it for profit, your help in spreading the knowledge will be much appreciated. If you have translated part or all of the manual, please contact me and share the translation, so that I can share it again with other children's homes.

UN GUIDELINES:

115. Training should be provided to all carers on the rights of children without parental care and on the specific vulnerability of children, in particularly difficult situations, such as emergency placements or placements outside their area of habitual residence. Cultural, social, gender and religious sensitisation should also be assured. States should also provide adequate resources and channels for the recognition of these professionals in order to favour the implementation of these provisions.

Chapter 5:   The Relationship between Management and Caregivers

It is not easy to decide how to best balance the relationship between management and caregivers. I have seen many different ways of doing it and have not yet come across anything that I would call ideal. I cannot provide you with a 'how to' for best practice on this subject. What I can do, is relate some of the situations that I have come across that resulted in less than ideal situations, and explain how and why they happened. Then it is up to you to try out a new approach with these warnings in the back of your mind, and see if that approach works any better.

✳ ──────────────   **Need for Hierarchy**

While I am in favour of a relatively egalitarian setup in any workplace, I believe that a dedicated management works well in the case of children's homes. There are places where someone who spends most of her time in the children's home, taking care of the children's day-to-day care, also has to deal with all of the administration, logistics, communications, and so on. This will inevitably lead to a work overload and to one or both parts of her job suffering. It is important to realise that administration, logistics, communication, accounting, and so on, take up a lot of time and energy and cannot be done as an afterthought. If they are not handled well, a lot of trouble may follow. Sometimes, badly kept records and accounts can even lead to the closing down of your children's home by officials.

When there is literally a wall between the management offices and the rest of the children's home, that is usually not a good sign for the relation between management and caregivers.

On the other end of the scale, there are children's homes where there is 'The Office', with its staff of managers, accountants, and social workers on the one hand, and 'The Home', where children live and are cared for by caregivers, on the other hand. Both are strictly separated, with only the occasional, brief visit from someone from management to the home. In my experience, this is not ideal either. In this situation, management is taken care of very thoroughly. Caregivers have been trained and know what to do. However, the gap between the two is very big. Caregiving staff is unaware of management issues and are only told of decisions once they have been taken and cannot be changed anymore. The caregiving staff often resents the management. A trace of resentment between caregivers and management will be present in any setup, but in my experience the bigger the gap between caregivers and management, the greater the resentment. Caregiving staff, in this case, feels that the management does not know what is going on and what they are making decisions about. There is often some truth in this feeling. Because of it, new decisions are met with hostility, regardless of what they are about.

> *Management had decided to hand out fireworks to each of the children, for the celebration of the upcoming holiday. The caregiver, who was responsible for 24 children aged three to eleven years old, was against this decision, as she foresaw a lot of burns and other accidents among the children. But it was not her place to speak. Instead, the only thing she could do once the children started setting off their fireworks, was to frantically run around to try to keep the serious accidents to a minimum.*

A gap between management and caregivers that is too big can also lead to dangerous situations. In a situation where upper management has made it clear that caregivers do not have the right to address them directly, and the person whom the caregiver *can* speak to is not available, is not interested, or refuses to act, the caregiver can only wait in despair, for what will happen.

> *A child had a fever of more than 40°C, he was very unwell. His caregiver was very worried. She left me with the boy and went to look for the doctor. When she came back, she was desperate. She had asked for the doctor, but he was not there, and she had asked for someone who might be able to help, but nothing happened. She did not have the right to take any further action, all she could do now was wait and hope the doctor would come today, at some point. I left her with the boy and went to speak to management. I explained the situation and the doctor was called and came within an hour. Without my intervention, as an outside link to management, the little boy's situation did not look good.*

It is very important that the staff know who is in charge and that they take orders from management seriously. To achieve this, instructions need to be given in a way that makes it clear that it is not just a suggestion. However, it is important to find a middle ground to have a good working relationship with your staff. If you are only authoritarian, you are essentially ruling through fear, something that we covered in Part 2, Chapter 6: 'Discipline'. Ruling through fear will not be any more effective with your staff than it is with children. It will not make them eager to please you. It will just make them try not to upset you, when they think it might be noticed.

It is not true that being authoritarian is the only way to effectively deal with staff. Letting staff—and children—see you as a person and a friend, rather than just as an authority figure, is likely to make them respect you more. When a member of staff feels acknowledged as a person rather than nothing more than a subordinate, it will make her much more likely to want to please you and go the extra mile.

Various children's home directors and other management staff are afraid that if the staff would see them as 'too human' or as a friend, they would not be taken seriously or they would seem weak. To prevent the impression of weakness, everything they say comes out as an order, in a stern authoritarian voice. Any dealings with the staff is strictly business: either informing them of a changed situation or upcoming events, instructing them to do things a certain way, reprimanding them harshly, or threatening them with consequences if mistakes are made. These managers often complain that their staff hardly ever volunteers for tasks or shows any initiative.

If necessary, when I tell someone to do something, I can make sure they are in no doubt that it needs to be done and that it had better be done as well and as quickly as possible. From the way I say it, my tone of voice, the way I look, this is clear. I can be very demanding. When I know someone is able to do something but did not do it and as a result, a child's well-being was put at risk, I can be quite sharp. People who have known me for a while tend to tremble when they realise I have found out they did something like that, because they know what is coming.

However, most of my time, I work and live alongside the caregivers: I help them with their work, we share stories from our different backgrounds, we joke and enjoy beautiful moments with the children. Most caregivers consider me a friend and they are sad to see me leave when I go. None of this makes them hesitate when I give them an order or makes them tremble any less if they realise I have found out about a serious, unnecessary mistake they made.

UN GUIDELINES:

114. Conditions of work, including remuneration, for carers employed by agencies and facilities should be such as to maximize motivation, job satisfaction and continuity, and enhance their disposition to fulfil their role in the most appropriate and effective manner.

✱ ——————— Elements for Good Practice
In my experience, to improve the level of care in a children's home, at least one member of staff should be part of management–call

her the children's home director, or children's home manager, for in-stance—as well as being actively involved inside the children's home every day. Part of her duties will take place in the office, where she is a part of the decision-making concerning administration and management. It will be her responsibility to take care of some man-agement issues herself, and she is kept informed about issues taken care of by other management and administrative staff. She knows when children will be coming or going, where they come from and where they go, and she has a voice in the decision-making process concerning the day-to-day running of the children's home. The other part of her duties takes place among the children, in the home.

The babies hold their own meeting, the director may sit in.

In a particular baby home, the supervisor is the link between the office and the children's home. He reports conditions in the baby home to the office and he passes on decisions from the management to the caregivers. However, when he is in the baby home, it seems like he is mostly enjoying his high status among the caregivers. Sometimes he will talk to a toddler, but he never holds a baby—even at times when the caregivers are understaffed and many babies are crying. Very often he will sit on a chair—while the caregivers sit on the floor with the babies—and be busy on his phone for half an hour or longer. Not a very good example to set.

The children's home manager has to be familiar with all children and their condition. Aside from her administrative responsibili-ties in the office, this person should spend about half of her time in the home. With the caregivers, to talk with them and answer their questions, and with the children, to get to know them, play with them and at the same time observe what goes on around her. When she notices problems with care, she will be able to intervene immediately. And if there is a problem with one of the children, concerning health, behaviour or otherwise, she should be notified so she can assess the situation—or bring in someone to do it and inform her of his conclusions.

Ideally, from time to time, someone from management should also visit the children's home during the night–or regularly have someone spend the night at the children's home–to check that the night-time standard of care is still acceptable. Unannounced checks are usually most effective. Especially if you have waking night shifts, doing this is important to maintain care standards.

In a medical children's home there was a separate night shift. Caregivers on the night shift were paid a slightly higher wage than caregivers on the day shift because they had to stay awake during the night, to make sure the same level of care was provided around the clock. This was necessary because the medically fragile babies needed constant care and monitoring. For an unannounced check, the children's home director visited the home at 3:00 a.m. She found all the caregivers and the shift supervisor asleep. They had not dozed off on the job; they had lain down on empty children's beds and covered themselves with the children's quilts. They were all fired.

Time Management

Most people want the caregiving staff to see themselves more as surrogate parents than as employees who just want to earn their salary. If you are serious about this, management will have to contribute to this mindset for it to have any chance of success.

The caregiving staff cannot be expected to fully take on a parental role for the children, if management treats them the same way they treat office staff or cleaning staff. In some places, caregivers are expected to always be available at the whim of anyone higher up in the management hierarchy. At any given moment, they can be told to go to the office to give information, receive information, sign something or bring something; they can be sent on an errand or be pulled in for a meeting or for training. When they are advised of any of these circumstances, they are expected to drop everything they are doing and report to their superior instantly.

Imagine being forced to abandon this situation to go to the office for something that is not urgent.

Can you imagine someone calling you away, at a moment's notice, when you are spending time with your family? It can happen while you are bathing your child, feeding your child, tending to your sick child, trying to discipline your child, or helping your child with homework or with emotional difficulties. Imagine this happening various times a day, day in day out. You never know how long you will be away for. And there is no backup, you just have to leave the children in whatever state they are in and go. Worst of all, most of the time you are called away for things that are not urgent: it was not absolutely necessary for management to do something about an issue at that moment, it was just convenient.

When you look at it this way, it sounds ridiculous and impossible to do a job under these circumstances. Yet it is the reality for many caregivers, and at the same time they are criticised for not spending enough time with the children and not providing more parent-like care. Some of the caregivers hardly spend three hours a day with their children because they are made to run around doing so many other things. If this happens in a children's home, you can be almost certain that most caregivers will not stay in their job very long, because it is made impossible for them to do the job properly.

I was told that a boy had had a serious seizure the evening before. I asked if he was on anti-seizure medication and was told that he was, but he had not been given it the past two days, because he had run out. When asked how that could happen, the explanation was that the caregiver in charge of the boy's dorm had been away the past few days because he had been put in charge of getting things ready for an upcoming event, so he had not been able to get new medicine. I explained to them that suddenly stopping anti-seizure medication is extremely dangerous and should never be done. I also explained that in a place where there was a great lack of caregivers, maybe assigning caregivers to duties such as organising an event and leaving their dorms without supervision is not the best way to go.

This is something management needs to become aware of and do something about. Some suggestions to avoid leaving children unsupervised and having caregivers walk away:

- Appoint a period of no more than one hour a day for each dorm or department—chosen at a time during the day that is usually least busy for the caregivers of that particular dorm or department—during which caregivers can be called in to give information, sign things, and so on. Management has to do everything in its power to organise things so that caregivers are not called out at other times. In absolute emergencies that cannot wait until the appointed time the next day, a caregiver can be called, but she has to be allowed to say: 'I'll be there in (for example) half an hour, when I have finished [...].' If the issue cannot wait that long, the management staff can go over to the caregiver personally and deal with it while the caregiver continues to do what she cannot abandon.

- Appoint a period of no more than two hours a week for meetings, and stick to that. This time does not need to be used if it is not necessary to hold a meeting. It could be used for training, if time is needed for that instead.
- If a caregiver needs more than 25% of her time to do other things than take care of her children, she should either be replaced as a caregiver and allowed to focus on the administration/logistic work (one person can then take on the administration/logistics for several dorms), or someone needs to be hired separately to take care of this work so the caregiver can focus on her children.
- One or two caregivers could be hired who are not placed 'in charge' of a dorm, but are 'floating', like baby sitters. Their job is to cover for caregivers who are ill, who are on leave, who are in hospital with one of their children, who have to attend training, and so on.

A caregiver was in charge of a dorm with 17 children. One of the children got sick and had to stay in hospital for several days. This meant that the caregiver had to stay in hospital with the child. For this entire time, there was no caregiver to look after the other 16 children. One morning, an eleven-year-old girl from that dorm arrived late at breakfast and was asked why. She said that she had had to wash and dress the smaller children before breakfast and they were not cooperating.

- Give the 'surrogate parents' a certain degree of autonomy. Parenting does not work if the 'parent' has to ask permission all the time before doing anything. Provide caregivers with a list of rules that provide a framework of things that are expected and things that are considered unacceptable in the care for the children—you can have them sign this, like a kind of contract—and then allow them to make their own decisions within that framework.

Communication

On my way to the office I am stopped by someone asking me why I am not attending the meeting being held in the great hall. Well, if I had known that there was a meeting and that I was supposed to attend it, I probably would have been there. Since nobody had told me about it, it was hard to make sure I would be there.

Communication between management and caregiving staff is vital. Keeping the staff informed of what is going on allows them to anticipate and to prepare the children for what is going to happen. At the same time, the staff is able to provide information about children and the way things are going, which is very valuable for good management.

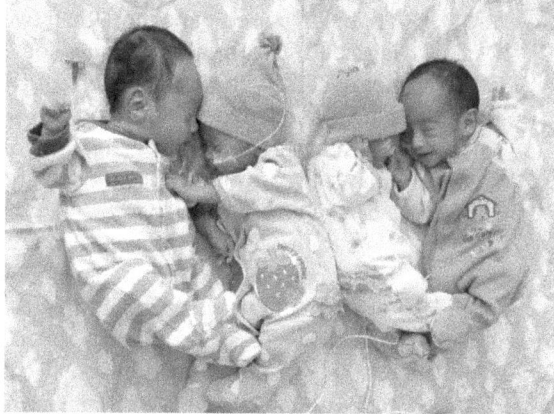

Communication is essential.

One option to ensure communication between management and staff is to hold monthly staff meetings–in two batches, as always, to make sure there are still people looking after the children–during which someone from management talks to the staff (caregivers as well as other staff), gives them feedback on things that have happened in the past month–both good and not so good–and gives them an update on what is expected to happen in the coming weeks. During this meeting, staff is also asked for their comments on how things are going and what problems and obstacles they have come across. This can be anything from relationships with management, between colleagues, with children and between children, to practical things to do with health, maintenance, events or activities, and supplies. The issues raised need to be taken seriously and the staff should get an update on any progress being made.

In an adoption centre, I had been asked to provide training for the caregiving staff by upper management. The home supervisor had been appointed as my translator by his superior. While upper management knew the kind of training I was going to give and wanted the caregivers to be told about these things, the supervisor was afraid that his job would get harder, so he did not agree with what I said. When I had started talking and then nodded to the supervisor to translate it for me, instead he turned to me and argued against what I had said. I told him that in a moment I would explain how it was possible to do what I suggested, and asked if he wanted me to provide the training, or whether I should just leave. His superior told the supervisor to just translate and me to keep going. Communication was clearly an issue here.

One more issue regarding communication is that in some places, part or even all of the caregiving staff may be **illiterate** or only partially **literate**. This does not need to negatively affect their ability to provide good childcare. However, it is important to be sensitive to how intimidating it is for illiterate people to be made to sign documents with conditions that affect their work and possibly their job security, because they cannot be sure whether they have fully been explained what they are signing or if there are things they do not know about. If you provide the possibility of a recorded verbal agreement, which holds the same binding force as a signed contract, this could go a long way to reassure them. In a recorded verbal agreement, the document is read out loud and this is audio recorded, and when the reading is finished, the staff member states his or her name, the date and that they agree with, or will be bound by what was just read out. This way, they are agreeing to exactly what they have heard, without fear of things being hidden, because they have not agreed to anything that was not read out.

UN Guidelines:

121. Carers should have, within fostering agencies and other systems involved with children without parental care, the opportunity to make their voice heard and to influence policy.

✳ ———————————— ***Not Undermining Caregivers***

In a family situation, when one parent tells the children they can or cannot do something and then the other parent (or a grandparent) goes against that, or reprimands the first parent in front of the children for saying such a thing, the authority of the first parent disappears. If it happens regularly, the children will see no reason to even listen to the first parent anymore, because they have learned not to put too much value on what this person says.

She needs to know that when her caregiver tells her something, everyone will follow through on it.

The same is true for caregivers. If their decisions or actions are regularly questioned or reversed, or if they are reprimanded in front of the children, their authority will be completely undermined and they will have no con-

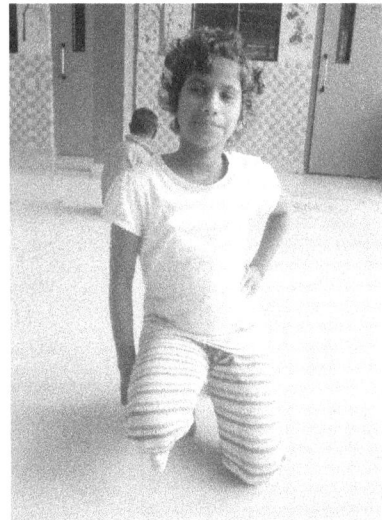

trol over the children anymore. They can hardly be blamed for being unable to keep order among the children under such circumstances. This is exactly what happens in many places where no thought is given to the parental role of the caregiver and where there is a strong focus on the employer-employee relationship. Worse yet, the blame for the consequences of this situation is almost always placed on the caregivers.

Obviously, if a caregiver is behaving in an inappropriate way, she needs to be reprimanded. But this should be done privately and most certainly not in front of the children. Also, management must realise that children will quickly discover if their word is seen as more important than that of the caregivers, and they will use this knowledge to threaten caregivers and manipulate management. The situation can become very extreme in places where management is very sensitive to the needs of the children. They may be afraid that adult caregivers will possibly abuse defenceless children. Children are taken as honest and caregivers as devious, but that is not necessarily always the truth, especially when it comes to older children who are figuring out how to get what they want. As was discussed in Part 2, Chapter 4: 'Interaction with Children', children will almost always learn to lie, as part of their normal development. And if they find out that it is in their advantage to lie, they will do it more often. Neither adults nor children should be automatically assumed to be honest, nor should they automatically be assumed to be lying. Information from more sources should always be sought, if there is any doubt about the truth on either side.

> *In one particular home the practice of physical punishment was put to an end. This caused quite a few problems, mostly because the children's word would generally be taken over that of the caregivers. Many caregivers were afraid to use any form of disciplining, because children would demand to talk to the director and threaten to say they had been beaten. After signing the agreement not to beat the children, many caregivers feared that they would lose their jobs, not because they had done something wrong, but because a child accused them of doing something. Some caregivers even considered quitting before this could happen.*

Children will always rebel against being restricted and disciplined.

> *As a nanny, I have often been told by the children that I was 'mean' or 'cruel' followed by: 'I am going to tell my mum.' My strength rested on the fact that I was able to say, 'Okay, shall I dial the number for you?' because I knew I would be backed up by the mother. If that*

would not have been the case, I might as well have packed up and left. The same is true in a children's home. The fastest way to put an end to the children's revolt in the example just given is to say, 'All right, you call the director.' Let them call and let them be told that whatever they did was unacceptable and that they will need to accept the disciplining as a consequence of it. That will put an end to the problem quite quickly.

By treating caregivers like the enemy, as the management does in some places, you end up actually making them the enemy. If you are serious about wanting staff to stay long-term, they need to feel empowered to do their job, they need to feel they are a part of a bigger whole–rather than just a subordinate–and they need to be validated for what they are doing. What I have been explaining about children goes for all people: unless reprimands are balanced with praise and signs of gratitude, caregivers will not stay. They will feel more and more worn down and they will not be able to continue if they are constantly reprimanded.

Just like adults should all get on the same line towards the children, it is important for management to have one way of dealing with the staff. If different members of management say different things to caregiving staff, or undermine each other's authority, caregivers are likely to become confused, or rebellious. When that happens, the chance of proper work being done becomes very small.

The manager found several caregivers sitting around chatting, while it was clear that right under their noses, there was work that needed to be done. The manager commented on this and pointed out what the caregivers should be doing, and reminded them that they had signed a document saying they would take care of these things. The caregivers did not get up, they just said that the superintendent never made them do it anyway, so why should they?

Hostage Situation

One pitfall I want to warn you about, very specifically, involves management being held hostage by the caregivers. This may sound outrageous, but it happens more often than you might think.

A certain amount of distance and sometimes tension between caregivers and management is usual. The two groups come from different backgrounds, different levels of education, and different layers of society. This can lead to a lack of open communication, miscommunication and sometimes even resentment from the caregivers towards the management in varying degrees.

It is generally true that management staff have little practical experience with these kinds of situations.

Management is sometimes perceived to be 'doing nothing'–just sitting behind computers and in meetings all day long, getting more money (which is generally true), and not realising the hardships of the work that the caregivers perform (which is sometimes true). Attempting to keep communication channels open and giving caregivers the opportunity to vent their frustration from time to time can help prevent this situation from escalating.

The management of a children's home brought me in with great enthusiasm. They wanted to know how they might be able to improve the care of the children and learn new things. I was told this in the office. Then I was led to the children's home, and on the way I was warned that a lot of the caregivers had been there for many years and they were not very open to change. In fact, it might be better if I did not tell the staff in the home exactly what I had come to do and just follow their instructions, and then I could give the management my recommendations. I spent some time at this children's home and there were various things that could have been improved very simply, but no progress was made. The management was too afraid of the staff leaving to dare to propose any changes.

What should be prevented is a situation where the caregivers hold all the power, because when that point is reached, it becomes impossible to effectively run a children's home. In a situation like that, you cannot be certain that the children's best interest will always be put first.

So, how can a situation like that possibly develop? It is frighteningly simple, really. In any situation where it is easier for your staff to find new jobs than it is for you to find new staff up to your standards, the caregivers have something to threaten you with. This is the case in quite a lot of places. The only other ingredient needed at that point is for you to allow them to use the situation against you.

When you propose a change, want your staff to do further training, or simply demand that the standards that they were originally taught are upheld, and a member of staff says she refuses cooperate and will quit if you insist on it, that is the moment when everything hangs in the balance. When this happens for the first time, all eyes and ears will be on you to see what you will do, because this will tell them exactly where you stand. If at this point you do not stand by your demands, you are officially handing power to your staff, and from then on, you are their hostage to do what they want. You have confirmed that they have a weapon and they will not be afraid to use it, because it will do them no harm.

A caregiver was hardly working at all, the children she was responsible for were badly neglected. Several times she had been warned by the manager that if she kept this up, she would be fired. However, the manager did not actually fire her, because there was already a shortage of caregivers and despite trying to recruit new ones, she had not found any yet. So pretty soon the lazy caregiver did not take the threats seriously anymore and became even lazier. This example had a bad effect on the other caregivers, who did not see the point in working hard anymore, if they would be able to keep their job anyway.

So, how do you avoid being taken hostage? When a person threatens to leave, you calmly let her know that you would of course be very sad to see her go, but that she has every right to leave if she feels that she cannot work up to your standards and by your rules. Depending on how humiliated she feels by having lost the standoff and how much she needs her salary, she may or may not leave.

In any case, if you are a fair employer, it is unlikely that all of your caregivers will leave. Because even if it may theoretically be easy for them to find a new job, very few people are willing to give up the security of the job they already have for the uncertainty of a job they still have to find. And now your point is made: you have shown you are not afraid to send away someone who is uncooperative or someone whose work is clearly below standard, which puts you in charge of running the children's home.

How do you escape from a caregiver-management hostage situation if you are already in one? In much the same way as you would prevent it. If you were too afraid to put through the measures that you feel have been necessary for some time, but you have decided to put an end to the hostage situation, all you need to do is create a situation in which your authority is challenged again and change the outcome. So, you call your staff together, propose whatever measure you wish to propose and wait for them to threaten you again. When they do, you fire *one* person—whoever is the least cooperative, most resistant and most active in whipping the entire staff up against you—stating their lack of compliance with your rules as the cause. And then you ask the rest of the staff if they would like to go too. They are likely to be quite shocked by this, and very unlikely to leave.

If finding staff is very hard, it might be a good idea to find a replacement *before* you set the stage for making your point. By having a replacement ready for the person who got fired, you signal that you are quite able to find replacements if necessary. Hopefully, it will never come to this in your institution, but if it does, do try to break out of the situation as quickly as possible.

Chapter 6:   Day-to-Day Issues

✳ ─────────── **Taking in New Children**

To be able to provide good care, it helps to have a system in place for taking in new children on arrival. This system needs to include assessing the child's condition, bathing her before letting her go amongst other children, and starting a file for the child.

Just arrived: The arm was said to be her problem, her severe heart defect was not mentioned.

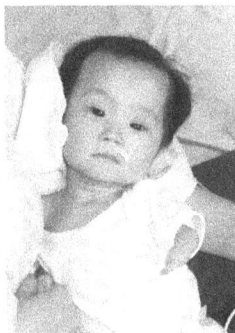

How much information you can get about a child depends on the way she arrives. When a child has been abandoned, usually almost nothing is known about her, while if she is brought in by the police or social services after losing her family or after being taken out of her family home, a name and date of birth should certainly be known, as well as some family and medical history. Some organisations do not only have an adoption centre where they take care of babies, but they also help single, pregnant women who stay with them until they give birth and then leave the baby if they have no way to take care of it. When that is the case, you have the opportunity to collect and record a full family medical history, which can be extremely valuable to the child later in life. It is essential to get as much information as possible about the child from whoever brings her in, or from the child herself if she is able to speak. Make notes of this information and put them in the child's file, together with the date of acceptance into your facility and her (estimated) age, weight, length, and general condition as far as you can determine.

ⓘ

Over time you will discover how reliable the information given by the people who drop the children off really is. Sometimes it can be very wrong:

- *A baby with Trisomy 13, a syndrome with poor chance of survival and obvious abnormalities of the face, was brought in with the diagnosis of 'cleft lip and palate'.*
- *A baby with a complicated heart defect was brought in with the diagnosis 'deformity to her left arm'.*
- *A baby whose umbilical stump had not started to dry yet–so he could not possibly be more than two days old–arrived with a date of birth, given to him by officials, that would make him three weeks old.*

So, you see why it is important to always do your own assessment to make sure.

Whether there is an official care agreement—on paper and signed— for every child will depend on the country you work in and the authorities you are dealing with. However, if it is at all possible, you should have some kind of official agreement for every child, that states that your organisation is the child's official guardian or that gives a similar legal authority. This is to prevent problems in case of any run-in with authorities, as well as to protect the child.

When a child arrives, her intake should be done privately, separate from the other children. In the case of a small child or baby, undress the child. In the case of an older child, ask the child to undress herself and give her some privacy to do this. Have the clothes washed

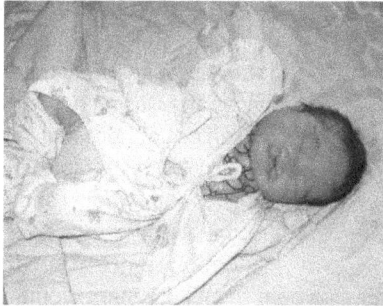

The baby as he is brought in.

thoroughly. If there is no other option, the clothes may have to be thrown away. However, it is important to be aware that the clothes the child came in with may be the only thing she has left that her parents gave her. This makes them quite precious to her, so if at all possible, keep the clothes she came in for her to have, even if they cannot be worn anymore.

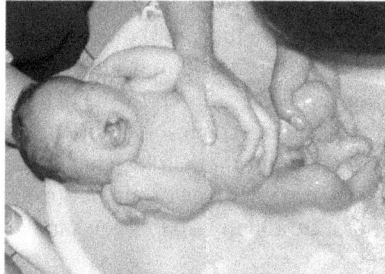

The same baby being washed ...

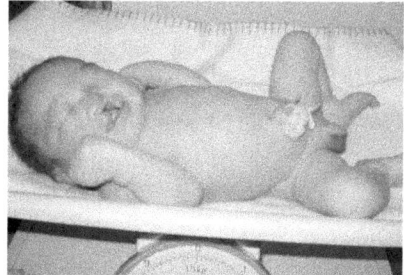

...and weighed ....

Do not let the child walk around or lie in the clothes she came in with, because you do not know what bacteria she may be bringing in with her, even if her clothes look clean. If there is a serious suspicion or certainty that the child might have or carry a contagious illness—

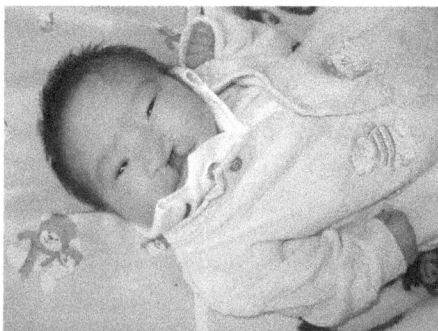

through a medical diagnosis, or because of what her relatives are known to have died from— isolate her completely until you can be certain that she is not or no longer contagious. Being HIV-positive is not a reason to isolate a child.

And finally dressed.

The new arrival should be:

- Washed thoroughly: only in the case of hypothermia or another critical medical situation does taking care of her medical needs take precedence over washing the child. Older children should be given the opportunity to wash themselves, without anyone watching, but they do need to be reminded to wash thoroughly.
- Checked for lice: if they are present, treat the child for lice straight away—or shave off the hair, depending on your policy—to prevent them from spreading to all the children and staff in your home.
- Weighed and measured: knowing her weight and height on arrival is important for several reasons. You will want to have a weight and height to compare to, to see if she is growing, to know the correct weight for calculating a dosage of medication if necessary, and to be able to calculate how much formula to offer to start with for a baby.
- Checked for any signs of obvious abnormalities or injuries: with small children, you can check their naked body for anything out of the ordinary, with older children, you can have the child cover up essential areas and check the rest, while asking the child for any problems or deformations in the areas covered.
- Have her age estimated, if date of birth is not available: age is assessed by looking at a combination of posture, size, developmental stage, presence of teeth, and so on. Children with severe heart or kidney conditions and severely malnourished children are almost always small for their age and behind in development, but they may, for instance, be much more advanced in their speech than expected based on their size and motor development stage. I have seen people wrongly estimate the ages of babies and toddlers with heart conditions by as much as six months too young. Of course, in the case of older children who are able to speak, you can ask them for their age and maybe even their birthday, and compare their answer to your own overall impression.

Dress the child in clean clothes and measure her height. To rule out fever—or in babies, hypothermia—it is wise to also take her temperature. With babies, this should be done before they are washed to make sure they are not hypothermic. Detailed information about how to check for any health issues in new arrivals can be found in *Sick Children Everywhere* Part 3, Chapter 2: 'Discovery'.

Then offer the child something to eat, formula for babies and food and a drink for older children. Monitor the way they eat: Are they able to manage an amount that is appropriate for their (estimated) age and size? Do they get tired quickly? Do they have the motor skills required to eat at the level you would expect for their age?

If possible, it is wise to have all new arrivals checked out by a doctor or another medically knowledgeable person soon–preferably within 24 to 48 hours–after they are taken in. This way, if there is a problem, you will know about it as soon as possible and you can take appropriate measures for good care.

> *A baby of probably about two weeks old arrives. He is given the usual look-over, is cleaned and dressed. He eats well and seems normal. After a few hours, he starts to seem weaker and weaker. He does not have the strength to suck for very long and eats less and less. After another few hours he starts turning blue. When he is taken to hospital, a serious heart defect is discovered. When he first arrived, only a doctor would have been able to find out about that. Only when things started to go really wrong did it become clear to everyone.*

If everything seems normal, or as expected, the child can become a part of the daily routine of the home, among the other children. However, the first couple of days, a close eye should be kept on the child to recognise any possible problems early on.

Giving older children instructions on what they are expected to do at different times is important to help make their start in a new place easier and less scary.

> *A ten-year-old boy had arrived at the children's home in the afternoon. He had been taken to an office, where he was asked for his name and age and he had to sit there and wait until many papers were filled in. Then he was taken to a dorm, where other boys were told to show him his bunk bed and to take care of him.*
>
> *At dinner time, the other boys took him to the dining hall and showed him where to get his plate and where to queue for food. The boy sat down at one of the long tables with his food, and he began to eat. Instantly one of the adults shouted at him to stop that immediately. What was he thinking to start eating! The boy got a scare. When he looked around, he noticed that everyone sat behind their plate, but no one touched the food. They were supposed to wait until everyone was served, and then pray together. Then they were allowed to eat. But no one had told him this.*

UN Guidelines:

19. No child should be without the support and protection of a legal guardian or other recognized responsible adult or competent public body at any time.

167. Appropriate records of any placement of a child should be made and kept in a safe and secure manner so that reunification can be facilitated in the future.

✳ —————————— **Record keeping**

In a family situation, parents know whether their child is eating well or not, whether there is a change in his bowel movements or urine output, if he is growing or losing weight, and what incidents have taken place. They know these things, because they are there to witness almost all of them, and if they have been absent for a brief period, they will ask about everything they have missed. This means that when there is any change in the normal situation, they will notice it quite quickly. Knowing this is very helpful for a doctor or a therapist to get an idea of what is wrong with the child and what should be done. In fact, in some cases this information can save the child's life.

Parents do not need to write everything down, because they are around most of the time.

In a children's home the situation is different. Often, there are many different caregivers. In some places:

- A child is taken care of by different caregivers at different parts of the day, in different shifts.
- A child does have one caregiver around the clock, but he has to share her attention with more than ten other children, not to mention the practical chores, leaving very little opportunity for changes to be noticed.
- A child has one caregiver for a few days around the clock, and then another caregiver for a few days.
- All children are taken care of by all caregivers and will be randomly fed by this one, changed by that one, and changed by yet another one the next time.
- A child's care is split up between caregivers: this person always changes him, that person always feeds him, and that person always takes him to play outside.

In all of these situations, no one has a full overview of the child's situation.

This way, very serious problems can go unnoticed for a long time, until the child becomes so weak and ill that it is impossible not to notice. This is why I strongly recommend to have caregivers make notes of these kinds of things, to make sure that any time something is out of the ordinary, a caregiver can look back over the notes and see if this is the first time that something like this has happened, if it can be explained or if action must be taken.

> *A caregiver might think: 'The child hardly ate anything. Oh, but maybe he has eaten more than normal just before my shift started.' Or: 'The baby's nappy is completely dry. Oh, but maybe someone else just changed her.'*

Records of Daily Condition

For children up to one year old, I recommend keeping records of all their wet and dirty nappies, with the time when they were changed. I would also recommend a record of everything they eat and drink, with the amounts. This will make it easy to see at a glance if the baby is peeing enough, if he has had a bowel movement and if he is eating and drinking enough.

> *A five-month-old baby is not drinking her milk very well. She will only take half the bottle and nothing the caregiver tries can make her take more. She also seems tired or sleepy, even though she just woke up. The caregiver takes her to change her nappy and finds it dry. Because her shift only started just over two hours ago, the caregiver is not sure if the baby has been like this all day or not. When the caregiver looks at the nappy changing list, she finds that even though it is already 4:30 p.m., the baby has only had two wet nappies today. When she checks how much she has been drinking, the caregiver discovers that the baby has been drinking much less than usual, starting yesterday evening.*
>
> *The caregiver tells the person in charge of the children's health about the situation. The baby is taken to see a doctor and is diagnosed with dehydration and a throat infection. She probably did not want to drink because of a sore throat. Both are in the early stages and can be treated easily, and within a few days the baby is back to having a normal, healthy appetite and producing plenty of wet nappies.*

Keeping these kinds of records can be done by having a notebook for every child and having the caregivers write down the relevant information in it. Or you can make things simpler for caregivers and create forms in which they only have to fill in a number, mark an 'x', or write the time. Especially for caregivers who are not fully literate, the option of marking an 'x' makes life much more manageable. If your caregivers are completely illiterate, you can have a literate supervisor keep track of recording essential information.

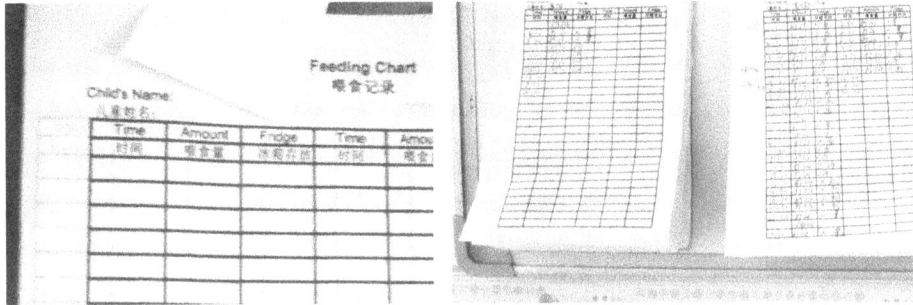

Example of a form for feeding records.

Here, each baby has a clipboard with forms.

For children over one year old, it is usually not necessary to keep such detailed records of everything that goes in and comes out unless they have a medical condition or special circumstances that require such information. Still, it is useful to make sure that certain information is recorded and passed on. In this case, having a notebook for every child is a good idea. In it, the caregivers–or their supervisor–can note down anything that happened out of the ordinary. Making such notes for a baby under one year old would also be a good idea.

So, write down things like: 'Did not want to eat at all', 'Ate less than usual', 'Only peed once', 'Did not have a bowel movement', 'Had diarrhoea', 'Fell on his head, doctor says he needs to be woken up every hour during the night, to check if he is okay', or, 'Has a fever and is coughing, highest temperature today 38.4°C'. Anything at all unusual that happened during the day or during the caregiver's shift can be written down.

Apart from making sure there are records of the things in a child's life that are out of the ordinary, it is a good idea to encourage your caregivers to talk with the people who take over from them when they finish their shift. During this change of staff, anything that happened that was out of the ordinary or that might need to be monitored should be mentioned.

Weight and Height

Certain information is essential to have on record, even if you choose not to keep the kind of records that were discussed in the previous section: the children's height and weight. Monitoring a child's growth and weight gain is an important way to get clues about their health. Also, if a child becomes ill or has something as simple as a fever requiring medication, it is necessary to know the child's weight to be able to calculate the dose of medicine he needs. It is inconvenient to have to weigh a child when he already feels terrible and needs his medication.

- Premature babies should be weighed every day. Their weight may go up or down a little bit from day to day, but over the course of a week they should have gained an average of approximately 20 grams per day, which is 140 grams per week. If a premature baby loses 10% or more of her weight in 24 hours, it is a sign of serious dehydration: the water lost from her body causes her weight to drop. When this happens, the baby needs to be taken straight to hospital.

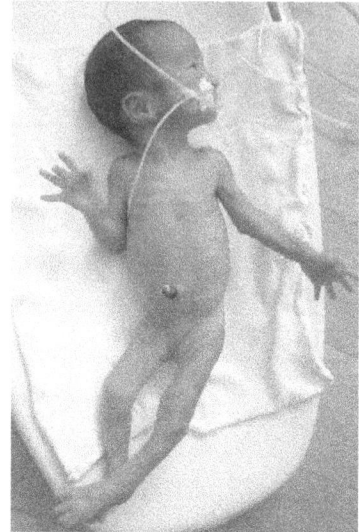

This preemie's weight went from 1.13kg to 1.08kg in 24 hours; she was rushed to hospital.

- Babies and children up to six years old–and older children with health issues or a history of weight loss–should be weighed once every week. This is both to make sure that you have an up-to-date weight record in case they need medication, and to make sure that they are gaining weight.
- Children over six should be weighed once a month, to make sure that they keep gaining weight while they are growing, especially if they live in a children's home.

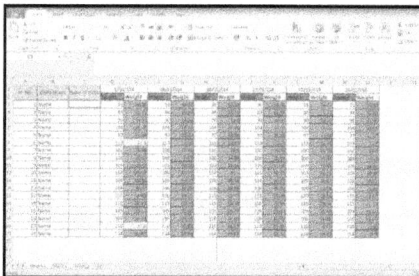

A growing child normally never loses weight. If he does lose weight, it is a sign that something is wrong and the cause of the weight loss should be investigated.

Example of a growth chart.

The monthly growth records of 204 children from one children's home showed that in the past month, 107 children had lost weight, some of them quite a lot, and 20 children had not gained any weight. Seeing the information in one document, rather than just thinking that this or that child was looking a bit thinner, made it clear that there was a serious problem. This led to an investigation into the children's diet and overall health, to solve the problem.

All children should also be measured, and records should be kept of their height.

- Up to six months old, babies should be measured every month.
- From six months up to six years old, children should be measured once every three months.
- From six up to twelve years, children should be measured once every six months.
- From twelve years onward, measuring children once a year is enough.

More detailed information about correctly weighing and measuring children and when it is necessary, can be found in *Sick Children Everywhere* Part 3, Chapter 2: 'Discovery'.

Over the course of several months, it became noticeable on the monthly growth reports that while most children in the children's home were growing well, two dorms had a lot of children who lost weight very often. This was odd, because all the children ate together in the dining hall, getting the same food. After more investigation, a strong suspicion arose that the children in these dorms were being terrorised by their caregivers. Their needs were met less than those of the other children and they lived in fear. This could be seen on the growth reports.

All children in children's homes are almost certain to be smaller than children of the same age in families, on whom the curves on the average growth chart are based. However, if you find that a particular child is much smaller than others of her age or that her growth is slowing down a lot, or if her weight for height is very low, she should be seen by a doctor to find out what is causing these problems and what can be done about it.

Visitors

A home with many orphans, abandoned children, or children with medical problems or handicaps, is often an attractive place for people to visit. Unless very strict rules are put in place and upheld, it will not take very long for your children's home to be turned into a 'petting zoo', which is not in the best interest of the children. Curious people come to places like these, sometimes bringing very small donations to pretend that they do not just want to have a look and feel good about themselves because of the interest they show in the 'poor little orphans'.

Looking up from the floor at this many strangers' legs is quite intimidating.

There are many ways in which a constant stream of curious visitors is a bad thing. First of all, it is a lot of work to supervise visitors and keep them under control, which is time taken out of the day of one of the caregivers or managers. Because if you want to guarantee the children's safety and well-being, someone has to be with the visitors at all times.

Secondly, it will not do the children's self-respect and self-esteem any good to have regularly changing crowds of people making exclamations about the poor, poor children who have nothing at all, and so on. It can be quite frightening for children to be confronted with a lot of strangers who all want to touch them, pinch their cheeks and just pick them up and hold them, regardless of protests. Usually very little attention is paid to the children's dignity and right to privacy. Not to mention the disturbance the invasion brings to the children's routine.

However well-meaning, visitors are not always aware of the right way to hold or treat children of a certain age or children with certain special needs. This can cause dangerous situations, both through improper physical contact and inappropriate things they might give a child to play with or to eat.

A group of young women have posted themselves in the doorway to a room where 13 children aged nine months to two years are playing. They have been told they cannot enter the room, to make sure they do not frighten the children too much. The children are still quite intimidated by the shouting from the group. The women are determined to touch and if possible hold the little ones, so they start luring them with sweets. Two or three of the babies crawl closer to find out what is going on. One of the women is about to give a hard boiled sweet to a ten-month-old baby when a caregiver steps in and takes the little girl back into the room, saving the baby from possibly choking on the sweet.

Both staff and visitors change into slippers when entering.

There is also a hygiene concern. It is very hard to make sure that nothing dangerous or contagious is brought in when many people regularly walk in and out. In the case of a home for children with medical conditions, it can simply be life threatening to allow many visitors. If you are dealing with children who already have a weak health, the slight cold of a visitor (or a caregiver) can very easily turn into a dangerously serious pneumonia in a child, particularly a baby.

Life would be a lot simpler if it were possible to simply ban all visitors. Unfortunately, it does not work that way. Substantial donors will always have to be indulged to a certain extent, and authorities—with the power to close the children's home—even more. With authorities, your hands are tied. Aside from kindly requesting that they spend as little time as possible with those who are seriously ill or contagious, and asking if they would not mind washing their hands before touching any of the children, there is nothing much you can do. With all other groups, it is important to impose very strict rules and make sure that these rules are followed.

Guidelines for such rules are:

- *Keep all visitors far away from any children who are currently ill or immuno-deficient. It is a good idea to have a 'sick room' that is considered isolated. This means that no visitors are allowed to go in and the children are not allowed to be taken out; you can allow visitors a look through the window into these rooms, but they cannot enter; you can explain that these rules are made both for the safety of the visitor and that of the child.*
- *Do not allow any sleeping children to be disturbed–allow a brief look from a distance as a maximum.*
- *Have all visitors strictly supervised by a single person who gives 'the tour' and provides them with information.*
- *Have all visitors wash their hands before touching any of the children, and if possible have them leave their shoes at the door.*
- *Instruct visitors not to talk about 'the terrible fate' of the children within the children's hearing, to prevent the children from feeling humiliated and worthless–whether the visitors will actually obey this is another matter.*
- *Have a maximum number of visitors allowed at any one time, otherwise the place will get overcrowded, children will be overwhelmed, and proper care will be hindered (in most cases ten visitors per day would be an absolute maximum, already quite a high number in many situations).*
- *Maybe have a set 'minimum value of donations' that entitles people to access to the children. This way, at least you will get something out of the effort you have to put into receiving the visitors.*
- *Never ever leave anyone (this includes volunteers and newly hired caregivers in their first days) alone in a room with the children or let them leave the facility with one of the children without a member of staff accompanying them.*

Aside from having rules for any visitors for the protection of the children, ideally you should simply not encourage people to come to visit your children's home. Even though it can at times help with donations coming in, a balance needs to be kept with the well-being of the children in mind. As mentioned in Part 3, Chapter 2: 'Ethics Involved in Running a Children's Home', there is often a grey area between helping the children and exploiting them. Signing up with organisations to have groups of local or foreign visitors come to

your children's home
to spend time with the
children and hopefully
leave donations falls on
the side of exploitation.

In certain situations,
such as in shelters and
respite care, you will
have parents or other
relatives who want to
visit. In most cases, this
is a good thing. How-
ever, it is not a good
thing if the visits are
unrestricted. If parents
have the right to walk
in whenever they want
and bother the staff
about their child, in the

Local and foreign volunteers helping to improve the living conditions.

end the care of all children will suffer. In case of parents or family
members, there need to be very clear rules concerning the times
they are allowed to visit, how long they are allowed to visit, and
which locations they can have access to while they are there. And
when visiting your institution, relatives have to commit to the same
hygiene rules as other visitors, even if they do not apply such rules
at home with their child.

Volunteers

Volunteers may find you themselves, contacting you after they have
heard about your organisation. You may look for volunteers, putting up an appeal on your website. Or you may cooperate with one
of the international volunteer organisations that take care of the
recruitment and selection process of volunteers abroad.

Having the help of volunteers can be a great blessing. They can help
lighten the load of the caregivers, give the children extra attention,
and give everyone a break from the sameness of everyday life. An
outsider—which is what a volunteer is—may be able to point out issues that you had never noticed because you take them for granted.
And they might be able to make valuable recommendations on how
certain things could be done easier or better. However, it is important to think about how you wish to manage volunteers and what
basic criteria they need to fulfil to be of use in your children's home.
Because, just like visitors, volunteers can also cause a lot of extra
work, and can do unintentional damage to the children's well-being.
Especially young volunteers who come from abroad for only a short
period may need a lot of guidance and support to make sure they
are suitable for the work.

A volunteer had agreed to spend three days a week at the children's home from 9.00 a.m. to 5.00 p.m. She was asked to spend those days helping the caregivers in a particular room, so that she would get to know the babies there and they would get to know her. She agreed to this. However, on the days that she came to the children's home, she could usually be found in the–already overcrowded–office for several hours. She would be working on her CV, or other things on her laptop. In the end, management added a new rule to the list of volunteer rules: volunteers were not allowed in the office, unless called in by management.

Children thanking a volunteer.

In any case, it is important to ask yourself:

- Do you want a minimum duration of stay for your volunteers? If so, how long? Having volunteers stay less than three months is not very good for children's psychological development, which is something to keep in mind.
- Do you want a minimum commitment of hours worked per week while they are with you?
- Do you want a minimum/maximum age?
- Do you require certain qualifications or experience?
- Do you want them to have a certain religious background?
- Will you provide them with accommodation and food, or should they take care of that themselves?
- Will you provide an airport/train/bus pick-up?
- Do you want to organise touristic outings for your volunteers?
- Will you charge volunteers for coming?
- Will you provide volunteers with pocket money?
- Will you provide volunteers with language classes?
- What duties do you want/are you willing to let volunteers undertake?

By thinking these things through, you will have a better idea both what you are looking for–which will simplify the selection process–and what you will need to prepare for. It is also important to be aware of laws concerning volunteering in the country where you have your children's home. In some countries, there are legal restrictions on volunteering.

In any case, all volunteers should be given a basic training. This does not need to be as extensive as that of the caregivers, but it should cover your rules on how to behave in the children's home, and issues of hygiene and basic care. The purpose is the same as with the caregivers, to ensure that they all have a basic level of knowledge, no matter what their background or experience is, and to ensure they are aware of what is expected of them. It is important to be aware that most volunteers have no real childcare experience. Rules that do not apply to caregivers but that you have set up for volunteers should be included in their basic training. It can be a good idea to explain your policy on smoking and use of alcohol or narcotics right from the start.

> *After a training on basic childcare for staff and volunteers, one of the volunteers came up to me. She told me that she never knew that girls are supposed to be wiped from front to back when changing their nappy. Even these little bits of new knowledge can make a big difference in the health of the children.*

Like with visitors, try to limit the number of volunteers who are in the children's home at any given time. This is both to make sure that it is possible to properly supervise the volunteers, and to make sure that the caregivers still are able to do their jobs well. If you have quite a lot of volunteers at any given time, see if you can organise them in different shifts. Have some of them work in the morning and some in the afternoon, for instance, or have them spend time with the children on alternate days.

> *A foreign volunteer has stretched out on the mat that is there to let the babies play on the floor. He is not paying any attention to the babies and the other people around him. His attention is absorbed by the music on his iPod. The caregivers are annoyed and give each other looks and whispers. The volunteer is in the way and the babies cannot play on the floor, but they are afraid to ask him to go. After all, he is an American, just like their boss…*

Caregivers need to know—meaning they need to be told explicitly—that they outrank volunteers, unless they have been advised that this is not the case for a specific volunteer. Generally, the only exceptions to this are experts brought in by management. This is important, because I have often seen caregivers despair at what was being done to their children, but afraid to take action against a stranger—often a foreigner—of whom they were not sure what their rank was. Sometimes the language barrier or miscommunication can lead to confusion, but in my experience, a lot of the time the caregiver is right to intervene when she feels something is going wrong. At least if she is really involved with the children in her care and has affection for them.

Until they have shown, over the course of some time, that they are capable and trustworthy with the children, volunteers should not, under any circumstances, be left alone in a room with the children. This sounds logical, yet I have seen it happen a lot.

In the very early days of Orphanage Projects when my name was not established yet, I arrived at a new project. The project had been set up through a third party and there had been no direct contact between me and the people of the organisation. They had not asked for any information such as my CV either, though I had offered to send it. On my very first evening there–at a group home for babies and toddlers–the director came to see me. He asked me three questions–which I was just about able to understand and answer, since I was still learning the language: 'Do you know how to make a bottle?', 'Do you know how to cook food for small children?' and 'Are you afraid to stay alone with the children at night?' The answers were two times yes and a no. The conclusion was 'she will do'. Three days later, the caregiver of the group home went on holiday for 15 days and I was left in charge.
I was well able to cope, but they could not have known that.

Local Volunteers

It can be very helpful to have local people volunteer at your children's home. It is a way for the community to connect to the children's home. It is also a wonderful way for the children to have a little interruption of the daily sameness and to get some extra attention and stimulation. Local volunteers can also be a great source of knowledge about where to get

One of a group of local volunteers who visit the home every Sunday afternoon and do activities with the children.

certain things or whom to talk to, to get things done. The advantage of local volunteers over foreign volunteers is that they are familiar with the children's culture and language and make good role models in those respects.

What you need to watch out for are people who only want to come in once or twice. They come to satisfy their curiosity rather than to do something for the children. They present themselves as volunteers, but they are more like visitors. Having people come in, introducing them to the children as a new friend or playmate, and having them disappear again very soon is scarring for the children and can affect their self-esteem; it makes them feel rejected and worthless.

To avoid a lot of people like this slipping in, it is a good idea to have people commit to coming for at least a minimum period of time, and coming at least once a week, at a set time. This way, the children will hopefully be able to count on someone coming and they can be warned in advance when the person is not able to come anymore after a longer period.

Physiotherapist volunteer works with babies who have cerebral palsy.

Every Sunday afternoon a local volunteer would visit the children's home. She was a professional street dancer and after spending some time chatting with the children, she would give a dance lesson every week. In the course of several weeks, she worked together with the children to learn the dance routine for an entire song. The children loved this, they worked hard every Sunday and looked forward to the lessons.

Specialist Volunteers

Generally speaking, volunteers who only come for a few weeks cost more time and effort than you get back from them. They need time to settle in, get over jetlag, and get familiar with the routines of the home. And by the time that has happened, they have to leave again. One group that is usually an exception to this rule are specialist volunteers. Specialist volunteers can have a huge variety of backgrounds. They may know things about medicine, physiotherapy, occupational therapy, speech therapy, nutrition, they may be a teacher or a psychologist who can help you by assessing and/or working with your children, or teach you how to deal with certain problems yourself. They could also be an engineer or builder who can help you with the construction, reconstruction, or transformation of buildings, a business manager who can help you to bring order in your management team, or an IT specialist who can set up your computer network and provide you with a website. Anyone who is a professional in an area of knowledge and skills that you need can be a very valuable specialist volunteer.

Most of the time, these specialists have full-time jobs and do not have the luxury to spend months volunteering at a children's home. If they manage to come and volunteer their time and knowledge, it is usually only for a few days to a week or two at the most. This is often time taken out of a holiday spent nearby or an extension of their stay after a local conference.

Yet, despite the limited time available, you can get a lot out of a situation like this by having someone on your staff (the person most suited to learning about the relevant subject, who is able to ask relevant questions and learn quickly) to accompany the expert and learn from them. This way, a tremendous advantage can be gained from the visit of a specialist volunteer, however brief the visit may be.

Long-Term Volunteers

The cost-benefit ratio you get from a long-term volunteer is generally better than that which you get from a short-term volunteer, and their visit is generally less damaging to the children. A long-term volunteer is anyone who commits to volunteering for you for longer than six months.

A long-term volunteer can really bond with children.

A long-term volunteer will need the same kind of guidance and training to start out with as a short-term volunteer, but after a month or two she will most likely be settled in and able to take care of herself and her assigned tasks, without too much need for constant guidance. Because she really gets to know the place, the staff, and the children through and through, a long-term volunteer can be very helpful in bringing things to your attention, and possibly in making recommendations and giving help to bring about improvements. They become a part of the children's lives and have a great impact on them. They can also be a great help in handling any short-term volunteers who might be visiting during their stay. If you have a good long-term volunteer, really the only downside is the sadness the children will feel when she leaves, possibly feeling 'abandoned' again, by a friend.

There is one thing I would like to warn against with regard to long-term volunteers. There are children's homes where foreign volunteers are required to commit to a minimum of six months or even a year of volunteering, where they are put in charge of a group of children as their regular caregiver. This I would strongly advise against, for several reasons.

First of all, even though a foreign volunteer may have good qualifications or extensive experience in childcare, you will not be able to assess how they actually deal with running a group home until they have arrived and taken charge. At that point, you have no replacement for this particular group, so however it works out: you are stuck with this person.

Secondly—and even more importantly—structurally speaking, running a children's home this way means that, by definition, the children will never be able to bond with their caregivers. Caregivers are only going to be there for less than a year and then they will be replaced by someone else the children do not know. This is bound to create severe attachment problems, as well as problems with the children's sense of security and self-esteem. After all, when children are routinely 'abandoned' once or twice every year by their volunteer caregivers who are going home again, how do you expect them to feel about their own worth? It is also likely to result in behavioural problems and severe depression. In Part 1, Chapter 5: 'Essential Psychological Needs', the crucial importance of attachment is discussed in more detail.

There are some 'minor' issues with having a volunteer as a main caregiver like:

- A foreign volunteer is probably not going to be fluent in local language
- Most volunteers have little or no childcare experience
- The volunteer may struggle to adjust to the foreign surroundings and as a result not be totally invested in the care of the children
- Someone who comes from the other side of the world is almost certain to get sick more often and therefore will be unable to care for children from time to time
- A foreigner is not able to make the children familiar with their own local culture

However, even if we ignore those there is still the issue that the children do not have anyone who cares for them long-term, no one who knows their history, who can reminisce with them and predict how something will affect them, because of something that has happened in the past. So, for the protection of the children, please do not give volunteers a role as main caregiver. It is all right for them to help as a caregiver's assistant, or to take on a big role in a different area—such as part of the medical team, part of the fundraising team and so on—but the children's main caregivers should be people who are going to be around for a much longer time, preferably many years.

In most places, volunteers will be welcomed and given the freedom to take on any role they want. This seems like a kind thing to do, to give so much freedom. However, the reality is that the volunteers are not quite sure what they should be doing and most of the time they would much rather hear from you what role you want them to play. So if you can give some thought to what you would like volunteers to do for you, and have a conversation with them shortly after they arrive, this might help to make the most of the help that is being offered.

Volunteers with Children Everywhere is a manual written for people who intend to volunteer in a children's home as a foreign volunteer. Advising people who are going to volunteer for your children's home to read this book, will help ensure a greater quality and responsibility of work from the volunteer. And having your volunteer coordinator read it, may help her understand some of the risks posed to the children by the presence of volunteers and some of the expectations from the volunteers better.

Afterword

The information provided in this book does not include *everything* involved in caring for children in an institution. I do not explain how to put clothes on a baby, nor do I take you through the steps of washing a child. This book is not meant as a guide that can be blindly followed to lead to excellent childcare conditions. I work from the presumption that I am providing information to sensible people, who know what they are getting into and have a basic idea of what is needed to care for children. The subjects that I have discussed are those that I have found to cause problems in certain children's homes.

Our thanks to all the hardworking caregivers who brighten our lives.

This entire manual is dedicated to creating awareness of approaches to childcare that can have a negative effect on children's well-being and development, and to providing alternatives that improve the child's quality of life—and in some cases, even chances of survival—both in the short term and in the long term. It has become clear throughout the manual that receiving physical contact and attention are part of our essential basic needs, starting at birth. Children who do not receive physical contact and attention, but only have their practical needs met for a long time—if they survive—become emotionally scarred and in some cases even mentally handicapped. Problems that are more common in children who grew up in children's homes than in children who grew up in regular families include a developmental delay—in extreme cases to the point of mental retardation—behavioural problems, depression—in extreme cases self-destructive behaviour—and attention deficit disorders.

If a child really cannot stay with family members, if adoption or foster care are not an option, and providing respite care is not enough, a group home structure should be considered for any children's home. The idea of a group home is to create a family-like situation for children who do not have families of their own and who cannot be placed in foster families. Instead of having children live as a tiny part of a big mass, they become a significant part of an artificial 'family'.

In most children's homes around the world, caregiving and management staff work very hard and very long hours to give the children in their care a better life. I applaud your dedication and efforts. And I want to be very clear that I did not write this manual to criticise you, but to help you with your goal. My own goal is to provide you with information and awareness of issues that you may not know about because no one told you about them. Issues that have a greater impact on the children's well-being than you might have guessed. With this book, I have tried to give you information and recommendations that will help you further improve the quality of life of the children in your care, and maybe make life of the caregiving and management staff a little easier too.

Institutional care will never have quite the same positive impact on a child's growth and development as growing up in a family does. That is why alternatives such as adoption and foster care, or if that is impossible, respite care or group home care, should always be explored. However, if all of these options are really completely impossible, there is still a lot that can be done to reduce the negative impact of institutionalisation on children. It requires a great deal of commitment and dedication and some investment on the part of the entire staff at a children's home to make a difference. However, it can be done. And once the investment of time and money has been made, the benefits will be there for both children and care-givers to enjoy.

If you want any more information or additional help from Orphanage Projects, please feel free to contact us, and we will see how we can help you.

Florence Koenderink, November 2012

Word List

Ability	Something you are able to do
Adequate	Good enough in quality or amount; meeting the most basic requirements
Appropriate	The thing that is the easiest, safest, and most likely to work in a particular situation
ART	Anti-Retroviral Therapy; this is a combination of different medication to slow down the spreading of the HIV virus
Aspiration	Inhaling liquids or food into the airways, it causes a choking /coughing episode and if the coughing does not get rid of the liquid or food particles, an infection like pneumonia can be caused
Assembly	A group of people who come together to listen to something together
Attachment	A close bond or relationship with another person
Authoritarian	An attitude of strictness, giving orders and reprimanding, without warmth or a show of interest in another person
Aversion	Very strong dislike or even fear of something
Awareness	The understanding of the existence and meaning of something
Behavioural Problems	Extremely problematic behaviour, which can include aggression, violent behaviour, problems with concentration, inability to control oneself or one's emotions, or being completely unresponsive
Bowels	Also called intestines, the organs that absorb nutrients from our food and turn the leftover waste into poop
Cerebral Palsy	A non-progressive paralysis of part of the brain that can lead to spasticity, mental retardation and seizure disorders among other things
Choke	To be unable to breathe because a liquid or something solid has gone into the airway, blocking it and not allowing air to reach the lungs, if the blockage lasts for too long, this can lead to death
Cleft	Divided; a cleft lip means the lip is not closed but divided into two parts, a cleft palate means the roof of the mouth is open, divided into two parts
Communicate	To share information, for example by talking or writing
Compliment	A praising remark
Consequence	The result of something that has happened or that has been done
Consistently	Every single time, without exceptions
Cooperate	Work together with you
Cruise	In this book: Walking while holding on to furniture or the wall
Dehydration	A situation where the body has lost more liquids than it has taken in
Deprive	To keep something away from someone
Development	Progress from one stage to the next, often involving improvement
Diet	Kinds and amounts of food that a person eats
Discouraged	Losing the hope that things will work out well or that something can be done
Disposable	Made to be thrown away after one use
Empathy	The ability to imagine or understand what someone else is feeling
Essential	Extremely important, a basic necessity
Ethical	What is morally right or wrong
Experiment	To try out how something works through trial and error
Eye Contact	Looking someone in the eyes
Focus	To concentrate on or to aim your efforts at
Formula	In this book: milk powder, usually made from cows' milk,

that has been put together especially to make sure it contains everything a baby needs to grow well and stay healthy, in a way that a baby's body is able to absorb

Gender — In this book: male or female

Hospice — An institution where people who are terminally ill receive care

Hygiene — Actions or practices of cleanliness that lead to good health

Hypothermia — A body temperature that is too low

Illiterate — Unable to read and write

Imitate — To copy behaviour

Immune System — A system of different kinds of white blood cells that fight invasions of the body by bacteria, viruses, fungi and parasites, to keep the body healthy

Impact — The result or effect of an action or situation

Improve — To make better

Inappropriate — Not the right or accepted thing to do

Incidental — Only happening once or once in a very long while

Independence — Being able to do things yourself, without relying on the help of others

Infant — A baby up to one year old

Infection — A sickness caused by bacteria or other germs

Infestation — A lot of insects invading a living space

Institutional Care — Care that is given outside of the family in a situation where caregivers are paid to provide care to a big group of people, who are given little or no room for making their own decisions

Lack — Not to have a thing that is needed

Liquidised — Mashed up so fine that you can pour it as a thick liquid

Literate — Able to read and write

Malnutrition — Health problems caused by not eating enough of the foods that the body needs

Manipulate — To make someone do what you want without them realising that is what is happening

Mental Retardation — A lower than normal IQ, the brain has only developed to the abilities of children under the age of 12

Midline — In this book: the central line in a child's body running along her nose and belly button

Milestone — The mastering of an important new skill during childhood

Morbidity — Being ill or physically compromised

Mortality — Death

Motor Development — The improvement of control over the muscles in the body and the use of hands, arms, feet, and legs to do things

Fine motor skills — Mostly related to hands, feet and mouth; the ability to perform very precise and detailed tasks

Gross motor skills — The ability to make big movements such as walking and throwing

Mould — The visible presence of a fungus

Nappy — Diaper, pamper

Nuisance — Something that is irritating

Oral — To do with the mouth

Outing — A trip away from home

Permanent — Without ending

Physical — To do with the body

Physiological — To do with the body's structural build

Pneumonia — Lung infection

Poop — Faeces, excrement, crap

Possession — Something you own, that belongs to you

Postpone — To push forward until a later time

Potty — A small bucket or specially designed stool with an open area below the bottom to catch urine and poo, used to help small children become toilet trained

Praise — To show admiration or gratitude; to tell someone they did something well

Prevent	To make sure something does not happen	Stigma	The idea that something is shameful or disgraceful
Protein	Body-building food necessary for proper growth and strength	Tantrum	An outburst of anger and frustration, often from a young child, who may start screaming and crying and throw himself to the floor, and may be very hard to calm down
Rash	In this book: the appearance of red spots or areas on the skin, which may or may not be itchy		
Reprimand	To tell someone they are doing something wrong		
Resentment	A negative feeling, often related to anger, toward someone else	Texture	The structure or feeling of a material
		Thrive	Grow and develop well
Resource	What is needed or available for doing or making something; this often means money	Throw up	Vomit, empty the contents of the stomach through the mouth
Respite Care	Daytime care given to people with complicated special needs, to give their family a break from caring for them	Toddler	A child aged between one and four years old
		Traumatic	Psychologically damaging
		Urine	Pee, piss, liquid waste from the body
Scabies	A skin condition where tiny animals burrow under the skin, usually between the fingers and toes, and lay their eggs there, it is extremely itchy	Unresponsive	Does not react in any way when called or sometimes even when touched
		Validate	To 'give value', to show that someone has worth and meaning
Segregation	To keep separated		
Self-Esteem	The feeling of what you think you are worth and how good you are	Vulnerable	Easily hurt, without defence; this can relate both to physical harm and/or psychological harm
Skill	An ability to do something well		
Soil	Make dirty, usually used when something is made dirty with poop	Weaning	To move from drinking only milk to starting to eat solid foods
Solids	Food, as opposed to liquids like milk	Worthy	To be worth something or to deserve something
Stage	In this book: A period of development		

References

Part 1   Basic Childcare

Kevin Browne (2009). *The Risk of Harm to Young Children in Institutional Care.* The Save the Children Fund, London.

Kendra Cherry. *The Science of Love: Harry Harlow and the Nature of Affection.* http://psychology.about.com/od/historyofpsychology/p/ harlow_love.htm (26/05/2012).

Corinna Csaky (2009). *Keeping Children out of Harmful Institutions. Why We Should Be Investing in Family-Based Care.* The Save the Children Fund, London.

KE Elizabeth (2010). *Nutrition and Child Development.* Paras Medical Publisher, Hyderabad.

Dr. Ronald S. Federici (2003). *Help for the Hopeless Child: A Guide for Families.* http://www.drfederici.com/ins_autism.htm (25/05/2011).

Craig Haney, Curtis Banks, Philip Zimbardo (1973). Interpersonal Dynamics in a Simulated Prison. *International Journal of Criminology and Penology 1973, 1, 69-97.* http://pdf.prisonexp.org/ijcp1973.pdf (29/08/2016).

Robert Goodman, Stephen Scott (2012). *Child and Adolescent Psychiatry, Third Edition.* Wiley-Blackwell, Oxford UK.

Marinus H. van IJzendoorn, Marian J. Bakermans-Kranenburg (2003). Attachment Disorders and Disorganised Attachment: Similar and Different. *Attachment and Human Development, vol. 5, no 3 (September 2003).*   (30/10/2012).

International HIV/AIDS Alliance (2003). Building Blocks: Africa-Wide Briefing Notes. *Psychosocial Support.* International HIV/AIDS Alliance, Brighton. http://www.womenchildrenhiv.org/pdf/p09-of/of-05-04.pdf (22/05/2011).

Florence Koenderink (2015). *Sick Children Everywhere. How to Provide Good Institutional Care. Book 2: Basic Medical Care for Childcare Institutions.* Orphanage Projects, Forfar.

Florence Koenderink (2016). *Volunteers with Children Everywhere. How to Provide Good Institutional Care. Book 3: Manual for Volunteers in Children's Homes.* Orphanage Projects, Forfar.

Terry M. Levy, Michael Orlans (2000). *Attachment Disorders as an Antecedent to Violence and Antisocial Patterns in Children.* http://www.hhs.csus.edu/sw/document/syllabus/fall%202008/sw224reader_gagerman.pdf (30/10/2012).

Tom Lissauder, Graham Clayden (2007). *Illustrated Textbook of Paediatrics.* Mosby Elsevier, Spain.

Jim Mann, A. Stewart Truswell (ed.) (2007). *Essentials of Human Nutrition.* Oxford University Press, Oxford.

Florence Nightingale (1969). *Notes on Nursing: What It Is, and What It Is Not.* Dover Publications Inc., New York, New York.

Bjarte Sanne (2008). *Understanding the Child. A Mental Needs Manual for Caretakers in Children's Homes, 2nd Edition.* http://www.myanmarorphanages.com/wp-content/uploads/2012/11/Understanding-the-child-English-2nd-edition.pdf (26/07/2015).

Maia Szalavitz. How Orphanages Kill Babies--and Why No Child Under 5 Should Be In One. *Huffington Post, 23 April 2010.* http://www.huffingtonpost.com/maia-szalavitz/how-orphanages-kill-babie_b_549608.html (25/05/2011).

UN Resolution 24 February 2010. *Guidelines for the Alternative Care of Children.* http://www.unhcr.org/refworld/publisher,UNGA,RESOLUTION,,4c3acd162,0.html (29/10/2012).

Unknown. *Early Brain Development, What We Know About Brain Development.* University of North Florida, Jacksonville, Florida. http://www.unf.edu/dept/fie/PDF%20Folder/early.pdf (25/05/2011).

Unknown. *How Much Sleep Do Babies and Kids Need?* National Sleep Foundation. https://sleepfoundation.org/sleep-news/how-much-sleep-do-babies-and-kids-need (04/06/2016).

Panayiota Vorria et al (2003). Early Experiences and Attachment Relationships of Greek Infants Raised in Residential Group Care. *Journal of Child Psychology and Psychiatry* 44:0 (2003), pp 1-13 http://scholar.google.co.uk/scholar_url?url=http://www.academia.edu/download/45399767/Early_experiences_and_attachment_relatio20160506-1071-7r3jh8.pdf&hl=en&sa=X&scisig=AAGBfm0EKwNKHKTKNm32p6_e7dPzse1qxA&nossl=1&oi=scholarr&ved=0ahUKEwiXlLHK4rbVAhVsKcAKHSl4DGsQgAMIJSgAMAA (01/08/2017).

David Werner with Carol Thurman, Jane Maxwell and Andrew Pearson (2010). *Where There is No Doctor: A Village Health Care Handbook for Africa.* The Hesperian Foundation, Berkeley, California.

World Health Organisation (2006). *Pocket Book of Hospital Care for Children.* World Health Organisation, New Delhi.

Janice Wood, Aberto August (2010). *Research Base 2009-10.* Florida Institute of Education at the University of North Florida, Jacksonville, Florida.

Part 2: Basic Child Psychology and Child Development

Jason W. Custer, MD, Rachel E. Rau, MD (ed.)*(2009). The Harriet Lane Handbook. A Manual for Pediatric House Officers.* P256-257. 2009 Elsevier Mosby, Philadelphia, Philadelphia.

KE Elizabeth (2010). *Nutrition & Child Development.* Paras Medical Publisher, Hyderabad. 448-452.

Dr. Ronald S. Federici (2003). *Help for the Hopeless Child: A Guide for Families.* http://www.drfederici.com/ins_autism.htm (25/05/2011).

Arlene F Harder (2002, revised 2009). *The Developmental Stages of Erik Erikson.* http://www.learningplaceonline.com/stages/organize/Erikson.htm (31/05/2011).

The Institute for Human Services for the Ohio Child Welfare Training Program (2007). *Developmental Milestones Chart.* http://uppua.org/pdfs/CW%20II%20Handouts/Effects%20of%20Abuse%20and%20Neglect%20on%20Child%20Development/Development_Chart_for_Booklet.pdf (31/05/2011).

Florence Koenderink (2016). *Volunteers with Children Everywhere. How to Provide Good Institutional Care. Book 3: Manual for Volunteers in Children's Homes.* Orphanage Projects, Forfar.

Bjarte Sanne (2008). *Understanding the Child. A Mental Needs Manual for Caretakers in Children's Homes, 2nd Edition.* http://www.myanmarorphanages.com/wp-content/uploads/2012/11/Understanding-the-child-English-2nd-edition.pdf (26/07/2015).

UN Resolution 24 February 2010. *Guidelines for the Alternative Care of Children.* http://www.unhcr.org/refworld/publisher,UNGA,RESO-LUTION,,4c3acd162,0.html (29/10/2012).

Unknown, website, 2007. The Institute of Human Services for the Ohio Welfare Training Program. http://uppua.org/pdfs/CW%20 II%20Handouts/Effects%20of%20Abuse%20and%20Neglect%20 on%20Child%20Development/Development_Chart_for_Booklet.pdf (25/09/2012).

Unknown, website, 2009. Congress of Neurological Surgeons University of Neurosurgery. http://w3.cns.org/university/pediatrics/Ch3Table2.pdf (25/09/2012).

Unknown, website. *Pippi Longstocking Quotes.* Goodreads. https://www.goodreads.com/work/quotes/2056462-pippi-l-ngstrump (08/06/2016).

Part 3:   **Running a Childcare Institution**

Alpay Alkan, Kaya Sarac, Ramazan Kutlu, Cengiz Yakinci, Ahmet Sigirci, Mehmet Aslan, Tamer Baysal (2003). Early and Late-State Subacute Sclerosing Panencephalitis: Chemical Shift Imaging and Single-Voxel MR Spectroscopy. *American Journal of Neuroradiology.* http://www.ajnr.org/content/24/3/501.full (29/10/2012).

Kevin Browne (2009). *The Risk of Harm to Young Children in Institutional Care.* The Save the Children Fund, London.

Corinna Csaky (2009). *Keeping Children out of Harmful Institutions. Why We Should Be Investing in Family Based Care.* The Save the Children Fund, London.

Dr. Ronald S. Federici (2003). *Help for the Hopeless Child: A Guide for Families.* http://www.drfederici.com/ins_autism.htm (25/05/2011).

Marinus H. van IJzendoorn, Marian J. Bakermans-Kranenburg (2003). Attachment Disorders and Disorganised Attachment Similar and Different. *Attachment and Human Development, vol 5, no 3 (September 2003).* http://www.kidscomefirst.info/SimilarDifferent-Ijzendoorn-Kranenburg.pdf (30/10/2012).

International HIV/AIDS Alliance (2003). Building Blocks: Africa-Wide Briefing Notes. *Psychosocial Support*. Brighton. http://www.women-childrenhiv.org/pdf/p09-of/of-05-04.pdf (22/05/2011).

Florence Koenderink (2015). *Sick Children Everywhere. How to Provide Good Institutional Care. Book 2: Basic Medical Care for Children in Children's Homes*. Orphanage Projects, Forfar.

Florence Koenderink (2015). *Orphanages for Money*. Orphanage Projects. http://www.orphanageprojects.org/orphanages-for-money/ (26/07/2015).

Florence Koenderink (2016). *Volunteers with Children Everywhere. How to Provide Good Institutional Care. Book 3: Manual for Volunteers in Children's Homes*. Orphanage Projects, Forfar.

Terry M. Levy, Michael Orlans (2000). *Attachment Disorders as an Antecedent to Violence and Antisocial Patterns in Children*. http://www.hhs.csus.edu/sw/document/syllabus/fall%202008/sw224reader_gagerman.pdf (30/10/2012).

Tom Lissauder, Graham Clayden (2007). *Illustrated Textbook of Paediatrics*. Mosby Elsevier, Spain.

Saul McLeod (2009). Attachment Theory. *Simply Psychology.* http://www.simplypsychology.org/attachment.html (07/11/2012).

Charlotte Philips (2011). *Child Headed Households: A Feasible Way Forward, or an Infringement on Children's Right to Alternative Care?* http://www.charlottephillips.org/eBook%20Child-headed%20Households.pdf (14/06/2016).

Bjarte Sanne (2008). *Understanding the Child. A Mental Needs Manual for Caretakers in Children's Homes, 2nd Edition*. http://www.myanmarorphanages.com/wp-content/uploads/2012/11/Understanding-the-child-English-2nd-edition.pdf (26/07/2015).

Maia Szalavitz. How Orphanages Kill Babies–and Why No Child Under 5 Should Be in One. *Huffington Post, 23 April 2010.* http://www.huffingtonpost.com/maia-szalavitz/how-orphanages-kill-babie_b_549608.html (25/05/2011).

UN Resolution 24 February 2010. *Guidelines for the Alternative Care of Children.* http://www.unhcr.org/refworld/publisher,UNGA,RESO-LUTION,,4c3acd162,0.html (29/10/2012).

Unknown. *Early Brain Development. What We Know About Brain Development.* University of North Florida. http://www.unf.edu/dept/fie/PDF%20Folder/early.pdf (25/05/2011).

Unknown (2014). *Ending the Institutionalisation of Children Glo-bally–The Time Is Now.* Lumos Foundation, London.

Janice Wood, Aberto August (2010). *Research Base 2009-10.* Florida Institute of Education at the University of North Florida, Jacksonville, Florida.

Index

positive attention *127, 138, 139, 140, 156, 158, 160, 230, 231, 233, 305*

possessions *104, 138, 194, 195, 264, 282*

potty training *37, 39, 40, 42*

control his bladder *36*

dry at night *39, 40*

power struggle *184, 185, 186, 187*

practical needs *13, 117, 118, 122, 258, 289, 293, 358*

premature baby *58, 59, 72, 346*

primary caregiver *119, 127, 128, 150, 171, 181, 229, 262*

psychologically damaging *259*

self-hate *159*

shame *40, 45, 154, 164, 221*

psychological needs

affection *117, 118, 122, 123, 125, 127, 128, 131, 132, 133, 140, 285, 307, 315, 321, 352*

attachment *117, 122, 123, 126, 127, 128, 129, 132, 136, 146, 260, 262, 271, 321, 356*

attention *28, 38, 39, 42, 44, 50, 65, 66, 92, 101, 109, 111, 117, 118, 119, 122, 123, 126, 127, 128, 131, 132, 133, 134, 135, 137, 138, 139, 140, 141, 142, 145, 151, 152, 154, 155, 156, 157, 158, 163, 176, 177, 178, 185, 186, 187, 195, 196, 197, 202, 210, 211, 217, 219, 222, 230, 231, 232, 233, 237, 238, 243, 245, 246, 247, 259, 266, 271, 272, 274, 279, 289, 301, 315, 316, 320, 321, 323, 343, 348, 350, 352, 353, 355, 358*

confidence *38, 40, 65, 110, 130, 137, 138, 142, 145, 150, 156, 215, 216, 217, 218, 221, 222, 289, 314*

dignity *36, 37, 141, 221, 248, 323, 348*

freedom *17, 107, 125, 144, 152, 156, 157, 158, 166, 168, 189, 191, 225, 226, 227, 356*

limits *76, 81, 113, 146, 181, 225, 226, 227, 229, 230, 237, 238, 241, 276, 299, 303*

physical contact *22, 101, 117, 118, 122, 123, 125, 132, 140, 141, 143, 146, 156, 161, 196, 271, 274, 321, 348, 358*

praise *42, 82, 137, 140, 154, 157, 198, 210, 216, 219, 222, 230, 231, 292, 305, 314, 316, 335*

relationship *119, 120, 126, 128, 129, 136, 137, 145, 159, 266, 270, 274, 287, 312, 316, 325, 326, 332, 334*

security *123, 124, 126, 136, 140, 154, 238, 262, 267, 333, 337, 356*

self-esteem *17, 37, 65, 133, 153, 154, 155, 156, 157, 159, 192, 195, 196, 215, 216, 218, 219, 220, 221, 222, 264, 289, 348, 353, 356*

self-respect *130, 348*

stimulation *76, 79, 92, 117, 122, 125, 131, 132,*

133, 142, 143, 150, 152, 170, 175, 177, 178, 236, 274, 279, 280, 315, 323, 353

validation *222, 223, 224, 335*

psychological problems

aggression *128, 155, 166, 188, 199, 215, 227, 228, 234*

depression *129, 131, 133, 199, 201, 220, 356, 358*

difficult behaviour *132, 145, 154, 264, 270*

feeling worthless *145, 215, 216, 217, 218, 222, 349, 353*

humiliation *37, 46, 153, 209, 218, 221, 245, 248, 309, 337, 349*

insecurity *40, 221*

respite care *13, 277, 278, 279, 350, 358, 359*

responsibility *135, 166, 226, 256, 288, 290, 292, 295, 300, 316, 328, 357*

reuniting *254, 286*

role model *121, 133, 208, 211, 212, 213, 214, 259, 315, 320, 353*

routine *42, 83, 84, 99, 100, 101, 103, 121, 140, 264, 304, 342, 348, 354*

safe water *22, 42, 55, 56, 297*

sleep *22, 25, 43, 56, 58, 70, 78, 92, 93, 94, 95, 96, 97, 98, 99, 100, 101, 102, 103, 117, 120, 121, 122, 144, 159, 165, 184, 196, 198, 261, 262, 268, 281, 288, 289, 305*

cot death *96, 97*

mosquito nets *96*

swaddling *98, 152*

special needs *34, 169, 256, 257, 260, 264, 267, 268, 273, 274, 277, 279, 280, 306, 348*

stereotypical behaviour *131*

supervision *44, 45, 65, 79, 89, 107, 108, 110, 112, 113, 114, 128, 163, 200, 233, 236, 246, 261, 263, 264, 278, 292, 298, 300, 302, 305, 316, 330, 347, 349, 352*

survival *14, 22, 117, 123, 163, 200, 208, 270, 274, 286, 319, 339, 358*

taking in new children *339*

tantrum *183, 186, 187, 197, 203, 204, 208, 223, 226, 230, 232, 238*

teenager *102, 123, 128, 144, 162, 164, 165,, 166, 167, 168, 191, 228, 256, 292, 316*

terminally ill *276, 277, 307, 317*

traditional orphanage *258, 259, 261, 265, 268, 271, 279*

trafficking *261, 286, 291, 318*

volunteer *224, 264, 270, 278, 288, 290, 296, 297, 299, 319, 327, 349, 350, 351, 352, 353, 354, 355, 356, 357*

www.ingramcontent.com/pod-product-compliance
Lightning Source LLC
Chambersburg PA
CBHW080226270326
41926CB00020B/4158